Learning Quranic Arabic

For Complete Beginners

A Step by Step Self-Teaching Guide to the Arabic Language of the Quran

Ikram Hawramani

2019
Stewards
Publishing

بسم الله الرحمن الرحيم

STEWARDS PUBLISHING

FIRST EDITION

FIRST PUBLISHED IN 2019 IN THE UNITED STATES

ISBN 9781796502404

HAWRAMANI.COM

CONTENTS

Introduction

بِسْمِ ٱللَّهِ ٱلرَّحْمَٰنِ ٱلرَّحِيمِ

This book is an introduction to Quranic Arabic which begins by teaching the Arabic alphabet. It uses the unique LTSDR method to familiarize learners with the Arabic language without overwhelming them with unnecessary technical details. A highly developed and detailed transliteration system is used to help learners know the exact pronunciation of each Arabic word even before mastering the alphabet.

LTSDR (Learning through Stimulated Decipherment of Representations) is a method of language learning that I invented after I became dissatisfied with educational books on human languages, computer languages and mathematics. Many teachers are under the impression that highly structured books, with long lists and tables, facilitate learning. Many language books delve into technicalities like grammar and ignore the fact that in the real world people successfully learn languages all the time without knowing anything about grammar.

I used this method to teach myself many computer languages in very short time. I went on to write many successful educational books on learning computer languages like JavaScript using this method. I have now adapted it to teaching Quranic Arabic. LTSDR breaks down any complex topic into small, easily digestible pieces that the brain easily picks up and remembers.

I hope that you will have as much joy learning from this book as I had in writing it.

This book has been enriched by numerous works of Quranic exegesis (*tafsīr*) and Quranic linguistics (*iʿrāb*), such as the Quran commentaries of al-Ṭabarī, al-Wāḥidī, al-Qurṭubī and al- Bayḍāwī, and the works of Quranic linguistics *al-Jadwal fī Iʿrāb al-Qurʾān* of Maḥmūd al-Ṣāfī and *Mujtabā min Mushkil al-Qurʾān* of Aḥmad al-Kharrāṭ.

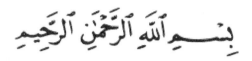

How to Use This Book

This book is training book designed to help you understand Quranic Arabic and train your ability to read it and comprehend it. Once you have learned the alphabet, do your best to read the Arabic and understand it, and use the translation and transliteration to help you when you need it. Difficult as it may be, it is essential that you do your best to struggle to understand the Arabic on its own. This is where your learning takes place.

Memorizing the meaning of the words is not as important as being able to understand the structure of the language. You can always look up the meaning of a word later during your normal reading of the Quran. What you should gain from this book is the ability to understand the structure and patterns of the language.

There is no way to make language learning effortless. Hundreds of hours of training are needed to gain a basic grasp of any language. Thousands of hours are needed to gain some expertise in it. This book is designed to help you get some of that training. To get the full benefits, once you finish the book, come back to the beginning and do all of the Lesson Reviews again. This will refresh your memory of things that will slowly escape your mind if you let them, while also helping you get a fuller grasp of the language's grammar.

You know you are ready to move on when the material in the Lesson Reviews becomes so familiar that you can effortlessly read through them without having to use the transliterations and translations underneath the Arabic script.

Lesson 1: al-Fātiḥa

بِسۡمِ ٱللَّهِ ٱلرَّحۡمَٰنِ ٱلرَّحِيمِ

Above is the first verse of the Quran, which translates as "In the name of God: the Most Gracious, the Most Merciful." This verse is part of the first chapter of the Quran. The chapter's name is *al-Fatiḥa* ("the Opening"). The Arabic word for a chapter of the Quran is *sūra*. We will use the word "chapter" in this book.

Below is the first part of the verse:

بسم

The above phrase is made up of only three letters: b-s-m, which means "In the name of." Arabic is an abjad language, meaning that the focus of the writing system is largely on consonants. Normal written Arabic lacks most vowels. A person simply learns to fill in the vowels as they progress in their learning. But important books like the Quran are written specially with all of the vowels filled in to help readers avoid misreading the text. Below is the same phrase with the vowels filled in:

بِسْمِ

While the b-s-m remains, the additional marks known as *ḥarakāt* now tell us that the b-s-m should be read as b(i)-s-m(i). The singular of *ḥarakāt* is *ḥaraka* ("vowel mark").

Below is the first letter of the earlier phrase:

بـ

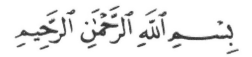

The above is the letter *bā'*, which is pronounced exactly the same as the English letter “b”. Below is the same letter with the vowel mark added:

بِ

The diagonal line underneath the *bā'* is a *kasra*, which is a vowel mark that stands for the sound “i” as in the English word “sit”. The “b” sound above is now followed by a “i” sound, becoming “bi”. The sound b^i is now a full word that means “with”, “in” or “by”. The meaning changes depending on the context.

Below is the next letter:

سـ

The above is the letter *sīn*, which sounds exactly like the letter “s” in English. Below is the same letter with the vowel mark added:

سْـ

The circle above the *sīn* is a vowel mark known as *sukūn*, which tells us that there is no vowel here. It looks like the number zero; you can think of it as “zero vowels here.” By having a *sukūn* above it, the “s” sound remains a “s”. While most Arabic fonts represent the *sukūn* as a circle, calligraphic fonts can represent it as follows:

That is a stylized *sukūn* and it is not used in ordinary Arabic writing.

The next letter is a *mīm*, which sounds exactly like “m” in English:

مـ

Below is the same letter with the vowel added:

Lesson 3: al-Raḥmān

بِسْمِ ٱللَّهِ ٱلرَّحْمَٰنِ ٱلرَّحِيمِ

We are still covering the first verse of the Quran. We will now move on to the "the Most Gracious, the Most Merciful" part.

ٱلرَّحْمَٰن

Above is one of the names of God in Islam, *al-R^{a}ḥmān*, which is often translated as "The Most Gracious". The word begins with an "al", which in Arabic means "the". Below is the "al" part by itself:

الـ

Next is the letter *rā'*, which is pronounced as the "r" in "random":

ر

Above the *rā'* there is a *shadda* which duplicates it:

رّ

Above the *shadda* there is a slanted line that is known as a *fatḥa* (pronounced *f^{a}t-ḥ^{a}*). This is a vowel mark that indicates a sound that is akin to the "u" in "cup". The vowel mark does not apply to the original *rā'* but to the duplicated one. The first *rā'* remains unvowelled, as if it has a *sukūn* above it. Therefore the following:

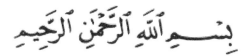

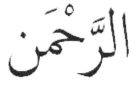

الرَّ

is identical with the following:

الرْرَ

The *shadda* is just a shorthand that helps us avoid having to write the same letter twice.

Let us take another look at the word we are working on:

الرَّحْمَن

The next letter is a *ḥā'*:

حـ

Notice the way this letter is not joined with the *rā'* before it. That is because some letters are joined and some letters are not. Over time it should become clear which ones are joined and which ones are not.

The letter *ḥā'* is also exists in the popular name Muḥammad. To find out how it is pronounced, I recommend that you do a search for "how to pronounce Muhammad" on websites like YouTube. Until you learn how to pronounce it, you can pronounce it like an "h". In fact Persians, despite using common Muslim names like Muhammad, pronounce it exactly like an "h" due to the fact that their language does not have the *ḥā'* sound.

The next letter is one that we have already seen. It is a *mīm*. Earlier we saw a *mīm* that looked like this:

ـم

Lesson 2: Allāh

In this lesson we will move onto the second word of the first verse of the Quran, which is the word *Allāh*. This is the Arabic word for "God" that is used by Arabic-speaking Muslims, Jews and Christians.

الله

The word *Allāh* begins with a letter known as *hamza*. This letter makes a sound that is produced by a constriction of the throat, it is the same as the "u" sound in "umbrella", but only the *first* part of the "u" sound (only the throat constriction).

The *hamza*, when it is at the start of a word, is generally represented as a vertical line:

ا

Next we have two occurrences of the letter *lām*, which is pronounced the same as "l" in "language":

لل

One *lām* by itself looks like this:

ل

After the two *lāms* we have a *shadda* which stands above the second *lām*:

ّ

The *shadda* mark simply duplicates the sound it stands above. It is not a vowel mark; it deals with consonants. Since it is above a *lām*, it causes a new *lām* to be created. It is therefore as if we now have three *lāms*. Therefore the following:

لّل

has the same meaning as the following:

للل

When reading the word, all these *lāms* get merged into a single "l" sound as in the English word "ball". Depending on the context, the "l" sound in *Allāh* can also be pronounced as "l" in "language".

Let us now take another look at the word *Allāh*:

اللّٰه

Above the *shadda* there is a short vertical line, stylized to make it look curvy. This line represents an *alif*, a letter which sounds similar to the "a" in "car". This letter is normally a vertical line. We differentiate it from a *hamza* by the fact that it only occurs in the middle or end of a word, and by special marks that are placed on the *hamza* when needed. But here the *alif* is not written in the normal way. A few special Arabic words are written in a way that does not follow the ordinary rules of spelling.

The final letter of the word *Allāh* is a *hā'*, which is pronounced the same as the "h" in "hill":

ه

We are now ready to cover the full phrase "In the name of God":

This page intentionally left blank

مِ

Now it reads like m^i.

Below is the full phrase again:

بِسْمِ

The b^i at the beginning is a word that means "with/by/in" as mentioned, while the sm^i means "name of". The whole phrase is read as $b^is\text{-}m^i$. Even though the "s" is part of the second word, during reading it is conjoined with the first word simply because this is the easiest way to pronounce it. Saying $b^i\text{-}sm^i$ feels unnatural, it is much easier on the tongue to say $b^is\text{-}m^i$.

The *sm* means "name". It is a shortened form of the Arabic word *ism* that we will see later.

Even though the phrase $b^is\text{-}m^i$ means "in the name of", we see no obvious word that stands for "of". That is because the "of" is *inferred* from the context. You just know it is there when you see a word end with a "i" sound in certain contexts.

The lessons in this book are not meant to be memorized. Readers are meant to pick up a few useful things from each lesson while casually moving on to the next one. Important concepts will be explained many times in different lessons until they become fully clear.

Lesson 4: al-Raḥīm

بِسْمِ ٱللَّهِ ٱلرَّحْمَٰنِ ٱلرَّحِيمِ

B^{i}*sm*^{i} (in the name [of]) *allāh*^{i} (God) *al-r*^{a}*ḥmān*^{i} (the Most Gracious) *al-r*^{a}*ḥīm* (the Most Merciful).

We will now move on to the final word, *al-R*^{a}*ḥīm* ("The Most Merciful"):

ٱلرَّحِيْم

The only new letter above is the *yā'* before the final *mīm*. This letter acts like the English letter "y" and the English digraph "ee" as in "see" depending on the context. The appearance of this letter changes greatly depending on where it is. Since the *ḥā'* before it has a *kasra* and the *yā'* has a *sukūn*, the resulting sound is "ḥī". The two names of God together are pronounced thus: al-R^{a}ḥ-mā-n^{i}l-R^{a}-ḥīm.

However, there is a complication here. Arabs say *ar-R*^{a}*ḥ-mā-n*^{i}*r-R*^{a}*-ḥīm*. The "l" sound becomes an "r" sound with a *shadda* when it comes to certain types of letters that come after "al". This is something that will become clear over time. The full verse is pronounced thus: *b*^{i}*s-m*^{i}*l-lā-h*^{i}*r-R*^{a}*ḥ-mā-n*^{i}*r-R*^{a}*-ḥīm*. There is a *kasra* on the last letter *al-Raḥīm* in the Quranic verse, as follows:

ٱلرَّحِيْمِ

This *kasra* is ignored because it is at the end of the verse. It would have been pronounced if there was something after it.

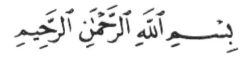

Lesson 5: al-Fātiḥa 2

ٱلْحَمْدُ لِلَّهِ رَبِّ ٱلْعَٰلَمِينَ

Praise is for God, Lord of the Worlds
Transliteration: al-ḥamd^{u} l^{i}-llāh^{i} rabb^{i} al-ʿālamīn
Pronunciation: al-ḥam-d^{u} l^{i}l-lā-h^{i} rab-b^{i}l-ʿā-la-mīn

Al-ḥ^{a}md^{u} (praise [is]) *l^{i}-llāh^{i}* (for God) *r^{a}bb^{i}* (Lord [of]) *al-ʿāl^{a}mīn* (the worlds).

An essential part of your learning is to try to read the Arabic while using the transliteration to help you figure out the letters you do not know. Take a minute to do that at the beginning of each lesson.

We will now move on to the second verse of the Quran (chapter 1, verse 2). The first phrase of the verse is *al-ḥamd^{u}*, which means "praise is". The word *ḥamd* means "praise", but not just any kind of praise. It means grateful praise; praise directed at someone who deserves it and has earned it by doing us a favor. The verse starts with *al-ḥamd* rather than merely *ḥamd* because in Arabic the "al" also serves the function of making the meaning of a word more general. If the word lacked "al", it would have meant "a praise", which sounds strange.

الْحَمْدُ

Above is the phrase *al-ḥamd^{u}*. The letters are all familiar except for the last one. That is the letter *dāl*, which is the same as the English letter "d". There is a vowel mark above it. This mark is known as the *ḍamma*, which makes the same sound as "u" in the English word "put".

As mentioned, *al-ḥamd^{u}* means "praise is". The context tells us that this is an "is" context. This is figured out by looking at the words that come after it. There is no shortcut to learning how this works; you just have to keep reading and learning until your brain starts to pick up the patterns.

The next word is *l^{i}llāh^{i}*, "for God":

The current *mīm* looks like this:

ـمـ

The reason is that this *mīm* is joined to another letter both at the beginning and at the end. Arabic letters can look different depending on what they are joined with.

There is a *fatḥa* above the *mīm*, as follows:

ـمَـ

This turns the "m" sound into a "mu" as in the English word "must".

The last letter of *al-R*^{a}*ḥmān* is a *nūn*, which sounds exactly like the English letter "n":

ـن

There is a hidden *alif* between the *mīm* and the *nūn*, which is why we say *al-R*^{a}*ḥmān* (no need to worry about hidden letters, only a few words are like this). We do not pronounce the *fatḥa* above the *mīm*, since it is difficult to say *al-R*^{a}*ḥm*^{a}*-ān*. The *fatḥa* is thrown away and only the hidden *alif* is pronounced, leading to the pronunciation *mān*.

This page intentionally left blank

لِلَّهِ

The beginning *l*^{i} is a word by itself that means "for". The rest of the phrase is the word *Allāh*. The word is compressed due to the context. Originally it was *l*^{i}*-Allāh*^{i}, but it is easier on the tongue to throw away the *A* and say *l*^{i}*llāh*^{i}.

Rather than writing

لِـاللّٰه

we write

لِلَّهِ

The next word in the verse is *rabb*, which means "lord", "master" and "mentor":

رَبّ

The first letter is a *rā'* (which makes the "r" sound). We have seen it before, but here it looks different due to the fact that it is not joined to anything. The next letter is a *bā'* which makes a "b" sound. The *shadda* on the *bā'* duplicates it, as if the word was as follows:

رَبْب

The next word is *al- 'āl*^{a}*mīn*, which is often translated as "the worlds":

الْعَلَمِينَ

The first letter of *‘āl*^{a}*mīn* is the letter *‘ayn*, which has no equivalent in English. Watch a video on how to pronounce the Arabic name Umar, which begins with an *‘ayn*, and you will get an idea about how it is pronounced.

عَـ

There is a hidden *alif* after the *‘ayn*, which is why the *fatḥa* on the *‘ayn* is ignored. If you look at a modern Arabic book, the *alif* would be there:

الْعَالَمِينَ

It is just a peculiarity of the Quranic text that it lacks the *alif*. I use the symbol ‘ to represent the letter *‘ayn* in my transliteration system.

The rest of the letters should be familiar. Let us look at the full phrase:

رَبِّ الْعَلَمِينَ

Note that there is a *kasra* underneath the *bā’* in *rabb*, so that it is actually *rabbi*. The ending "i" sound functions as an "of", so that the full phrase is "Lord of the worlds".

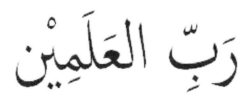

Lesson 6: al-Fātiḥa 3-4

ٱلرَّحْمَٰنِ ٱلرَّحِيمِ

The Most Gracious, the Most Merciful
Transliteration: *al-R^{a}ḥmān^{i} al-R^{a}ḥīm*
Pronunciation: *al-R^{a}ḥ-mā-n^{i}r-R^{a}-ḥī-m*

Al-R^{a}ḥmān^{i} (the Most Gracious) *al-R^{a}ḥīm* (the Most Merciful).

The third verse of the Quran is merely a repetition of the names of God from before: *al-Raḥmān al-Raḥīm* ("the Most Gracious, the Most Merciful"). We will therefore move on to the next verse:

مَٰلِكِ يَوْمِ ٱلدِّينِ

Translation: Sovereign of the Day of Repayment
Transliteration: māl^{i}k^{i} y^{a}wm^{i} al-dīn
Pronunciation: mā-l^{i}-k^{i} y^{a}w-m^{i}d-dīn

Māl^{i}k^{i} (Sovereign [of]) *y^{a}wm^{i}* (the day [of]) *al-dīn* (repayment).

The fourth verse of the Quran starts with the word is *māl^{i}k* ("sovereign", "keeper").

مَٰلِكِ

The first letter is *mīm* (making a "m" sound). There is hidden *alif* right after it which would be shown in standard Arabic writing:

مَالِكِ

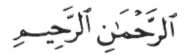

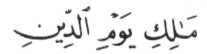

The next letter is a *lām* (making a "l" sound). The final letter is a *kāf* which makes a "k" sound. The symbol above the *kāf* is part of the letter; it is not a special mark. It is only written when the *kāf* is at the end of a word.

The second word of the verse is *y*^{a}*wm*, which means "day".

يَوْمِ

The first letter is a *yā'*, which as mentioned functions as the English "y" or "ee" depending on its context. Here it functions as a "y". Since it has a *fatḥa* above it, we say "y^{a}". The "a" is a short "a", pronounced as the "u" in "cup". In the transliteration system I use in this book, the long "a" sound (as in "car") has a line above it: ā.

The second letter of the word *y*^{a}*wm* is a *wāw*, which functions as the English "w" or "oo" depending on context. Here it functions as a "w". It has a *sukūn* above it which tells us it is unvowelled.

The final letter of the word *y*^{a}*wm* is a *mīm*. It looks like that because it is not joined with anything.

The *mīm* has a *kasra* underneath it, so in context (when reading it as part of the verse) we say *y*^{a}*wm*^{i}, and this tells us that it means "day of" rather than merely "day".

The final word of verse four of the Quran is the word *dīn*, which means "religion", "creed", "repayment", "recompense". In this particular verse it means "repayment", "recompense".

الدِّينِ

After the "al" there is a *dāl* ("d") with a *shadda* above it, which duplicates it. When we pronounce the word with the "al" before it, we say *ad-dīn* similar to the way we said *ar-Raḥmān* ("the Most Gracious"). After the *dāl* there is a *yā'* with a *sukūn* above it, making the sound "ee" as in "see". This long "ee" sound is represented in my transliteration system by the "i" with a line above it: ī.

This full phrase *y*^{a}*wm al-dīn* (pronounced *y*^{a}*w-m*^{i}*d-dīn*) means "Day of Repayment", meaning the Day of Judgment.

Lesson 7: al-Fātiḥa 5

إِيَّاكَ نَعْبُدُ وَإِيَّاكَ نَسْتَعِينُ

You we worship and You we ask for help
Transliteration: *Iyyāk*^{a} *n*^{a}*ʿb*^{u}*d*^{u} *w*^{a}*-iyyāk*^{a} *n*^{a}*st*^{a}*ʿīn*
Pronunciation: *Iy-yā-k*^{a} *n*^{a}*ʿ-b*^{u}*-d*^{u} *w*^{a} *iy-yā-k*^{a} *n*^{a}*s-t*^{a}*-ʿīn*

Iyyāk^{a} (You) *n*^{a}*ʿb*^{u}*d*^{u} (we worship) *w*^{a}*-iyyāk*^{a} (and You) *n*^{a}*st*^{a}*ʿīn* (we ask for help).

The first word of the fifth verse of the Quran is *iyyāk*^{a}, which means "you" (singular). This is not an ordinary "you"; it is only used to express high regard for the addressed person. It almost means "your highness".

إِيَّاكَ

Above, the vertical line at the beginning is a *hamza* as has been mentioned. The symbol underneath it indicates that this *hamza* is pronounced "i" rather than "a". If the symbol was above the vertical line, it would have told us that it is pronounced "a". The *kasra* is additional help that tells us the word starts with a "i" sound, but it is not necessary because whenever you see the special *hamza* symbol underneath the vertical line, you immediately know there is a *kasra* underneath whether it is written or not. Many Arabs when writing omit both the *hamza* symbol and the *kasra*, as follows:

اياك

One simply learns to figure out the meaning and pronunciation based on the word and its context.

The fourth letter (the vertical line after the *yāʾ*) is an *alif*. Here we finally see a proper *alif*, which is a vertical line that can be joined with what comes before it. The vertical line in the middle or end of a word is always an *alif* rather than *hamza* unless it has the special symbol of the *hamza* underneath or above it, in which case it becomes a *hamza*.

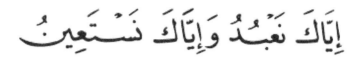

The second word is *naʿb*^{u}*d*^{u}, which means “we worship”:

نَعْبُدُ

The third letter is a *bā’* (“b”), which we have seen before.

Next we have the phrase *w*^{a}*-iyyāk*^{a}, which means “and you”:

وَإِيَّاكَ

The first part of the phrase is *w*^{a}, which is Arabic for “and”. There is no space between this *wāw* letter that means “and” and the word after it. The special *hamza* mark and *kasra* appear to be underneath the *wāw*, but they actually belong to the vertical line and form part of the word *iyyāka* (“you”) that we saw earlier.

The final word is *n*^{a}*st*^{a}*ʿīn*^{u} (“we ask for help”):

نَسْتَعِينُ

The only new letter here is the third one, which is a *tā’* and makes a “t” sound:

ـتـ

If this letter is at the beginning of a word, it looks like this:

تـ

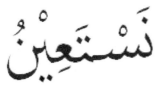

Lesson 8: al-Fātiḥa 6

اَهْدِنَا الصِّرَاطَ الْمُسْتَقِيمَ

Guide us to the Straight Path
Transliteration: *Ihd^{i}nā al-ṣ^{i}rāt al-m^{u}st^{a}qīm*
Pronunciation: *Ih-d^{i}-nāṣ-ṣ^{i}-rā-t^{a}l-m^{u}s-t^{a}-qīm*

Ihd^{i}nā (guide us) *al-ṣ^{i}rāt* (the path) *al-m^{u}st^{a}qīm* (the straight).

The first word of the sixth verse of the Quran is *ihd^{i}nā* ("guide us"):

اهْدِنَا

The second letter is a *ḥā'* which makes a "h" sound as in "hill". We have seen as the last letter of the word *Allāh*. It looks different here because it is not joined with anything before it. You recognize it by the double holes or "eyes". When the ḥā' is in the middle of a word, it looks like this:

ـهـ

The next word is al-ṣ^{i}rāt, which means "the path":

الصِّرَاط

There are two new letters in this word. The first one after the "al" is a *ṣād*. This has no English equivalent; you can pronounce it as an "s" for now. You can look up "how to pronounce Mustafa" online to find out how the letter sounds (the "s" in Mustafa is a *ṣād*). In the Quranic text, the *alif* is missing and is represented by a short vertical line. Here I have chosen to place a full *alif*.

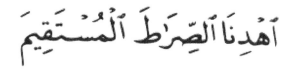

Do not confuse *ṣād* with *ḥā'*:

ص ح

The letter on the left is a *ḥā'*, while the one on the right is a *ṣād*. The *ṣād* has no sharp edges while the top part of the *ḥā'* has a sharp angle, although calligraphers may soften the angle a little as seen above.

The last letter of al-ṣirāt is a *ṭa'*. This letter looks like a *ṣād* with a vertical line at its end:

ط

The letter *ṭa'* has no English equivalent. For now you can pronounce it as a "t". The "t" in the name Mustafa is a *ṭa'*.

The final word in the verse is *al-m^{u}st^{a}qīm*, "the straight":

المُسْتَقِيْم

The first letter after the "al" is a *mīm*. Some fonts show an "eye" for the *mīm*, as follows:

المُ

But other fonts represent the *mīm* without an eye. In some fonts, as in the earlier image, the *mīm* is directly beneath the letter that comes before it, in this case the *lām*, while in the image right above the *lām* is elongated for a bit before the *mīm*.

The one new letter in this word is the second before last, a *qāf*:

ق

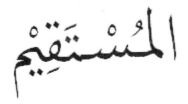

The *qāf* looks like a *mīm* with two dots above it. It has no English equivalent. The country name Iraq has a *qāf* at the end.

Let us now look at the full phrase "the Straight Path":

الصِّرَاطَ الْمُسْتَقِيمْ

The first means "the path" while the second one means "the straight". But when they are together, the meaning is "the Straight Path". The second word, *al-m*^{u}*st*^{a}*qīm,* is an adjective or *ṣifa*—it describes the word that comes before it. In Arabic, the adjective follows the format of the word before it. If the previous word has an "al", the adjective must have an "al" too.

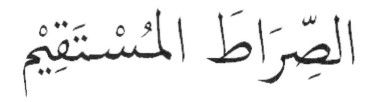

This page intentionally left blank

Lesson 9: al-Fātiḥa 7a

صِرَٰطَ ٱلَّذِينَ أَنْعَمْتَ عَلَيْهِمْ غَيْرِ ٱلْمَغْضُوبِ عَلَيْهِمْ وَلَا ٱلضَّآلِّينَ

We are now at the final verse of the first chapter of the Quran. Due to its length, we will break it up into multiple parts:

صِرَٰطَ ٱلَّذِينَ أَنْعَمْتَ عَلَيْهِمْ

The path of those whom You bestowed your favor upon
Transliteration: Ṣ^{i}rāt^{a} all^{a}dhīn^{a} an^{ʿa}mt^{a} ^{ʿa}l^{a}yh^{i}m
Pronunciation: Ṣ^{i}-rā-t^{a}l-l^{a}-dhī-n^{a} an-^{ʿa}m-t^{a} ^{ʿa}-l^{a}y-h^{i}m

Ṣ^{i}rāt^{a} (path) *all^{a}dhīn^{a}* (those whom) *an^{ʿa}mt^{a}* (You bestowed) *^{ʿa}l^{a}yh^{i}m* (upon them).

The first word is *ṣ^{i}rāt* ("path"), which we saw in the previous lesson. In this verse it lacks an "al". However, its context makes it definite, as if it has an "al". This will be explained further in future lessons.

The second word is *all^{a}dhīn^{a}* ("those who", "those whom").

ٱلَّذِينَ

The "al" at the beginning is part of the word—it is not the usual "al" that means "the". The third letter is a *dhāl*, which is pronounced exactly like the "th" in "that". In my transliteration system I use *dh* to represent it. The word *all^{a}dhīn^{a}* is the plural form of *all^{a}dhī* ("he who", "he whom"):

ٱلَّذِي

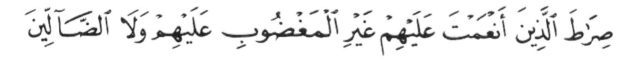

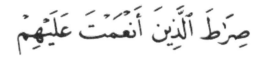

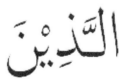

That is used when referring to a masculine item. When referring to a feminine, we say *all^{a}tī* ("she who", "she whom"):

الَّتِي

And when referring to a plural feminine, we say *allātī* ("those who", "those whom"):

اللَّاتِي

Back to the Quranic verse, the third word is *an^{a}mt^{a}* ("you bestowed"):

أَنْعَمْتَ

The first letter is a *hamza*. This *hamza* has the *hamza* symbol above it. This tells us that this particular *hamza* cannot be neglected even when reading it in context (the same is true when the *hamza* symbol is beneath the vertical line). If you remember, the word *Allāh* would become *l^{i}-llāh* if it had a *l^{i}* before it (the *A* would disappear). But when you see the *hamza* symbol, you know this cannot happen to it. So even if we place the emphatic word *l^{a}* ("truly") before *an^{a}mt^{a}*, it becomes *l^{a}-an^{a}mt^{a}* ("You truly bestowed"). It does not become *l^{a}n^{a}mt^{a}*.

The final part of the part of the verse we are working on is *^{a}l^{a}yh^{i}m* ("upon them"):

عَلَيْهِمْ

The first letter is an *'ayn* which we have already seen. This is what it looks like if it is at the beginning of a word. To refresh your memory, here is what it looked like when it was in the middle of a word:

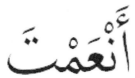

ـعَـ

The ʿ*ayn* can also have an eye depending on the font, as follows:

ـعَـ

The way we differentiate it from a *mīm* is that the ʿ*ayn* has sharper angles, looking somewhat like an inverted triangle.

The letter before last of ʿ$^{a}l^{a}yh^{i}m$ is a *ḥā*ʾ. Here it is stylized in a way that makes it lack any eyes.

ه ـهـ مهن يهم

Above are four examples of the shapes the letter *ḥā*ʾ can take. The one on the right is the shape it takes when it is alone by itself at the end of a word.

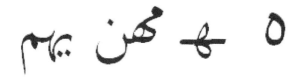

This page intentionally left blank

Lesson 10: al-Fātiḥa 7b

Below is the second part of the final verse of the chapter we are in:

غَيْرِ ٱلْمَغْضُوبِ عَلَيْهِمْ وَلَا ٱلضَّآلِّينَ

Not those who have evoked anger and not the misguided
Transliteration: gh^{a}yr^{i} al-m^{a}ghḍūb^{i} ^{ca}l^{a}y-h^{i}m w^{a}-lā al-ḍālīn
Pronunciation: gh^{a}y-r^{i}l-m^{a}gh-ḍū-b^{i} ^{ca}-l^{a}y-h^{i}m w^{a}-l^{a}ḍ-ḍā-līn

Gh^{a}yr^{i} (not) *al-m^{a}ghḍūb^{i} ^{ca}l^{a}y-h^{i}m* (those upon whom anger is directed) *w^{a}-lā* (and not) *al-ḍālīn* (the misguided [ones]).

The first word of this fragment is *gh^{a}yr^{i}*, which means "except for", "not [that thing]", "apart from":

غَيْرِ

The first letter is a *ghayn* which has no English equivalent. It is present in the city name Baghdad. You can pronounce it as a "g" in "girl" until you learn how to pronounce it accurately. Below are some of the different shapes this letter takes:

غـ ـغـ غ

The second word is *al-m^{a}ghḍūb^{i}*, which means "thing that is experiencing someone's anger", something that someone is angry at. There is no simple English word for it, and it makes more sense when read with the word after it:

الْمَغْضُوبِ

After the "al" the first letter is a *mīm*. The next letter is a *ghayn* which we just saw above. The third letter is a *ḍād*, which we have not seen before. This letter has no English equivalent. You can pronounce it as a "d" for now. If you try to say "d" while making your whole tongue touch the roof of your mouth, you would be close to making the correct sound. Below are the different shapes this letter takes:

ضـ ـضـ ـض

The next letter is ${}^{a}l^{a}yh^{i}m$ ("upon them"). We already covered this phrase in the previous lesson. The full phrase *al-*$m^{a}gh\d{d}\bar{u}b^{i}$ ${}^{a}l^{a}yh^{i}m$ means "those upon whom is anger is directed".

The next phrase is w^{a}*-lā* ("and not"):

وَلَا

The above letters are all familiar. After the *wāw* there is a *lām* and then an *alif*. Here is another way of writing it to clarify it further:

وَلَـا

The word *lā* is Arabic for "no", "not", "do not", the meaning depends on the context.

The final word in the current fragment is *al-ḍālīn* ("the misguided [ones]"):

الضَّالِّيْن

This page intentionally left blank

Lessons 1-10 Review

At the end of each there will be a Lesson Review meant to help you practice your learning. Do your best to read the Arabic text and make sense of it. Use the transliteration and translation underneath it to help you when you need it.

According to LTSDR theory the act of comprehension is the act of learning. Your efforts to "decipher" the meaning of each word is what helps your brain learn, this is what the "D" in LTSDR stands for. Trying to decipher words in a language you do not speak is very taxing on the brain, but by performing it you force your brain to build new neuronal connections that cause the new language's vocabulary and grammar to be embedded in your brain (i.e. to be learned). Doing the deciphering at the end of each lesson is therefore essential; it is in fact the most important part of the learning you will get from this book.

بِسۡمِ ٱللَّهِ ٱلرَّحۡمَٰنِ ٱلرَّحِيمِ

B^{i}*sm*^{i} (in the name [of]) *allāh*^{i} (God) *al-r*^{a}*ḥmān*^{i} (the Most Gracious) *al-r*^{a}*ḥīm* (the Most Merciful).

ٱلۡحَمۡدُ لِلَّهِ رَبِّ ٱلۡعَٰلَمِينَ

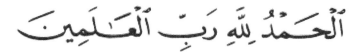

Al-ḥ^{a}*md*^{u} (praise [is]) *l*^{i}*-llāh*^{i} (for God) *r*^{a}*bb*^{i} (Lord [of]) *al-ʿāl*^{a}*mīn* (the worlds).

ٱلرَّحۡمَٰنِ ٱلرَّحِيمِ

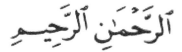

Al-R^{a}*ḥmān*^{i} (the Most Gracious) *al-R*^{a}*ḥīm* (the Most Merciful).

مَٰلِكِ يَوۡمِ ٱلدِّينِ

Māl^{i}*k*^{i} (Sovereign [of]) *y*^{a}*wm*^{i} (the day [of]) *al-dīn* (repayment).

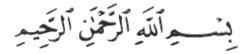

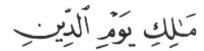

إِيَّاكَ نَعْبُدُ وَإِيَّاكَ نَسْتَعِينُ

Iyyāk^{a} (You) *n*^{a}*ʿb*^{u}*d*^{u} (we worship) *w*^{a}*-iyyāk*^{a} (and You) *n*^{a}*st*^{a}*ʿīn* (we ask for help).

ٱهْدِنَا ٱلصِّرَٰطَ ٱلْمُسْتَقِيمَ

Ihd^{i}*nā* (guide us) *al-ṣ*^{i}*rāt* (the path) *al-m*^{u}*st*^{a}*qīm* (the straight).

صِرَٰطَ ٱلَّذِينَ أَنْعَمْتَ عَلَيْهِمْ

Ṣ^{i}*rāt*^{a} (path) *all*^{a}*dhīn*^{a} (those whom) *an*^{a}*ʿmt*^{a} (You bestowed) ^{a}*l*^{a}*yh*^{i}*m* (upon them).

غَيْرِ ٱلْمَغْضُوبِ عَلَيْهِمْ وَلَا ٱلضَّآلِّينَ

Gh^{a}*yr*^{i} (not) *al-m*^{a}*ghḍūb*^{i} ^{a}*l*^{a}*yh*^{i}*m* (those upon whom anger is directed) *w*^{a}*-lā* (and not) *al-ḍālīn* (the misguided [ones]).

Lesson 11: al-Ikhlās

We will now move on to another short chapter of the Quran—chapter 112. The name of this chapter is *al-Ikhlās* ("sincere devotion") and it has only four verses.

بِسْمِ ٱللَّهِ ٱلرَّحْمَٰنِ ٱلرَّحِيمِ

Muslims pronounce the the *basmala* (the phrase "In the name of God: Most Gracious, Most Merciful") at the beginning of the recitation of every chapter of the Quran (except chapter 9), therefore we will placed at the top of the start of each new chapter we deal with. While the *basmala* is part of the first chapter of the Quran, when it comes to the rest of the chapters it is placed ahead of them outside the chapters.

Verse 1

قُلْ هُوَ ٱللَّهُ أَحَدٌ

Say: "He is God, [Who is] One."
Transliteration: q^{u}l h^{u}w^{a} Allāh^{u} aḥ^{a}d
Pronunciation: q^{u}l h^{u}-w^{a}l-lā-h^{u} a-ḥ^{a}d

Q^{u}l (say) *h^{u}w^{a}* (He is) *Allāh^{u}* (God) *aḥ^{a}d* (One/Individual).

The first word is *q^{u}l,* which is a command that means "Say!" The second word is *h^{u}w^{a}*, which means "he [is]". The third word is *Allāh,* and the fourth word *aḥad,* which means "one", "individual", "solitary". The word for the number one in Arabic is actually *wāḥ^{i}d.* The word *aḥad* emphasizes the individuality of the thing described.

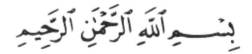

Verse 2

ٱللَّهُ ٱلصَّمَدُ

God: the Eternal
Transliteration: Allāh^{u} al-ṣ^{a}m^{a}d
Pronunciation: Al-lā-h^{u}ṣ-ṣ^{a}-m^{a}d

Allāh^{u} (God) *al-ṣ^{a}m^{a}d* (the Eternal, or the Absolute).

The second word *al-ṣ^{a}m^{a}d*, which means “eternal”, “absolute”.

Verse 3

لَمْ يَلِدْ وَلَمْ يُولَدْ

He did not beget, and he was not begotten
Transliteration: *l^{a}m y^{a}l^{i}d w^{a}-l^{a}m yūl^{a}d*
Pronunciation: *l^{a}m y^{a}-l^{i}d w^{a}-l^{a}m yū-l^{a}d*

L^{a}m (did not) *y^{a}l^{i}d* (He begets) *w^{a}-l^{a}m* (and did not) *yūl^{a}d* (He gets begotten).

The first word is *l^{a}m*, which means “did not”. The second word *y^{a}l^{i}d* means “he begets”. Next, the phrase *w^{a}-l^{a}m* means “and did not”. The final word *yūl^{a}d* means “he gets begotten”.

Verse 4

وَلَمْ يَكُن لَّهُۥ كُفُوًا أَحَدٌۢ

And there was not to Him any equivalent
Transliteration: w^{a}-l^{a}m y^{a}k^{u}n l^{a}-h^{u} k^{u}f^{u}w^{an} aḥ^{a}d
Pronunciation: w^{a}-l^{a}m y^{a}-k^{u}n l^{a}-h^{u} k^{u}-f^{u}-w^{an} a-ḥ^{a}d

W^{a}-l^{a}m (and did not) *y^{a}k^{u}n* (was/existed) *l^{a}-h^{u}* (for Him) *k^{u}f^{u}w^{an}* (an equal) *aḥ^{a}d* (one/anyone).

We are now at the final verse. The word $y^a k^u n$ means "was", "existed". But it can refer to an action or state that continued from the past to the present. For this reason this verse is often translated as "And there is not to Him any equivalent."

The phrase l^a-h^u is made up of two words: l^a, which means "for", and h^u, which is a pronoun that means "him". If it was referring to a female, it would have been l^a-*hā* ("for her"):

لَهَا

And if it was referring to a plural male group, it would have been l^a-$h^u m$ ("for them"):

لَهُمْ

As for a plural female group: l^a-$h^u nn^a$ ("for them"):

لَهُنَّ

The tiny *wāw* after l^a-h^u in the Quranic text is to help with recitation. It tells the reciter that the sound before it should be voiced for double the time of a normal sound:

لَّهُۥ

The reason the *lām* has a *shadda* above it is that when reciting it in context, according to the rules of Quran recitation (the art of *tajwīd*), the letter before it can be omitted and the *lām* can be doubled. Instead of saying $y^a k^u n$ l^a-h^u the reciter says $y^a k^u l$ l^a-h^u. This is not essential for understanding the Quran therefore there is no need to be concerned about it.

The word $k^u f^u w^{an}$ ("an equal", "an equivalent") starts with the letter *kāf*. Here it does not have the special *kāf* symbol which we saw in the past: because that symbol only shows up when the *kāf* is at the end of a word:

كـ ـكـ ـك

The second letter of the word $k^u f^u w^{an}$ is a *fā'* which makes a "f" sound. It looks like a *qāf* but it has only one dot instead of two:

فـ ـفـ ـف ف

The *wāw* after the *fā'* has a double slanted line above it that we have not seen before:

كُفُوًا

This symbol is known as a *tanwīn*. It creates a vowel sound followed by an "n" sound. There are three types of *tanwīn*, each corresponding to one of the vowel marks:

ـً ـٍ ـٌ

The one on the right is *tanwīn al-fatḥ:* it creates the sound ^{an}. The one in the middle is *tanwīn al-kasr* and creates the sound ^{in}. The one on the left is *tanwīn al-ḍamm* and creates the sound ^{un}. The *tanwīn* performs various grammatical functions, one of which is to turn a word into its singular form. For example, below is the word $b^a yt$, which means "house":

بَيْتْ

Below is the same word with a *tanwīn al-ḍamm* at its end, making it $b^{a}yt^{un}$:

بَيْتٌ

Now the meaning is "a house" rather than just "house". All of the *tanwīns* can perform this function of turning a name into a singular instance.

In the Quranic verse, $k^{u}f^{u}w^{an}$ means "an equivalent". Notice that this word has an *alif* at the end:

كُفُوًا

The *alif* is only written when it is *tanwīn al-fatḥ*, which is why $b^{a}yt^{un}$ above has no *alif*. The reason why an *alif* exists here is that this *alif* is pronounced when the word is at the end of a sentence. If there had been nothing after $k^{u}f^{u}w^{an}$, or if we paused here before going on, we would have said $k^{u}f^{u}$*wā*, taking away the ^{un} sound and replacing it with a long *ā*. The meaning remains the same; it is just the reading that changes.

As for the other types of *tanwīn*, if the word is at the end of a sentence or if someone pauses at them, the *tanwīn* becomes a *sukūn*. For example, below is Arabic for "a tall man":

رَجُلٌ طَوِيلٌ

If this phrase is part of a longer sentence, you would say $r^{a}j^{u}l^{u}n$ ("a man") $ṭ^{a}$*wīl*^{u}n ("a tall [one]"). But if it is at the end of a sentence, you would ignore the *tanwīn* and say $r^{a}j^{u}l^{u}n$ $ṭ^{a}$*wīl*.

The second letter above is a *jīm*, with sounds like the "j" in "juice". It looks exactly like a ḥā' except that it has a dot underneath it:

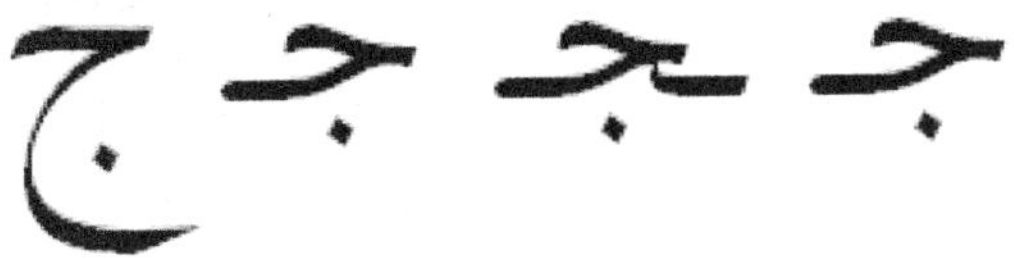

The last word of the verse is *aḥ*^{a}*d* (“one”), which we have already seen.

Lesson 11 Review

بِسْمِ ٱللَّهِ ٱلرَّحْمَٰنِ ٱلرَّحِيمِ

قُلْ هُوَ ٱللَّهُ أَحَدٌ

Q^{u}*l* (say) *h*^{u}*w*^{a} (he is) *Allāh*^{u} (God) *aḥad* (one/individual).

ٱللَّهُ ٱلصَّمَدُ

Allāh^{u} (God) *al-ṣ*^{a}*m*^{a}*d* (the Eternal, or the Absolute).

لَمْ يَلِدْ وَلَمْ يُولَدْ

L^{a}*m* (did not) *y*^{a}*l*^{i}*d* (he begets) *w*^{a}*-l*^{a}*m* (and did not) *yūl*^{a}*d* (he gets begotten).

وَلَمْ يَكُن لَّهُۥ كُفُوًا أَحَدٌۢ

W^{a}*-l*^{a}*m* (and did not) *y*^{a}*k*^{u}*n* (was/existed) *l*^{a}*-h*^{u} (for him) *k*^{u}*f*^{a}*w*^{an} (an equal) *aḥ*^{a}*d* (one/anyone).

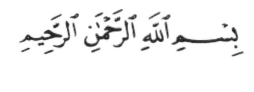

This page intentionally left blank

Lesson 12: al-ʿAṣr

In this chapter we will move on to chapter 103 of the Quran, which is called *al-ʿAṣr* ("time", "the age", the word age has the same meaning as the "age" in "the Middle Ages"). This chapter has only three verses.

بِسْمِ ٱللَّهِ ٱلرَّحْمَٰنِ ٱلرَّحِيمِ

Verse 1

وَٱلْعَصْرِ

[I swear] by the age
Transliteration: w^{a}-al^{ʿa}ṣr
Pronunciation: w^{a}l-^{ʿa}ṣr

The first letter of this very short verse is a *wāw*, which usually means "and". Here, however, it means "by". It is used to express an oath, as when you say "By God, I did not do that!" Here God swears by the age.

Verse 2

إِنَّ ٱلْإِنسَٰنَ لَفِى خُسْرٍ

Indeed, humanity is in loss.
Transliteration: inn^{a} al-insān^{a} l^{a}-fī kh^{u}sr
Pronunciation: in-n^{a}l-in-sā-n^{a} l^{a}-fī kh^{u}sr

Inn^{a} (truly) *al-insān*^{a} (humanity) *l*^{a}*-fī* (truly in) *kh*^{u}*sr* (loss).

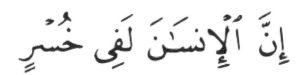

The first of this verse is *inn*^{a}, which is used for emphasis. It means "truly", "indeed", "verily". The second word is a*l-*^{i}*nsān*, which literally means "the human". As has been mentioned, the "al" before a word sometimes functions to make the meaning of a word more general, therefore while the word literally means "the human", we know it actually means "humanity", "mankind".

There is a hidden *alif* after the *sīn* in a*l-insān* in the Quranic calligraphy. The short vertical line, known as a dagger, represents this *alif*. In standard Arabic writing the *alif* is present:

الإِنْسَان

After the "al" at the beginning of the word, there is a *hamza* with a *hamza* symbol and *kasra* beneath it. Below is a different way of writing the same word in order to clarify it:

الـإِنْسَان

To clarify further, below I have separated the "al" completely from the word:

الـ إِنْسَان

The next phrase in the verse is *l*^{a}*-fī* ("truly in"):

لَفِي

The *l*^{a} is used for emphasis, it means "truly", "verily". The word *fī* means "in". Notice that the *yā'* at the end has two dots underneath it, while in the Quranic calligraphy the dots are missing. The dot is not essential, it merely helps readers know this is a *yā'*. Calligraphers may avoid them for stylistic purposes.

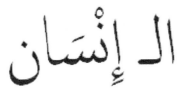

The final word of the verse is *kh*^{u}*sr*, which means "[a state of] loss".

خُسْرٍ

The first letter is a *khāʾ*, which we have not seen before. It is present in the city name Khartoum. You can pronounce it as a "k" until you learn the correct pronunciation. Below are the different forms this letter takes:

خـ ـخـ ـخ خ

Notice that there is a *tanwīn al-kasr* at the end of the word. Since the word is at the end of a verse, this *tanwīn* is ignored and is treated as if it was a *sukūn*. We say *kh*^{u}*sr* rather than *kh*^{u}*sr*^{in} unless we continue the recitation to the next verse without pausing, it which point we would pronounce the *tanwīn*.

Verse 3, part 1

We are now at the third and final verse. Since it is a little long, we will break it up into two fragments:

إِلَّا ٱلَّذِينَ ءَامَنُوا۟ وَعَمِلُوا۟ ٱلصَّٰلِحَٰتِ

Translation: Except those who have believed and done righteous deeds
Transliteration: illā all^{a}dhīn^{a} ām^{a}nū w^{a}-ʿam^{i}lū al-ṣāl^{i}ḥāt
Pronunciation: il-l^{a}l-l^{a}-dhī-n^{a} ā-m^{a}-nū w^{a}-ʿa-m^{i}-lūṣ ṣā-l^{i}-ḥāt

Illā (except) *all*^{a}*dhīn*^{a} (those who) *ām*^{a}*nū* (they believed) *w*^{a}*-ʿam*^{i}*lū* (and they did) *al-ṣāl*^{i}*ḥāt* (good deeds).

The word *illā* means "except". The second word *all*^{a}*dhīn*^{a} ("those") is familiar.

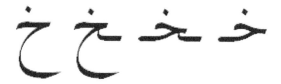

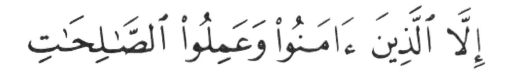

The third word is *ām*^{a}*nū* ("they believed", "they acquired faith"). It starts with a *hamza* followed by an *alif*. The vertical line is not above the *hamza* because that would make it part of the *hamza*. It is written to its left to tell us that it is an independent letter.

ءَامَنُوا

In standard Arabic, this word would be written as follows:

آمَنُوا

The two have exactly the same meaning and pronunciation. Standard Arabic uses the letter you see at the beginning to represent a *hamza* that has an *alif* after it.

The *alif* at the end of the word is not pronounced. It is only there in past verbs referring to a plural masculine. Its only purpose is to help us know that the word is a plural verb rather than a plural noun. Instead of using an *alif*, they could have used any other symbol for this purpose, but they settled on an *alif*. If you forget to write the *alif*, this would suggest that the word *ām*^{a}*nū* is a noun rather than a verb, which is nonsensical. As you progress in your learning, you will come to recognize these silent *alifs*.

To turn this verb into the singular masculine, we say *ām*^{a}*n*^{a} ("he believed"):

آمَنَ

As for a singular female, we say *ām*^{a}*n*^{a}*t* ("she believed"):

آمَنَت

For a plural female group, we say *ām^{a}nn^{a}* (“they believed”):

آمَنَّ

And if you wanted to say “I believed”, you would say *ām^{a}nt^{u}*:

آمَنْتُ

To say “we believed”, you would say *ām^{a}nnā*:

آمَنَّا

These different verb forms all follow a familiar pattern that you will pick up over time.

The next word of the verse is *w^{a}-ʿam^{i}lū* (“and they did”, “and they performed”):

وَعَمِلُوا

Similar to the previous word, there is a silent *alif* at the end. In Arabic past verbs can refer to actions or states that continue to the present, which is why this verb is translated as “those who have done righteous deeds”, and similarly the previous verb is translated as “those who have believed”. One determines from the context whether the action started and ended in the past or whether it is implied that the action continues to the present.

The next word is *al-ṣāl^{i}ḥāt* (“righteous deeds”, “good deeds”), literally “the wholesome [things]”:

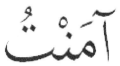

الصَّالِحَات

In the Quranic calligraphy shown earlier both the *alif* after the ṣād and the *alif* after the *ḥāʾ* are hidden, while above I have written them both in their usual places. The word *al-ṣāl*^{i}*ḥāt* is the feminine plural of *al-ṣāl*^{i}*ḥ* ("the sound [one]", "the wholesome [one]", "the good [one]", "the pious [one]"):

الصَّالِح

To say "The pious man," we say *al-r*^{a}*j*^{u}*l al-ṣāl*^{i}*ḥ*:

الرَّجُل الصَّالِح

To say "The pious woman", we say *al-m*^{a}*r*^{ʾa}*t*^{u} *al-ṣāl*^{i}*ḥ*^{a}:

المَرْأَة الصَّالِحَة

The word *al-m*^{a}*r*^{ʾa}*t*^{u} ("the woman") ends with what is called a *tāʾ marbūṭa* or closed *tāʾ*. It looks like a *hāʾ* but has two dots above it, and it only occurs at the end of words to indicate the feminine:

ة ـة

The closed *tāʾ* is only pronounced if there comes something after it. If we had "the woman" without anything after it, we would not pronounce it:

المَرْأَة

The above is pronounced *al-m*^{a}*r*^{a}. The word *al-ṣāl*^{i}*ḥ*^{a} ("the pious") also has a closed *tā'* because in Arabic adjectives must follow the pattern of the word they describe. Since "the pious" is applying to a female, *al-ṣāl*^{i}*ḥ* acquires a closed *tā'* at its end to becomes *al-ṣāl*^{i}*ḥ*^{a} in order to match the word it describes.

Verse 3, part 2

We will now move on to the second and last fragment of the final verse of chapter 103:

وَتَوَاصَوْا بِالْحَقِّ وَتَوَاصَوْا بِالصَّبْرِ

And advised each other to truth and advised each other to patience
Transliteration: w^{a}-t^{a}wāṣ^{a}w b^{i}-al-ḥ^{a}qq^{i} w^{a}-t^{a}wāṣ^{a}w b^{i}-al-ṣ^{a}br
Pronunciation: w^{a}-t^{a}-wā-ṣ^{a}w b^{i}l-ḥ^{a}q-q^{i} w^{a}-t^{a}-wā-ṣ^{a}w b^{i}l-ṣ^{a}br

W^{a}*-t*^{a}*wāṣ*^{a}*w* (and they recommended to each other) *b*^{i}*-al-ḥ*^{a}*qq*^{i} (by the truth) *w*^{a}*-t*^{a}*wāṣ*^{a}*w* (and they recommended to each other) *b*^{i}*-al-ṣ*^{a}*br* (by patience).

The word *t*^{a}*wāṣ*^{a}*w* means "they recommended to each other", "they advised each other", but it has no exact equivalent in English.

The phrase *b*^{i}*-al-ḥ*^{a}*qq*^{i} is made up of the word *b*^{i} ("with", "by") and *al- ḥ*^{a}*qq*^{i} ("the truth"). The last phrase is *b*^{i}*-al-ṣ*^{a}*br*. We again have the word *b*^{i} followed by *al-ṣ*^{a}*br* ("patience").

This page intentionally left blank

Lesson 12 Review

بِسۡمِ ٱللَّهِ ٱلرَّحۡمَٰنِ ٱلرَّحِيمِ

وَٱلۡعَصۡرِ

W^{a}*-al*^{a}*ṣr* (by the age).

إِنَّ ٱلۡإِنسَٰنَ لَفِي خُسۡرٍ

Inn^{a} (truly) *al-insān*^{a} (humanity) *l*^{a}*-fī* (truly in) *kh*^{u}*sr* (loss).

إِلَّا ٱلَّذِينَ ءَامَنُواْ وَعَمِلُواْ ٱلصَّٰلِحَٰتِ

Illā (except) *all*^{a}*dhīn*^{a} (those) *ām*^{a}*nū* (they believed) *w*^{a}*-ʿam*^{i}*lū* (and they did) *al-ṣāl*^{i}*ḥāt* (good deeds).

Illā (except) *all*^{a}*dhīn*^{a} *ām*^{a}*nū* (those who believed) *w*^{a}*-ʿam*^{i}*lū al-ṣāl*^{i}*ḥāt* (and did good deeds).

وَتَوَاصَوۡاْ بِٱلۡحَقِّ وَتَوَاصَوۡاْ بِٱلصَّبۡرِ

W^{a}*-t*^{a}*wāṣ*^{a}*w* (and they recommended to each other) *b*^{i}*-al-ḥ*^{a}*qq*^{i} (by the truth) *w*^{a}*-t*^{a}*wāṣ*^{a}*w* (and they recommended to each other) *b*^{i}*-al-ṣ*^{a}*br* (by patience).

W^{a}*-t*^{a}*wāṣ*^{a}*w b*^{i}*-al-ḥ*^{a}*qq*^{i} (the recommended the truth to each other) *w*^{a}*-t*^{a}*wāṣ*^{a}*w b*^{i}*-al-ṣ*^{a}*br* (the recommended patience to each other).

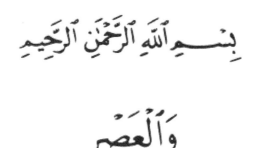

This page intentionally left blank

Lesson 13: al-Ḍuḥā

We will now move on to the 93rd chapter of the Quran. This chapter has 11 verses and is called *al-Ḍuḥā* ("the forenoon", "the [time of] the morning brightness"). It refers to the part of the morning where the sun has risen for a while so that it has become very bright.

بِسْمِ ٱللَّهِ ٱلرَّحْمَٰنِ ٱلرَّحِيمِ

Verse 1

وَٱلضُّحَىٰ

By the [time of] the morning brightness
Transliteration: wa-al-ḍuḥā
Pronunciation: wad-ḍu-ḥā

The verse begins with the letter *wāw*. Like we saw before, the letter means "by" (for oaths) rather than having the usual meaning of "and". The one new thing above is the final letter, which is actually an *alif*. This *alif* is known as *alif maqṣūra* ("shortened *alif*"). It looks like a *yā'* but has nothing to do with a *yā'*. Some Arabic words simply end with an *alif* that is written in this way. In the Quranic calligraphy a dagger is placed above it to hint that it is an *alif* rather than a *yā'*.

Verse 2

وَٱلَّيْلِ إِذَا سَجَىٰ

By the night when it covers
Transliteration: w^{a}-al-l^{a}yl^{i} idhā s^{a}jā
Pronunciation: w^{a}-al-l^{a}yl^{i} idhā s^{a}jā

W^{a}-al-l^{a}yl^{i} (by the night) *idhā* (when) *s^{a}jā* (covers with darkness).

After the oath-taking *wāw*, the first word is *al-l^{a}yl* ("night"). The word *idhā* means "when". The word *s^{a}jā* means "it covered", for example when you cover something with a blanket. The full verse therefore means "I swear by the night when it covers [the world like a blanket]." The word *s^{a}jā* also ends with a shortened *alif*. The word *s^{a}jā* is in the past tense format, but due to the fact that there is an *idhā* before it, we know it is referring to the present tense. The word *idhā* turns the past tense into the present tense.

Verse 3

مَا وَدَّعَكَ رَبُّكَ وَمَا قَلَىٰ

Your Lord has not abandoned you, and He has not detested [you]
Transliteration: mā w^{a}dd$^{a\text{ʿ}a}$-k^{a} r^{a}bb^{u}-k^{a} w^{a}-mā q^{a}lā
Pronunciation: mā w^{a}d-d^{a}-$^{\text{ʿ}a}$-k^{a} r^{a}b-b^{u}-k^{a} w^{a}-mā q^{a}-lā

Mā (has not) *w^{a}dd$^{a\text{ʿ}a}$k^{a}* (abandoned you) *r^{a}bb^{u}-k^{a}* (your Lord) *w^{a}-mā* (and has not) *q^{a}lā* (detested).

The word *mā* means "has not". The phrase *w^{a}dd$^{a\text{ʿ}a}$k^{a}* means "abandoned you". It is made up of two words: *w^{a}dd$^{a\text{ʿ}a}$* ("[he] abandoned") and *k^{a}* (singular "you"). The *wāw* at the beginning of *w^{a}dd$^{a\text{ʿ}a}$* is part of the word—it is not the independent *wāw* that means "and" or "by". If we wanted to say "abandoned you" directed at a female, we would say *w^{a}dd$^{a\text{ʿ}a}$kī*:

وَدَّعَكِي

Arabic differentiates between a plural made up of only two people and a plural made up of three or more people. If we said "abandoned you" and the speech was directed at two males or two females, or a male and a female, then we would say *w^{a}dd$^{a\text{ʿ}a}$k^{u}mā*:

وَدَّعَكُمَا

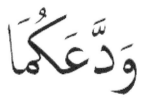

In this unique case, there is no differentiation between speech directed at males or females. But if the speech was directed at a group of males (three or more), we would say $w^{a}dd^{a\,a}k^{u}m$:

وَدَّعَكُم

As for a group of females, we would say $w^{a}dd^{a\,a}k^{u}nn^{a}$ ("he abandoned you [O group of females]"):

وَدَّعَكُنَّ

The next phrase of the verse is $r^{a}bb^{u}k^{a}$ ("your Lord", "your Master"), made up of $r^{a}bb$ ("lord", "master") and k^{a} (singular "you"):

رَبُّكَ

Below are different versions of this word all of which mean "your Lord". From right to left: directed at one female, at two males or females, a group of males, and a group of females.

رَبُّكِي — رَبُّكُمَا — رَبُّكُم - رَبُّكُنَّ

Next we have the phrase w^{a}-*mā* ("and has not"):

وَمَا

The final word of the verse is q^{a}*lā*, which ends with a shortened *alif* and means "he detested":

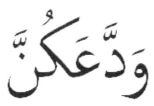

قَلَىٰ

Verse 4

وَلَلْءَاخِرَةُ خَيْرٌ لَّكَ مِنَ ٱلْأُولَىٰ

And truly the Hereafter is better for you than the first [life]
Transliteration: w^{a}-l^{a}-l-ākh^{i}r^{a}t^{u} kh^{a}yr^{un} l^{a}-k^{a} m^{i}n^{a} al-ūlā
Pronunciation: w^{a}-l^{a}l-ā-kh^{i}-r^{a}-t^{u} kh^{a}y-r^{un} l^{a}-k^{a} m^{i}-n^{a}l-ū-lā

W^{a} (and) *l*^{a} (truly) *l-ākh*^{i}*r*^{a}*t*^{u} (the Hereafter) *kh*^{a}*yr*^{un} ([is] better) *l*^{a}*-k*^{a} (for you) *m*^{i}*n*^{a} (than) *al-ūlā* (the first).

The phrase *w*^{a}*-l*^{a}*-al-ākh*^{i}*r*^{a}*t*^{u} is made up of three words: *w*^{a} ("and"), *l*^{a} ("truly"), *al-ākh*^{i}*r*^{a}*t*^{u} ("the Hereafter"). The "al" of *al-ākh*^{i}*r*^{a}*t*^{u} merges with the *l*^{a} that comes before it, as follows:

لَـ الآخِرَة لَلآخِرَة

The *hamza* at the beginning of *al-ākh*^{i}*r*^{a}*t*^{u} disappears, so that we say *l*^{a}*l-ākh*^{i}*r*^{a}*t*^{u}. Above, I have used the standard letter to represent the *ā,* while in the Quranic calligraphy above a *hamza* symbol is used, followed by an *alif.* As has been mentioned, the two things have the same meaning.

The next word is *kh*^{a}*yr*^{un} ("better", "best"). In Arabic the comparative and the superlative forms of adjectives are the same word. We determine whether "better" or "best" is meant from the context. The rest of the verse shows us that here "better" is meant.

خَيْرٌ

Above, I have used the usual symbol for *tanwīn al-ḍamm* on the end of the final letter, while in the Quranic calligraphy another symbol is used that looks like two small *wāw* letters. This was done by the calligrapher for decorative purposes; it is still a *tanwīn al-ḍamm*.

The next word is $l^a k^a$ ("for you"):

لَكَ

In the Quranic calligraphy the *lām* has a *shadda*:

خَيْرٌ لَّكَ

The reason is that according to the art of Quran recitation (*tajwīd*), a person can duplicate the *lām* and merge it with the sound before it, saying: $kh^a yr^{ul}$ $l^a k^a$ (note that the "n" sound of the *tanwīn* has now become a "l" sound).

The final two words of the verse are:

مِنَ الأُولَى

The first word is $m^i n^a$ ("than", "from"), while the second one is *al-ūlā* ("the first one"), which refers to the life of this world. Notice that the *hamza* symbol on *al-ūlā* is directly above the vertical line, which means that the vertical line along with the *hamza* symbol together make up a single letter: a *hamza*. But if you look at w^a-l^al-$ākh^i r^a t^u$ in the Quranic calligraphy, you see the *hamza* symbol is in the middle between the lām and vertical line rather than hovering at the tip of the vertical line:

وَلَلْأَخِرَةُ

That tells you that the *hamza* does not belong with the vertical line. It is independent and the vertical line is a different letter (an *alif*) that follows it. Below I have broken down w^a-l^al-$ākh^i r^a t^u$ so that you

can see the independent *hamza*, while on the right you can see the way the *hamza* of *al-ūlā* belongs with the vertical line:

وَلَلْءاخِرَةَ — الْأُولَى

Verse 5

وَلَسَوْفَ يُعْطِيكَ رَبُّكَ فَتَرْضَىٰٓ

And your Lord is going to give you, and you will be satisfied
Transliteration: w^{a}-l^{a}-s^{a}wf^{a} y^{uʿ}ṭī-k^{a} r^{a}bb^{u}-k^{a} f^{a}-t^{a}rḍā
Pronunciation: w^{a}-l^{a}-s^{a}w-f^{a} y^{uʿ}-ṭī-k^{a} r^{a}b-b^{u}-k^{a} f^{a}-t^{a}r-ḍā

W^{a} (and) l^{a} (truly) *s*^{a}*wf*^{a} (will) *y*^{u}*ʿṭīk*^{a} (give you) *r*^{a}*bb*^{u}*k*^{a} (your Lord) *f*^{a} (then) *t*^{a}*rḍā* (you will be satisfied).

The first phrase of the verb is made up three words: w^{a} (and) l^{a} (truly) s^{a}wf^{a} (will). The second phrase is *y*^{u}*ʿṭīk*^{a}, made up of the verb *y*^{u}*ʿṭī* ("gives") and *k*^{a} ("you"). The word *y*^{u}*ʿṭī* is a verb (*fiʿl*) in the present tense, known as the *muḍāriʿ* tense. To turn it into the past (*māḍī*) tense we say aʿṭā ("he gave"):

أَعْطَى

Below are other forms of this verb:

أَعْطَتْ أَعْطَيَا أَعْطَوْا أَعْطَيْنَ

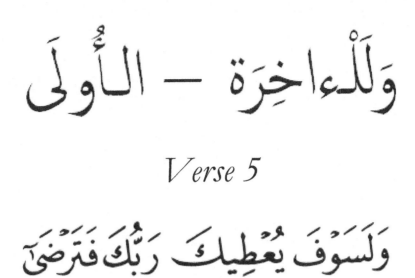

From right to left: *aʿṭ^{a}t* (“she gave”), *aʿṭ^{a}yā* (“they [two of them] gave”), *aʿṭ^{a}w* (“they [male plural] gave”, *aʿṭ^{a}yn^{a}* (“they [female plural] gave”).

When I place the different permutations of a word, they are not for memorization, but for exposure to the way the language works. Try to read each word and make sense of it. As you continue doing this throughout this book, the patterns of the language become embedded in your mind so that you get an intuitive sense for how it works.

Notice the way the *alif* at the end becomes a *yāʾ* in the word second from the right. That is the reason this type of *alif* is written to look like a *yāʾ*.

Below, all four are shown in their present tense:

تُعْطِي تُعْطِيَا تُعْطُونَ تُعْطَيْنَ

The *hamza* at the beginning of the word disappears according to the rules of Arabic grammar. This is something that becomes familiar as you continue your learning.

Moving onto the last part of the verse:

رَبُّكَ فَتَرْضَىٰٓ

The first word is *r^{a}bb^{u}-k^{a}* (“your Lord”). The second item is a phrase made up of *f^{a}* (“then”, “and then”) and *t^{a}rḍā* (“you will be satisfied”).

The symbol at the end of the very last word of the verse is there to tell reciters to elongate that final *ā* sound.

Verse 6

أَلَمْ يَجِدْكَ يَتِيمًا فَـَٔاوَىٰ

Did He not find you an orphan and then give [you] refuge?

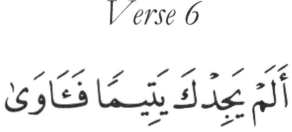

Transliteration: a-l^{a}m y^{a}j^{i}d-k^{a} y^{a}tīm^{an} f^{a}-āwā
Pronunciation: a-l^{a}m y^{a}-j^{i}d-k^{a} y^{a}-tī-m^{an} f^{a}-ā-wā

A-l^{a}m (did not) *y^{a}j^{i}d-k^{a}* (He found you) *y^{a}tīm^{an}* (an orphan) *f^{a}* (and then, so) *āwā* (gave refuge).

The phrase *a-l^{a}m* means “is it not the case that...?”, “is it not true that...?” It is made up of *a*, which is a *hamza* used for asking questions, and *lam* (“did not”, “is not”).

The word *y^{a}j^{i}dk^{a}* means “he found you”. Therefore the full phrase *a-l^{a}m y^{a}j^{i}dk^{a}* means “Is it not true that He found you...?”, “Did He not find you...” *L^{a}m y^{a}j^{i}dk^{a}* means “he did not find you”; adding the *a* to the beginning turns it into a question.

The word *y^{a}tīm* means “orphan” while *y^{a}tīm^{an}* means “an orphan”. The last part of the verse is *f^{a}* (“then”, “and then”) and *āwā* (“gave refuge”). Below are the two different ways of writing this phrase:

فَـَٔاوَىٰ فآوَىٰ

In the Quranic calligraphy the letter *fā’* is joined with the *alif* and the *hamza* symbol is placed above the joined area.

Verse 7

وَوَجَدَكَ ضَآلًّا فَهَدَىٰ

And He found you lost and then guided [you]
Transliteration: w^{a}-w^{a}j^{a}d^{a}-k^{a} ḍāl^{an} f^{a}-h^{a}dā
Pronunciation: w^{a}-w^{a}-j^{a}-d^{a}-k^{a} ḍā-l^{an} f^{a}-h^{a}-dā

W^{a} (and) *w^{a}j^{a}d^{a}-k^{a}* (He found you) *ḍāl^{an}* (a lost one) *f^{a}* (and then) *h^{a}dā* (he guided).

The first *wāw* is an “and”, while the second one is part of the verb *w^{a}j^{a}d^{a}k^{a}* (“he found you”). The word *ḍāl* means “lost”, “misguided”. We already saw this word in its plural form: *ḍālīn* (“misguided ones”).

Verse 8

وَوَجَدَكَ عَآئِلًا فَأَغْنَىٰ

And He found you poor and made [you] self-sufficient.
Transliteration: w^{a}-w^{a}j^{a}d^{a}-k^{a} ‘ā^{ʾi}l^{a}n f^{a}-aghnā
Pronunciation: w^{a}-w^{a}-j^{a}-d^{a}-k^{a} ‘ā-^{ʾi}-l^{a}n f^{a}-agh-nā

W^{a} (and) *w^{a}j^{a}d^{a}-k^{a}* (he found you) *‘ā^{i}l^{a}n* (a poor one, a poor person) *f^{a}* (and then) *aghnā* (he made [someone] rich, he made [someone] self-sufficient).

Notice that in the transliteration of *‘ā^{i}l^{a}n* ("a poor one") there is a new symbol: ʾ. This stands for a *hamza* and faces in the opposite direction to the *‘ayn* symbol. The standard way of writing this word is as follows:

عَائِلًا

In the Quranic calligraphy the *hamza* symbol is underneath. The wavy symbol above the second letter of *‘ā^{i}l^{a}n* merely tells the reciter to elongate that sound. In the Quranic calligraphy it never stands for the *hamza-alif* combination that is used in standard Arabic writing.

Verse 9

فَأَمَّا ٱلْيَتِيمَ فَلَا تَقْهَرْ

So as for the orphan: then do not oppress [him]
Transliteration: f^{a}-ammā al-y^{a}tīm^{a} f^{a}-lā t^{a}qh^{a}r
Pronunciation: f^{a}-am-m^{a}l-y^{a}-tī-m^{a} f^{a}-lā t^{a}q-h^{a}r

F^{a} (so) *ammā* (as for) *al-y^{a}tīm^{a}* (the orphan) *f^{a}* (then) *lā* (do not) *t^{a}qh^{a}r* (you oppress).

The *f^{a}* at the beginning is the same as the one from the previous verse, but here it is more correct to translate it as "so". The word *ammā* means "as for".

Verse 10

وَأَمَّا ٱلسَّآئِلَ فَلَا تَنْهَرْ

And as for the asker, so do not repel [him].

Transliteration: w^{a}-ammā al-sā^{ʾi}l^{a} f^{a}-lā t^{a}nh^{a}r

Pronunciation: w^{a}-am-mal-sā-^{ʾi}-l^{a} f^{a}-lā t^{a}n-h^{a}r

W^{a} (and) *ammā* (as for) *al-sā*^{ʾi}*l*^{a} (the asker) *f*^{a} (then) *lā* (do not) *t*^{a}*nh*^{a}*r* (repel).

The word *al-sā*^{ʾi}*l* means "asker", both one who asks a question and one who asks for something. Here it is generally considered to refer to one who asks for material assistance.

Verse 11

وَأَمَّا بِنِعْمَةِ رَبِّكَ فَحَدِّثْ

And of the favor of your Lord, then speak

Transliteration: w^{a}-ammā b^{i}-n^{iʿ}m^{a}t^{i} r^{a}bb^{i}k^{a} f^{a}-ḥ^{a}dd^{i}th

Pronunciation: w^{a}-am-mā b^{i}-n^{iʿ}-m^{a}-t^{i} r^{a}b-b^{i}-k^{a} f^{a}-ḥ^{a}d-d^{i}th

W^{a} (and) *ammā* (as for) *b*^{i}*-n*^{iʿ}*m*^{a}*t*^{i} (of the favor) *r*^{a}*bb*^{i}*k*^{a} (your Lord) *f*^{a} (then) *ḥaddith* (speak).

The phrase *w*^{a}*-ammā* still means "and as for", but now that there is an "of" right after it, in English it sounds strange to say "And as for of the favor", therefore in the translation I wrote "And of the favor". The word *n*^{iʿ}*m*^{a} means "favor", "blessing", "bounty", something that is bestowed by someone on someone. Since it ends with a closed *tāʾ*, we simply say *n*^{iʿ}*m*^{a} if we say the word by itself. But in context we read the closed *tāʾ*, saying *n*^{iʿ}*m*^{a}*t*^{i} *r*^{a}*bb*^{i}*k*^{a}. The final phrase is *f*^{a}*-ḥ*^{a}*dd*^{i}*th* ("then speak!"). The final letter is a *thāʾ* which is pronounced the same as the "th" in "thing". In this book I always use *th* to represent this letter, while using *dh* to represent the "th" sound in "that".

The words in the Quranic verse are arranged to create a poetic effect. Below I have rephrased them to make them sound more like ordinary Arabic:

فَحَدِّث بِنِعْمَةِ رَبِّك

The above says *f*^{a}-*ḥ*^{a}*dd*^{i}*th* (“then speak”) *b*^{i}-*n*^{i}*ʿm*^{a}*t*^{i} (“of the favor [of]”) *r*^{a}*bb*^{i}*k* (your Lord).

While there is no “of” in “the favor of your Lord”, the phrase *b*^{i}-*n*^{i}*ʿm*^{a}*t*^{i} *r*^{a}*bb*^{i}*k* “favor [of] your Lord” tells us there is an “of” there based on the way the vowels are placed.

This page intentionally left blank

Lesson 13 Review

بِسۡمِ ٱللَّهِ ٱلرَّحۡمَٰنِ ٱلرَّحِيمِ

وَٱلضُّحَىٰ

Wa-al-ḍuḥā (by the morning brightness).

وَٱلَّيۡلِ إِذَا سَجَىٰ

W^{a}*-al-l*^{a}*yl*^{i} (by the night) *idhā* (when) *s*^{a}*jā* (covers with darkness).

مَا وَدَّعَكَ رَبُّكَ وَمَا قَلَىٰ

Mā (has not) *w*^{a}*dd*^{a}^{a}*k*^{a} (abandoned you) *r*^{a}*bb*^{u}*k*^{a} (your Lord) *w*^{a}*-mā* (and has not) *q*^{a}*lā* (detested).

وَلَلۡأٓخِرَةُ خَيۡرٞ لَّكَ مِنَ ٱلۡأُولَىٰ

W^{a} (and) *l*^{a} (truly) *l-ākh*^{i}*r*^{a}*t*^{u} (the Hereafter) *kh*^{a}*yr*^{un} ([is] better) *l*^{a}*k*^{a} (for you) *m*^{i}*n*^{a} (than) *al-ūlā* (the first).

وَلَسَوۡفَ يُعۡطِيكَ رَبُّكَ فَتَرۡضَىٰٓ

W^{a} (and) l^{a} (truly) *s*^{a}*wf*^{a} (will) *y*^{u}*ʿṭīk*^{a} (give you) *r*^{a}*bb*^{u}*k*^{a} (your Lord) *f*^{a} (then) *t*^{a}*rḍā* (you will be satisfied).

أَلَمْ يَجِدْكَ يَتِيمًا فَـَٔاوَىٰ

A-l^{a}m (did not) y^{a}j^{i}d-k^{a} (He found you) y^{a}tīm^{an} (an orphan) f^{a} (and then, so) *āwā* (gave refuge).

وَوَجَدَكَ ضَآلًّا فَهَدَىٰ

W^{a} (and) w^{a}j^{a}d^{a}-k^{a} (he found you) ḍāl^{an} (a lost one) f^{a} (and then) h^{a}dā (he guided).

وَوَجَدَكَ عَآئِلًا فَأَغْنَىٰ

W^{a} (and) w^{a}j^{a}d^{a}k^{a} (he found you) ʿā^{i}l^{a}n (a poor one, a poor person) f^{a} (and then) *aghnā* (he made [someone] rich, he made [someone] self-sufficient).

فَأَمَّا ٱلْيَتِيمَ فَلَا تَقْهَرْ

F^{a} (so) *ammā* (as for) al-y^{a}tīm^{a} (the orphan) f^{a} (then) *lā* (do not) t^{a}qh^{a}r (you oppress).

F^{a}-ammā (so as for) al-y^{a}tīm^{a} (the orphan) f^{a}-lā t^{a}qh^{a}r (then do not oppress).

وَأَمَّا ٱلسَّآئِلَ فَلَا تَنْهَرْ

W^{a} (and) *ammā* (as for) al-sā^{i}l^{a} (the asker) f^{a} (then) *lā* (do not) t^{a}nh^{a}r (repel).

W^{a} *ammā* (and as for) al-sā^{i}l^{a} (the asker) f^{a}-lā t^{a}nh^{a}r (so do not repel).

وَأَمَّا بِنِعْمَةِ رَبِّكَ فَحَدِّثْ

W^{a} (and) *ammā* (as for) b^{i}-n^{i}ʿm^{a}t^{i} (of the favor) r^{a}bb^{i}k^{a} (your Lord) f^{a} (then) *ḥaddith* (speak).

Lesson 14: al-Sharḥ

We will now move on to chapter 94 of the Quran, known as *al-Sharḥ* ("the expansion of the chest", "the opening of the heart"), referring to the feeling of open-heartedness a person feels when they finally accept something and open their heart toward it.

بِسْمِ ٱللَّهِ ٱلرَّحْمَٰنِ ٱلرَّحِيمِ

Verse 1

أَلَمْ نَشْرَحْ لَكَ صَدْرَكَ

Did we not expand your chest for you?
Transliteration: a-l^{a}m n^{a}shr^{a}ḥ l^{a-}k^{a} ṣ^{a}dr^{a}k
Pronunciation: a-l^{a}m n^{a}sh-r^{a}ḥ l^{a}-k^{a} ṣ^{a}d-r^{a}k

A-l^{a}m (did not) *n^{a}shr^{a}ḥ* (we expand) *l^{a}-k^{a}* (for you) *ṣ^{a}dr^{a}k* (your chest).

A-l^{a}m means "is it not true that...?" while *n^{a}shr^{a}ḥ* means "we expand", "we cause to be open-hearted". The *sīn*-like letter with three dots above it is a *shīn* which makes a "sh" sound as in "should". I use "sh" to represent it in the transliteration. The full phrase *Al^{a}m n^{a}shr^{a}ḥ* then means "Did we not expand...?". The word *ṣ^{a}dr^{a}k* literally means "your chest", metaphorically referring to a person's heart.

Verse 2

وَوَضَعْنَا عَنكَ وِزْرَكَ

And we removed from you your burden
Transliteration: w^{a}-w^{a}ḍ^{aʿ}-nā ^{ʿa}n-k^{a} w^{i}zr^{a}-k
Pronunciation: w^{a}-w^{a}-ḍ^{aʿ}-nā ^{ʿa}n-k^{a} w^{i}z-r^{a}k

W^{a} (and) *w^{a}ḍ^{aʿ}-nā* (we removed) *^{ʿa}n-k^{a}* (from you) *w^{i}zr^{a}-k* (your burden).

The first phrase is *w^{a}-w^{a}ḍ^{a}ʿnā* ("and we removed"). The verb *w^{a}ḍ^{a}ʿnā* ("we removed") is the first person plural of *w^{a}ḍ^{a}ʿ^{a}* ("he removed"):

وَضَعَ

The phrase *ʿ^{a}n-k^{a}* is made up of *ʿ^{a}n* ("from") and *k^{a}* ("you"). The phrase *w^{i}zr^{a}k* ("your burden") is made up of the noun *w^{i}zr* ("burden") and the pronoun *k^{a}* ("you").

وِزْرَكَ

I have written *w^{i}zr^{a}k* rather than *w^{i}zr^{a}k^{a}* in the transliteration because the word is at the end of the verse, meaning that its final vowel is not pronounced. The second letter of *w^{i}zr* is a *zāy*, which is pronounced like the "z" in "zebra". It looks like a *rā'* with a dot above it.

Verse 3

ٱلَّذِىٓ أَنقَضَ ظَهْرَكَ

The one which weighed upon your back
Transliteration: all^{a}dhī anq^{a}ḍa ẓ^{a}hr^{a}-k
Pronunciation: al-l^{a}-dhī an-q^{a}-ḍa ẓ^{a}h-r^{a}k

All^{a}dhī (which, the one which) *anq^{a}ḍa* (weighed upon) *ẓ^{a}hr^{a}-k* (your back).

The verb *anq^{a}ḍa* means "it weighed upon". The phrase *ẓ^{a}hr^{a}k* means "your back". The first letter is a *ẓā'*, which is pronounced like a "z" but with the back part of the tongue lifted up. It is presented in the city name Abu Dhabi (the "Dh").

Verse 4

وَرَفَعْنَا لَكَ ذِكْرَكَ

And we raised for you your repute
Transliteration: w^{a}-r^{a}f^{aʿ}nā l^{a}-k^{a} dh^{i}kr^{a}k
Pronunciation: w^{a}-r^{a}-f^{aʿ}-nā l^{a}-k^{a} dh^{i}k-r^{a}k

W^{a} (and) *r*^{a}*f*^{aʿ}*nā* (we raised) *l*^{a}*-k*^{a} (for you) *dh*^{i}*kr*^{a}*-k* (your repute).

The verb *r*^{a}*f*^{aʿ}*nā* is the first person plural of *r*^{a}*f*^{aʿa} ("he raised"):

رَفَعَ يَرْفَعُ

Above, on the right is the past tense *r*^{a}*f*^{aʿa} ("he raised"), while on the left is the present tense *y*^{a}*rf*^{aʿu} ("he raises").

رَفَعْنَا نَرْفَعُ

Above is the past and present for the plural form: *r*^{a}*f*^{aʿ}*nā* ("we raised") on the right and *n*^{a}*rf*^{aʿu} ("we raise") on the left.

The phrase *dh*^{i}*kr*^{a}*k* means "your repute", "your mention", "your remembrance".

Verse 5

فَإِنَّ مَعَ ٱلْعُسْرِ يُسْرًا

Then truly with hardship is relief

Transliteration: f^{a}-inn^{a} m^{aʿa} al-^{ʿu}sr^{i} y^{u}srā

Pronunciation: f^{a}-in-n^{a} m^{a}-^{ʿa}l-^{ʿu}s-r^{i} y^{u}s-rā

F^{a} (then) *inn^{a}* (truly is) *m^{aʿa}* (with) *al-^{ʿu}sr^{i}* (hardship) *y^{u}srā* (relief).

The meaning of the verse is that relief always follows after hardship. The word inn^{a} is used for emphasis, it means "truly is". I have written *y^{u}srā* at the end of the verse even though it has a *tanwīn* because the *tanwīn* is not pronounced when it is at the end of a sentence or verse, and instead the *alif* is pronounced.

As we progress, there will be fewer explanations for each verse since their contents will become familiar.

Make sure to do all of the Training Points, since that is where most of your learning will take place. Do your best to read the Arabic and understand it, using the transliteration above it for help when needed.

Verse 6

إِنَّ مَعَ ٱلْعُسْرِ يُسْرًا

Truly with hardship is relief

Transliteration: inn^{a} m^{aʿa} al-^{ʿu}sr^{i} y^{u}srā

Pronunciation: in-n^{a} m^{a}-^{ʿa}l-^{ʿu}s-r^{i} y^{u}s-rā

Inn^{a} (truly is) *m^{aʿa}* (with) *al-^{ʿu}sr^{i}* (hardship [is]) *y^{u}srā* (relief).

The sixth verse is a repetition of the previous verse. The only difference is that this verse does not start with a *f^{a}* (then).

Verse 7

فَإِذَا فَرَغْتَ فَٱنصَبْ

So when you finish [your work] then devote [yourself to worship]

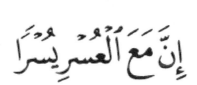

Transliteration: f^{a}-idhā f^{a}r^{a}ght^{a} f^{a}-inṣ^{a}b
Pronuncianation: f^{a}-i-dhā f^{a}-r^{a}gh-t^{a} f^{a}n-ṣ^{a}b

F^{a} (then) *idhā* (when) *f^{a}r^{a}ght^{a}* (you finish) *f^{a}-inṣ^{a}b* (then devote!).

F^{a}r^{a}ght^{a} means "you finish", "you become free [from whatever busies you]".

The command *f^{a}-nṣ^{a}b* ("then devote!") is made up of *f^{a}* and *inṣ^{a}b*. The *hamza* at the beginning of *inṣ^{a}b* is silent when there is a vowel before it, which is why we say *f^{a}-nṣ^{a}b*.

Verse 8

وَإِلَىٰ رَبِّكَ فَٱرْغَب

And to your Lord turn with longing.
Transliteration: w^{a}-ilā r^{a}bb^{i}-k^{a} f^{a}-irgh^{a}b
Pronunciation: w^{a}-ilā r^{a}b-b^{i}-k^{a} f^{a}r-gh^{a}b

W^{a} (and) *ilā* (toward) *r^{a}bb^{i}-k^{a}* (your Lord) *f^{a}* (then) *irgh^{a}b* (turn with longing).

The word *ilā* means "to", "toward". The word *irgh^{a}b* (the *hamza* at the beginning is silent in context) means "turn [toward something] with desire", "turn [toward something] with longing". The past tense is *r^{a}gh^{i}b^{a}* ("he turned [toward something] with longing"):

رَغِبَ يَرْغَبُ

On the right is the past tense, while on the left is the present tense *y^{a}rgh^{a}b^{u}* ("he turns [toward something] with longing").

This page intentionally left blank

Lesson 14 Review

بِسْمِ ٱللَّهِ ٱلرَّحْمَٰنِ ٱلرَّحِيمِ

أَلَمْ نَشْرَحْ لَكَ صَدْرَكَ

Al^{a}*m* (did not) *n*^{a}*shr*^{a}*ḥ* (we expand) *l*^{a}*k*^{a} (for you) *ṣ*^{a}*dr*^{a}*k* (your chest).

وَوَضَعْنَا عَنكَ وِزْرَكَ

W^{a} (and) *w*^{a}*ḍ*^{a}*ʿ-nā* (we removed) ^{a}*n-k*^{a} (from you) *w*^{i}*zr*^{a}*-k* (your burden).

ٱلَّذِىٓ أَنقَضَ ظَهْرَكَ

All^{a}*dhī* (which, the one which) *anq*^{a}*ḍa* (weighed upon) *ẓ*^{a}*hr*^{a}*-k* (your back).

وَرَفَعْنَا لَكَ ذِكْرَكَ

W^{a} (and) *r*^{a}*f*^{a}*ʿnā* (we raised) *l*^{a}*-k*^{a} (for you) *dh*^{i}*kr*^{a}*-k* (your repute).

فَإِنَّ مَعَ ٱلْعُسْرِ يُسْرًا

F^{a} (then) *inn*^{a} (truly is) *m*^{a} ^{a} (with) *al-*^{u}*sr*^{i} (hardship) *y*^{u}*srā* (relief).

إِنَّ مَعَ ٱلْعُسْرِ يُسْرًا

Inn^{a} (truly is) *m*$^{a\,a}$ (with) *al-*^{u}*sr*^{i} (hardship [is]) *y*^{u}*srā* (relief).

فَإِذَا فَرَغْتَ فَٱنصَبْ

F^{a} (then) *idhā* (when) *f*^{a}*r*^{a}*ght*^{a} (you finish) *f*^{a}*-nṣ*^{a}*b* (then devote!).

وَإِلَىٰ رَبِّكَ فَٱرْغَب

W^{a} (and) *ilā* (toward) *r*^{a}*bb*^{i}*-k*^{a} (your Lord) *f*^{a} (then) *irgh*^{a}*b* (turn with longing).

Lesson 15: al-ʿAlaq Part 1

We will next move onto chapter 96 of the Quran. This chapter is named *al-ʿAlaq* ("the Clinging Substance"), which is a reference to a fetus in the womb. This chapter is considered to be the first chapter of the Quran revealed to the Prophet Muhammad (pbuh).

بِسۡمِ ٱللَّهِ ٱلرَّحۡمَٰنِ ٱلرَّحِيمِ

Verse 1

ٱقۡرَأۡ بِٱسۡمِ رَبِّكَ ٱلَّذِي خَلَقَ

Recite in the name of your Lord who created
Transliteration: iqr^{a}ʾ b^{i}-sm^{i} r^{a}bb^{i}-k^{a} all^{a}dhī kh^{a}l^{a}q
Pronunciation: iq-r^{a}ʾ b^{i}s-m^{i} r^{a}b-b^{i}-k^{a}l-l^{a}-dhī kh^{a}-l^{a}q

Iqr^{a}ʾ (read) *b*^{i} (in) *sm*^{i} (name [of]) *r*^{a}*bb*^{i}*-k*^{a} (your Lord) *all*^{a}*dhī* (who) *kh*^{a}*l*^{a}*q* (He created).

The verb *iqr*^{a}ʾ is a command that means "read!" or "recite!" There is a *hamza* at the end that is always pronounced. You know that because it has the *hamza* symbol. You do not say *iqr*^{a}, you say *iqr*^{a}ʾ with a "throat constriction" at the end.

قَرَأَ يَقۡرَأُ

Above on the right is *q*^{a}*r*^{a}ʾ^{a} ("he read") and on the left is *y*^{a}*qr*^{a}ʾ^{u} ("he reads").

The final word is *kh*^{a}*l*^{a}*q*^{a} ("he created"). Below is its present tense *y*^{a}*khl*^{u}*q*^{u} ("he creates"):

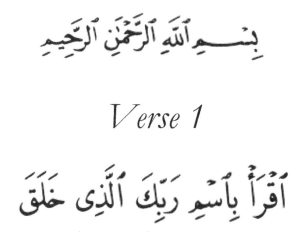

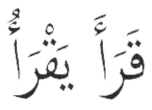

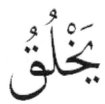

يَخْلُقُ

The dots of the *yāʾ* are stylized in a way that makes them appear underneath the *khāʾ*, which can be confusing to beginners. Below is the same word written to take away the stylization:

يَخْلُقُ

Verse 2

خَلَقَ ٱلْإِنسَٰنَ مِنْ عَلَقٍ

He created the human from a clinging substance
Transliteration: kh^{a}l^{a}q^{a} al-insān^{a} m^{i}n ^{ʿa}l^{a}q
Pronunciation: kh^{a}-l^{a}-q^{a}l-in-sā-n^{a} m^{i}n ^{ʿa}-l^{a}q

Kh^{a}l^{a}q^{a} (He created) *al-insān^{a}* (the human) *m^{i}n* (from) *^{ʿa}l^{a}q* (a clinging substance).

While *al-insān* literally means "the human", note that here it is used as a generic reference to all humans. It means "humanity", "mankind".

Since the *tanwīn* at the end of *^{ʿa}l^{a}q* is *tanwīn al-kasr*, it becomes a *sukūn* when the word is at the end of a verse or sentence, so we say *^{ʿa}l^{a}q* rather than *^{ʿa}l^{a}q^{in}*.

Verse 3

ٱقْرَأْ وَرَبُّكَ ٱلْأَكْرَمُ

Translation: Read, and your Lord is the Most Generous

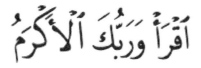

Tranlsiteration: iqr^{aʾ} w^{a}-r^{a}bb^{u}-k^{a} al-akr^{a}m
Pronunciation: iq-r^{aʾ} w^{a}-r^{a}b-b^{u}-k^{a}l-ak-r^{a}m

Iqr^{aʾ} (read) *w^{a}* (and) *r^{a}bb^{u}-k^{a}* (your Lord [is]) *al-akr^{a}m* (the Most Generous).

The word *akr^{a}m* means “more generous”, “most generous”. From the context we know that “most generous” is meant here.

Verse 4

ٱلَّذِى عَلَّمَ بِٱلْقَلَمِ

The One Who taught by the pen
Transliteration: all^{a}dhī ^{ʿa}ll^{a}m^{a} b^{i}-al-q^{a}l^{a}m
Pronunciation: al-l^{a}-dhī ^{ʿa}l-l^{a}-m^{a} b^{i}l-q^{a}-l^{a}m

All^{a}dhī (the One Who) *^{ʿa}ll^{a}m^{a}* (taught) *b^{i}* (by) *al-q^{a}l^{a}m* (the pen).

The verb *^{ʿa}ll^{a}m^{a}* means “he taught”, “he imparted knowledge”. That *shadda* is part of the verb. Without the *shadda* the word would become a completely different word *^{ʿa}l^{a}m^{a}* which means “he placed a marker on it”. It also means “he dominated [another person] in knowledgeability” (he was more knowledgeable than another person).

عَلَمَ

And if we turn the *fatḥa* on the second letter into a kasra, it again becomes a different word that means “he knew”:

عَلِمَ

The noun *al-q^{a}l^{a}m* means "the pen". It does not refer to a particular pen, it just means pens in general. However, some interpretations of the Quran assume it refers to a particular metaphorical/theological "pen".

Therefore the vowel and *shadda* on the second letter of a verb are highly important and determine its meaning.

Verse 5

عَلَّمَ ٱلْإِنسَٰنَ مَا لَمْ يَعْلَمْ

He taught the human that which he did not know
Transliteration: ^{ca}ll^{a}m^{a} al-insān^{a} mā l^{a}m y^{ac}l^{a}m
Pronunciation: ^{ca}l-l^{a}m^{a}l-in-sā-n^{a} mā l^{a}m y^{ac}-l^{a}m

^{a}ll^{a}m^{a} (he taught) *al-insān^{a}* (the human) *mā* (what, that which) *l^{a}m* (did not) *y^{a}l^{a}m* (he knows).

The final word is *y^{a}l^{a}m* ("he knows"), which is the present tense form of *^{a}l^{i}m^{a}* ("he knew"):

عَلِمَ يَعْلَمُ

Unlike the first word of the verse, this final word lacks a *shadda* since it is a different word as mentioned earlier.

While *y^{a}l^{a}m* is in the present tense, the *l^{a}m* before it turns its meaning into the past tense, so that the full phrase *l^{a}m y^{a}l^{a}m* means "he did not know". If we wanted to say "he does not know" (in the present tense), we would say *lā y^{a}l^{a}m*:

لَا يَعْلَمُ

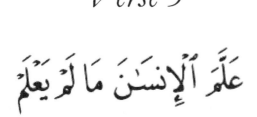

Verse 6

كَلَّآ إِنَّ ٱلْإِنسَٰنَ لَيَطْغَىٰٓ

No! But indeed man truly transgresses
Transliteration: k^{a}llā inn^{a} al-insān^{a} l^{a}-y^{a}ṭghā
Pronunciation: k^{a}l-lā in-n^{a}l-in-sā-n^{a} l^{a}-y^{a}ṭ-ghā

K^{a}llā (No! But) *inn^{a}* (indeed) *al-insān^{a}* (the human) *l^{a}* (truly) *y^{a}ṭghā* (he transgresses).

The word *k^{a}llā* means "No! But..." It is one word and has no English equivalent. The final phrase *l^{a}-y^{a}ṭghā* is made up of *l^{a}* (truly) and *y^{a}ṭghā* ("he transgresses", "he acts despotically"). It is the present tense form of *ṭaghā* ("he transgressed", "he acted despotically"):

طَغَى يَطْغَى

Verse 7

أَن رَّءَاهُ ٱسْتَغْنَىٰٓ

When he sees himself [as] self-sufficient
Transliteration: an r^{a}'ā-h^{u} ist^{a}ghnā
Pronunciation: an r^{a}-'ā-h^{u}s-t^{a}gh-nā

An (when) *r^{a}'ā-h^{u}* (sees him) *ist^{a}ghnā* (became needless).

The word *an* ("when"), which lacks a *shadda*, is different from *inn^{a}* ("indeed"). The verb *r^{a}'ā-h^{u}* means "he saw him". It is made up of *r^{a}'ā* ("he saw") and the pronoun *h^{u}* ("him"). We know from the context that it is referring to the person himself, so it means "he saw himself". Below are the past and present tense of the verb *r^{a}'ā* written using standard Arabic spelling:

رَأَىٰ يَرَىٰ

On the right is the verb *r^{a}ʾā* ("he saw") while on the left is *y^{a}rā* ("he sees").

The verb *ist^{a}ghnā* means "he became rich", "he became needless", "he became self-sufficient".

Verse 8

إِنَّ إِلَىٰ رَبِّكَ ٱلرُّجْعَىٰٓ

Truly to your Lord is the return
Transliteration: inn^{a} ilā r^{a}bb^{i}-k^{a} al-r^{u}jʿā
Pronunciation: in-n^{a} ilā r^{a}b-b^{i}-k^{a}r-r^{u}-jʿā

Inn^{a} (truly) *ilā* (to) *r^{a}bb^{i}-k^{a}* (your Lord [is]) *al-r^{u}jʿā* (the return).

Al-r^{u}jʿā literally means "the return". It refers to the return of all humans to God.

Verse 9

أَرَءَيْتَ ٱلَّذِى يَنْهَىٰ

Have you seen the one who forbids
Transliteration: a-r^{a}ʾ^{a}yt^{a} all^{a}dhī y^{a}nhā
Pronunciation: a-r^{a}-ʾ^{a}y-t^{a}l-l^{a}-dhī y^{a}n-hā

A-r^{a}ʾ^{a}yt^{a} (have you seen) *all^{a}dhī* (the one who) *y^{a}nhā* (forbids).

The beginning *hamza* turns the sentence into a question. *r^{a}ʾ^{a}yt^{a}* means "you saw", while *a-r^{a}ʾ^{a}yt^{a}* means "did you seen?" Since the rest of the verse is in the present tense, we know that meaning is actually "have you seen?" We already saw the verb *r^{a}ʾ^{a}yt^{a}* in its third person singular form *r^{a}ʾā* ("he saw") in verse 7.

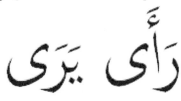

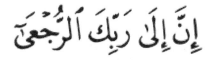

رَأَيْتُ رَأَيْنَا

Above are the first person singular and plural of the verb. On the right there is $r^{a\,a}yt^{u}$ ("I saw"). On the left there is $r^{a\,a}yn\bar{a}$ ("we saw").

رَأَيْتَ رَأَيْتِي رَأَيْتُمَا رَأَيْتُم رَأَيْتُنَّ

Above are the second person forms. From right to left: $r^{a\,a}yt^{a}$ ("you saw" addressed to a male, although it can be used with a female as well), $r^{a\,a}yt\bar{\imath}$ ("you saw" addressed specifically to a female), $r^{a\,a}yt^{u}m\bar{a}$ ("you saw", addressed to two males or females), $r^{a\,a}yt^{u}m$ ("you saw", addressed to three or more males, although it can be used with females), $r^{a\,a}yt^{u}nn^{a}$ ("you saw", addressed specifically to three or more females).

رَأَى رَأَتْ رَأَيَا رَأَوا رَأَيْنَ

Above are the third person forms. From right to left: $r^{a}\text{'}\bar{a}$ ("he saw"), $r^{a\,a}t$ ("she saw"), $r^{a\,a}y\bar{a}$ ("they saw", meaning two males or females), $r^{a\text{'}a}w$ ("they saw", meaning a group of males), $r^{a\text{'}a}yn^{a}$ ("they saw", meaning a group of females).

Back to the Quranic verse, the word $y^{a}nh\bar{a}$ means "he forbids", "he blocks". It has no exact English equivalent because it means both to forbid and to take action to enforce it, for example by telling someone not do something and by getting in their way if they try to do it. The past tense form is $na\d{h}^{a}$ ("he forbad"):

نَهَى يَنْهَى

Below are the various permutations of this verb:

نَهَيْتُ نَهَيْنَا

نَهَيْتَ نَهَيْتِ نَهَيْتُمَا نَهَيْتُمْ نَهَيْتُنَّ

نَهَى نَهَتْ نَهَيَا نَهَوْا نَهَيْنَ

Above, the first line is the first person, second line is the second person, and the third line is the third person.

أَنْهَى نَنْهَى

تَنْهَى تَنْهَيَا تَنْهَوْا تَنْهَيْنَ

يَنْهَى تَنْهَى يَنْهَيَا يَنْهَوْا يَنْهَيْنَ

Above, the present tense forms are shown. Note that when it comes to the second person (second line), the first word on the right t^{a}*nhā* ("you forbid") applies to both males and females, which is why we have four words on the second line, while above in the past tense there are five words on the second line.

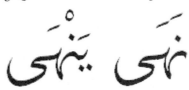

Verse 10

عَبۡدًا إِذَا صَلَّىٰٓ

Translation: A servant when he prays
Transliteration: ^{ca}bd^{an} idhā ṣ^{a}llā
Pronunciation: ^{ca}b-d^{an} i-dhā ṣ^{a}l-lā

^{a}bd^{an} (a servant) *idhā* (when) *ṣ^{a}llā* (he prayed).

This verse completes the meaning of the verse before it: "Have you seen the one who forbids a servant when he prays?" The word *^{a}bd* means "slave", "servant". Here it is referring to a servant of God, so the intent is anyone who prays. The verb *ṣ^{a}llā* means "he prayed", "he performed worship". It does not mean prayer that asks for something, but prayer that is made up of praise and remembrance of God. The *idhā* before it turns this past tense verb into the present tense.

This page intentionally left blank

Lesson 15 Review

بِسْمِ ٱللَّهِ ٱلرَّحْمَٰنِ ٱلرَّحِيمِ

ٱقْرَأْ بِٱسْمِ رَبِّكَ ٱلَّذِى خَلَقَ

Iqr^{a}ʾ (read) *b*^{i} (in) *sm*^{i} (name [of]) *r*^{a}*bb*^{i}*-k*^{a} (your Lord) *all*^{a}*dhī* (who) *kh*^{a}*l*^{a}*q* (He created).

خَلَقَ ٱلْإِنسَٰنَ مِنْ عَلَقٍ

Kh^{a}*l*^{a}*q*^{a} (He created) *al-insān*^{a} (the human) *m*^{i}*n* (from) ^{a}*l*^{a}*q* (a clinging substance).

ٱقْرَأْ وَرَبُّكَ ٱلْأَكْرَمُ

Iqr^{a}ʾ (read) *w*^{a} (and) *r*^{a}*bb*^{u}*-k*^{a} (your Lord [is]) *al-akr*^{a}*m* (the Most Generous).

ٱلَّذِى عَلَّمَ بِٱلْقَلَمِ

All^{a}*dhī* (the One Who) ^{a}*ll*^{a}*m*^{a} (taught) *b*^{i} (by) *al-q*^{a}*l*^{a}*m* (the pen).

عَلَّمَ ٱلْإِنسَٰنَ مَا لَمْ يَعْلَمْ

^{a}*ll*^{a}*m*^{a} (he taught) *al-insān*^{a} (the human) *mā* (what, that which) *l*^{a}*m* (did not) *y*^{a}*ʿl*^{a}*m* (he knows).

كَلَّآ إِنَّ ٱلْإِنسَٰنَ لَيَطْغَىٰٓ

K^{a}*llā* (No! But) *inn*^{a} (indeed) *al-insān*^{a} (the human) *l*^{a} (truly) *y*^{a}*ṭghā* (he transgresses).

أَن رَّءَاهُ ٱسْتَغْنَىٰٓ

An (when) *r*^{a}*ʾā-h*^{u} (sees him) *ist*^{a}*ghnā* (became needless).

إِنَّ إِلَىٰ رَبِّكَ ٱلرُّجْعَىٰٓ

Inn^{a} (truly) *ilā* (to) *r*^{a}*bb*^{i}*-k*^{a} (your Lord [is]) *al-r*^{u}*jʿā* (the return).

أَرَءَيْتَ ٱلَّذِى يَنْهَىٰ

A-r^{a}^{a}*yt*^{a} (have you seen) *all*^{a}*dhī* (the one who) *y*^{a}*nhā* (forbids).

عَبْدًا إِذَا صَلَّىٰٓ

^{a}*bd*^{an} (a servant) *idhā* (when) *ṣ*^{a}*llā* (he prayed).

Lesson 16: al-ʿAlaq Part 2

Verse 11

أَرَءَيْتَ إِن كَانَ عَلَى ٱلْهُدَىٰٓ

Have you seen if he was upon guidance
Transliteration: a-r^{aʾa}yt^{a} in kān^{a} ^{ʿa}l^{a} al-h^{u}dā
Pronunciation: a-r^{a}-^{ʾa}y-t^{a} in kā-n^{a} ^{ʿa}-l^{a}l-h^{u}-dā

A-r$^{a\,a}$*yt*^{a} (Have you seen) *in* (if) *kān*^{a} (he was) ^{a}*l*^{a} (upon) al-*h*^{u}*dā* (guidance).

This verse is asking the Prophet (pbuh): This man who is forbidding people from praying—have you seen him to be upon right guidance? It is a rhetorical question.

Verse 12

أَوْ أَمَرَ بِٱلتَّقْوَىٰٓ

Or if he commanded piety?
Transliteration: aw am^{a}r^{a} b^{i}-al-t^{a}qwā
Pronunciation: aw a-m^{a}-r^{a} b^{i}t-t^{a}q-wā

Aw (or) *am*^{a}*r*^{a} (he commanded) *b*^{i} (with/to) *al-t*^{a}*qwā* (piety, fear of God).

The word *aw* is Arabic for "or". The verse continues the question from the previous verse: "Have you seen if he was upon right guidance, or if he commanded piety?" Even though the literal meaning of the verses is in the past tense, we know that it is asking about the present because in verse 9 it used "the one who forbids" rather than "the one who forbad". For this reason these verses are generally shown in Quran translations in the present tense: "Have you seen if he is upon right guidance, or if he commands piety?"

The phrase *am*^{a}*r*^{a} *b*^{i}*-al-t*^{a}*qwā* means "he commanded piety". The *b*^{i} means "with", "to". It does not seem to have a place in the English, but in the Arabic it is necessary. You can think of the verse as saying "he commanded to piety" which sounds a little strange but not entirely wrong.

Verse 13

أَرَءَيْتَ إِن كَذَّبَ وَتَوَلَّىٰٓ

Have you seen if he denied and turned away?
Transliteration: a-r^{aʾa}yt^{a} in k^{a}dhdh^{a}b^{a} w^{a}-t^{a}w^{a}llā
Pronunciation: a-r^{a}-^{ʾa}y-t^{a} in k^{a}dh-dh^{a}-b^{a} w^{a}-t^{a}-w^{a}l-lā

A-r^{a} ^{a}*yt*^{a} (have you seen) *in* (if) *k*^{a}*dhdh*^{a}*b*^{a} (he denied) *w*^{a} (and) *t*^{a}*w*^{a}*llā* (turned away).

The word *k*^{a}*dhdh*^{a}*b*^{a} means "he denied [the truth of]", "he considered something to be a lie or considered someone to be a liar". Without the *shadda*, the word becomes *k*^{a}*dh*^{a}*b*^{a} which means "he lied".

Verse 14

أَلَمْ يَعْلَم بِأَنَّ ٱللَّهَ يَرَىٰ

Did he not know that God sees?
Transliteration: a-l^{a}m y^{aʿ}l^{a}m b^{i}-ann^{a} Allāh^{a} y^{a}rā
Pronunciation: a-l^{a}m y^{aʿ}-l^{a}m b^{i}-an-n^{a}l-lā-h^{a} y^{a}-rā

A-l^{a}*m* (did not) *y*^{a}*ʿl*^{a}*m* (he knows) *b*^{i}*-ann*^{a} (about the fact that) *Allāh*^{a} (God) *y*^{a}*rā* (sees).

The phrase *y*^{a}*ʿl*^{a}*m b*^{i}*-ann*^{a} means "he knows about the fact that…". The verb *y*^{a}*ʿl*^{a}*m* means "he knows", *b*^{i} here means "about", and *ann*^{a} means "[the fact] that…" So the verse literally means "Did he not know about the fact that God sees?", but it can be simplified to "Did he not know that God sees?"

Verse 15

كَلَّا لَئِن لَّمْ يَنتَهِ لَنَسْفَعًا بِالنَّاصِيَةِ

No! But truly if he does not desist, We will surely drag him by the forelock

Transliteration: k^{a}llā l^{a}-in l^{a}m y^{a}nt^{a}h^{i} l^{a}-n^{a}sf^{aʿa}n b^{i}-al-nāṣīy^{a}

Pronunciation: k^{a}l-lā l^{a}-in l^{a}m y^{a}n-t^{a}-h^{i} l^{a}-n^{a}s-f^{a}-^{ʿa}m b^{i}n-nā-ṣī-y^{a}

K^{a}*llā* (No! But...) *l*^{a} (truly) *in* (if) *l*^{a}*m* (does not) *y*^{a}*nt*^{a}*h*^{i} (he desists) *l*^{a} (truly) *n*^{a}*sf*^{a} ^{a}*n* (we surely drag him) *b*^{i} (by/with) *al-nāṣīy*^{a} (the forelock).

The phrase *l*^{a}*-in* means “truly if”. In standard Arabic writing it looks like this:

لَئِن

The word *y*^{a}*nt*^{a}*h*^{i} (“he desists”, “he stops doing something”) would actually be *y*^{a}*nt*^{a}*hī* in standard Arabic:

يَنْتَهِي

In the Quranic Arabic, the final *yā’* is thrown away. This is just a peculiarity of the Quranic text.

The phrase *n*^{a}*sf*^{a} ^{a}*n* (“we will surely drag him”) would be written as follows in standard Arabic:

نَسْفَعَنْ

It is a peculiarity of the Quranic text that it is written with an *alif*. The verb is *n*^{a}*sf*^{a}*ʿ* (“we drag”):

نَسْفَعْ

But for added emphasis, a *nūn* added to the end.

The tiny *mīm* on the *ʿayn* in the Quranic text indicates to reciters that the *nūn* should be pronounced as a *mīm* here:

لَنَسْفَعًا

The *n*^{a}*sf*^{a}^{a}*n* is pronounced *n*^{a}*sf*^{a}^{a}*m*.

Verse 16

نَاصِيَةٍ كَٰذِبَةٍ خَاطِئَةٍ

A lying, sinning forelock.
Transliteration: nāṣ^{i}y^{a}t^{in} kādh^{i}b^{a}t^{in} khāṭ^{iʾa}
Pronunciation: nā-ṣ^{i}-y^{a}-t^{in} kā-dh^{i}-b^{a}-t^{in} khā-ṭ^{i}-^{ʾa}

Nāṣ^{i}*y*^{a}*t*^{in} (a forlock) *kādh*^{i}*b*^{a}*t*^{in} (a lying [one]) *khāṭ*^{iʾa} (a sinning [one]).

We already saw *nāṣ*^{i}*y*^{a} in the previous verse, which means "forelock" (a lock of hair growing just above the forehead). It can also refer to front part of the head. This verse refers to the person's forlock as a lying and sinning thing, rather than referring to the person himself. The next two words are adjectives that describe *nāṣ*^{i}*y*^{a} and follow its format. They too are in the feminine form (they end with a closed *tāʾ*) and they have the *tanwīn al-kasr*. The word *kādh*^{i}*b*^{a}*t*^{in} means "a [female] lying person/thing". It is the feminine form of *kādh*^{i}*b* ("lying person/thing", "liar"). The reason it is feminine is because the word it describes, *nāṣ*^{i}*y*^{a}, is a feminine word. in Arabic some words are masculine and some words are feminine. The word for "forlock" happens to be feminine.

The word *khāṭ*^{iʾa} ("an erring one", "a sinning one") also describes *nāṣ*^{i}*y*^{a}.

Verse 17

فَلْيَدْعُ نَادِيَهُۥ

Then let him call his associates
Transliteration: f^{a}-l-y^{a}d^{ʿu} nādiy^{a}-h
Pronunciation: f^{a}l-y^{a}d-^{ʿu} nā-d^{i}-y^{a}h

F^{a} (then) *l* (let him) *y^{a}d^{ʿu}* (he calls) *nādiy^{a}-h* (his associate).

In *f^{a}-l-y^{a}d^{ʿu}* ("then let him call", "so let him call") the second word is a *l^{i}* which means "let [him/her/it/them]". Normally this word would have a *kasra,* as follows, while *y^{a}d^{ʿu}* would normally have a *wāw* at the end so that it would be pronounced *y^{a}dʿū*:

لِيَدْعُو

The reason that in the Quranic text the *l^{i}* has a *sukūn* is that it is preceded by *f^{a}*. A reciter is supposed to join both sounds and ignore the *kasra,* saying *f^{a}l-y^{a}d^{ʿu}*. Since the Quranic text is designed to help reciters, the grammatically correct *kasra* is omitted from the text. It is also a peculiarity of the Quranic text that the final grammatically correct *ū* is omitted and turned into a ^{u}.

دَعَوْتُ دَعَوْنَا

دَعَيْتَ دَعَيْتُمَا دَعَيْتُمْ دَعَيْتُنَّ

دَعَى دَعَتْ دَعَيَا دَعَوا دَعَيْنَ

Above are the various past tense forms of this verb:

Top line (from right to left): I called; we called.

Middle line: You (singular male or female) called; you (two) called; you (plural male) called; you (plural female) called.

Bottom line: He called; she called; they (two males or females) called; they (group of males) called; they (group of females) called.

أَدْعُو نَدْعُو

تَدْعُو تَدْعَيَا تَدَعَو تَدْعَيْنَ

يَدْعُو تَدْعُو يَدْعَيَا يَدْعَوا يَدْعَيْنَ

Above are the present tense forms.

Top: I call; we call.

Middle: you (singular male or female) call; you (two) call; you (male group) call; you (female group) call.

Bottom: he calls; she calls; they (two) call; they (male group) call; they (female group) call.

The last phrase of the verse is *nād^{i}y^{a}-h*. Because it is at the end of the verse, we ignore its final vowel. We say *nād^{i}y^{a}-h* rather than *nād^{i}y^{a}-h^{u}*:

نَادِيَهُ

The noun is *nādī* ("a person that one usually calls for help", "associate"). The *h* at the end is a pronoun that means "his". So the full phrase *nād^{i}y^{a}-h* means "his associate".

Verse 18

سَنَدْعُ ٱلزَّبَانِيَةَ

We will call the angels of Hell.
Tranliteration: s^{a}-$n^{a}d^{ʿu}$ al-$z^{a}bān^{i}y^{a}$
Pronunciation: s^{a}-$n^{a}d$-^{ʿu}z-z^{a}-bā-n^{i}-y^{a}

S^{a}-$n^{a}d^{ʿu}$ (We will call) *al-$z^{a}bān^{i}y^{a}$* (the angels of Hell).

This verse says in regards to the man who forbids people from praying; let him call whomever he wishes to support him. We (God) can always call the angels of Hell on him (once he dies). In the Quran sometimes God refers to Himself in the singular and sometimes in the plural. When God uses "We", He is referring to Himself and His establishment: His angels and other servants.

The word *s^{a}* turns the verb that comes after it into the future tense. For example *$akt^{u}b^{u}$* means "I write":

أَكْتُبُ

But *s^{a}-$akt^{u}b^{u}$* means "I will write":

سَأَكْتُبُ

The verb *$n^{a}d^{ʿu}$* again has a non-standard spelling here. It would be written as follows in standard Arabic:

سَنَدْعُو

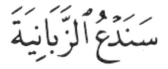

Al-z^{a}bān^{i}y^{a} is the plural of *al-zabān*, which literally means "one who thrusts", "one who shoves". This word refers to the angels who are in charge of Hell.

Verse 19

كَلَّا لَا تُطِعْهُ وَٱسْجُدْ وَٱقْتَرِب

No! But do not obey him, and prostrate yourself, and draw near [to God].

Transliteration: k^{a}llā lā t^{u}ṭ^{iʿ}-h^{u} w^{a}-usj^{u}d w^{a}-qt^{a}r^{i}b

Pronunciation: k^{a}l-lā lā t^{u}-ṭ^{iʿ}-h^{u} w^{a}s-j^{u}d w^{a}q-t^{a}-r^{i}b

K^{a}llā (No! But...) *lā* (do not) *t^{u}ṭ^{iʿ}-h^{u}* (you obey him) *w^{a}-sj^{u}d* (and prostrate yourself) *w^{a}-qt^{a}r^{i}b* (and draw near).

The phrase *t^{u}ṭ^{iʿ}-h^{u}* means "you obey him", while *lā t^{u}ṭ^{iʿ}-h^{u}* means "do not obey him". The verb *t^{u}ṭ^{iʿ}* becomes *aṭ^{aa}* ("he obeyed") in the past tense.

أَطَاعَ

The line above *w^{a}-usj^{u}d* tells readers that there is a voluntary prostration (*s^{a}jd^{a}*) here. When reaching this point in their reading, Muslims can prostrate themselves as a voluntary (rather than obligatory) act of piety. The phrase *w^{a}-usj^{u}d* is made up of *w^{a}* ("and") and *usj^{u}d* ("prostrate yourself!"). Below are three forms of this verb:

سَجَدَ يَسْجُدُ أُسْجُدْ

From right to left: he prostrated himself; he prostrates himself; prostrate yourself!

The last phrase is also a command: *w^{a}-qt^{a}r^{i}b*. The verb is *iqt^{a}r^{i}b* ("draw near!", "come closer!").

اقْتَرَبَ يَقْتَرِبُ اقْتَرِبْ

From right to left: he drew near; he draws near; draw near!

The *hamza* at the beginning of $iqt^{a}r^{a}b^{a}$ is part of the verb. Without it it becomes a different word:

قَرَبَ قَرَّبَ قَرِبَ قَرُبَ

From right to left: $qar^{a}b^{a}$ ("he sheathed a sword"); $q^{a}rr^{a}b^{a}$ ("he brought it near", "he advanced it", "he offered a sacrifice"), $q^{a}r^{i}b^{a}$ ("he drew near"), $q^{a}r^{u}b^{a}$ ("it was near", "it became near").

As you can see, the vowel on the second letter is essential in determining the meaning. Among them $q^{a}r^{i}b^{a}$ has the same meaning as $iqt^{a}r^{a}b^{a}$, but $iqt^{a}r^{a}b^{a}$ sounds stronger, more emphatic.

This page intentionally left blank

Lesson 16 Review

أَرَءَيْتَ إِن كَانَ عَلَى ٱلْهُدَىٰٓ

A-r^{a}^{ʾa}*yt*^{a} (Have you seen) *in* (if) *kān*^{a} (he was) ^{ʿa}*l*^{a} (upon) al-*h*^{u}*dā* (guidance).

أَوْ أَمَرَ بِٱلتَّقْوَىٰٓ

Aw (or) *am*^{a}*r*^{a} (he commanded) *b*^{i} (with/to) *al-t*^{a}*qwā* (piety, fear of God).

أَرَءَيْتَ إِن كَذَّبَ وَتَوَلَّىٰٓ

A-r^{a}^{ʾa}*yt*^{a} (have you seen) *in* (if) *k*^{a}*dhdh*^{a}*b*^{a} (he denied) *w*^{a} (and) *t*^{a}*w*^{a}*llā* (turned away).

أَلَمْ يَعْلَم بِأَنَّ ٱللَّهَ يَرَىٰ

A-l^{a}*m* (did not) *y*^{a}^{ʿ}*l*^{a}*m* (he knows) *b*^{i}*-ann*^{a} (about the fact that) *Allāh*^{a} (God) *y*^{a}*rā* (sees).

كَلَّا لَئِن لَّمْ يَنتَهِ لَنَسْفَعًۢا بِٱلنَّاصِيَةِ

نَاصِيَةٍ كَـٰذِبَةٍ خَاطِئَةٍ

Nāṣ^{i}*y*^{a}*t*^{in} (a forlock) *kādh*^{i}*b*^{a}*t*^{in} (a lying [one]) *khāṭ*^{i}^{ʾa} (a sinning [one]).

فَلْيَدْعُ نَادِيَهُۥ

F^{a} (then) *l* (let him) *y*^{a}*d*^{u} (he calls) *nādiy*^{a}*-h* (his associate).

سَنَدْعُ ٱلزَّبَانِيَةَ

S^{a}*-n*^{a}*d*^{u} (We will call) *al-z*^{a}*bān*^{i}*y*^{a} (the angels of Hell).

كَلَّا لَا تُطِعْهُ وَٱسْجُدْ وَٱقْتَرِب

K^{a}*llā* (No! But...) *lā* (do not) *t*^{u}*ṭ*^{i}*ʿ-h*^{u} (you obey him) *w*^{a}*-sj*^{u}*d* (and prostrate yourself) *w*^{a}*-qt*^{a}*r*^{i}*b* (and draw near).

Lesson 17: al-Layl Part 1

We will move on to chapter 92 of the Quran, *al-Layl* ("the Night").

بِسْمِ ٱللَّهِ ٱلرَّحْمَٰنِ ٱلرَّحِيمِ

Verse 1

وَٱلَّيْلِ إِذَا يَغْشَىٰ

By the night when it covers
Transliteration: w^{a}-al-l^{a}yl^{i} idhā y^{a}ghshā
Pronunciation: w^{a}l-l^{a}y-l^{i} i-dhā y^{a}gh-shā

W^{a} (by) *al-l^{a}yl^{i}* (the night) *idhā* (when) *y^{a}ghshā* (it covers).

The word *l^{a}yl* is Arabic for "night". The phrase "the night" does not refer to any particular night, it refers to nights in general.

Its plural is *l^{a}yāl* ("nights"):

لَيَالٍ

In lesson 14, verse 2 we saw the verb *s^{a}jā* ("it becomes covered with darkness"). In this verse the verb *y^{a}ghshā* is used to mean "it covers". The word *s^{a}jā* has a connotation of silence, quietness, and darkness, while *y^{a}ghshā* has no such connotations.

غَشِيَ يَغْشَى اغْشَ

Above are three forms of the verb: it covered; it covers; cover [it]!

The purpose of showing these different forms is not that you should memorize them. They are only there for you to try to read and make sense of so that you become familiar with the way the language works.

Verse 2

وَالنَّهَارِ إِذَا تَجَلَّى

By the daytime when it radiantly appears
Transliteration: w^{a}-al-n^{a}hār^{i} idhā t^{a}j^{a}llā
Pronunciation: w^{a}-al-n^{a}hār^{i} idhā t^{a}j^{a}llā

W^{a} (by) *al-n^{a}hār^{i}* (the daytime) *idhā* (when) *t^{a}j^{a}llā* (it radiantly appeared).

The word *al-n^{a}hār* (day, daytime) is the opposite of *al-l^{a}yl* (night, nighttime).

The verb *t^{a}j^{a}llā* means “it appeared radiantly”, “it appeared and shone brightly”. While it is in the past tense, the *idhā* before it turns it into the present tense.

تَجَلَّى يَتَجَلَّى تَجَلَّ

Above from right to left: it radiantly appeared; it radiantly appears; appear radiantly!

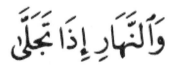

Verse 3

وَمَا خَلَقَ ٱلذَّكَرَ وَٱلْأُنثَىٰٓ

And that which created the male and the female
Transliteration: w^{a}-mā kh^{a}l^{a}q^{a} al-dh^{a}k^{a}r^{a} w^{a}-al-unthā
Pronunciation: w^{a}-mā kh^{a}-l^{a}-q^{a} al-dh^{a}-k^{a}-r^{a} w^{a}l-un-thā

W^{a} (and) *mā* (what) *kh^{a}l^{a}q^{a}* (he created) *al-dh^{a}k^{a}r^{a}* (the male) *w^{a}* (and) *al-unthā* (the female).

The word *mā* "that which", "what", as in "that is what I wrote":

ذَٰلِكَ مَا كَتَبْتُ

The first word above is *dhāl^{i}k^{a}* (masculine "that"). There is an *alif* sound after the "dh", but it does not show up in writing. The word *mā* can also be used to create a negative, as follows:

مَا كَتَبْتُ ذَٰلِكَ

Above we have *mā k^{a}t^{a}bt^{u} dhāl^{i}k^{a}* ("I did not write that"). It depends on the context whether *mā* means "that which" or "did not/was not".

The plural of *al-dh^{a}k^{a}r* ("the male") is *al-dh^{u}kūr* and *al-dh^{u}krān* ("the males"):

الذكُوْر الذُّكْران

The plural of *al-unthā* ("the female") is *al-ināth* ("the females"):

الإِنَاث

Verse 4

إِنَّ سَعْيَكُمْ لَشَتَّىٰ

Indeed your efforts are truly diverse
Transliteration: inn^{a} s^{a}ʿy^{a}-k^{u}m l^{a}-sh^{a}ttā
Pronunciation: in-n^{a} s^{a}ʿ-y^{a}-k^{u}m l^{a}-sh^{a}t-tā

Inn^{a} (indeed) *s^{a}ʿy^{a}-k^{u}m* (your efforts) *l^{a}-sh^{a}ttā* (truly diverse, truly various).

S^{a}ʿy^{a}-k^{u}m is made up of *saʿī* ("effort", "efforts") and the pronoun *k^{u}m* (plural "your"). While *saʿī* is singular, it is often used, as in here, to mean a bundle of efforts, so it is correct to translate it both as "effort" and "efforts".

The word *sh^{a}ttā* ("diverse things", "various things") is the plural of *shatīt* ("differing", "varying", "scattered"). The word *shatīt* is rarely used, the plural *sh^{a}ttā* is the commonly used word to mean "diverse", "various".

Verse 5

فَأَمَّا مَنْ أَعْطَىٰ وَاتَّقَىٰ

So as for he who gives and fears [God]
Transliteration: F^{a}-ammā m^{a}n aʿṭā w^{a}-itt^{a}qā
Pronunciation: F^{a}-am-mā m^{a}n aʿ-ṭā w^{a}t-t^{a}-qā

F^{a} (then) *ammā* (as for) *m^{a}n* (he who) *aʿṭā* (gives) *w^{a}-itt^{a}qā* (and fears [God]).

The word *m^{a}n* means "he/she who".

أَنَا مَنْ كَتَبَ ذَلِك

Above is the sentence *anā* (I [am]) $m^{a}n$ (he who) $k^{a}t^{a}b^{a}$ (wrote) $dh\bar{a}l^{i}k$ (that) (I am he who wrote that). Depending on the context, $m^{a}n$ can also be used to ask a question:

مَنْ كَتَبَ ذَلِك؟

Above is the sentence $m^{a}n$ (who) $k^{a}t^{a}b^{a}$ (wrote) $dh\bar{a}l^{i}k$ (that) (Who wrote that?)

The verb $itt^{a}q\bar{a}$ means “he was cautiously mindful [of God]”, it is generally translated shortly as “he feared [God]”. We already saw a word from the same root in Lesson 16: $t^{a}qw\bar{a}$ (“fear of God”).

تَقْوَى

Below are the different tenses of $itt^{a}q\bar{a}$:

اتَّقَى يَتَّقِي اتَّقِ

From right to left: he feared [God]; he fears [God]; fear [God]!

Verse 6

وَصَدَّقَ بِٱلْحُسْنَىٰ

And affirms the most beautiful

Transliteration: w^{a}-ṣ^{a}dd^{a}q^{a} b^{i}-al-ḥ^{u}snā

Pronunciation: w^{a}-ṣ^{a}d-d^{a}-q^{a} b^{i}l-ḥ^{u}s-nā

W^{a}-ṣ^{a}dd^{a}q^{a} (and affirmed) *b^{i}* (with/by) *al-ḥ^{u}snā* (the most beautiful).

The verb *ṣ^{a}dd^{a}q^{a}* ("he affirmed", "he considered it to be true", "he considered him a teller of truth") is the opposite of *k^{a}dhdh^{a}b^{a}* ("he denied", "he considered it a lie", "he considered him a liar").

The word *al-ḥ^{u}snā* ("the most beautiful") is the feminine form if *al-aḥsan* ("the more beautiful", "the most beautiful"). However, the feminine form only means "most", not "more". There are different interpretations of what may be meant by *al-ḥ^{u}snā.* Some consider it to refer to the reward of the Hereafter, while others consider it to refer to words that affirm the truth of God's oneness and other attributes and items of faith.

The *bi* ("by", "with") before *al-ḥ^{u}snā* is necessary in Arabic while in English it has no place.

Verse 7

فَسَنُيَسِّرُهُۥ لِلْيُسْرَىٰ

Then we will ease him toward ease

Transliteration: f^{a}-s^{a}-n^{u}y^{a}ss^{i}r^{u}-h^{u} l^{i}-l-y^{u}srā

Pronunciation: f^{a}-s^{a}-n^{u}-y^{a}s-s^{i}-r^{u}-h^{u} l^{i}-l-y^{u}s-rā

F^{a} (then) *s^{a}* (will) *n^{u}y^{a}ss^{i}r^{u}* (we make easy) *h^{u}* (him) *l^{i}* (for) *l-y^{u}srā* (ease).

The meaning of the verse is that God will facilitate things for such a person toward that which is easiest and most problem-free for them.

The verb *n^{u}y^{a}ss^{i}r^{u}* means "we make it easy", "we facilitate". While *n^{u}y^{a}ss^{i}r^{u}-h^{u}* literally means "we make him easy", the meaning is that the way is made easy for him.

يَسَّرَ يُيَسِّرُ يَسِّرْ

Above are the different tenses of $n^{u}y^{a}ss^{i}r^{u}$ when converted to the singular: he made [it] easy; he makes [it] easy; make it easy!

The next word is *al-*y^{u}*srā* which comes from the same root as $n^{u}y^{a}ss^{i}r^{u}$ and means "ease". It is the feminine form of *ays*^{a}*r* ("easier", "easiest"). Since it has a l^{i} before it, the *hamza* of the *al* is removed. The word originally is:

لِ الْيُسْرَى

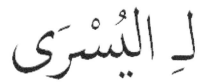

When the l^{i} joins it, it becomes:

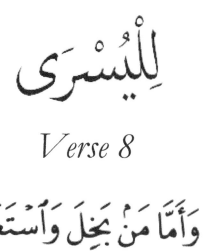

لِلْيُسْرَى

Verse 8

وَأَمَّا مَنۢ بَخِلَ وَٱسْتَغْنَىٰ

And as for one who withholds and considers himself needless
Transliteration: w^{a}-ammā m^{a}n $b^{a}kh^{i}l^{a}$ w^{a}-ist^{a}ghnā
Pronunciation: w^{a}-am-mā m^{a}n b^{a}-kh^{i}-l^{a} w^{a}s-t^{a}gh-nā

W^{a}-ammā (and as for) *$m^{a}n$* (he who) *$b^{a}kh^{i}l^{a}$* (he withheld) *w^{a}-ist^{a}ghnā* (and considered himself needless/self-sufficient).

The verb *$b^{a}kh^{i}l^{a}$* means "he withheld [his money] in a miserly manner", "he was ungenerous".

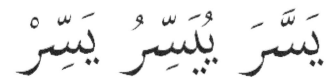

بَخِلَ يَبْخَلُ ابْخَلْ

From right to left: he withheld; he withholds; withhold!

Verse 9

وَكَذَّبَ بِٱلْحُسْنَىٰ

And denied the most beautiful
Translation: w^{a}-k^{a}dhdh^{a}b^{a} b^{i}-al-ḥ^{u}snā
Pronunciation: w^{a}-k^{a}dh-dh^{a}-b^{a} b^{i}l-ḥ^{u}s-nā

W^{a}-k^{a}dhdh^{a}b^{a} (and denied) *b^{i}-al-ḥ^{u}snā* (the most beautiful).

As mentioned in verse 7, *k^{a}dhdh^{a}b^{a}* ("he denied", "he considered him a liar") is the opposite of *ṣ^{a}dd^{a}q^{a}* ("he affirmed").

Verse 10

فَسَنُيَسِّرُهُۥ لِلْعُسْرَىٰ

Then we will ease him toward difficulty
Transliteration: f^{a}-s^{a}-n^{u}y^{a}ss^{i}r^{u}-h^{u} l^{i}-l- ^{ʿu}srā
Pronunciation: f^{a}-s^{a}-n^{u}-y^{a}s-s^{i}-r^{u}-h^{u} l^{i}l- ^{ʿu}s-rā

F^{a}-s^{a}-n^{u}y^{a}ss^{i}r^{u}-h^{u} (then we will ease him) *l^{i}* (to, toward) *l- ^{ʿu}srā* (difficulty).

The meaning of the verse is that God will arrange matters for such a person so that they easily fall into difficulties, although by "difficulty" the punishment of the Hereafter can also be meant.

The first part of the verse is the same as verse 8. The word *al-^{ʿu}srā* means "the most difficult", and more generally means "difficulty". It is the feminine of *aʿs^{a}r* ("more difficult", "most difficult"):

أَعْسَر

Verse 11

وَمَا يُغْنِى عَنْهُ مَالُهُۥٓ إِذَا تَرَدَّىٰٓ

And his wealth avails him not when he falls
Transliteration: w^{a}-mā y^{u}ghnī ^{ca}n-h^{u} māl^{u}-h^{u} idhā t^{a}r^{a}ddā
Pronunciation: w^{a}-mā y^{u}gh-nī ^{ca}n-h^{u} mā-l^{u}-h^{u} idhā t^{a}-r^{a}d-dā

W^{a}-mā (and it does not) *y^{u}ghnī ^{ca}n-h^{u}* (avails him) *māl^{u}-h^{u}* (his wealth, his property) *idhā* (when) *t^{a}r^{a}ddā* (he fell [into the Hellfire]).

The verb *y^{u}ghnī* means "it makes [him] needless", "it avails [him]". The phrase *y^{u}ghnī ^{ca}n-h^{u}* means "it avails him". The phrase *^{ca}n-h^{u}* literally means "from him" and is necessary for the Arabic phrasing while in English it has no place.

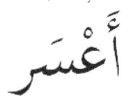

This page intentionally left blank

Lesson 17 Review

بِسْمِ ٱللَّهِ ٱلرَّحْمَٰنِ ٱلرَّحِيمِ

وَٱلَّيْلِ إِذَا يَغْشَىٰ

W^{a} (by) *al-l*^{a}*yl*^{i} (the night) *idhā* (when) *y*^{a}*ghshā* (it covers).

وَٱلنَّهَارِ إِذَا تَجَلَّىٰ

W^{a} (by) *al-n*^{a}*hār*^{i} (the daytime) *idhā* (when) *t*^{a}*j*^{a}*llā* (it radiantly appeared).

وَمَا خَلَقَ ٱلذَّكَرَ وَٱلْأُنثَىٰٓ

W^{a} (and) *mā* (what) *kh*^{a}*l*^{a}*q*^{a} (he created) *al-dh*^{a}*k*^{a}*r*^{a} (the male) *w*^{a} (and) *al-unthā* (the female).

إِنَّ سَعْيَكُمْ لَشَتَّىٰ

Inn^{a} (indeed) *s*^{a}*ʿy*^{a}*-k*^{u}*m* (your efforts) *l*^{a}*-sh*^{a}*ttā* (truly diverse, truly various).

فَأَمَّا مَنْ أَعْطَىٰ وَٱتَّقَىٰ

F^{a} (then) *ammā* (as for) *m*^{a}*n* (he who) *aʿṭā* (gives) *w*^{a}*-itt*^{a}*qā* (and fears [God]).

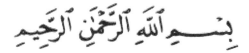

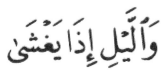

وَصَدَّقَ بِٱلْحُسْنَىٰ

W[a]-ṣ[a]dd[a]q[a] (and affirmed) *b[i]* (with/by) *al-ḥ[u]snā* (the most beautiful).

فَسَنُيَسِّرُهُۥ لِلْيُسْرَىٰ

F[a] (then) *s[a]* (will) *n[u]y[a]ss[i]r[u]* (we make easy) *h[u]* (him) *l[i]* (for) *l-y[u]srā* (ease).

وَأَمَّا مَنۢ بَخِلَ وَٱسْتَغْنَىٰ

W[a]-ammā (and as for) *m[a]n* (he who) *b[a]kh[i]l[a]* (he withheld) *w[a]-ist[a]ghnā* (and considered himself needless/self-sufficient).

وَكَذَّبَ بِٱلْحُسْنَىٰ

W[a]-k[a]dhdh[a]b[a] (and denied) *b[i]-al-ḥ[u]snā* (the most beautiful).

فَسَنُيَسِّرُهُۥ لِلْعُسْرَىٰ

F[a]-s[a]-n[u]y[a]ss[i]r[u]-h[u] (then we will ease him) *l[i]* (to, toward) *l- ʿ[u]srā* (difficulty).

وَمَا يُغْنِى عَنْهُ مَالُهُۥٓ إِذَا تَرَدَّىٰٓ

W[a]-mā (and it does not) *y[u]ghnī ʿ[a]n-h[u]* (avail him) *māl[u]-h[u]* (his wealth, his property) *idhā* (when) *t[a]r[a]ddā* (he fell [into the Hellfire]).

Lesson 18: al-Layl Part 2

Verse 12

إِنَّ عَلَيْنَا لَلْهُدَىٰ

Indeed, truly upon us is guidance
Transliteration: inn^{a} ^{ca}l^{a}y-nā l^{a}-l-h^{u}dā
Pronunciation: in-n^{a} ^{ca}-l^{a}y-nā l^{a}l-h^{u}-dā

Inn^{a} (indeed) *^{ca}l^{a}y-nā* (upon us) *l^{a}* (truly) *l-h^{u}dā* (guidance).

The phrase *^{ca}l^{a}y-nā* is made up of ʿalā ("upon") and the pronoun *nā* ("us"). The meaning is "it is our duty". The word *ʿalā* when combined with a pronoun becomes *^{ca}l^{a}y*, as follows:

عَلَى نَا — عَلَيْنَا

The emphatic *l^{a}* before *al-h^{u}dā* ("truly guidance") serves to strengthen the original emphatic *inn^{a}*. It English it is strange to say "Indeed, upon us is truly guidance", the correct meaning is "Indeed, truly upon us is guidance".

Verse 13

وَإِنَّ لَنَا لَلْآخِرَةَ وَالْأُولَىٰ

And indeed for us truly is the Hereafter and the first [life]
Transliteration: w^{a}-inn^{a} l^{a}nā l^{a}-l-ākh^{i}r^{a}t^{a} w^{a}-al-ūlā
Pronunciation: w^{a}-in-n^{a} l^{a}-nā l^{a}l-ā-kh^{i}-r^{a}-t^{a} w^{a}l-ū-lā

W^{a}-inn^{a} (and indeed) *l^{a}-nā* (for us) *l^{a}-al-ākh^{i}r^{a}t^{a}* (truly the Hereafter) *w^{a}-al-ūlā* (and the first).

The word *al-ūlā* ("the first one") is the feminine of *al-^{a}ww^{a}l* ("the first one"):

الأَوَّل

It depends on the context whether one uses the feminine or the masculine form of an adjective.

Verse 14

فَأَنذَرۡتُكُمۡ نَارٗا تَلَظَّىٰ

So I have warned you of a fire that blazes.
Transliteration: f^{a}-andh^{a}rt^{u}k^{u}m nār^{an} t^{a}l^{a}ẓẓā
Pronunciation: f^{a}-an-dh^{a}r-t^{u}-k^{u}m nā-r^{an} t^{a}-l^{a}ẓ-ẓā

F^{a}-andh^{a}rt^{u}k^{u}m (so I have warned you [of]) *nār^{an}* (a fire) *t^{a}l^{a}ẓẓā* (it blazed violently).

The verb *andh^{a}rt^{u}* can mean "I warned" and "I warned [him] of [something]" The "of" is part of the meaning of the verb (in Arabic we say the verb takes two objects). Here the first object is *k^{u}m* ("you") and the second object is *nār^{an}* ("a fire"), so the full meaning is "I warned you of a fire". The verb *t^{a}l^{a}ẓẓā* "it blazes violently" would actually be *tat^{a}l^{a}ẓẓā* in standard Arabic. The first *tā'* is removed for poetic effect.

Verse 15

لَا يَصۡلَىٰهَآ إِلَّا ٱلۡأَشۡقَى

None experiences its heat and burn except the most wretched
Transliteration: lā y^{a}ṣlā-hā illā al-ashqā
Pronunciation: lā y^{a}ṣ-lā-hā il-l^{a}l-ash-qā

Lā (does not) *y^{a}ṣlā-hā* (experiences its heat and burn) *illā* (except) *al-ashqā* (the most wretched).

The verb *y^{a}ṣlā* means "experiences the heat and burn [of a fire]". The word *al-ashqā* ("the more wretched", "the most wretched") is not a feminine superlative like the ones we saw before, so it means "more" or "most" depending on the context.

Verse 16

ٱلَّذِى كَذَّبَ وَتَوَلَّىٰ

Who denies and turns away
Translation: all^{a}dhī k^{a}dhdh^{a}b^{a} w^{a}-t^{a}w^{a}llā
Pronunciation: al-l^{a}-dhī k^{a}dh-dh^{a}-b^{a} w^{a}-t^{a}-w^{a}l-lā

All^{a}dhī (who, the one who) *k^{a}dhdh^{a}b^{a}* (denied) *w^{a}-t^{a}w^{a}llā* (and turned away).

This verse and the two before it are worded as if they are in the past tense but from the context of the chapter we know they are referring to the present.

تَوَلَّى يَتَوَلَّى تَوَلَّ

From right to left: he turned away; he turns away; turn away!

Verse 17

وَسَيُجَنَّبُهَا ٱلْأَتْقَى

And the most pious will be made to avoid it.
Transliteration: w^{a}-s^{a}-y^{u}j^{a}nn^{a}b^{u}-hā al-atqā
Pronunciation: w^{a}-s^{a}-y^{u}-j^{a}n-n^{a}-b^{u}-h^{a}l-at-qā

W^{a} (and) *s^{a}* (will) *y^{u}j^{a}nn^{a}b^{u}* (will be made to avoid) *hā* (it) *al-atqā* (the most pious).

جَنَّبَ يُجَنِّبُ جَنِّبْ

From right to left: he avoided; he avoids; avoid! The verb used in the Quran is none of the above exactly; it is *y*^{u}*j*^{a}*nn*^{a}*b* which means "he is made to avoid it". It is in the present third person passive voice.

يُجَنَّب

The person is an object who is *made* to avoid it [by God], and the subject (the doer of the action), who is God, is hidden. The meaning is that while we can work toward avoiding the Hellfire, God's guidance and help is essential in succeeding.

Al-atqā means "the more pious", "the most pious". Here it means "the most pious". The meaning is not that only the most pious will be made to avoid the Hellfire. "The most pious" is being used to contrast with "the most wretched" from verse 15.

Verse 18

ٱلَّذِى يُؤْتِى مَالَهُۥ يَتَزَكَّىٰ

Who gives his wealth to purify himself
Translation: all^{a}dhī y^{u}'tī māl^{a}-hū y^{a}t^{a}z^{a}kkā
Pronunciation: al-l^{a}-dhī y^{u}'-tī mā-l^{a}-hū y^{a}-t^{a}-z^{a}k-kā

All^{a}*dhī* (the one who) *y*^{u}*'tī* (gives) *māl*^{a}*-hū* (his money) *y*^{a}*t*^{a}*z*^{a}*kkā* (he purifies himself).

The verb *y*^{u}*'tī* means "he gives":

آتَى يُؤْتِي آتِ

From right to left: he gave; he gives; give!

The verb *y^u'tī* has a similar meaning to *yu'ṭi* ("he gives", "he bestows"):

يُعْطِي

But *yu'ṭi* has a connotation of bestowal and favor. The verb *y^u'tī* (the one in the current verse) merely means "to give", whether it is to give away money or to hand someone an object in any other context.

تَزَكَّى يَتَزَكَّى تَزَكَّ

From right to left: he purified himself; he purifies himself; purify yourself! The word *zakāt*, which in Islam refers to the alms tax on wealth, comes from the same root as this word and literally means "purification".

زَكَاة

Verse 19

وَمَا لِأَحَدٍ عِندَهُۥ مِن نِّعْمَةٍ تُجْزَىٰٓ

And there is not for anyone with him a favor to be recompensed

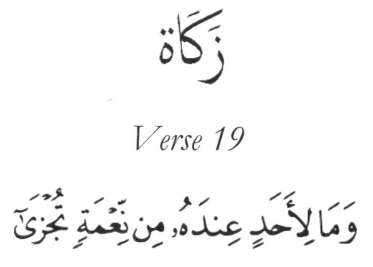

Transliteration: w^{a}-mā l^{i}-aḥ^{a}d^{in} ʿind^{a}-hū m^{i}n n^{iʿ}m^{a}t^{in} t^{u}jzā

Pronunciation: w^{a}-mā l^{i}-a-ḥ^{a}-d^{i}n ʿin-d^{a}-hū m^{i}n n^{iʿ}-m^{a}-t^{in} t^{u}j-zā

W^{a} (and) *mā* (is not) *l*^{i} (for) *aḥ*^{a}*d*^{in} (anyone) *ʿind*^{a}*-hū* (with him, by him) *m*^{i}*n* (of) *n*^{i}*ʿm*^{a}*t*^{in} (a favor, a blessing) *t*^{u}*jzā* (is recompensed).

The meaning of this verse is that this doer of charity does not have any favor that he has to return to someone. He is giving his wealth purely for God's sake; he is not rewarding anyone for past favors.

جَزَى يَجْزِي اجْزِ

From right to left: he recompensed; he recompenses; recompense! The verb used in the Quranic verse is *t*^{u}*jzā* ("is recompensed") which is in the passive voice:

تُجْزَى

Verse 20

إِلَّا ٱبْتِغَآءَ وَجْهِ رَبِّهِ ٱلْأَعْلَىٰ

Except only to seek the countenance of his Lord, Most High

Transliteration: illā ibt^{i}ghā^{ʾa} w^{a}jh^{i} r^{a}bb^{i}-h^{i} al-aʿlā

Pronunciation: il-l^{a}b-t^{i}-ghā-^{ʾa} w^{a}j-h^{i} r^{a}b-b^{i}-h^{i}l-a^{ʿ}-lā

Illā (except, only) *ibt*^{i}*ghā*^{a} (to seek) *w*^{a}*jh*^{i} (face [of], countenance [of]) *r*^{a}*bb*^{i}*-h*^{i} (his Lord) *al-aʿlā* (the highest).

Ibt^{i}*ghā'* means "to seek", from the verb *ibt*^{a}*ghā* ("he sought"):

ابْتَغَى يَبْتَغِي ابْتَغِ

From right to left: he sought; he seeks; seek!

Verse 21

وَلَسَوْفَ يَرْضَىٰ

And he truly will be satisfied
Transliteration: w^a-l^a-s^{a}wf^a y^{a}rḍā
Pronunciation: w^a-l^a-s^{a}w-f^a y^{a}r-ḍā

W^a (and) *l^a* (truly) *s^{a}wf^a* (will) *y^{a}rḍā* (he is satisfied)

The word *s^{a}wf^a* ("will") is like *s^a*, it turns the verb that comes after it into the future tense.

This page intentionally left blank

Lesson 18 Review

إِنَّ عَلَيْنَا لَلْهُدَىٰ

Inn^{a} (indeed) ^{a}*l*^{a}*y-nā* (upon us) *l*^{a} (truly) *l-h*^{u}*dā* (guidance).

وَإِنَّ لَنَا لَلْءَاخِرَةَ وَٱلْأُولَىٰ

W^{a}*-inn*^{a} (and indeed) *l*^{a}*-nā* (for us) *l*^{a}*-al-ākh*^{i}*r*^{a}*t*^{a} (truly the Hereafter) *w*^{a}*-al-ūlā* (and the first).

فَأَنذَرْتُكُمْ نَارًا تَلَظَّىٰ

F^{a}*-andh*^{a}*rt*^{u}*k*^{u}*m* (so I have warned you [of]) *nār*^{an} (a fire) *t*^{a}*l*^{a}*ẓẓā* (it blazed violently).

لَا يَصْلَىٰهَآ إِلَّا ٱلْأَشْقَى

Lā (does not) *y*^{a}*ṣlā-hā* (experiences its heat and burn) *illā* (except) *al-ashqā* (the most wretched).

ٱلَّذِى كَذَّبَ وَتَوَلَّىٰ

All^{a}*dhī* (who, the one who) *k*^{a}*dhdh*^{a}*b*^{a} (denied) *w*^{a}*-t*^{a}*w*^{a}*llā* (and turned away).

وَسَيُجَنَّبُهَا ٱلْأَتْقَى

W^{a} (and) *s*^{a} (will) *y*^{u}*j*^{a}*nn*^{a}*b*^{u} (will be made to avoid) *hā* (it) *al-atqā* (the most pious).

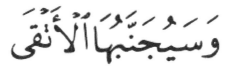

ٱلَّذِى يُؤْتِى مَالَهُۥ يَتَزَكَّىٰ

All^{a}*dhī* (the one who) *y*^{u}*'tī* (gives) *māl*^{a}*-hū* (his money) *y*^{a}*t*^{a}*z*^{a}*kkā* (he purifies himself).

وَمَا لِأَحَدٍ عِندَهُۥ مِن نِّعْمَةٍ تُجْزَىٰٓ

W^{a} (and) *mā* (is not) *l*^{i} (for) *aḥ*^{a}*d*^{in} (anyone) *ʿind*^{a}*-hū* (with him, by him) *m*^{i}*n* (of) *n*^{i}*ʿm*^{a}*t*^{in} (a favor, a blessing) *t*^{u}*jzā* (is recompensed).

إِلَّا ٱبْتِغَآءَ وَجْهِ رَبِّهِ ٱلْأَعْلَىٰ

Illā (except, only) *ibt*^{i}*ghā*^{a} (to seek) *w*^{a}*jh*^{i} (face [of], countenance [of]) *r*^{a}*bb*^{i}*-h*^{i} (his Lord) *al-aʿlā* (the highest).

وَلَسَوْفَ يَرْضَىٰ

W^{a} (and) *l*^{a} (truly) *s*^{a}*wf*^{a} (will) *y*^{a}*rḍā* (he is satisfied)

W^{a} (and) *l*^{a} (truly) *s*^{a}*wf*^{a} *y*^{a}*rḍā* (he will be satisfied)

Lesson 19: al-Fajr Part 1

In this lesson we will move to chapter 89 of the Quran; *al-Fajr* (the Dawn).

بِسۡمِ ٱللَّهِ ٱلرَّحۡمَٰنِ ٱلرَّحِيمِ

Verse 1

وَٱلۡفَجۡرِ

By the dawn
Transliteration: w^{a}-al-f^{a}jr
Pronunciation: w^{a}l-f^{a}jr

Verse 2

وَلَيَالٍ عَشۡرٖ

And by ten nights
Transliteration: w^{a}-l^{a}yāl^{in} ʿ^{a}shr
Pronunciation: w^{a}-l^{a}-yā-l^{in} ʿ^{a}shr

W^{a} (by) *l*^{a}*yāl*^{in} (nights) ʿ^{a}*shr* (ten).

The ten nights referred to here are the first ten nights of the Islamic month of Dhul Ḥijja according Quran exegetes.

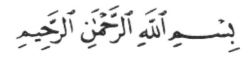

Verse 3

وَٱلشَّفْعِ وَٱلْوَتْرِ

By the even and the odd
Transliteration: w^a-al-sh^{a}f^{ʿi} w^a-al-w^{a}tr
Pronunciation: w^{a}sh-sh^{a}f-^{ʿi} w^{a}l-w^{a}tr

W^a (by) *al-sh*^{a}*f*^{ʿi} (the even) *w*^{a}*-al-w*^{a}*tr* (and the odd).

The even and odd could refer to numbers. They can also be references to pairs and individuals. According to some *al-sh*^{a}*f*^{ʿ} ("even") refers to Adam and Eve while *al-w*^{a}*tr* ("the odd", "the individual") refers to God.

Verse 4

وَٱلَّيْلِ إِذَا يَسْرِ

By the night when it passes
Transliteration: w^a-al-l^{a}yl^i idhā y^{a}sr
Pronunciation: w^{a}l-l^{a}y-l^i i-dhā y^{a}sr

W^a (by) *al-l*^{a}*yl*^{i} (the night) *idhā* (when) *y*^{a}*sr* (it passes).

The verb *y*^{a}*sr*^{i} is *y*^{a}*srī* in standard Arabic:

سَرَى يَسْرِي اسْرِ

From right to left: he passed; he passes; pass!

Verse 5

هَلْ فِي ذَٰلِكَ قَسَمٌ لِّذِي حِجْرٍ

Is there in that an oath for one who posses perception?
Transliteration: h^{a}l fī dhāl^{i}k^{a} q^{a}s^{a}m^{un} l^{i}-dhī ḥ^{i}jr
Pronunciation: h^{a}l fī dhā-l^{i}-k^{a} q^{a}-s^{a}-m^{un} l^{i}-dhī ḥ^{i}jr

H^{a}l (is there) *fī* (in) *dhāl^{i}k^{a}* (that) *q^{a}s^{a}m^{un}* (an oath) *l^{i}* (for) *dhī* (possessor of) *ḥ^{i}jr* (perception, rationality).

The *h^{a}l* at the beginning turns the sentence into a question. The phrase *dhī ḥ^{i}jr* means "possessor of perception", "possessor of rationality". The word *dhī* is used to express possession.

Verse 6

أَلَمْ تَرَ كَيْفَ فَعَلَ رَبُّكَ بِعَادٍ

Have you not seen how your Lord dealt with ʿĀd?
Transliteration: a-l^{a}m t^{a}r^{a} k^{a}yf^{a} f^{aʿa}l^{a} r^{a}bb^{u}k^{a} b^{i}-ʿād
Pronunciation: a-l^{a}m t^{a}-r^{a} k^{a}y-f^{a} f^{a}-^{ʿa}-l^{a} r^{a}b-b^{u}-k^{a} b^{i}-ʿād

A-l^{a}m (have not) *t^{a}r^{a}* (you see) *k^{a}yf^{a}* (how) *f^{a} ^{a}l^{a}* (he dealt) *r^{a}bb^{u}k^{a}* (your Lord) *b^{i}* (with) *ʿād*.

The verb *t^{a}r^{a}* (you see) is *t^{a}rā* in standard Arabic with an *alif* at the end. *Faʿala* means "he did", "he performed an action". The phrase is *Faʿala...b^{i}*, the meaning is "he dealt with". ʿĀd is the name of a pre-Islamic civilization that existed in Arabia until it was destroyed by God.

Verse 7

إِرَمَ ذَاتِ ٱلْعِمَادِ

Iram, the possessor pillars

Transliteration: Ir^{a}m^{a} dh^{a}t^{i} al-ʿimād

Pronunciation: Ir^{a}-m^{a} dh^{a}-t^{i}l-ʿi-mād

Ir^{a}m^{a} dh^{a}t^{i} (possessor of) *al-ʿimād* (the pillars).

Iram is the name of the main city of ʿĀd. The word *dh^{a}t^{i}*, similar to *dh^{u}*, means “possessor of”. It is the feminine form of *dh^{u}*.

Verse 8

ٱلَّتِي لَمْ يُخْلَقْ مِثْلُهَا فِي ٱلْبِلَٰدِ

Which the like of had not been created in the cities

Transliteration: all^{a}tī l^{a}m y^{u}khl^{a}q m^{i}thl^{u}-hā f^{i}-al-b^{i}lād

Pronunciation: al-l^{a}tī l^{a}m y^{u}kh-l^{a}q m^{i}th-l^{u}-hā f^{i}l-b^{i}l-ād

All^{a}tī (which) *l^{a}m y^{u}khl^{a}q* (had not been created) *m^{i}thl^{u}-hā* (its like) *f^{i}-al-b^{i}lād* (in the cities).

The word *all^{a}tī* (“which”) is the feminine of *all^{a}dhī*.

Verse 9

وَثَمُودَ ٱلَّذِينَ جَابُوا۟ ٱلصَّخْرَ بِٱلْوَادِ

And Thamud, who carved out the rocks in the valley?

Transliteration: w^{a}-th^{a}mūd^{a} all^{a}dhīn^{a} jābū al-ṣ^{a}khr^{a} b^{i}-al-wād

Pronunciation: w^{a}-th^{a}-mū-d^{a}l-l^{a}-dhī-n^{a} jā-būṣ-ṣ^{a}kh-r^{a} b^{i}l-wād

W^{a}-th^{a}mūd^{a} (and Thamud) *all^{a}dhīn^{a}* (those who) *jābū* (carved out) *al-ṣ^{a}khr^{a}* (the rocks) *b^{i}-al-wād* (in/at the valley).

Thamud is the name of another pre-Islamic Arabian civilization destroyed by God. *Al-ṣ^{a}khr* (“the rocks”) is the plural of *al-ṣ^{a}khra* (“the rock”).

الصَّخْرَة الصَّخْر

الشَّجَرَة الشَّجَر

Above, the first line shows *al-ṣ*^{a}*khra* ("the rock") on the right and its plural on the left. On the second line there is another word whose plural follows the same pattern. On the right is *al-sh*^{a}*j*^{a}*r*^{a} ("the tree"), on the left is *al-sh*^{a}*j*^{a}*r* ("the trees").

The word wād has a *yā'* at the end which is thrown away in the Quranic text:

الوَادِي

Verse 10

وَفِرْعَوْنَ ذِى ٱلْأَوْتَادِ

And Pharaoh, possessor of the stakes
Transliteration: w^{a}-f^{i}r^{ʿa}wn^{a} dhī al-awtād
Pronunciation: w^{a}-f^{i}r-^{ʿa}w-n^{a} dhīl-aw-tād

W^{a}*-f*^{i}*r*^{a}*wn*^{a} (and Pharaoh) *dhī* (possessor of) *al-awtād* (the stakes).

F^{i}*r*^{a}*wn* is Arabic for Pharaoh, the title of the rulers of ancient Egypt. The word *dhī* ("possessor of") is the same as *dhū*. The word changes based on context. The word *al-awtād* ("the stakes") is the plural of *al-w*^{a}*t*^{a}*d* ("the stake").

الوَتَد

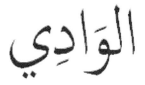

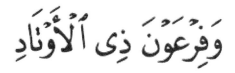

It may refer to largeness of Pharaoh's army, which had to use a large number of stakes for its camping tents. It may also refer to a form of punishment by stakes (impalement) practiced by Pharaoh.

Verse 11

ٱلَّذِينَ طَغَوْا۟ فِى ٱلْبِلَـٰدِ

Those who oppressed in the cities

Transliteration: all^{a}dhīn^{a} ṭ^{a}gh^{a}w fī al-b^{i}lād

Pronunciation: al-l^{a}-dhī-n^{a} ṭ^{a}-gh^{a}w fīl-b^{i}-lād

Alladhīna (those who) *ṭaghaw* (oppressed) *fī* (in) *al-bilād* (the cities, the land).

The verb *ṭaghaw* ("they oppressed", "they acted despotically") is the plural third person form of *ṭaghā*:

طَغَى يَطْغَى اطْغَ

From right to left: he oppressed; he oppresses; oppress!

The word *al-bilād* is written with an *alif* in standard Arabic:

البِلَاد

While this word literally means "the cities", it is also used to mean "the land". For example the phrase *bilād al-shām* means "the lands of the Levant".

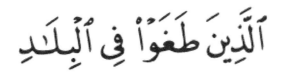

Verse 12

فَأَكْثَرُوا۟ فِيهَا ٱلْفَسَادَ

So they increased in it corruption
Transliteration: f^{a}-akth^{a}rū fī-hā al-f^{a}sād
Pronunciation: f^{a}-ak-th^{a}-rū fī-h^{a}l-f^{a}-sād

F^{a} (so) *akth^{a}rū* (they increased) *fī-hā* (in it) *al-f^{a}sād* (corruption).

The verb *akth^{a}rū* ("they increased [it]") is the third person plural of *akth^{a}r^{a}* ("he increased [it]").

أَكْثَرَ يُكْثِرُ اكْثِرْ

From right to left: he increased [it]; he increases [it]; *ikth^{i}r* (increase [it]!)

Verse 13

فَصَبَّ عَلَيْهِمْ رَبُّكَ سَوْطَ عَذَابٍ

So your Lord poured upon them a scourge of punishment.
Transliteration: f^{a}-ṣ^{a}bb^{a} ^{ca}l^{a}y-h^{i}m r^{a}bb^{u}k^{a} s^{a}wṭa ^{ca}dhāb
Pronunciation: f^{a}-ṣ^{a}b-b^{a} ^{ca}-l^{a}y-h^{i}m r^{a}b-b^{u}-k^{a} s^{a}w-ṭa ^{ca}-dhāb

F^{a} (so) *ṣ^{a}bb^{a}* (he poured) *^{ca}l^{a}y-h^{i}m* (upon them) *r^{a}bb^{u}k^{a}* (your Lord) *s^{a}wṭa* (scourge [of]) *^{ca}dhāb* (punishment).

صَبَّ يَصُبُّ صُبَّ

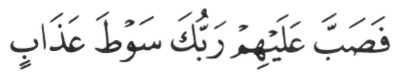

From right to left: he poured; he pours; pour!

The word *s^{a}wṭ* means “scourage” (a whip used for punishment). The word *^{a}dhāb* means “punishment” and “torture”.

Verse 14

إِنَّ رَبَّكَ لَبِالْمِرْصَادِ

Indeed, your Lord truly is [waiting] in ambush
Transliteration: inn^{a} r^{a}bb^{a}-k^{a} l^{a}-b^{i}-al-m^{i}rṣād
Pronunciation: in-n^{a} r^{a}b-b^{a}-k^{a} l^{a}-b^{i}l-m^{i}r-ṣād

Inn^{a} (indeed) *r^{a}bb^{a}k^{a}* (your Lord) *l^{a}-b^{i}-al-m^{i}rṣād* (truly waits in ambush).

The word *al-m^{i}rṣād* means “ambush”. When you say he is *b^{i}-al-m^{i}rṣād* it means “he is lying in ambush”, “he is waiting in ambush” (he is waiting and observing from a hidden place in order to attack an enemy when the time is right). The meaning of the verse is that God keeps Himself hidden and observes patiently until the time is right to punish His enemies.

Lesson 19 Review

بِسْمِ ٱللَّهِ ٱلرَّحْمَٰنِ ٱلرَّحِيمِ

وَٱلْفَجْرِ

W^{a}*-al-f*^{a}*jr* (by the dawn).

وَلَيَالٍ عَشْرٍ

W^{a} (by) *l*^{a}*yāl*^{in} (nights) ^{a}*shr* (ten).

وَٱلشَّفْعِ وَٱلْوَتْرِ

W^{a} (by) *al-sh*^{a}*f*^{i} (the even) *w*^{a}*-al-w*^{a}*tr* (and the odd).

وَٱلَّيْلِ إِذَا يَسْرِ

W^{a} (by) *al-l*^{a}*yl*^{i} (the night) *idhā* (when) *y*^{a}*sr* (it passes).

هَلْ فِى ذَٰلِكَ قَسَمٌ لِّذِى حِجْرٍ

H^{a}*l* (is there) *fī* (in) *dhāl*^{i}*k*^{a} (that) *q*^{a}*s*^{a}*m*^{un} (an oath) *l*^{i} (for) *dhī* (possessor of) *ḥ*^{i}*jr* (perception, rationality).

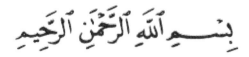

أَلَمْ تَرَ كَيْفَ فَعَلَ رَبُّكَ بِعَادٍ

A-l^{a}*m* (have not) *t*^{a}*r*^{a} (you see) *k*^{a}*yf*^{a} (how) *f*^{a} ^{a}*l*^{a} (he dealt) *r*^{a}*bb*^{u}*k*^{a} (your Lord) *b*^{i} (with) *ʿād*.

A-l^{a}*m t*^{a}*r*^{a} (have you not seen) *k*^{a}*yf*^{a} (how) *f*^{a} ^{a}*l*^{a} *r*^{a}*bb*^{u}*k*^{a} *b*^{i}*-ʿād* (your Lord dealt with ʿĀd).

إِرَمَ ذَاتِ ٱلْعِمَادِ

Ir^{a}*m*^{a} *dh*^{a}*t*^{i} (possessor of) *al-ʿimād* (the pillars).

ٱلَّتِي لَمْ يُخْلَقْ مِثْلُهَا فِي ٱلْبِلَـٰدِ

All^{a}*tī* (which) *l*^{a}*m y*^{u}*khl*^{a}*q* (had not been created) *m*^{i}*thl*^{u}*-hā* (its like) *f*^{i}*-al-b*^{i}*lād* (in the cities).

وَثَمُودَ ٱلَّذِينَ جَابُوا۟ ٱلصَّخْرَ بِٱلْوَادِ

W^{a}*-th*^{a}*mūd*^{a} (and Thamud) *all*^{a}*dhīn*^{a} (those who) *jābū* (carved out) *al-ṣ*^{a}*khr*^{a} (the rocks) *b*^{i}*-al-wād* (in/at the valley).

وَفِرْعَوْنَ ذِى ٱلْأَوْتَادِ

W^{a}*-f*^{i}*r*^{a}*wn*^{a} (and Pharaoh) *dhī* (possessor of) *al-awtād* (the stakes).

ٱلَّذِينَ طَغَوْا۟ فِى ٱلْبِلَـٰدِ

Alladhīna (those who) *ṭaghaw* (oppressed) *fī* (in) *al-bilād* (the cities, the land).

فَأَكۡثَرُواْ فِيهَا ٱلۡفَسَادَ

F^{a} (so) *akth*^{a}*rū* (they increased) *fī-hā* (in it) *al-f*^{a}*sād* (corruption).

فَصَبَّ عَلَيۡهِمۡ رَبُّكَ سَوۡطَ عَذَابٍ

F^{a} (so) *ṣ*^{a}*bb*^{a} (he poured) ^{a}*l*^{a}*y-h*^{i}*m* (upon them) *r*^{a}*bb*^{u}*k*^{a} (your Lord) *s*^{a}*wṭa* (scourge [of]) ^{a}*dhāb* (punishment).

إِنَّ رَبَّكَ لَبِٱلۡمِرۡصَادِ

Inn^{a} (indeed) *r*^{a}*bb*^{a}*k*^{a} (your Lord) *l*^{a}*-b*^{i}*-al-m*^{i}*rṣād* (truly waits in ambush).

This page intentionally left blank

Lesson 20: al-Fajr Part 1

Verse 15, part 1

The next verse is long, so we will discuss it in multiple parts.

فَأَمَّا ٱلْإِنسَٰنُ إِذَا مَا ٱبْتَلَىٰهُ رَبُّهُۥ

So as for the human, when His Lord tests him
Transliteration: f^{a}-ammā al-insān^{u} idhā mā ibt^{a}lā-h^{u} r^{a}bb^{u}-h^{u}
Pronunciation: f^{a}-am-m^{a}l-in-sā-n^{u} i-dhā m^{a}b-t^{a}-lā-h^{u} r^{a}b-b^{u}-h^{u}

F^{a}-ammā (so as for) *al-insān^{u}* (the human) *idhā mā* (when) *ibt^{a}lā-h^{u}* (he tested him) *r^{a}bb^{u}-h^{u}* (his Lord).

The phrase *ibt^{a}lāh^{u}* ("he tested him") uses a non-standard spelling in the Quranic text. In standard Arabic it would be:

ابْتَلَاهُ

This word has connotations of trials and hardship. It does not mean a simple test, but a test that causes the person difficulty in order to bring out their true character and test their faith. Below are the different permutations of this word:

ابْتَلَى يَبْتَلِي ابْتَلِ ابْتِلَاء مُبْتَلّ مُبْتَلَى

From right to left: *ibt^{a}lā* (he tested); *y^{a}bt^{a}lī* (he tests); *ibt^{a}l^{i}* test! (a command); *ibt^{i}lā'* (test [this is a noun that means "test"]); *m^{u}bt^{a}ll* (tester [a person who tests someone]); *m^{u}bt^{a}lā* (tested [person] [a person who is tested]).

The word *idhā* means "when". *Idhā mā* means the same, it is just more emphatic.

Verse 15, part 2

فَأَكْرَمَهُۥ وَنَعَّمَهُۥ

So He honored him with generosity and bestowed favors upon him

Transliteration: f^{a}-akr^{a}m^{a}-h^{u} w^{a}-n^{aʿʿa}m^{a}-h^{u}

Pronunciation: f^{a}-ak-r^{a}-m^{a}-h^{u} w^{a}-n^{aʿ}-^{ʿa}-m^{a}-h^{u}

F^{a} (so) *akr*^{a}*m*^{a}*-h*^{u} (he honored him) *w*^{a}*-n*^{aʿʿa}*m*^{a}*-h*^{u} (and bestowed favors upon him).

The verb *akr*^{a}*m*^{a} means "he treated [him] with graciousness and generosity", "he honored [him]".

أَكْرَمَ يُكْرِمُ اَكْرِمْ اِكْرَام مُكْرِم مُكْرَم

From right to left: he honored; he honors; honor!; to honor [someone]; one who honors; one who is honored [by someone].

The verb *n*^{aʿʿa}*m*^{a} means "he bestowed favors and blessings upon [him]". We already saw the noun *n*^{i}*ʿm*^{a} which comes from the same root and means "favor", "blessing".

نِعْمَة

Below are the different permutations of *n*^{aʿʿa}*m*^{a}:

نَعَّمَ يُنَعِّمُ نَعِّمْ تَنَعُّم مُنَعِّم مُنَعَّم

From right to left: he bestowed a favor upon; he bestows a favor upon; bestow a favor upon!; to bestow a favor upon; bestower of favor; one who has been bestowed a favor upon.

Verse 15, part 3

فَيَقُولُ رَبِّيٓ أَكۡرَمَنِ

Then he says, "My Lord has honored me."
Transliteration: f^{a}-y^{a}qūl^{u} r^{a}bb-ī akr^{a}m^{a}-n
Pronunciation: f^{a}-y^{a}-qū-l^{u} r^{a}b-bī ak-r^{a}-m^{a}n

F^{a} (so) *y^{a}qūl^{u}* (he says) *r^{a}bb-ī* (my Lord) *akr^{a}m^{a}n* (honored me).

قَالَ يَقُولُ قُلْ قَوْل قَائِل مَقُول

From right to left: he said; he says; say!; [a] saying; sayer (one who says something); said thing (a thing that was said).

The word *akr^{a}m^{a}-n* (he honored me) would be *akr^{a}m^{a}-nī* in standard Arabic:

أَكْرَمَنِي

Verse 16, part 1

وَأَمَّآ إِذَا مَا ٱبۡتَلَىٰهُ فَقَدَرَ عَلَيۡهِ رِزۡقَهُۥ

And as for when He tests him so he restricts upon him his provision
Transliteration: w^{a}-ammā idhā mā ibt^{a}lā-h^{u} f^{a}-q^{a}d^{a}r^{a} ʿ^{a}l^{a}y-h^{i} r^{i}zq^{a}-h^{u}
Pronunciation: w^{a}-am-mā idhā m^{a}b-t^{a}-lā-h^{u} f^{a}-q^{a}-d^{a}-r^{a} ʿ^{a}-l^{a}y-h^{i} r^{i}z-q^{a}-h^{u}

W^{a}*-ammā idhā mā* (and as for when) *ibt*^{a}*lā-h*^{u} (he tested him) *f*^{a}*-q*^{a}*d*^{a}*r*^{a} (so he restricted) ^{a}*l*^{a}*y-h*^{i} (upon him) *r*^{i}*zq*^{a}*-h*^{u} (his provision, his livelihood).

The verb *q*^{a}*d*^{a}*r*^{a} means "he measured", "he rationed", "he restricted".

قَدَرَ يَقْدُرُ قَدِّرْ قَدْر قَادِر مَقْدُور

From right to left: he restricted; he restricted; restrict!; restriction; restricter; restricted [thing].

Verse 16, part 2

فَيَقُولُ رَبِّيٓ أَهَٰنَنِ

Then he says, "My Lord has humiliated me."
Transliteration: f^{a}-y^{a}qūl^{u} r^{a}bb-ī ahān^{a}-n
Pronunciation: f^{a}-y^{a}-qū-l^{u} r^{a}b-bī ahā-n^{a}n

F^{a}*-y*^{a}*qūl*^{u} (then he says) *r*^{a}*bb-ī* (my Lord) *ahān*^{a}*-n* (he humiliated me).

The meaning of this verse with the one before it is that when God favors a human with blessings, the human is happy with God. But when God tests him with hardship, the human becomes disgruntled and unappreciative and forgets the favors God bestowed upon them in the past.

The phrase *ahān*^{a}*-n* ("he humiliated me") would be *ahān*^{a}*-nī* in standard Arabic. It is shortened for poetic effect.

أَهَانَنِي

Below are the different permutations of the word:

أَهَانَ يُهِينُ أَهِنْ إِهَانَةٌ مُهِينٌ مُهَانٌ

From right to left: he humiliated; he humiliates; humiliate!; (an act of) humiliation; one who humiliates; one who is humiliated.

Verse 17

كَلَّا ۖ بَل لَّا تُكْرِمُونَ ٱلْيَتِيمَ

No! But rather, you do not honor the orphan
Transliteration: k^{a}llā b^{a}l lā t^{u}kr^{i}mū-n^{a} al-y^{a}tīm^{a}
Pronunciation: k^{a}l-lā b^{a}l lā t^{u}k-r^{i}-mū-n^{a}l-y^{a}-tī-m^{a}

K^{a}llā (No! But) *b^{a}l* (rather) *lā* (do not) *t^{u}kr^{i}mū-n^{a}* (you [plural] honor) *al-y^{a}tīm^{a}* (the orphan).

The symbol above the *k^{a}llā* tells reciters that it is permitted for them to pause at that point before going on, but that it is recommended that they do not pause.

Verse 18

وَلَا تَحَٰٓضُّونَ عَلَىٰ طَعَامِ ٱلْمِسْكِينِ

And you do not encourage one another upon the feeding of the poor
Transliteration: w^{a}-lā taḥ^{a}ḍḍ-ūn^{a} ‘^{a}lā ṭ^{a}‘ām^{i} al-m^{i}skīn
Pronunciation: w^{a}-lā ta-ḥ^{a}ḍ-ḍū-n^{a} ‘^{a}-lā ṭ^{a}-‘ā-m^{i}l-m^{i}s-kīn

W^{a}-lā (and do not) *taḥ^{a}ḍḍ-ūn^{a}* (you [plural] encourage one another) *‘^{a}lā* (upon) *ṭ^{a}‘ām^{i} al-m^{i}skīn* (the food of the poor).

The phrase *taḥ^{a}ḍḍ-ūn^{a}* ("you [plural] encourage one another") is the second person present form of *taḥ^{a}ḍḍ^{a}* ("the [two persons] encouraged one another"). This is a verb that can only be correctly used when referring to two or more persons, so its third person singular actually applies to two people.

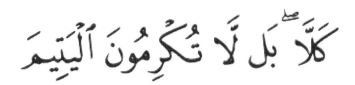

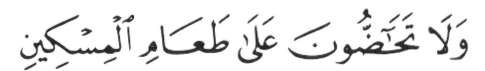

The word *ṭ*^{a}*ʿām* means "food". The phrase *ṭ*^{a}*ʿām*^{i} *al-m*^{i}*skīn* literally means "food of the poor", but from the context we know it is referring to the *feeding* of the poor.

Verse 19

وَتَأْكُلُونَ ٱلتُّرَاثَ أَكْلًا لَّمًّا

And you consume inheritance a total devouring
Transliteration: w^{a}-t^{a}ʾk^{u}lū-n^{a} al-t^{u}rāth^{a} akl^{an} l^{a}mmā
Pronunciation: w^{a}-t^{a}ʾ-k^{u}-lū-n^{a}t-t^{u}-rā-th^{a} ak-l^{an} l^{a}m-mā

W^{a}*-t*^{a}*ʾk*^{u}*lū-n*^{a} (and you consume) *al-t*^{u}*rāth*^{a} (inheritance) *akl*^{an} (an eating) *l*^{a}*mmā* (total).

The phrase *t*^{a}*ʾk*^{u}*lūn*^{a} ("you eat", "you consume", "you devour") is the second person plural if *ak*^{a}*l*^{a} ("he ate", "he consumed", "he devoured").

أَكَلَ يَأْكُلُ كُلْ أَكْل آكِل مَأْكُول

From right to left: he ate; he eats; eat!; [the act of] eating (also used in this verse); eater; eaten [thing]

أَكَلْتَ تَأْكُلُ كُلْ

أَكَلْتُمْ تَأْكُلُونَ كُلُوا

Above are the second-person singular and plural forms. Top from right to left: you ate; you eat; eat!

Bottom from right to left: you [plural] ate; you [plural] eat; eat! (addressed to a group). The one used in the Quranic verse is the one at the middle of the second line.

The noun *l*^{a}*mm* means the act of gathering together. When used as an adjective, it means "in a complete and total way".

The wording of the verse "And you consume inheritance a total devouring" may sound strange since it seems to be made up of two disjoined parts: "And you consume inheritance" and "a total devouring". This is a very common form of expression used in the Quran. The second part as a whole describes the first part; it means "you consume inheritance in the form of a total devouring". This is a highly poetic form of expression that rarely used in ordinary Arabic.

Verse 20

وَتُحِبُّونَ ٱلْمَالَ حُبًّا جَمًّا

And you love wealth an immense love
Transliteration: w^{a}-t^{u}ḥ^{i}bbū-n^{a} al-māl^{a} ḥ^{u}bb^{an} j^{a}mmā
Pronunciation: w^{a}-t^{u}-ḥ^{i}b-bū-n^{a}l-mā-l^{a} ḥ^{u}b-b^{an} j^{a}m-mā

W^{a}-t^{u}ḥ^{i}bbū-n^{a} (and you [plural] love) *al-māl^{a}* (wealth) *ḥ^{u}bb^{a}n* (a love) *j^{a}mmā* (immense).

The phrase *t^{u}ḥ^{i}bbūn^{a}* ("you [plural] love") is the second person plural of *ḥ^{a}bb^{a}* ("he loved").

حَبَّ يُحِبُّ احْبِب حُبّ حابّ مَحْبوب

From right to left: he loved; he loves; love [him]! (a command); love (a noun, also used in the verse); one who loves; one who is loved.

The word *j^{a}mm* ("immense", "vast") is from *jamm^{a}* ("it accumulated and increased").

Verse 21

كَلَّآ إِذَا دُكَّتِ ٱلْأَرْضُ دَكًّا دَكًّا

No! But when the earth has been razed an utter razing
Transliteration: k^{a}llā idhā d^{u}kk^{a}-t^{i} al-arḍ^{u} d^{a}kk^{an} d^{a}kkā
Pronunciation: k^{a}l-lā idhā d^{u}k-k^{a}-t^{i}l-ar-ḍ^{u} d^{a}k-k^{an} d^{a}k-kā

K^{a}llā (No! But) *idhā* (when) *d^{u}kk^{a}-t^{i}* (it was razed) *al-arḍ^{u}* (the earth) *d^{a}kk^{a}n d^{a}kkā* (an utter razing).

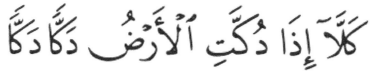

The verb *d*^{u}*kk*^{a} means "it was crushed and razed", "it was violently flattened". It is the passive third person form of *d*^{a}*kk*^{a} ("he razed").

دَكَّ يَدُكُّ اُدْكُكْ دَكٌّ دَاكٌّ مَدْكُوك

From right to left: he razed; he razes; raze [it]!; [an act of] razing; one who razes; razed [thing].

At the end of the verse the noun *d*^{a}*kk* ([an act of] razing; the fourth word from the right above) is repeated twice for emphasis: *d*^{a}*kk*^{a}*n d*^{a}*kkā* literally means "a razing and razing", its normal meaning "utter razing".

Verse 22

وَجَآءَ رَبُّكَ وَٱلْمَلَكُ صَفًّا صَفًّا

And came your Lord and the angels rank upon rank
Transliteration: w^{a}-jā'a r^{a}bb^{u}-k^{a} w^{a}-al-m^{a}l^{a}k^{u} ṣaff^{a}n ṣaffā
Pronunciation: w^{a}-jā-'a r^{a}b-b^{u}-k^{a} w^{a}l-m^{a}-l^{a}-k^{u} ṣaf-f^{a}n ṣaf-fā

W^{a}*-jā'a* (and came) *r*^{a}*bb*^{u}*-k*^{a} (your Lord) *w*^{a}*-al-m*^{a}*l*^{a}*k*^{u} (and the angels) *ṣaff*^{a}*n ṣaffā* (rank upon rank).

The verb *jā'a* means "it came". In some contexts a singular verb is applied to a plural group.

جَاءَ يَجِيْءُ جِئْ جِيئَةٌ جَاءٍ مَجِيْءٌ

This verb can be both non-transitive (as in the verse) and transitive. Non-transitive from right to left: he came; he comes; come!; a coming; comer; [the last word only applies to the transitive]

Transitive from right to left: he brought; he brings; bring!; a bringing; bringer; brought [thing].

The third word from the right is *ji'* ("come!", "bring!"). Its final letter is a *hamza* that looks like a *yā'* with a *hamza* symbol above it. This is not a *yā'*, it just a *hamza* with no *yā'* before it. In some contexts the *hamza* is written in this way.

The word *al-m*^{a}*l*^{a}*k* ("the angels") is the plural of *al-m*^{a}*lā*^{i}*k*^{a} ("the angel").

The word *ṣaff* means “line”, “row”, “rank”, “column” (as in “a column of troops”). The word is duplicated for poetic effect and emphasis, creating the meaning “rank by rank”, “rank upon rank”.

Verse 23, part 1

وَجِاْىٓءَ يَوْمَئِذٍۭ بِجَهَنَّمَ ۚ

And on that day Hell will be brought

Transliteration: wa-jī^{ʾa} y^{a}wm^{aʾi}dh^{in} b^{i}-j^{a}h^{a}nn^{a}m

Pronunciation: wa-jī-^{ʾa} y^{a}w-m^{a}-^{ʾi}-dh^{im} b^{i}-j^{a}-h^{a}-n-n^{a}m

Wa-jī^{ʾa} (and was brought) *y^{a}wm^{aʾi}dh^{in}* (on the day) *b^{i}-j^{a}h^{a}nn^{a}m* (Hell).

The verb *jī^{ʾa}* (“it was brought”) is the passive form of *j^{āʾa}* (“he brought”, “he came”). In standard Arabic *jī^{ʾa}* is written as follows:

جِيْءَ

You just have to ignore the strange way the Quranic word is spelled and read it as if it was just like the above.

The word *y^{a}wm^{aʾi}dh^{in}* is one word that means “on that day”. It was originally *y^{a}wm* (“day”) and *idh* (“when”), but the two were combined to create this new word. This word always has a *tanwīn al-kasr* at its end:

يَوْمَئِذٍ

In the Quranic text there is a small *mīm* at the end to tell reciters that according to the art of *tajwīd* this word should be pronounced *y^{a}wm^{aʾi}dh^{im}* rather than *y^{a}wm^{aʾi}dh^{in}*.

The *b^{i}* is necessary in the Arabic as a companion for *jī^{ʾa}* to create the meaning of “was brought”. The verb *jī^{ʾa}* does not make sense by itself in Arabic, it has to be *jī^{ʾa}...b^{i}*.

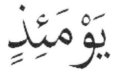

The tiny *jīm* at the end of the Quranic text is another *tajwīd* symbol that tells reciters they may pause here.

Verse 23, part 2

يَوْمَئِذٍ يَتَذَكَّرُ ٱلْإِنسَٰنُ وَأَنَّىٰ لَهُ ٱلذِّكْرَىٰ

On that day the human remembers, but how is remembrance for him?
Transliteration: y^{a}wm^{aʾi}dh^{i}n y^{a}t^{a}dh^{a}kk^{a}r^{u} al-insān^{u} w^{a}-annā l^{a}-h^{u} al-dh^{i}krā
Pronunciation: y^{a}w-m^{a}-^{ʾi}-dh^{i}n y^{a}-t^{a}-dh^{a}k-k^{a}-r^{u}l-in-sā-n^{u} w^{a}-an-nā l^{a}-h^{u}dh-dh^{i}-krā

Y^{a}wm$^{a\,i}$dh^{i}n (on that day) *y^{a}t^{a}dh^{a}kk^{a}r^{u}* (he remembers) *al-insān^{u}* (the human) *w^{a}-annā* (and how) *l^{a}-h^{u}* (for him) *al-dh^{i}krā* (remembrance).

The meaning of the verse is that on that day (the Day of Judgment) a human will remember (that they should have been pious), but what good is remembrance for him?

تَذَكَّرَ يَتَذَكَّرُ تَذَكَّرْ تَذَكُّر مُتَذَكِّر مُتَذَكَّر

From right to left: he remembered; he remembers; remember!; [the act of] remembering; one who remembers; that which is remembered.

The word *annā* means "how...?", "from where...?"

The word *al-dh^{i}krā* is from the same root as *y^{a}t^{a}dh^{a}kk^{a}r^{u}* and means "remembrance", "the act of remembering". It has the same meaning as *t^{a}dh^{a}kk^{u}r* (fourth word from the right above) in this verse.

Verse 24

يَقُولُ يَٰلَيْتَنِي قَدَّمْتُ لِحَيَاتِي

He says "Oh, I wish I had sent ahead [some good] for my life!"

Transliteration: y^{a}qūl^{u} yā-l^{a}yt^{a}-nī q^{a}dd^{a}m-t^{u} l^{i}-ḥ^{a}yāt-ī
Pronunciation: y^{a}-qū-l^{u} yā-l^{a}y-t^{a}-nī q^{a}d-d^{a}m-t^{u} l^{i}-ḥ^{a}-yā-tī

Y^{a}qūl^{u} (he says) *yā-l^{a}yt^{a}-nī* (Oh, I wish…!) *q^{a}dd^{a}m-t^{u}* (I advanced) *l^{i}-ḥ^{a}yāt-ī* (for my life).

Here the person wishes he had "sent ahead" some good deeds for his afterlife. He uses "my life" to refer to the life he has after his resurrection.

The phrase *yā-l^{a}yt^{a}* is made up of *yā*, which is a word used for grabbing attention, *l^{a}yt^{a}* is a special type of word that is used to express a wish. The full phrase *yā-l^{a}yt^{a}-nī* means "Oh, I wish…!". The phrase *q^{a}dd^{a}m-t^{u}* ("I sent [something] ahead", "I advanced [something]") is the first person singular of *q^{a}dd^{a}m^{a}* ("he sent ahead").

قَدَّمَ يُقَدِّمُ قَدِّمْ تَقْدِيمٌ مُقَدِّمٌ مُقَدَّمٌ

From right to left: he sent forth; he sends forth; send forth!; to send forth; one who sends forth; that which is sent forth.

Verse 25

فَيَوْمَئِذٍ لَّا يُعَذِّبُ عَذَابَهُۥٓ أَحَدٌ

So on that day no one is tortured his torture
Transliteration: f^{a}-y^{a}wm^{aʾi}dh^{i}n lā y^{uʿa}dhdh^{a}b^{u} ^{ʿa}dhāb^{a}-h^{u} aḥ^{a}d
Pronunciation: f^{a}-y^{a}w-m^{a}-^{ʾi}-dh^{i}n lā y^{u}-^{ʿa}dh-dh^{a}-b^{u} ^{ʿa}-dhā-b^{a}-h^{u} a-ḥ^{a}d

F^{a}-y^{a}wm$^{a\,i}$dh^{i}n (so on that day) *lā y$^{u\,a}$dhdh^{a}b^{u}* (is not tortured) *^{a}dhāb^{a}-h^{u}* (his torture) *aḥ^{a}d* (anyone).

The meaning of the verse is controversial. It may mean that the torture on that day will be something that no human (on earth) has suffered.

عَذَّبَ يُعَذِّبُ عَذِّبْ تَعْذِيبٌ مُعَذِّبٌ مُعَذَّبٌ

From right to left: he tortured; he tortures; torture!; torture; torturer; one who is tortured.

Verse 26

وَلَا يُوثِقُ وَثَاقَهُۥٓ أَحَدٌ

And no one is bound his binding
Transliteration: w^{a}-lā yūth^{a}q^{u} w^{a}thāq^{a}-h^{u} aḥ^{a}d
Pronunciation: w^{a}-lā yū-th^{a}-q^{u} w^{a}-thā-q^{a}-h^{u} a-ḥ^{a}d

W^{a}-lā yūth^{a}q^{u} (and is not bound) *w^{a}thāq^{a}-h^{u}* (his binding) *aḥ^{a}d* (anyone).

أَوْثَقَ يُوثِقُ أَوْثِقْ إِيثَاق مُوثِق مُوثَق

From right to left: he bound (someone with chains); he binds; bind!; to bind; one who binds; one who is bound.

The word *w^{a}thāq*, which comes from the same root as the words above, means "binding", "chains", "shackles".

Verse 27

يَٰٓأَيَّتُهَا ٱلنَّفْسُ ٱلْمُطْمَئِنَّةُ

O soul at ease!
Transliteration: yā-ayy^{a}t^{u}hā al-n^{a}fs^{u} al-m^{u}ṭm^{aʾi}nn^{a}
Pronunciation: yā-ay-y^{a}t^{u}-h^{a}n-n^{a}f-s^{u}l-m^{u}ṭ-m^{a}-^{ʾi}n-n^{a}

Y^{a}-ayy^{a}t^{u}hā (O) *al-n^{a}fs^{u}* (the soul) *al-m^{u}ṭm^{aʾi}nn^{a}* (at ease).

The phrase *yā-ayy^{a}t^{u}hā* is used for grabbing attention, it means "O..." It is stronger and more emphatic than merely *yā*. *Al-n^{a}fs* means different things in different contexts. It can mean "soul", "self" and "ego". *Al-m^{u}ṭm^{aʾi}nn^{a}* is a feminine adjective that means "reassured", "at peace", "at ease"

Verse 28

ٱرْجِعِىٓ إِلَىٰ رَبِّكِ رَاضِيَةً مَّرْضِيَّةً

Return to your Lord, pleased and pleasing
Transliteration: irj^{iʿ}-ī ilā r^{a}bb^{i}k^{i} rādh^{i}y^{a}t^{a}n m^{a}rdhīya
Pronunciation: ir-j^{i}-^{ʿ}ī ilā r^{a}b-b^{i}-k^{i} rā-dh^{i}-y^{a}-t^{a}n m^{a}r-dhī-ya

Irj^{i}ʿ-ī (return) *ilā* (to) *r^{a}bb^{i}k^{i}* (your Lord) *rādh^{i}y^{a}t^{a}n* (pleased) *m^{a}rdhīya* (pleasing [to God]).

The verb irj^{iʿ} is the command (*amr*) form of *rajaʿa* ("he returned"):

رَجَعَ يَرْجِعُ ارْجِعْ رُجُوْع رَاجِع مَرْجُوْع

From right to left: he returned; he returns; return!; return; returner; returned [thing].

In verb used in the Quranic text is *irj^{i}ʿ-ī* with the feminine *yā'* pronoun at the end because the speech is directed at a feminine noun (the *al-n^{a}fs* in the previous verse).

In standard Arabic *r^{a}bb^{i}k^{i}* would be *r^{a}bb^{i}kī*; in the Quranic text the *yā'* is removed for poetic effect:

Verse 29

فَٱدْخُلِى فِى عِبَٰدِى

So enter among my servants
Transliteration: f^{a}-udkh^{u}l-ī fī ^{ʿi}b^{a}d-ī
Pronunciation: f^{a}d-kh^{u}-lī fī ^{ʿi}-b^{a}-dī

F^{a}-udkh^{u}l-ī (so enter) *fī* (in, among) *^{ʿi}b^{a}d-ī* (my servants).

دَخَلَ يَدْخُلُ أُدْخُلْ دُخُوْل دَاخِل مَدْخُوْل

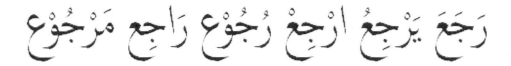

Non-transitive from right to left: he entered; he enters; enter!; to enter; one who enters; [n/a]

Transitive from right to left: he put [it] in; he puts [it] in; put [it] in; to put [something] in; one who puts [something] in; [a thing that was] put in.

The word *ʿ*^{i}*b*^{a}*d* (“servants”) is the plural of *ʿabd* (“servant”) and it would be written as follows in standard Arabic:

عِبَاد

Verse 30

وَٱدۡخُلِي جَنَّتِي

And enter my Paradise
Tranlsiteration: w^{a}-udkh^{u}l-ī j^{a}nn^{a}t-ī
Pronunciation: w^{a}d-kh^{u}-lī j^{a}n-n^{a}-tī

W^{a}*-udkh*^{u}*l-ī* (and enter) *j*^{a}*nn*^{a}*t-ī* (my Paradise).

J^{a}*nn*^{a} literally means “garden”. It is the word used for Paradise in Islam.

Lesson 20 Review

فَأَمَّا ٱلْإِنسَٰنُ إِذَا مَا ٱبْتَلَىٰهُ رَبُّهُۥ

F^a*-ammā* (so as for) *al-insān*^{u} (the human) *idhā mā* (when) *ibt*^{a}*lā-h*^{u} (he tested him) *r*^{a}*bb*^{u}*-h*^{u} (his Lord).

فَأَكْرَمَهُۥ وَنَعَّمَهُۥ

F^a (so) *akr*^{a}*m*^{a}*-h*^{u} (he honored him) *w*^{a}*-n*^{a}ʿʿ^a*m*^{a}*-h*^{u} (and bestowed favors upon him).

فَيَقُولُ رَبِّىٓ أَكْرَمَنِ

F^a (so) *y*^{a}*qūl*^{u} (he says) *r*^{a}*bb-ī* (my Lord) *akr*^{a}*m*^{a}*n* (honored me).

وَأَمَّآ إِذَا مَا ٱبْتَلَىٰهُ فَقَدَرَ عَلَيْهِ رِزْقَهُۥ

W^a*-ammā idhā mā* (and as for when) *ibt*^{a}*lā-h*^{u} (he tested him) *f*^{a}*-q*^{a}*d*^{a}*r*^{a} (so he restricted) ʿ^a*l*^{a}*y-h*^{i} (upon him) *r*^{i}*zq*^{a}*-h*^{u} (his provision, his livelihood).

فَيَقُولُ رَبِّىٓ أَهَٰنَنِ

F^a*-y*^{a}*qūl*^{u} (then he says) *r*^{a}*bb-ī* (my Lord) *ahān*^{a}*-n* (he humiliated me).

كَلَّا ۖ بَل لَّا تُكْرِمُونَ ٱلْيَتِيمَ

K^{a}llā (No! But) *b^{a}l* (rather) *lā* (do not) *t^{u}kr^{i}mū-n^{a}* (you [plural] honor) *al-y^{a}tīm^{a}* (the orphan).

وَلَا تَحَـٰٓضُّونَ عَلَىٰ طَعَامِ ٱلْمِسْكِينِ

W^{a}-lā (and do not) *taḥ^{a}ḍḍ-ūn^{a}* (you [plural] encourage one another) *^{a}lā* (upon) *ṭ^{a}ʿām^{i} al-m^{i}skīn* (the food of the poor).

وَتَأْكُلُونَ ٱلتُّرَاثَ أَكْلًا لَّمًّا

W^{a}-t^{a}ʾk^{u}lū-n^{a} (and you consume) *al-t^{u}rāth^{a}* (inheritance) *akl^{an}* (an eating) *l^{a}mmā* (total).

وَتُحِبُّونَ ٱلْمَالَ حُبًّا جَمًّا

W^{a}-t^{u}ḥ^{i}bbū-n^{a} (and you [plural] love) *al-māl^{a}* (wealth) *ḥ^{u}bb^{a}n* (a love) *j^{a}mmā* (immense).

كَلَّآ إِذَا دُكَّتِ ٱلْأَرْضُ دَكًّا دَكًّا

K^{a}llā (No! But) *idhā* (when) *d^{u}kk^{a}-t^{i}* (it was razed) *al-arḍ^{u}* (the earth) *d^{a}kk^{a}n d^{a}kkā* (an utter razing).

وَجَآءَ رَبُّكَ وَٱلْمَلَكُ صَفًّا صَفًّا

W^{a}-jāʾa (and came) *r^{a}bb^{u}-k^{a}* (your Lord) *w^{a}-al-m^{a}l^{a}k^{u}* (and the angels) *ṣaff^{a}n ṣaffā* (rank upon rank).

وَجِاْيٓءَ يَوْمَئِذٍۭ بِجَهَنَّمَۚ

Wa-jī^{a} (and was brought) *y*^{a}*wm*$^{a\,i}$*dh*^{in} (on the day) *b*^{i}*-j*^{a}*h*^{a}*nn*^{a}*m* (Hell).

يَوْمَئِذٍ يَتَذَكَّرُ ٱلْإِنسَٰنُ وَأَنَّىٰ لَهُ ٱلذِّكْرَىٰ

Y^{a}*wm*$^{a\,i}$*dh*^{i}*n* (on that day) *y*^{a}*t*^{a}*dh*^{a}*kk*^{a}*r*^{u} (he remembers) *al-insān*^{u} (the human) *w*^{a}*-annā* (and how) *l*^{a}*-h*^{u} (for him) *al-dh*^{i}*krā* (remembrance).

يَقُولُ يَٰلَيْتَنِى قَدَّمْتُ لِحَيَاتِى

Y^{a}*qūl*^{u} (he says) *yā-l*^{a}*yt*^{a}*-nī* (Oh, I wish...!) *q*^{a}*dd*^{a}*m-t*^{u} (I advanced) *l*^{i}*-ḥ*^{a}*yāt-ī* (for my life).

فَيَوْمَئِذٍ لَّا يُعَذِّبُ عَذَابَهُۥٓ أَحَدٌ

F^{a}*-y*^{a}*wm*$^{a\,i}$*dh*^{i}*n* (so on that day) *lā y*$^{u\,a}$*dhdh*^{a}*b*^{u} (is not tortured) ^{a}*dhāb*^{a}*-h*^{u} (his torture) *aḥ*^{a}*d* (anyone).

وَلَا يُوثِقُ وَثَاقَهُۥٓ أَحَدٌ

W^{a}*-lā yūth*^{a}*q*^{u} (and is not bound) *w*^{a}*thāq*^{a}*-h*^{u} (his binding) *aḥ*^{a}*d* (anyone).

يَٰٓأَيَّتُهَا ٱلنَّفْسُ ٱلْمُطْمَئِنَّةُ

Y^{a}*-ayy*^{a}*t*^{u}*hā* (O) *al-n*^{a}*fs*^{u} (the soul) *al-m*^{u}*ṭm*$^{a\,i}$*nn*^{a} (at ease).

Y^{a}*-ayy*^{a}*t*^{u}*hā* (O) *al-n*^{a}*fs*^{u} *al-m*^{u}*ṭm*$^{a\,i}$*nn*^{a} (soul at ease, at ease soul, i.e. a soul that is at ease).

ارْجِعِيٓ إِلَىٰ رَبِّكِ رَاضِيَةً مَّرْضِيَّةً

Irj^{i}ʿ*-ī* (return) *ilā* (to) *r*^{a}*bb*^{i}*k*^{i} (your Lord) *rādh*^{i}*y*^{a}*t*^{a}*n* (pleased) *m*^{a}*rdhīya* (pleasing [to God]).

فَادْخُلِي فِي عِبَٰدِى

F^{a}*-udkh*^{u}*l-ī* (so enter) *fī* (in, among) ʿ^{i}*b*^{a}*d-ī* (my servants).

وَادْخُلِي جَنَّتِي

W^{a}*-udkh*^{u}*l-ī* (and enter) *j*^{a}*nn*^{a}*t-ī* (my Paradise).

Lesson 21: al-Balad Part 1

In this lesson we will move on to chapter 90 of the Quran, *al-Balad* ("The Town").

بِسۡمِ ٱللَّهِ ٱلرَّحۡمَٰنِ ٱلرَّحِيمِ

Verse 1

لَآ أُقۡسِمُ بِهَٰذَا ٱلۡبَلَدِ

I swear by this town
Transliteration: lā uqs^{i}m^{u} b^{i}-hādhā al-b^{a}l^{a}d
Pronunciation: lā uq-s^{i}-m^{u} b^{i}-hā-dh^{a}l-b^{a}-l^{a}d

Lā uqs^{i}m^{u} (I swear) *b^{i}-hādhā* (by this) *al-b^{a}l^{a}d* (town).

The town that is sworn by in this verse is considered to be Mecca.

The seemingly negative *lā* here is used for grabbing attention. While the verse literally seems to say "I do not swear by this town", the meaning actually is "I swear by this town". *uqs^{i}m^{u}* is the first person singular of *aqs^{a}m^{a}* ("he swore", "he took an oath").

أَقْسَمَ يُقْسِمُ اقْسِم إِقْسَام مُقْسِم مُقْسَم

From right to left: he swore; he swears; swear!; to swear; one who swears; that which is sworn [by].

The word *hādhā* is Arabic for "this". It is written without the first *alif* in standard Arabic as well.

هَٰذَا

Verse 2

وَأَنتَ حِلٌّۢ بِهَٰذَا ٱلْبَلَدِ

And you are free of restriction at this town
Transliteration: w^{a}-ant^{a} ḥ^{i}ll^{un} b^{i}-hādhā al-b^{a}l^{a}d
Pronunciation: w^{a}-an-t^{a} ḥ^{i}l-l^{um} b^{i}-hā-dh^{a}l-b^{a}-l^{a}d

W^{a}-ant^{a} (and you) *ḥ^{i}ll^{un}* (free of restriction) *b^{i}-hādhā* (at this) *al-b^{a}l^{a}d* (town).

The word *ḥ^{i}ll* means "free of restriction", "not in a state where things are forbidden from [the person]". It comes from the same root as the word *ḥalāl* ("permitted", a thing that is not forbidden in Islam).

Verse 3

وَوَالِدٍ وَمَا وَلَدَ

And by a parent and that which it begets
Transliteration: w^{a}-wāl^{i}d^{in} w^{a}-mā w^{a}l^{a}d
Pronunciation: w^{a}-wā-l^{i}-d^{iw} w^{a}-mā w^{a}-l^{a}d

W^{a}-wāl^{i}d^{in} (by a parent) *w^{a}-mā* (and that which) *w^{a}l^{a}d* (he/she begot).

The word *wāl^{i}d* means "parent", "begetter". In modern Arabic it means "father" and its feminine form *wāl^{i}d^{a}* is used for "mother". But in Quranic Arabic it can mean either parent.

W^{a}l^{a}d^{a} means "he/she begot". In modern Arabic it is used to mean "she gave birth", but in Quranic Arabic it can refer to a man begetting a child or a woman giving birth to a child.

وَلَدَ يَلِدُ لِدْ وِلَادَة وَالِد مَوْلُوْد

From right to left: he begot; he begets; beget!; to beget; begetter/parent; begotten thing/child/infant.

Verse 4

لَقَدْ خَلَقْنَا ٱلْإِنسَٰنَ فِى كَبَدٍ

Truly we have created man in hardship
Transliteration: l^{a}-q^{a}d kh^{a}l^{a}qnā al-insān^{a} fī k^{a}b^{a}d
Pronunciation: l^{a}-q^{a}d kh^{a}-l^{a}q-n^{a}l-in-sā-n^{a} fī k^{a}-b^{a}d

L^{a}-q^{a}d (truly [we] have) *kh^{a}l^{a}qnā* (we created) *al-insān^{a}* (the human) *fī k^{a}b^{a}d* (in hardship).

L^{a}-q^{a}d means "truly [we] have". The word *q^{a}d* is used to emphasize something that happened in the past. *K^{a}b^{a}d* means "hardship", "toil".

Verse 5

أَيَحْسَبُ أَن لَّن يَقْدِرَ عَلَيْهِ أَحَدٌ

Does he think that no one will overpower him?
Transliteration: a-y^{a}ḥs^{a}b^{u} an l^{a}n y^{a}qd^{i}r^{a} ^{ca}l^{a}y-h^{i} aḥ^{a}d
Pronunciation: a-y^{a}ḥ-s^{a}-b^{u} *al* l^{a}n y^{a}q-d^{i}-r^{a} ^{ca}-l^{a}y-h^{i} a-ḥ^{a}d

A-y^{a}ḥs^{a}b^{u} (does he think) *an* (that) *l^{a}n* (will not) *y^{a}qd^{i}r^{a}* (he is capable/powerful) *^{ca}l^{a}y-h^{i}* (upon him) *aḥ^{a}d* (anyone).

In the pronunciation above I have italicized *al* to the way the "n" sound becomes a "l" during recitation.

The verb y^{a}ḥs^{a}b^{u} means "he thought", "he assumed".

حَسِبَ ، يَحْسَبُ وَيَحْسِبُ ، احْسِب ،

حِسْبَان ، حَاسِب ، مَحْسُوب

Above are the different permutations of the verb. I have used commas because the third-person singular present has two equally valid forms (the second and third word from right to left above).

Top from right to left: he thought; he thinks; assume!; to assume; one who assumes; assumed [thing].

Verse 6

يَقُولُ أَهْلَكْتُ مَالًا لُّبَدًا

He says, "I have consumed an abundant wealth."
Transliteration: y^{a}qūl^u ahl^{a}k-t^u māl^{a}n l^{u}b^{a}dā
Pronunciation: y^a-qū-l^u ah-l^{a}k-t^u mā-l^{a}n l^u-b^a-dā

Y^{a}qūl^u (he says) ahl^{a}k-t^u (I consumed) māl^{a}n (a wealth) l^{u}b^{a}dā (abundant, vast).

Ahl^{a}k-t^u means "I spent", "I consumed", "I caused it to cease existing".

أَهْلَكَ يُهْلِكُ اهْلِكْ إِهْلَاكٌ مُهْلِكٌ مُهْلَكٌ

From right to left: he consumed; he consumes; consume!; to consume; consumer; consumed [thing].

Verse 7

أَيَحْسَبُ أَن لَّمْ يَرَهُۥٓ أَحَدٌ

Does he think that no one saw him?
Transliteration: a-y^{a}ḥs^{a}b^u an l^{a}m y^{a}r^a-h^u aḥ^{a}d
Pronunciation: a-y^{a}ḥ-s^a-b^u an l^{a}m y^a-r^a-h^u a-ḥ^{a}d

A-y^{a}ḥs^{a}b^u (does he think, does he assume) *an* (that) *l^{a}m* (did not) *y^{a}r^a-h^u* (he sees him) *aḥ^{a}d* (anyone).

The phrase *y^{a}r^a-h^u* would be *y^{a}rā-h^u* in standard Arabic:

يَرَاهُ

رَأَى يَرَى رَهْ رُؤْيَة رَاءٍ مَرْئِي

From right to left: he saw; he sees; see!; to see; one who sees; seen [thing].

Verse 8

أَلَمْ نَجْعَل لَّهُۥ عَيْنَيْنِ

Did we not make for him two eyes?
Transliteration: a-l^{a}m n^{a}j^{ʿa}l l^{a}-h^{u} ^{ʿa}yn^{a}yn
Pronunciation: a-l^{a}m n^{a}j-^{ʿa}l l^{a}-h^{u} ^{ʿa}y-n^{a}yn

A-l^{a}m (did not) *n^{a}j^{a}l* (we create) *l^{a}-h^{u}* (for him) *^{a}yn^{a}yn* (two eyes).

The verb *n^{a}j^{a}l* is the first person plural of *j^{a} ^{a}l^{a}* (“he created”, “he made”, “he assigned”).

جَعَلَ يَجْعَلُ اجْعَل جَعْل جَاعِل مَجْعُول

From right to left: he made; he makes; make!; to make; maker; made [thing].

The word *^{a}yn^{a}yn* is the dual of *^{a}yn* (“eye”).

عَيْن، عَيْنَان وعَيْنَيْن، أَعْيُن وعُيُوْن

Above, the first word on the right is ^{a}*yn* ("eye"). The next towards are its duals ("two eyes"), it depends on the context which one is used. The last two words are the plural "eyes". Both can be used interchangeably (the context does not decide it).

Verse 9

وَلِسَانًا وَشَفَتَيْنِ

And a tongue, and two lips?
Transliteration: w^{a}-lisān^{an} w^{a}-sh^{a}f^{a}t^{a}yn
Pronunciation: w^{a}-li-sā-n^{an} w^{a}-sh^{a}-f^{a}-t^{a}yn

W^{a}-lisān^{an} (and a tongue) *w^{a}-sh^{a}f^{a}t^{a}yn* (and two lips).

The word *sh^{a}f^{a}t^{a}yn* ("two lips") is the dual of *sh^{a}f^{a}* ("lip").

شَفَة، شَفَتَان وشَفَتَيْن، شَفَهَات وشِفَاه وشَفَايِف

Above on the right is the singular, the next two are duals, and the last three are all plurals.

Verse 10

وَهَدَيْنَٰهُ ٱلنَّجْدَيْنِ

And we guided him to the two heights/ways
Transliteration: w^{a}-h^{a}d^{a}y-nā-h^{u} al-n^{a}jd^{a}yn
Pronunciation: w^{a}-h^{a}-d^{a}y-nā-*h^{u}n*-n^{a}j-d^{a}yn

W^{a}-h^{a}d^{a}y-nā-h^{u} (and we guided him) *al-n^{a}jd^{a}yn* (the two heights, the two ways).

The meaning of this verse is controversial. It may refer to God's guidance of a person to the two ways of good and evil. But the "two heights" can also refer to a woman's breasts, in which case the verse would be referring to the fact that God gave human infants the instinct to seek the breasts of their mothers.

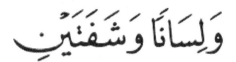

Al-n^{a}*jd*^{a}*yn* is the dual of *najd* ("height", "way"). Najd is also the name of the central highland part of Arabia where the city of Riyadh is located.

The verb *h*^{a}*d*^{a}*y-nā* ("we guided") is the first person plural of *hadā* ("he guided").

This page intentionally left blank

Lesson 21 Review

بِسْمِ ٱللَّهِ ٱلرَّحْمَٰنِ ٱلرَّحِيمِ

لَآ أُقْسِمُ بِهَٰذَا ٱلْبَلَدِ

Lā uqs^{i}*m*^{u} (I swear) *b*^{i}*-hādhā* (by this) *al-b*^{a}*l*^{a}*d* (town).

وَأَنتَ حِلٌّۢ بِهَٰذَا ٱلْبَلَدِ

W^{a}*-ant*^{a} (and you) *ḥ*^{i}*ll*^{un} (free of restriction) *b*^{i}*-hādhā* (at this) *al-b*^{a}*l*^{a}*d* (town).

W^{a}*-ant*^{a} *ḥ*^{i}*ll*^{un} (and you are free of restriction) *b*^{i}*-hādhā* (at this) *al-b*^{a}*l*^{a}*d* (town).

وَوَالِدٍ وَمَا وَلَدَ

W^{a}*-wāl*^{i}*d*^{in} (by a parent) *w*^{a}*-mā* (and that which) *w*^{a}*l*^{a}*d* (he/she begot).

لَقَدْ خَلَقْنَا ٱلْإِنسَٰنَ فِى كَبَدٍ

L^{a}*-q*^{a}*d* (truly [we] have) *kh*^{a}*l*^{a}*qnā* (we created) *al-insān*^{a} (the human) *fī k*^{a}*b*^{a}*d* (in hardship).

أَيَحْسَبُ أَن لَّن يَقْدِرَ عَلَيْهِ أَحَدٌ

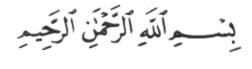

A-y^{a}ḥs^{a}b^{u} (does he think) *an* (that) *l^{a}n* (will not) *y^{a}qd^{i}r^{a}* (he is capable/powerful) *^{a}l^{a}y-h^{i}* (upon him) *aḥ^{a}d* (anyone).

يَقُولُ أَهْلَكْتُ مَالًا لُّبَدًا

Y^{a}qūl^{u} (he says) ahl^{a}k-t^{u} (I consumed) māl^{a}n (a wealth) l^{u}b^{a}dā (abundant, vast).

أَيَحْسَبُ أَن لَّمْ يَرَهُۥٓ أَحَدٌ

A-y^{a}ḥs^{a}b^{u} (does he think, does he assume) *an* (that) *l^{a}m* (did not) *y^{a}r^{a}-h^{u}* (he sees him) *aḥ^{a}d* (anyone).

أَلَمْ نَجْعَل لَّهُۥ عَيْنَيْنِ

A-l^{a}m (did not) *n^{a}j^{a}l* (we create) *l^{a}-h^{u}* (for him) *^{a}yn^{a}yn* (two eyes).

وَلِسَانًا وَشَفَتَيْنِ

W^{a}-lisān^{an} (and a tongue) *w^{a}-sh^{a}f^{a}t^{a}yn* (and two lips).

وَهَدَيْنَٰهُ ٱلنَّجْدَيْنِ

W^{a}-h^{a}d^{a}y-nā-h^{u} (and we guided him) *al-n^{a}jd^{a}yn* (the two heights, the two ways).

Lesson 22: al-Balad Part 2

Verse 11

فَلَا اقْتَحَمَ الْعَقَبَةَ

But he does not break through the difficult pass
Transliteration: f^{a}-lā iqt^{a}ḥam^{a} al-^{ʿa}q^{a}b^{a}
Pronunciation: f^{a}-l^{a}q-t^{a}-ḥa-m^{a}l-^{ʿa}-q^{a}-b^{a}

F^{a}-lā (but does not) *iqt^{a}ḥam^{a}* (he break through) *al-^{ʿa}q^{a}b^{a}* (the difficult pass).

In this verse "the difficult pass" may refer to the difficult task of overcoming one's ego and base desires.

While literally *f^{a}-lā* means "so does not", what is meant is more correctly "but does not".

اقْتَحَمَ يَقْتَحِمُ اقْتَحِمْ اقْتِحَام مُقْتَحِم مُقْتَحَم

From right to left: he broke through; he breaks through; break through!; to break through; one who breaks through; broken through [thing].

^{ʿa}q^{a}b^{a} means "mountain pass", "stumbling block", "disadvantage".

Verse 12

وَمَآ أَدْرَىٰكَ مَا الْعَقَبَةُ

And what can make you know what the difficult pass is?
Transliteration: w^{a}-mā adrā-k^{a} mā al-ʿaqaba
Pronunciation: w^{a}-mā ad-rā-k^{a} m^{a}l-^{ʿa}-q^{a}-b^{a}

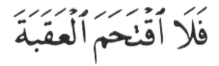

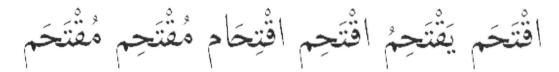

W^a-mā (and what) *adrā-k^a* (made you know) *mā* (what) *al-ʿaqaba* (the difficult pass [is]).

Adrā-k^a means "it made you know", "it made you understand". The phrase *mā adrā-k^a* means "what makes you know?", "what is there to make you know?", "what is there to make you understand?". It is rhetorical question that implies "you know little about", "you know nothing about".

أَدْرَى يُدْرِي أَدْرِ إِدْرَاء مُدْرِ مُدْرَى

From right to left: he made [him] know; he makes [him] know; make [him] know!; to make [someone] know; one who makes [others] know; one who has been made to know.

Verse 13

فَكُّ رَقَبَةٍ

The freeing of a slave
Transliteration: f^akk^u r^aq^ab^a
Pronunciation: f^ak-k^u r^a-q^a-b^a

F^akk^u (the freeing [of], to free) *r^aq^ab^a* (a slave).

This verse and the ones that follow answer the question from the previous verses. The difficult pass is the freeing of a slave and what follows.

The word *f^akk* means "to undo", "to dissolve [a bond or contract]", "to free [a prisoner or slave]".

فَكَّ ، يَفُكُّ ، افْكُكْ وفُكَّ ، فِكَاك ، فَاكّ ، مَفْكُوك

From right to left: he freed; he frees; free! (the command has to forms); to free; one who frees; freed [person].

The word *r^aq^ab^a* literally means "neck". It is used metaphorically to mean a slave since their neck is held in bond.

Verse 14

أَوْ إِطْعَٰمٌ فِى يَوْمٍ ذِى مَسْغَبَةٍ

Or feeding on a day that possesses severe hunger
Transliteration: aw iṭʿām^{un} fī y^{a}wm^{in} dhī m^{a}sgh^{a}b^{a}
Pronunciation: aw iṭ-ʿā-m^{un} fī y^{a}w-m^{in} dhī m^{a}s-gh^{a}-b^{a}

Aw iṭʿām^{un} (or feeding) *fī* (on) *y*^{a}*wm*^{in} (a day) *dhī* (possessing) *m*^{a}*sgh*^{a}*b*^{a} (great hunger).

Iṭʿām means "to feed [someone]", "feeding [someone]", from the verb *aṭ*^{a}*m*^{a} ("he fed [someone]").

أَطْعَمَ يُطْعِمُ اطْعِمْ إِطْعَام مُطْعِم مُطْعَم

From right to left: he fed [someone or something]; he feeds; feed [him]!; to feed; one who feeds [another person or animal]; one who is fed [by someone].

Verse 15

يَتِيمًا ذَا مَقْرَبَةٍ

An orphan possessing nearness [of relationship]
Transliteration: yatīm^{an} dhā m^{a}qr^{a}b^{a}
Pronunciation: ya-tī-m^{an} dhā m^{a}q-r^{a}-b^{a}

Yatīm^{an} (an orphan) *dhā* (possessing) *m*^{a}*qr*^{a}*b*^{a} (nearness).

This verse continues from the previous verse; it is saying that feeding an orphan who is a near relation is one of the actions that define passing the "difficult pass".

The phrase *dhā m*^{a}*qr*^{a}*b*^{a} literally means "possessing nearness", meaning an orphan who is also a near relation (a close relative).

Verse 16

أَوْ مِسْكِينًا ذَا مَتْرَبَةٍ

Or a needy person possessing great misery
Transliteration: aw m^{i}skīn^{an} dhā m^{a}tr^{a}b^{a}
Pronunciation: aw m^{i}s-kī-n^{an} dhā m^{a}-tr^{a}-b^{a}

Aw (or) *m^{i}skīn^{an}* (a needy person) *dhā* (possessing) *m^{a}tr^{a}b^{a}* (great misery).

The word *m^{a}tr^{a}b^{a}* means “great poverty”, “great misery”, “destitution”.

Verse 17, part 1

ثُمَّ كَانَ مِنَ ٱلَّذِينَ ءَامَنُوا۟

Next, he was of those who believed
Transliteration: th^{u}mma kān^{a} m^{i}n all^{a}dhīna ām^{a}nū

Th^{u}mma (then, next) *kān^{a}* (he was) *m^{i}n* (of) *all^{a}dhīna* (those) *ām^{a}nū* (they believed).

The verb *ām^{a}nū* is the third person plural of *ām^{a}n^{a}* (“he believed”).

آمَنَ يُؤْمِنُ آمِنْ إِيمَان مُؤْمِن مُؤْمَن

From right to left: he believed; *y^{u}'m^{i}n^{u}* (he believes [the *wāw*-like letter with the *hamza* symbol is a mere *hamza*, there is no *wāw* there]); believe!; to believe / belief; believer; that which is believed in (or one who is believed in).

Verse 18, part 2

وَتَوَاصَوْا۟ بِٱلصَّبْرِ وَتَوَاصَوْا۟ بِٱلْمَرْحَمَةِ

And they encouraged each other to patience and encouraged each other to compassion
Transliteration: w^{a}-t^{a}wāṣ^{a}w b^{i}-al-ṣ^{a}br^{i} w^{a}-t^{a}wāṣ^{a}w b^{i}-al-m^{a}rḥam^{a}
Pronunciation: w^{a}-t^{a}-wā-ṣ^{a}w *b^{i}ṣ*-ṣ^{a}b-r^{i} w^{a}-t^{a}-wā-ṣ^{a}w b^{i}l-m^{a}r-ḥa-m^{a}

W^{a}-t^{a}wāṣ^{a}w (and they encouraged each other) *b^{i}-al-ṣ^{a}br^{i}* (to patience) *w^{a}-t^{a}wāṣ^{a}w* (and they encouraged each other) *b^{i}-al-m^{a}rḥam^{a}* (to compassion).

Verse 18

أُو۟لَـٰٓئِكَ أَصْحَـٰبُ ٱلْمَيْمَنَةِ

Those are the companions of the right
Transliteration: ulā'^{i}k^{a} aṣḥāb^{u} al-m^{a}ym^{a}n^{a}
Pronunciation: u-lā-'^{i}-k^{a} aṣ-ḥā-b^{u}l-m^{a}y-m^{a}-n^{a}

Ulā'^{i}k^{a} (those [are]) *aṣḥāb^{u}* (companions [of]) *al-m^{a}ym^{a}n^{a}* (the right).

"Companions of the right" refers to those who will be on the right side on the Day of Judgment and/or who will receive their record of deeds with their right hand. It refers to those who will attain success on the Day of Judgment.

Aṣḥāb ("companion") is the plural of *ṣāḥib* ("companion").

Al-m^{a}ym^{a}n^{a} means "the right side", "the direction of the right". The more common word for "right" is *y^{a}mīn*.

Verse 19

وَٱلَّذِينَ كَفَرُوا۟ بِـَٔايَـٰتِنَا هُمْ أَصْحَـٰبُ ٱلْمَشْـَٔمَةِ

And those who denied our signs are the companions of left
Transliteration: w^{a}-all^{a}dhīn^{a} k^{a}f^{a}rū b^{i}-āyāt^{i}-nā h^{u}m aṣḥāb^{u} al-m^{a}sh^{ʾa}m^{a}
Pronunciation: w^{a}l-l^{a}-dhī-n^{a} k^{a}-f^{a}-rū b^{i}-ā-yā-t^{i}-nā h^{u}m aṣ-ḥā-b^{u}l-m^{a}sh-^{ʾa}-m^{a}

W^{a}-all^{a}dhīn^{a} (and those who) *k^{a}f^{a}rū* (denied) *b^{i}-āyāt^{i}-nā* (our signs) *h^{u}m* (they are) *aṣḥāb^{u}* (companions [of]) *al-m^{a}sh^{a}m^{a}* (the left).

The verb *k^{a}f^{a}rū* is the third person plural of *k^{a}f^{a}r^{a}* ("he denied"). *K^{a}f^{a}rū b^{i}* means "they expressed disbelief about..."

كَفَرَ يَكْفُرُ اُكْفُرْ كُفْر كَافِر مَكْفُوْر

From right to left: he denied; he denies; deny!; denial; denier; denied [thing or person].

The word *āyāt* ("signs") is the plural of *āya* ("sign"). It refers to the signs around us that point to God's existence and the truth of His scriptures. The word *āya* is also used to refer to a Quranic verse. Each verse of the Quran is an *āya.*

آيَة

The word *al-m^{a}sh^{a}m^{a}* ("the left") is the opposite of *al-m^{a}ym^{a}n^{a}* ("the right") from the previous verse. The more common word for "left" is *yasār.*

Verse 20

عَلَيْهِمْ نَارٌ مُّؤْصَدَةٌۢ

Upon them is a shut-in fire

Transliteration: ^{ʿa}l^{a}yh^{i}m nār^{un} m^{uʾ}ṣ^{a}d^{a}

Pronunciation: $^{ʿa\text{-}}$l^{a}y-h^{i}m nā-r^{un} m^{uʾ}-ṣ^{a}-d^{a}

^{ʿa}l^{a}yh^{i}m (upon them [is]) *nār^{un}* (a fire) *m^{u}ʾṣ^{a}d^{a}* (shut-in, enclosed).

This page intentionally left blank

Lesson 22 Review

فَلَا ٱقۡتَحَمَ ٱلۡعَقَبَةَ

F^{a}*-lā* (but does not) *iqt*^{a}*ḥam*^{a} (he break through) *al-*^{a}*q*^{a}*b*^{a} (the difficult pass).

وَمَآ أَدۡرَىٰكَ مَا ٱلۡعَقَبَةُ

W^{a}*-mā* (and what) *adrā-k*^{a} (made you know) *mā* (what) *al-ʿaqaba* (the difficult pass [is]).

W^{a}*-mā adrā-k*^{a} (what is there to make you know) *mā al-ʿaqaba* (what the difficult pass [is]).

فَكُّ رَقَبَةٍ

F^{a}*kk*^{u} (the freeing [of], to free) *r*^{a}*q*^{a}*b*^{a} (a slave).

أَوۡ إِطۡعَٰمٞ فِي يَوۡمٖ ذِي مَسۡغَبَةٖ

Aw iṭʿām^{un} (or feeding) *fī* (on) *y*^{a}*wm*^{in} (a day) *dhī* (possessing) *m*^{a}*sgh*^{a}*b*^{a} (great hunger).

يَتِيمٗا ذَا مَقۡرَبَةٍ

Yatīm^{an} (an orphan) *dhā* (possessing) *m*^{a}*qr*^{a}*b*^{a} (nearness).

أَوْ مِسْكِينًا ذَا مَتْرَبَةٍ

Aw (or) *m^{i}skīn^{an}* (a needy person) *dhā* (possessing) *m^{a}tr^{a}b^{a}* (great misery).

ثُمَّ كَانَ مِنَ ٱلَّذِينَ ءَامَنُوا۟

Th^{u}mma (then, next) *kān^{a}* (he was) *m^{i}n* (of) *all^{a}dhīna* (those) *ām^{a}nū* (they believed).

Th^{u}mma (then, next) *kān^{a}* (he was) *m^{i}n* (of) *all^{a}dhīna ām^{a}nū* (those who believed).

وَتَوَاصَوْا۟ بِٱلصَّبْرِ وَتَوَاصَوْا۟ بِٱلْمَرْحَمَةِ

W^{a}-t^{a}wāṣ^{a}w (and they encouraged each other) *b^{i}-al-ṣ^{a}br^{i}* (to patience) *w^{a}-t^{a}wāṣ^{a}w* (and they encouraged each other) *b^{i}-al-m^{a}rḥam^{a}* (to compassion).

أُو۟لَٰٓئِكَ أَصْحَٰبُ ٱلْمَيْمَنَةِ

Ulā^{i}k^{a} (those [are]) *aṣḥāb^{u}* (companions [of]) *al-m^{a}ym^{a}n^{a}* (the right).

وَٱلَّذِينَ كَفَرُوا۟ بِـَٔايَٰتِنَا هُمْ أَصْحَٰبُ ٱلْمَشْـَٔمَةِ

W^{a}-all^{a}dhīn^{a} (and those who) *k^{a}f^{a}rū* (denied) *b^{i}-āyāt^{i}-nā* (our signs) *h^{u}m* (they are) *aṣḥāb^{u}* (companions [of]) *al-m^{a}sh^{a}m^{a}* (the left).

عَلَيْهِمْ نَارٌ مُّؤْصَدَةٌۢ

^{a}l^{a}yh^{i}m (upon them [is]) *nār^{un}* (a fire) *m^{u}ʾṣ^{a}d^{a}* (shut-in, enclosed).

Lesson 23: al-Shams

In this lesson we will discuss chapter 91 of the Quran: *al-Shams* ("The Sun").

بِسْمِ ٱللَّهِ ٱلرَّحْمَٰنِ ٱلرَّحِيمِ

Verse 1

وَٱلشَّمْسِ وَضُحَىٰهَا

By the sun and her morning brightness
Transliteration: w^{a}-al-sh^{a}ms^{i} w^{a}-ḍ^{u}ḥā-hā
Pronunciation: *w^{a}sh*-sh^{a}m-s^{i} w^{a}-ḍ^{u}-ḥā-hā

W^{a}-al-sh^{a}ms^{i} (by the sun) *w^{a}-ḍ^{u}ḥā-hā* (and her morning brightness).

The phrase *ḍ^{u}ḥā-hā* has the feminine pronoun *hā* (here it means "its", "her") at the end because it is referring to *al-sh^{a}ms*, which is a feminine word. The feminine pronouns are generally translated as "it" and "its" in English rather than "her". Both are correct.

الرَّجُلِ وَكِتَابُهُ

الْمَرْأَةِ وَكِتَابُهَا

Above, on the first line we have "the man and his book". On the second line we have "the woman and her book". Notice the way the ending pronouns change: *k^{i}tāb^{u}-h^{u}* becomes *k^{i}tāb^{u}-hā* when it is referring to a woman.

Verse 2

وَٱلْقَمَرِ إِذَا تَلَىٰهَا

And the moon when it follows her
Transliteration: w^{a}-al-q^{a}m^{a}r^{i} idhā t^{a}lā-hā
Pronunciation: w^{a}l-q^{a}-m^{a}-r^{i} i-dhā t^{a}-lā-hā

W^{a}-al-q^{a}m^{a}r^{i} (and the moon) *idhā* (when) *t^{a}lā-hā* (it followed her).

Above, "her" continues to refer to the sun from the previous verse. The verse means "By the moon when it follows the sun".

تَلَا يَتْلُو اتْلُ تُلُوّ تَال مَتْلُوّ

From right to left: he followed; he follows; *utl^{u}* ("follow!"); *t^{u}l^{u}ww* ("to follow"); follower; [that which is] followed.

Verse 3

وَٱلنَّهَارِ إِذَا جَلَّىٰهَا

And the daytime when it clearly displays her
Transliteration: w^{a}-al-n^{a}hār^{i} idhā j^{a}llā-hā
Pronunciation: *w^{a}n*-n^{a}-hā-r^{i} i-dhā j^{a}l-lā-hā

W^{a}-al-n^{a}hār^{i} (and the daytime) *idhā* (when) *j^{a}llā-hā* (it displays her clearly).

The verb *j^{a}llā* means "he made it clear", "he displayed it with clarity", "he caused it to be clear".

جَلَّى يُجَلِّي جَلِّ تَجْلِيَة مُجَلِّ مُجَلًّى

From right to left: he displayed it clearly; he displays it clearly; display it clearly!; to display clearly; [one who] displays [something] clearly; [that which is made to be] displayed clearly.

Verse 4

وَٱلَّيۡلِ إِذَا يَغۡشَىٰهَا

And the night when it covers her
Transliteration: w^{a}-al-l^{a}yl^{i} idhā y^{a}ghshā-hā
Pronunciation: w^{a}l-l^{a}y-l^{i} i-dhā y^{a}gh-shā-hā

W^{a}-al-l^{a}yl^{i} (and the night) *idhā* (when) *y^{a}ghshā-hā* (it covers her).

غَشِيَ يَغْشَى اغْشَ غَشْي غَاش مَغْشِيّ

From right to left: he covered; he covers; *ighsh^{a}* ("cover!"); to cover; coverer; covered [thing].

Verse 5

وَٱلسَّمَآءِ وَمَا بَنَىٰهَا

And the sky and that which built her
Transliteration: w^{a}-al-s^{a}mā'i w^{a}-mā b^{a}nā-hā
Pronunciation: *w^{a}s*-s^{a}-mā-'i w^{a}-mā b^{a}-nā-hā

W^{a}-al-s^{a}mā'i (and the sky) *w^{a}-mā* (and that which) *b^{a}nā-hā* ([he/it] built it).

Here the ending pronoun in *b^{a}nā-hā* ("he built her") no longer refers to the sun but to the sky mentioned earlier in this verse. Again "her" is used because *al-s^{a}mā'* ("the sky") is feminine.

بَنَى يَبْنِي ابْنِ بِنَاء بَان مَبْنِي

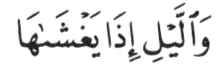

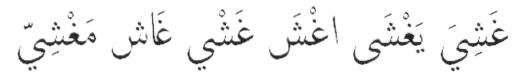

From right to left: he built; he builds; *ibn*^{i} ("build!"); to build (or building, both the physical structure known as a building and the act of building); builder; built [thing].

In the verse, the word *mā* ("that which") is used to refer to God who "built" the sky. Instead of *mā*, *m*^{a}*n* ("he who") could have been used:

مَنْ بَنَاهَا

In the Quran, sometimes God is referred to with *mā* even though normally this word is used to refer to non-living or non-conscious things, as in:

الكِتَاب وَمَا فِيه

"The book and that which is in it." Since the things inside a book are not conscious, we use *mā* ("that which") to refer to them. But below we have to use *m*^{a}*n*:

البَيْتِ وَمَن فِيهَا

"The house and those who are in it." Since those who are in the house are conscious beings, we have to use *m*^{a}*n*. If we had used *mā*, it would have referred to the non-conscious things in the house, such as its furniture.

Verse 6

وَالْأَرْضِ وَمَا طَحَـٰهَا

By the earth and that which spread her
Transliteration: w^{a}-al-arḍ^{i} w^{a}-mā ṭ^{a}ḥā-hā
Pronunciation: w^{a}l-ar-ḍ^{i} w^{a}-mā ṭ^{a}-ḥā-hā

W^{a}*-al-arḍ*^{i} (and the earth) *w*^{a}*-mā* (and that which) *ṭ*^{a}*ḥā-hā* ([he/it] spread her).

The phrase *ṭ*^{a}*ḥā-hā* means "he extended her", "he spread her", "he threw her". It refers to God's creation of the earth.

طَحَا يَطْحُو اطْحُ طَحْو طَاح مَطْحُوّ

From right to left: he spread; he spreads; *uṭḥ*^{u} ("spread [it]!"); to spread [it]; spreader; spread [thing].

Verse 7

وَنَفْسٍ وَمَا سَوَّىٰهَا

And a soul and that which proportioned her
Transliteration: w^{a}-n^{a}fs^{in} w^{a}-mā s^{a}wwā-hā
Pronunciation: w^{a}-n^{a}f-s^{in} w^{a}-mā s^{a}w-wā-hā

W^{a}*-n*^{a}*fs*^{in} (and a soul) *w*^{a}*-mā* (and that which) *s*^{a}*wwā-hā* ([he/it] proportioned her).

The verb *s*^{a}*wwā* has various meanings; here it means "he balanced it", "he proportioned it in a balanced way", "he caused it to be in a way that lacks unevenness and disorder".

سَوَّى يُسَوِّي سَوِّ تَسْوِيَة مُسَوّ مُسَوَّى

From right to left: he proportioned [it]; he proportions [it]; proportion [it]!; to proportion; proportioner; proportioned [thing].

Verse 8

فَأَلْهَمَهَا فُجُورَهَا وَتَقْوَىٰهَا

So he inspired in her her wickedness and righteousness
Transliteration: f^{a}-alh^{a}m^{a}-ḥā f^{u}jūr^{a}-hā w^{a}-t^{a}qwā-hā
Pronunciation: f^{a}-al-h^{a}-m^{a}-ḥā f^{u}-jū-r^{a}-hā w^{a}-t^{a}q-wā-hā

F^a-alh^{a}m^a-ḥā (so he inspired [in] her) *f^{a}jūr^a-hā* (her wickedness) *w^a-t^{a}qwā-hā* (her righteousness).

The meaning of this verse is controversial. It may refer to God inspiring in the soul the ability to discern good and evil. It may also refer to the concept that God increases good souls in righteousness and wicked souls in wickedness. While the soul is free to choose to be righteous or wicked, God inspires it with more righteousness or wickedness based on its choices.

أَلْهَمَ يُلْهِمُ إِلْهَام مُلْهِم مُلْهَم

From right to left: he inspires; he inspired; to inspire (or inspiration); inspirer; inspired [thing]. The command form is almost never used therefore it is omitted here.

Verse 9

قَدْ أَفْلَحَ مَن زَكَّىٰهَا

Truly has succeeded he who purifies her
Transliteration: q^{a}d afl^{a}ḥa m^{a}n z^{a}kkā-hā
Pronunciation: q^{a}d af-l^a-ḥa m^{a}n z^{a}k-kā-hā

Q^{a}d (truly has) *afl^{a}ḥa* (he succeeded) *m^{a}n* (he who) *z^{a}kkā-hā* ([he] purified her).

"Her" above continues to refer to the soul.

أَفْلَحَ يُفْلِحُ إِفْلَاح مُفْلِح مُفْلَح

From right to left: he succeeded; he succeeds; success; successful [person]; one who has been made to attain success.

This page intentionally left blank

بِسْمِ اللّٰهِ

As mentioned earlier, the first phrase above is *b*^{i}*s-m*^{i}. Now that the word *Allāh* comes after it, the pronunciation changes. The whole phrase is pronounced as *b*^{i}*s-m*^{i}*l-lā-h*^{i}. We say *h*^{i} because the *hā'* has a *kasra* underneath it (the final vowel mark in the above picture). The first "l" sound of *Allāh* is merged with the "m^{i}" before it, becoming "m^{i}l". The *hamza* at the beginning of *Allāh* completely disappears.

In Quranic calligraphy, these silent *hamza*s are written with a special mark above them, as follows:

ٱللّٰهِ

Muslims often say *b*^{i}*sm*^{i}*llāh* when starting something in hope of gaining God's blessing, for example when leaving or entering a house. When this phrase is by itself, there is no *kasra* underneath the final *hā'*. But when the phrase is in context, for example in a verse of the Quran, there it will have a *kasra*.

Verse 10

وَقَدْ خَابَ مَن دَسَّىٰهَا

And truly has lost he who corrupts it
Transliteration: w^{a}-q^{a}d khāb^{a} m^{a}n d^{a}ssā-hā
Pronunciation: w^{a}-q^{a}d khā-b^{a} m^{a}n d^{a}s-sā-hā

W^{a}-q^{a}d (and truly has) *khāb^{a}* (lost) *m^{a}n* (he who) *d^{a}ssā-hā* (he hid her).

The verb *khāb^{a}* means "he lost", "he failed", "he suffered disappointment".

خَابَ يَخِيبُ خِبْ خَيْبَة خَائِب

From right to left: he lost; he loses; lose!; loss; loser.

The verb *d^{a}ssā* literally means "he hid it". Here it means the person hid his soul's good qualities through evil deeds.

دَسَّى يُدَسِّي دَسِّ تَدْسِيَة مُدَسّ مُدَسَّى

From right to left: he hid; he hides; hide!; to hide; hider; hidden [thing].

Verse 11

كَذَّبَتْ ثَمُودُ بِطَغْوَىٰهَآ

Thamud denied by her transgression
Transliteration: k^{a}dhdh^{a}b^{a}-t th^{a}mūd^{u} b^{i}-ṭ^{a}ghwā-hā
Pronunciation: k^{a}dh-dh^{a}-b^{a}t th^{a}-mū-d^{u} b^{i}-ṭ^{a}gh-wā-hā

K^{a}dhdh^{a}b^{a}-t (she denied) *th^{a}mūd^{u}* (Thamud) *b^{i}-ṭ^{a}ghwā-hā* (by her transgression).

The meaning of the verse is that Thamud, by their transgression, denied the truth of their Prophet's message.

The word *ṭ*^{a}*ghwā* is a rare poetic word that means "transgression", "despotism", from *ṭ*^{a}*ghā* ("he acted despotically").

طَغَى طَغْوَى

Verse 12

إِذِ ٱنۢبَعَثَ أَشْقَىٰهَا

When her most wretched went forth
Transliteration: idh inb^{aʿa}th^{a} ashqā-hā
Pronunciation: i-*dh*^{i}*n*-b^{a}-^{ʿa}-th^{a} ash-qā-hā

Idh (when) *inb*^{a}$^{\text{ʿ}a}$*th*^{a} (he went forth) *ashqā-hā* (her most wretched).

This verse refers to a person among Thamud who went forth in order to carry out a deed that God had forbidden. The verb *inb*^{a}$^{\text{ʿ}a}$*th*^{a} means "he went forth". It is not *inb*^{a}$^{\text{ʿ}a}$*th*^{a}*-t* because the subject (*fāʿil*, the doer of the action) is a male, described here *ashqā-hā* ("her most wretched"). "Her" refers to Thamud.

انْبَعَثَ يَنْبَعِثُ انْبِعَاث مُنْبَعِث

From right to left: he went forth; he goes forth; to go forth, [one who] goes forth.

Verse 13

فَقَالَ لَهُمۡ رَسُولُ ٱللَّهِ نَاقَةَ ٱللَّهِ وَسُقۡيَٰهَا

So the Messenger of God said to them: "The she-camel of God and her water-portion."
Transliteration: f^{a}-qāl^{a} l^{a}-h^{u}m r^{a}sūl^{u} allāh^{i} nāq^{a}t^{a} allāh^{i} w^{a}-s^{u}qyā-hā
Pronunciation: f^{a}-qā-l^{a} l^{a}-h^{u}m r^{a}-sū-l^{u}l-lā-h^{i} nā-q^{a}-t^{a}l-lā-h^{i} w^{a}-s^{u}q-yā-hā

F^{a}-qāl^{a} (so he said) *l^{a}-h^{u}m* (to them) *r^{a}sūl^{u}* (messenger [of]) *allāh^{i}* (God) *nāq^{a}t^{a}* (she-camel [of]) *allāh^{i}* (God) *w^{a}-s^{u}qyā-hā* (and her water-portion).

This verse expresses in a very compressed way the fact that God's Messenger told Thamud: "This is God's she-camel and you should not obstruct her water-portion." They had asked for a miracle and their miracle was that a she-camel appeared to them. They were promised severe punishment if they did anything to obstruct or harm the camel.

The word *s^{u}qyā* means "water-portion", a specific amount of water assigned to an animal or person. It comes from the verb *saqā* ("he watered [an animal or person]", "he provided water"):

سَقَى يَسْقِي اسْقِ سَقْي سَاقٍ مَسْقِيّ

From right to left: he watered; he waters; *isq^{i}* ("water [it]!"); *s^{a}qī* ("to water"); server of water; watered [person or animal].

Verse 14, part 1

فَكَذَّبُوهُ فَعَقَرُوهَا

So they denied his truthfulness and they hamstrung her
Transliteration: f^{a}-k^{a}dhdh^{a}bū-h^{u} f^{a}-^{ca}q^{a}rū-hā
Pronunciation: f^{a}-k^{a}dh-dh^{a}-bū-h^{u} f^{a}-^{ca}-q^{a}-rū-hā

F^{a}-k^{a}dhdh^{a}bū-h^{u} (so they denied his truthfulness, they called him a liar) *f^{a}-^{ca}q^{a}rū-hā* (and they hamstrung her, and they hamstrung her).

As has been mentioned *k^{a}dhdh^{a}bū* means "they denied the truthfulness of", "they called him a liar or considered something to be a lie". The verb *ʿ^{a}q^{a}rū* ("they hamstrung", "they cut the legs") is the third person plural of *ʿ^{a}q^{a}r^{a}*.

When we have two *f*'s following each other as above, it is more correct to treat the first one as a "so" or "then" and the second one as an "and".

Verse 14, part 2

فَدَمْدَمَ عَلَيْهِمْ رَبُّهُم بِذَنۢبِهِمْ فَسَوَّىٰهَا

So their Lord brought destruction down upon them for their sin so He levelled her
Transliteration: f^{a}-d^{a}md^{a}m^{a} ʿ^{a}l^{a}y-h^{i}m r^{a}bb^{u}-h^{u}m b^{i}-dh^{a}nb^{i}-h^{i}m f^{a}-s^{a}wwā-hā
Pronunciation: f^{a}-d^{a}m-d^{a}-m^{a} ʿ^{a}-l^{a}y-h^{i}m r^{a}b-b^{u}-h^{u}m b^{i}-dh^{a}n-b^{i}-h^{i}m f^{a}-s^{a}w-wā-hā

F^{a}-d^{a}md^{a}m^{a} (so he brought destruction down) *ʿ^{a}l^{a}y-h^{i}m* (upon them) *r^{a}bb^{u}-h^{u}m* (their Lord) *b^{i}-dh^{a}nb^{i}-h^{i}m* (by their sin, for their sin) *f^{a}-s^{a}wwā-hā* (so He leveled her, i.e. He leveled Thamud).

D^{a}md^{a}m^{a} is a rare Arabic word that means "he crushed wrathfully", "he brought destruction down [upon it]". We already saw the verb *s^{a}wwā* in verse 7, where it meant "he proportioned [it]". Here it means "he leveled it", "he razed it to the ground".

Verse 15

وَلَا يَخَافُ عُقْبَٰهَا

And He fears not her consequence.
Transliteration: w^{a}-lā y^{a}khāf^{u} ʿ^{u}qbā-hā
Pronunciation: w^{a}-lā y^{a}-khā-f^{u} ʿ^{u}q-bā-hā

F^{a}-lā (so does not) *y^{a}khāf^{u}* (he fears) *ʿ^{u}qbā-hā* (her consequence, literally "what follows her").

The meaning of the verse is that God does not fear the consequence of "her". "Her" refers to God's action of destroying Thamud. So the meaning is that God does not fear the consequence of His destruction of Thamud, since there is no one to take Him to account; He can do whatever He wishes without fearing consequences.

The verb *y*^{a}*khāf*^{u} means "he fears". It is the third person present form of *khāf*^{a} ("he feared").

خَافَ، يَخَافُ، خَفْ، خَوْف وَخِيْفَة، خَائِف

From right to left: he feared; he fears; fear!; fear (two variants); [one who is] afraid.

This page intentionally left blank

Lesson 23 Review

بِسْمِ ٱللَّهِ ٱلرَّحْمَٰنِ ٱلرَّحِيمِ

وَٱلشَّمْسِ وَضُحَىٰهَا

W^{a}*-al-sh*^{a}*ms*^{i} (by the sun) *w*^{a}*-ḍ*^{u}*ḥā-hā* (and her morning brightness).

وَٱلْقَمَرِ إِذَا تَلَىٰهَا

W^{a}*-al-q*^{a}*m*^{a}*r*^{i} (and the moon) *idhā* (when) *t*^{a}*lā-hā* (it followed her).

وَٱلنَّهَارِ إِذَا جَلَّىٰهَا

W^{a}*-al-n*^{a}*hār*^{i} (and the daytime) *idhā* (when) *j*^{a}*llā-hā* (it displays her clearly).

وَٱلَّيْلِ إِذَا يَغْشَىٰهَا

W^{a}*-al-l*^{a}*yl*^{i} (and the night) *idhā* (when) *y*^{a}*ghshā-hā* (it covers her).

وَٱلسَّمَآءِ وَمَا بَنَىٰهَا

W^{a}*-al-s*^{a}*mā'i* (and the sky) *w*^{a}*-mā* (and that which) *b*^{a}*nā-hā* ([he/it] built it).

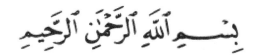

وَٱلْأَرْضِ وَمَا طَحَىٰهَا

W^{a}*-al-arḍ*^{i} (and the earth) *w*^{a}*-mā* (and that which) *ṭ*^{a}*ḥā-hā* ([he/it] spread her).

وَنَفْسٍ وَمَا سَوَّىٰهَا

W^{a}*-n*^{a}*fs*^{in} (and a soul) *w*^{a}*-mā* (and that which) *s*^{a}*wwā-hā* ([he/it] proportioned her).

فَأَلْهَمَهَا فُجُورَهَا وَتَقْوَىٰهَا

F^{a}*-alh*^{a}*m*^{a}*-ḥā* (so he inspired [in] her) *f*^{u}*jūr*^{a}*-hā* (her wickedness) *w*^{a}*-t*^{a}*qwā-hā* (her righteousness).

قَدْ أَفْلَحَ مَن زَكَّىٰهَا

Q^{a}*d* (truly has) *afl*^{a}*ḥa* (he succeeded) *m*^{a}*n* (he who) *z*^{a}*kkā-hā* ([he] purified her).

Q^{a}*d afl*^{a}*ḥa* (truly he has succeeded) *m*^{a}*n z*^{a}*kkā-hā* (he who purified her).

وَقَدْ خَابَ مَن دَسَّىٰهَا

W^{a}*-q*^{a}*d* (and truly has) *khāb*^{a} (lost) *m*^{a}*n* (he who) *d*^{a}*ssā-hā* (he hid her).

كَذَّبَتْ ثَمُودُ بِطَغْوَىٰهَآ

K^{a}*dhdh*^{a}*b*^{a}*-t* (she denied) *th*^{a}*mūd*^{u} (Thamud) *b*^{i}*-ṭ*^{a}*ghwā-hā* (by her transgression).

K^{a}*dhdh*^{a}*b*^{a}*-t th*^{a}*mūd*^{u} (Thamud denied) *b*^{i}*-ṭ*^{a}*ghwā-hā* (by her transgression).

إِذِ ٱنۢبَعَثَ أَشۡقَىٰهَا

Idh (when) *inb*^{a}^{ʿa}*th*^{a} (he went forth) *ashqā-hā* (her most wretched).

فَقَالَ لَهُمۡ رَسُولُ ٱللَّهِ نَاقَةَ ٱللَّهِ وَسُقۡيَٰهَا

F^{a}*-qāl*^{a} (so he said) *l*^{a}*-h*^{u}*m* (to them) *r*^{a}*sūl*^{u} (messenger [of]) *allāh*^{i} (God) *nāq*^{a}*t*^{a} (she-camel [of]) *allāh*^{i} (God) *w*^{a}*-s*^{u}*qyā-hā* (and her water-portion).

فَكَذَّبُوهُ فَعَقَرُوهَا

F^{a}*-k*^{a}*dhdh*^{a}*bū-h*^{u} (so they denied his truthfulness, they called him a liar) *f*^{a}*-*^{ʿa}*q*^{a}*rū-hā* (and they hamstrung her, and they hamstrung her).

فَدَمۡدَمَ عَلَيۡهِمۡ رَبُّهُم بِذَنۢبِهِمۡ فَسَوَّىٰهَا

F^{a}*-d*^{a}*md*^{a}*m*^{a} (so he brought destruction down) ^{ʿa}*l*^{a}*y-h*^{i}*m* (upon them) *r*^{a}*bb*^{u}*-h*^{u}*m* (their Lord) *b*^{i}*-dh*^{a}*nb*^{i}*-h*^{i}*m* (by their sin, for their sin) *f*^{a}*-s*^{a}*wwā-hā* (so He leveled her, i.e. He leveled Thamud).

وَلَا يَخَافُ عُقۡبَٰهَا

F^{a}*-lā* (so does not) *y*^{a}*khāf*^{u} (he fears) ^{ʿu}*qbā-hā* (her consequence, literally "what follows her").

This page intentionally left blank

Lesson 24: al-Aʿlā Part 1

In this lesson we will discuss chapter 87 of the Quran: *al-Aʿlā* ("The Most High").

بِسْمِ ٱللَّهِ ٱلرَّحْمَٰنِ ٱلرَّحِيمِ

Verse 1

سَبِّحِ ٱسْمَ رَبِّكَ ٱلْأَعْلَى

Exalt the name of your Lord the Most High
Transliteration: s^{a}bb^{i}ḥ ism^{a} r^{a}bb^{i}-k^{a} al-aʿlā
Pronunciation: s^{a}b-b^{i}ḥ is-m^{a} r^{a}b-b^{i}-k^{a}l-a^{ʿ}-lā

S^{a}bb^{i}ḥ (exalt) *ism^{a}* (name [of]) *r^{a}bb^{i}-k^{a}* (your Lord) *al-aʿlā* (the Most High, the Highest).

The verb *s^{a}bb^{i}ḥ* is a command that means "exalt [it]", "chant it [with exaltation]".

سَبَّحَ يُسَبِّحُ سَبِّحْ تَسْبِيح مُسَبِّح

From right to left: he exalted; he exalts; exalt!; to exalt; exalter.

Verse 2

ٱلَّذِى خَلَقَ فَسَوَّىٰ

The One Who created then proportioned
Transliteration: all^{a}dhī kh^{a}l^{a}q^{a} f^{a}-s^{a}wwā
Pronunciation: all^{a}dhī kh^{a}l^{a}q^{a} f^{a}-s^{a}wwā

All^{a}dhī (the one who) *kh^{a}l^{a}q^{a}* (created) *f^{a}-s^{a}wwā* (then proportioned).

خَلَقَ يَخْلُقُ اخْلُقْ خَلْق خَالِق مَخْلُوق

From right to left: he created; he creates; *ukhl^{u}q*(“create!”); creation; creator; created [thing].

Verse 3

وَٱلَّذِى قَدَّرَ فَهَدَىٰ

And the One Who measured then guided
Transliteration: w^{a}-all^{a}dhī q^{a}dd^{a}r^{a} f^{a}-h^{a}dā
Pronunciation: w^{a}l-l^{a}-dhī q^{a}d-d^{a}-r^{a} f^{a}-h^{a}-dā

W^{a}-all^{a}dhī (and the one who) *q^{a}dd^{a}r^{a}* (measured) *f^{a}-h^{a}dā* (then guided).

Verse 4

وَٱلَّذِىٓ أَخْرَجَ ٱلْمَرْعَىٰ

And the One Who brought out the pastureland
Transliteration: w^{a}-all^{a}dhī akhr^{a}j^{a} al-m^{a}rʿā
Pronunciation: w^{a}l-l^{a}-dhī akh-r^{a}-j^{a}l-m^{a}r-ʿā

W^{a}-all^{a}dhī (and the one who) *akhr^{a}j^{a}* (brought out) *al-m^{a}rʿā* (the pasture, the pastureland).

Verse 5

فَجَعَلَهُۥ غُثَآءً أَحْوَىٰ

So He makes it black dried and broken herbage

Transliteration: f^{a}-j^{aʿa}l^{a}h^{u} gh^{u}thā^{ʾan} aḥwā

Pronunciation: f^{a}-j^{a}-^{ʿa}-l^{a}-h^{u} gh^{u}-thā-^{ʾan} aḥ-wā

F^{a}-j^{aʿa}l^{a}h^{u} (then He made it [into]) *gh^{u}thā^{ʾan}* (dried and broken herbage) *aḥwā* (black).

The word *gh^{u}thāʾ* means "dried and broken pieces of herbage". The word *aḥwā* means "so dark as to be black".

Verse 6

سَنُقْرِئُكَ فَلَا تَنسَىٰٓ

We will cause you to recite so that you will not forget

Transliteration: s^{a}-n^{u}qr^{iʾu}-k^{a} f^{a}-lā t^{a}nsā

Pronunciation: s^{a}-n^{u}q-r^{i}-^{ʾu}-k^{a} f^{a}-lā t^{a}n-sā

S^{a}-n^{u}qr^{iʾu}-k^{a} (we will make you recite") *f^{a}-lā* (so do not) *t^{a}nsā* (you forget).

N^{u}qr^{iʾu} means "we cause [him] to recite", "we make [him] recite", from the verb *aqr^{aʾa}* ("he caused [him] to recite", rather than *q^{a}r^{aʾa}* ("he recited").

قَرَأَ أَقْرَأَ

From right to left: he read or recited; he caused [someone] to read or recite.

The verb t^{a}nsā is the second person singular of *n^{a}s^{i}y^{a}* ("he forgot"):

نَسِيَ

Verse 7

إِلَّا مَا شَآءَ ٱللَّهُۚ إِنَّهُۥ يَعۡلَمُ ٱلۡجَهۡرَ وَمَا يَخۡفَىٰ

Except that which God wills; indeed He knows what is declared and what is hidden
Transliteration: illā mā shā^{ʾa} allāh^{u} inn^{a}-h^{u} y^{aʿ}lam^{u} al-j^{a}hr^{a} w^{a}-mā y^{a}khfā
Pronunciation: il-lā mā shā-^{ʾa}l-lā-h^{u} in-n^{a}-h^{u} y^{aʿ}-la-m^{u}l-j^{a}h-r^{a} w^{a}-mā y^{a}kh-fā

Illā (except) *mā* (that which) *shā^{a}* (he wills) *allāh^{u}* (God) *inn^{a}-h^{u}* (truly He) *y^{a}ʿlam^{u}* (he knows) *al-j^{a}hr^{a}* (the declared) *w^{a}-mā* (and that which) *y^{a}khfā* (hides [itself], is/stays hidden).

The word *al-j^{a}hr* means "that which is loudly spoken" and "to speak loudly" (in a way that others may be able to hear it). The verb *y^{a}khfā* means "it hides [itself]", "it becomes hidden".

Verse 8

وَنُيَسِّرُكَ لِلۡيُسۡرَىٰ

And we ease you toward ease
Transliteration: w^{a}-n^{u}y^{a}ss^{i}r^{u}-k^{a} l^{i}-al-y^{u}srā
Pronunciation: w^{a}-n^{u}-y^{a}s-s^{i}-r^{u}-k^{a} l^{i}l-y^{u}s-rā

W^{a}-n^{u}y^{a}ss^{i}r^{u}-k^{a} (and we ease you) *l^{i}-al-y^{u}srā* (to ease, toward ease).

Verse 9

فَذَكِّرۡ إِن نَّفَعَتِ ٱلذِّكۡرَىٰ

So remind [them], if the reminder benefits
Transliteration: f^{a}-dh^{a}kk^{i}r in n^{a}f^{aʿa}t^{i} al-dh^{i}krā
Pronunciation: f^{a}-dh^{a}k-k^{i}r in n^{a}-f^{a}-^{ʿa}-*t^{i}dh*-dh^{i}k-rā

F^{a}-dh^{a}kk^{i}r (so remind!) *in* (if) *n^{a}f^{a}ʿ^{a}t^{i}* (it benefits) *al-dh^{i}krā* (the reminder, the remembrance).

Verse 10

سَيَذَّكَّرُ مَن يَخْشَىٰ

He who fears [God] will be reminded
Transliteration: s^{a}-y^{a}dhdh^{a}kk^{a}r^{u} m^{a}n y^{a}khshā
Pronunciation: s^{a}-y^{a}dh-dh^{a}k-k^{a}-r^{u} m^{a}n y^{a}kh-shā

S^{a}-y^{a}dhdh^{a}kk^{a}r^{u} (he will remember) *m^{a}n* (who) *y^{a}khshā* (he fears).

In standard Arabic *y^{a}dhdh^{a}kk^{a}r^{u}* would be *y^{a}t^{a}dh^{a}kk^{a}r^{u}* ("he is reminded [of something]", "he remembers [something]"):

يَتَذَكَّرُ

Verse 11

وَيَتَجَنَّبُهَا ٱلْأَشْقَى

And the most wretched will avoid it
Transliteration: w^{a}-y^{a}t^{a}j^{a}nn^{a}b^{u}-hā al-ashqā
Pronunciation: w^{a}-y^{a}-t^{a}-j^{a}n-n^{a}-b^{u}-h^{a}l-ash-qā

W^{a}-y^{a}t^{a}j^{a}nn^{a}b^{u}-hā (and avoid it) *al-ashqā* (the most wretched).

The meaning of the verse is that the most wretched will avoid the remembrance of God.

Verse 12

ٱلَّذِى يَصْلَى ٱلنَّارَ ٱلْكُبْرَىٰ

The one who experiences the burn of the greatest fire
Transliteration: all^{a}dhī y^{a}ṣlā al-nār^{a} al-k^{u}brā
Pronunciation: al-l^{a}-dhī y^{a}ṣ-*l^{a}n*-nā-r^{a}l-k^{u}b-rā

All^{a}dhī (the one who) *y^{a}ṣlā* (experiences the burn [of]) *al-nār^{a}* (the fire) *al-k^{u}brā* (the greatest).

The word *al-k^{u}brā* is the feminine of *al-k^{a}bīr* ("greater", "greatest"). The feminine adjective is used because *nār* ("fire") is a feminine word.

Verse 13

ثُمَّ لَا يَمُوتُ فِيهَا وَلَا يَحْيَىٰ

Then he does not die in it and he does not live
Transliteration: th^{u}mm^{a} l^{a} y^{a}mūt^{u} fī-hā w^{a}-lā y^{a}ḥyā
Pronunciation: th^{u}m-m^{a} l^{a} y^{a}-mū-t^{u} fī-hā w^{a}-lā y^{a}ḥ-yā

Th^{u}mm^{a} (then, next) *l^{a}* (does not) *y^{a}mūt^{u}* (he dies) *fī-hā* (in it) *w^{a}-lā* (and does not) *y^{a}ḥyā* (he lives).

Lesson 24 Review

بِسْمِ ٱللَّهِ ٱلرَّحْمَٰنِ ٱلرَّحِيمِ

سَبِّحِ ٱسْمَ رَبِّكَ ٱلْأَعْلَى

S^{a}bb^{i}ḥ (exalt) ism^{a} (name [of]) r^{a}bb^{i}-k^{a} (your Lord) al-aʿlā (the Most High, the Highest).

ٱلَّذِى خَلَقَ فَسَوَّىٰ

All^{a}dhī (the one who) kh^{a}l^{a}q^{a} (created) f^{a}-s^{a}wwā (then proportioned).

وَٱلَّذِى قَدَّرَ فَهَدَىٰ

W^{a}-all^{a}dhī (and the one who) q^{a}dd^{a}r^{a} (measured) f^{a}-h^{a}dā (then guided).

وَٱلَّذِىٓ أَخْرَجَ ٱلْمَرْعَىٰ

W^{a}-all^{a}dhī (and the one who) akhr^{a}j^{a} (brought out) al-m^{a}rʿā (the pasture, the pastureland).

فَجَعَلَهُۥ غُثَآءً أَحْوَىٰ

F^{a}-j^{a}ʿ^{a}l^{a}h^{u} (then He made it [into]) gh^{u}thā^{ʾan} (dried and broken herbage) aḥwā (black).

سَنُقۡرِئُكَ فَلَا تَنسَىٰٓ

S^{a}*-n*^{u}*qr*$^{i\,u}$*-k*^{a} (we will make you recite") *f*^{a}*-lā* (so do not) *t*^{a}*nsā* (you forget).

S^{a}*-n*^{u}*qr*$^{i\,u}$*-k*^{a} (we will make you recite") *f*^{a}*-lā t*^{a}*nsā* (so you will not forget).

إِلَّا مَا شَآءَ ٱللَّهُۚ إِنَّهُۥ يَعۡلَمُ ٱلۡجَهۡرَ وَمَا يَخۡفَىٰ

Illā (except) *mā* (that which) *shā*^{a} (he wills) *allāh*^{u} (God) *inn*^{a}*-h*^{u} (truly He) *y*^{a}*ʿlam*^{u} (he knows) *al-j*^{a}*hr*^{a} (the declared) *w*^{a}*-mā* (and that which) *y*^{a}*khfā* (hides [itself], is/stays hidden).

وَنُيَسِّرُكَ لِلۡيُسۡرَىٰ

W^{a}*-n*^{u}*y*^{a}*ss*^{i}*r*^{u}*-k*^{a} (and we ease you) *l*^{i}*-al-y*^{u}*srā* (to ease, toward ease).

فَذَكِّرۡ إِن نَّفَعَتِ ٱلذِّكۡرَىٰ

F^{a}*-dh*^{a}*kk*^{i}*r* (so remind!) *in* (if) *n*^{a}*f*^{a}^{a}*t*^{i} (it benefits) *al-dh*^{i}*krā* (the reminder, the remembrance).

F^{a}*-dh*^{a}*kk*^{i}*r* (so remind!) *in* (if) *n*^{a}*f*^{a}^{a}*t*^{i} *al-dh*^{i}*krā* (the reminder benefits).

سَيَذَّكَّرُ مَن يَخۡشَىٰ

S^{a}*-y*^{a}*dhdh*^{a}*kk*^{a}*r*^{u} (he will remember) *m*^{a}*n* (who) *y*^{a}*khshā* (he fears).

S^{a}*-y*^{a}*dhdh*^{a}*kk*^{a}*r*^{u} (he will remember) *m*^{a}*n y*^{a}*khshā* (he who fears).

وَيَتَجَنَّبُهَا ٱلۡأَشۡقَى

W^{a}*-y*^{a}*t*^{a}*j*^{a}*nn*^{a}*b*^{u}*-hā* (and avoid it) *al-ashqā* (the most wretched).

ٱلَّذِى يَصْلَى ٱلنَّارَ ٱلْكُبْرَىٰ

All^{a}dhī (the one who) *y^{a}ṣlā* (experiences the burn [of]) *al-nār^a* (the fire) *al-k^{u}brā* (the greatest).

ثُمَّ لَا يَمُوتُ فِيهَا وَلَا يَحْيَىٰ

Th^{u}mm^a (then, next) *l^a* (does not) *y^{a}mūt^u* (he dies) *fī-hā* (in it) *w^a-lā* (and does not) *y^{a}ḥyā* (he lives).

Th^{u}mm^a (then, next) *l^a y^{a}mūt^u* (he does not die) *fī-hā* (in it) *w^a-lā y^{a}ḥyā* (and he does not live).

This page intentionally left blank

Lesson 25: al-Aʿlā Part 2

Verse 14

قَدۡ أَفۡلَحَ مَن تَزَكَّىٰ

Truly he has succeeded who purifies himself
Transliteration: q^{a}d afl^{a}ḥ^{a} m^{a}n t^{a}z^{a}kkā
Pronunciation: q^{a}d af-l^{a}-ḥ^{a} m^{a}n t^{a}-z^{a}k-kā

Q^{a}d (truly has) *afl^{a}ḥ^{a}* (he succeeded) *m^{a}n* (he who) *t^{a}z^{a}kkā* (he purified himself).

Verse 15

وَذَكَرَ ٱسۡمَ رَبِّهِۦ فَصَلَّىٰ

And remembered the name of his Lord then worshiped
Transliteration: w^{a}-dh^{a}k^{a}r^{a} ism^{a} r^{a}bb^{i}-h^{i} f^{a}-ṣ^{a}llā
Pronunciation: w^{a}-dh^{a}-k^{a}-r^{a}s-m^{a} r^{a}b-b^{i}-h^{i} f^{a}-ṣ^{a}l-lā

W^{a}-dh^{a}k^{a}r^{a} (and remembered) *ism^{a} r^{a}bb^{i}-h^{i}* (the name of his Lord) *f^{a}-ṣ^{a}llā* (then worshiped, then performed the formal Islamic prayer).

Verse 16

بَلۡ تُؤۡثِرُونَ ٱلۡحَيَوٰةَ ٱلدُّنۡيَا

But rather, you give preference to the life of the world
Transliteration: b^{a}l t^{uʾ}th^{i}rū-n^{a} al-ḥ^{a}yāt al-d^{u}nyā
Pronunciation: b^{a}l t^{uʾ}-th^{i}-rū-n^{a}l-ḥ^{a}-yā-*t^{a}d*-d^{u}nyā

B^{a}l (but rather) *t^{u}'th^{i}rū-n^{a}* (you [plural] give preference [to]) *al-ḥ^{a}yāt* (the life [of]) *al-d^{u}nyā* (this world).

The word *b^{a}l* means "but rather". The word *t^{u}'th^{i}rū-n^{a}* ("you [plural] give preference [to]") is the second person plural of *āth^{a}r^{a}* ("he gave preference [to]").

آثَرَ يُؤْثِرُ إِيثَار مُؤْثِر مُؤْثَر

From right to left: he gave preference [to]; he gives preference [to]; to give preference [to]; one who gives preference [to]; [something that is] given preference.

The word *al-ḥ^{a}yāt* ("the life") would be written as follows in standard Arabic:

الحَيَاة

The word *al-d^{u}nyā* is used in the Quran to refer to the life of this world as opposed to the Hereafter. It is the opposite of *al-ākh^{i}r^{a}* ("the Hereafter"), literally "the last one".

Verse 17

وَٱلْءَاخِرَةُ خَيْرٌ وَأَبْقَىٰٓ

And the Hereafter is better and more enduring
Transliteration: w^{a}-al-ākh^{i}r^{a}t^{u} kh^{a}yr^{un} w^{a}-abqā
Pronunciation: w^{a}l-ā-kh^{i}-r^{a}-t^{u} kh^{a}y-r^{un} w^{a}-ab-qā

W^{a}-al-ākh^{i}r^{a}t^{u} (and the Hereafter) *kh^{a}yr^{un}* ([is] better) *w^{a}-abqā* (and more enduring).

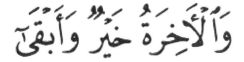

The word *kh^{a}yr* means "better" when it is used in comparisons. Originally the word was *akhy^{a}r*, but the *a* was removed by Arabs to shorten it and make it easier to say, which is why this word does not follow the ordinary patterns of Arabic adjectives. The word comes from *khār^{a}* ("it was good", "it was superior"). The word *abqā* ("more enduring", "most enduring") is the comparative and superlative form of *b*^{a}*qī* ("remaining", "lasting", "enduring"). The word comes from the verb *b*^{a}*qā* ("it remained", "it endured").

بَقِيَ

Verse 18

إِنَّ هَٰذَا لَفِي ٱلصُّحُفِ ٱلْأُولَىٰ

Indeed, this is truly in the first scriptures
Transliteration: inn^{a} hādhā l^{a}-fī al-ṣ^{u}ḥ^{u}f^{i} al-ūlā
Pronunciation: in-n^{a} hā-dhā l^{a}-*f*^{i}*ṣ* -ṣ^{u}-ḥ^{u}-f^{i}l-ū-lā

Inn^{a} (indeed) *hādhā* (this) *l*^{a}*-fī* (truly [is] in) *al-ṣ*^{u}*ḥ*^{u}*f*^{i} (the scriptures) *al-ūlā* (the first).

The word *ṣ*^{u}*ḥ*^{u}*f* ("written pages", "scriptures") is the plural of *ṣ*^{a}*ḥīf*^{a} ("written page"), anything that has writing upon it, whether it is paper or some other material.

صَحِيفَة

Verse 19

صُحُفِ إِبْرَٰهِيمَ وَمُوسَىٰ

The scriptures of Abraham and Moses
Transliteration: ṣ^{u}ḥ^{u}f^{i} ibrāhīm^{a} w^{a}-mūsā
Pronunciation: ṣ^{u}-ḥ^{u}-f^{i} ib-rā-hī-m^{a} w^{a}-mū-sā

Ṣ^{u}*ḥ*^{u}*f*^{i} (the scriptures [of]) *ibrāhīm*^{a} (Abraham) *w*^{a}*-mūsā* (and Moses).

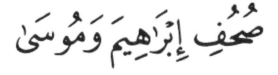

This page intentionally left blank

Lesson 25 Review

قَدۡ أَفۡلَحَ مَن تَزَكَّىٰ

Q^{a}d (truly has) *afl^{a}ḥ^a* (he succeeded) *m^{a}n* (he who) *t^{a}z^{a}kkā* (he purified himself).

Q^{a}d afl^{a}ḥ^a (truly he has succeeded) *m^{a}n t^{a}z^{a}kkā* (he who purified himself).

وَذَكَرَ ٱسۡمَ رَبِّهِۦ فَصَلَّىٰ

W^a-dh^{a}k^{a}r^a (and remembered) *ism^a r^{a}bb^i-h^i* (the name of his Lord) *f^a-ṣ^{a}llā* (then worshiped, then performed the formal Islamic prayer).

بَلۡ تُؤۡثِرُونَ ٱلۡحَيَوٰةَ ٱلدُّنۡيَا

B^{a}l (but rather) *t^u'th^{i}rū-n^a* (you [plural] give preference [to]) *al-ḥ^{a}yāt* (the life [of]) *al-d^{u}nyā* (this world).

وَٱلۡأٓخِرَةُ خَيۡرٞ وَأَبۡقَىٰٓ

W^a-al-ākh^{i}r^{a}t^u (and the Hereafter) *kh^{a}yr^{un}* ([is] better) *w^a-abqā* (and more enduring).

إِنَّ هَٰذَا لَفِي ٱلصُّحُفِ ٱلۡأُولَىٰ

Inn^a (indeed) *hādhā* (this) *l^a-fī* (truly [is] in) *al-ṣ^{u}ḥ^{u}f^i* (the scriptures) *al-ūlā* (the first).

صُحُفِ إِبْرَٰهِيمَ وَمُوسَىٰ

Ṣ^{u}*ḥ*^{u}*f*^{i} (the scriptures [of]) *ibrāhīm*^{a} (Abraham) *w*^{a}*-mūsā* (and Moses).

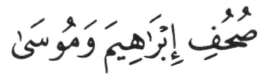

Lesson 26: al-Ṭāriq Part 1

This lesson is about chapter 86 of the Quran; *al-Ṭāriq* (“The Night Comer”).

بِسۡمِ ٱللَّهِ ٱلرَّحۡمَٰنِ ٱلرَّحِيمِ

Verse 1

وَٱلسَّمَآءِ وَٱلطَّارِقِ

By the sky and the night comer
Transliteration: wa-al-s^{a}mā^{ʾi} w^{a}-al-ṭār^{i}q
Pronunciation: *w^{a}s*-s^{a}-mā-^{ʾi} w^{a}ṭ-ṭār^{i}q

Wa-al-s^{a}mā^{i} (by the sky) *w^{a}-al-ṭār^{i}q* (and the night comer).

Al-ṭār^{i}q means “the night comer” and “the knocker”, from the verb *ṭ^{a}r^{a}q^{a}* (“[the star] appeared”, “he knocked”).

Verse 2

وَمَآ أَدۡرَىٰكَ مَا ٱلطَّارِقُ

And what can make you know what the night comer is?
Transliteration: w^{a}-mā adrā-k^{a} mā al-ṭār^{i}q
Pronunciation: w^{a}-mā ad-rā-k^{a} *m^{a}ṭ*-ṭā-r^{i}q

W^{a}-mā (and what) *adrā-k^{a}* (it made you know) *mā* (what [is]) *al-ṭār^{i}q* (the night comer).

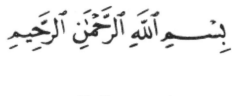

Verse 3

ٱلنَّجْمُ ٱلثَّاقِبُ

The piercingly bright star
Transliteration: al-n^{a}jm^{u} al-thāq^{i}b
Pronunciation: *an*-n^{a}j-*m^{u}th*-thā-q^{i}b

Al-n^{a}jm^{u} (the star) *al-thāq^{i}b* (the piercingly bright).

This verse answers the question from the previous verse. The "night comer" is the piercing star.

Al-thāq^{i}b literally means "the piercer", metaphorically meaning extremely bright. It comes from the word *th^{a}q^{a}b^{a}* ("he pierced", "it shone brightly").

Verse 4

إِن كُلُّ نَفْسٍ لَّمَّا عَلَيْهَا حَافِظٌ

Truly there is no soul except that upon it is a keeper
Transliteration: in k^{u}ll^{u} n^{a}fs^{in} l^{a}mmā ^{ca}l^{a}yhā ḥāf^{i}ẓ
Pronunciation: in k^{u}l-l^{u} n^{a}f-s^{in} l^{a}m-mā ^{ca}-l^{a}y-hā ḥā-f^{i}ẓ

In (truly not) *k^{u}ll^{u}* (every) *n^{a}fs^{in}* (a soul) *l^{a}mmā* (except that) *^{ca}l^{a}yhā* (upon her [is]) *ḥāf^{i}ẓ* (a keeper).

The first *in* is for negative emphasis, it means "truly not". *K^{u}ll^{u}* means "every", "all of".

The *l^{a}mmā* means "except that". The word *ḥāf^{i}ẓ* ("keeper", "protector") could refer to angels who watch over every human, recording their deeds and protecting them according to God's wishes.

Verse 5

فَلْيَنظُرِ ٱلْإِنسَٰنُ مِمَّ خُلِقَ

So let the human look from what he was made

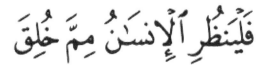

Transliteration: f^{a}-l-y^{a}nẓ^{u}r^{i} al-insān^{u} m^{i}-mm^{a} kh^{u}l^{i}q

Pronunciation: f^{a}l-y^{a}n-ẓ^{u}-r^{i}l-in-sā-n^{u} m^{i}m-m^{a} kh^{u}-l^{i}q

F^{a} (then) *l* (let) *y^{a}nẓ^{u}r^{i}* (he looks) *al-insān^{u}* (the human) *m^{i}-mm^{a}* (from what) *kh^{u}l^{i}q* (he was made).

M^{i}-mm^{a} is a shortened form of *min mā* (“of what”, “from what”).

مِنْ مَا

The word *kh^{u}l^{i}q^{a}* (“it was made”) is the passive form of *kh^{a}l^{a}q^{a}* (“he created”).

Verse 6

خُلِقَ مِن مَّآءٍ دَافِقٍ

He wade from an ejected fluid

Transliteration: kh^{u}l^{i}q^{a} m^{i}n mā^{ʾin} dāf^{i}q

Pronunciation: kh^{u}-l^{i}-q^{a} m^{i}n mā’-^{in} dā-f^{i}q

Kh^{u}l^{i}q^{a} (he was created) *m^{i}n* (from) *mā^{ʾin}* (a fluid) *dāf^{i}q* (thing that comes out ejectingly).

The word *mā’* literally means “water”, but it can also be used to mean “fluid”, “liquid”.

Verse 7

يَخْرُجُ مِنۢ بَيْنِ ٱلصُّلْبِ وَٱلتَّرَآئِبِ

It comes out from between the backbone and the ribs

Transliteration: y^{a}khr^{u}j^{u} m^{i}n b^{a}yn^{i} al-ṣ^{u}lb^{i} w^{a}-al-t^{a}rā^{ʾi}b

Pronunciation: y^{a}kh-r^{u}-j^{u} *m^{i}m* b^{a}y-*n^{i}ṣ*-ṣ^{u}l-b^{i} w^{a}t-t^{a}-rā-^{ʾi}b

Y^{a}khr^{u}j^{u} (it comes out) *m^{i}n* (from) *b^{a}yn^{i}* (between) *al-ṣ^{u}lb^{i}* (the backbone) *w^{a}-al-t^{a}rā^{ʾi}b* (and the ribs).

The word *al-t^{a}rā^{ʾi}b* is the plural of *tarīb^{a}* (“rib”):

تَرِيْبَة

Verse 8

إِنَّهُۥ عَلَىٰ رَجْعِهِۦ لَقَادِرٌ

Truly He is upon returning him truly capable
Transliteration: inn^{a}-hū ^{ʿa}lā r^{a}j^{ʿi}-h^{i} l^{a}-qād^{i}r
Pronunciation: in-n^{a}-hū ^{ʿa}-lā r^{a}j-^{ʿi}-h^{i} l^{a}-qā-d^{i}r

Inn^{a}-hū (truly He) *^{ʿa}lā* (upon) *r^{a}j^{ʿi}-h^{i}* (his returning, the act of returning him) *l^{a}-qād^{i}r* (truly capable).

The meaning of the verse is that God is totally capable of returning the human from the dead.

Verse 9

يَوْمَ تُبْلَى ٱلسَّرَآئِرُ

The day personal secrets will be put on trial
Transliteration: y^{a}wm^{a} t^{u}blā al-s^{a}rā^{ʾi}r
Pronunciation: y^{a}w-m^{a} t^{u}b-l^{a}s-s^{a}-rā-^{ʾi}r

Y^{a}wm^{a} ([the] day) *t^{u}blā* (are put on trial) *al-s^{a}rā^{ʾi}r* (the personal secret).

The verb *t^{u}blā* ("it is put on trial") is the third person present passive form of *b^{a}lā* ("he put [it] on trial", "he tested it").

Al-s^{a}rā^{ʾi}r ("personal secrets") is the plural of *s^{a}rīr^{a}* ("personal secret"), the things a person keeps hidden and private. It comes from the word *s^{i}rr* ("secret"), which comes from the verb *s^{a}rr^{a}* ("he kept it secret").

سَرِيْرَة

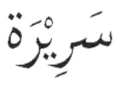

Verse 10

فَمَا لَهُۥ مِن قُوَّةٍ وَلَا نَاصِرٍ

So there is not for him any power or helper
Transliteration: f^{a}-mā l^{a}-h^{u} m^{i}n q^{u}ww^{a}t^{in} w^{a}-lā nāṣ^{i}r
Pronunciation: f^{a}-mā l^{a}-h^{u} m^{i}n q^{u}w-w^{a}-t^{in} w^{a}-lā nā-ṣ^{i}r

F^{a}-mā (so there is not) *l^{a}-h^{u}* (for him) *m^{i}n* ([any]) *q^{u}ww^{a}t^{in}* (strength, power) *w^{a}-lā* (and not) *nāṣ^{i}r* (supporter).

The phrase *mā…m^{i}n* means “there is not any”, “there is none”.

This page intentionally left blank

Lesson 26 Review

بِسْمِ ٱللَّهِ ٱلرَّحْمَٰنِ ٱلرَّحِيمِ

وَٱلسَّمَآءِ وَٱلطَّارِقِ

Wa-al-s^{a}*mā*^{i} (by the sky) *w*^{a}*-al-ṭār*^{i}*q* (and the night comer).

وَمَآ أَدْرَىٰكَ مَا ٱلطَّارِقُ

W^{a}*-mā* (and what) *adrā-k*^{a} (it made you know) *mā* (what [is]) *al-ṭār*^{i}*q* (the night comer).

ٱلنَّجْمُ ٱلثَّاقِبُ

Al-n^{a}*jm*^{u} (the star) *al-thāq*^{i}*b* (the piercingly bright).

إِن كُلُّ نَفْسٍ لَّمَّا عَلَيْهَا حَافِظٌ

In (truly not) *k*^{u}*ll*^{u} (every) *n*^{a}*fs*^{in} (a soul) *l*^{a}*mmā* (except that) ^{a}*l*^{a}*yhā* (upon her [is]) *ḥāf*^{i}*ẓ* (a keeper).

In k^{u}*ll*^{u} *n*^{a}*fs*^{in} (truly there is not any soul) *l*^{a}*mmā* (except that) ^{a}*l*^{a}*yhā ḥāf*^{i}*ẓ* (upon her is a keeper).

فَلْيَنظُرِ ٱلْإِنسَٰنُ مِمَّ خُلِقَ

F^{a} (then) *l* (let) *y*^{a}*nẓ*^{u}*r*^{i} (he looks) *al-insān*^{u} (the human) *m*^{i}*-mm*^{a} (from what) *kh*^{u}*l*^{i}*q* (he was made).

F^{a}*-l-y*^{a}*nẓ*^{u}*r*^{i} (so let him look) *al-insān*^{u} (the human) *m*^{i}*-mm*^{a} *kh*^{u}*l*^{i}*q* (from what he was made).

خُلِقَ مِن مَّآءٍ دَافِقٍ

Kh^{u}l^{i}q^{a} (he was created) *m^{i}n* (from) *mā^{in}* (a fluid) *dāf^{i}q* (thing that comes out ejectingly).

Kh^{u}l^{i}q^{a} (he was created) *m^{i}n* (from) *mā^{in}* *dāf^{i}q* (a fluid that comes out ejectingly).

يَخْرُجُ مِنۢ بَيْنِ ٱلصُّلْبِ وَٱلتَّرَآئِبِ

Y^{a}khr^{u}j^{u} (it comes out) *m^{i}n* (from) *b^{a}yn^{i}* (between) *al-ṣ^{u}lb^{i}* (the backbone) *w^{a}-al-t^{a}rā^{i}b* (and the ribs).

إِنَّهُۥ عَلَىٰ رَجْعِهِۦ لَقَادِرٌ

Inn^{a}-hū (truly He) *^{a}lā* (upon) *r^{a}j^{i}-h^{i}* (his returning, the act of returning him) *l^{a}-qād^{i}r* (truly capable).

يَوْمَ تُبْلَى ٱلسَّرَآئِرُ

Y^{a}wm^{a} ([the] day) *t^{u}blā* (are put on trial) *al-s^{a}rā^{i}r* (the personal secret).

فَمَا لَهُۥ مِن قُوَّةٍ وَلَا نَاصِرٍ

F^{a}-mā (so there is not) *l^{a}-h^{u}* (for him) *m^{i}n* ([any]) *q^{u}ww^{a}t^{in}* (strength, power) *w^{a}-lā* (and not) *nāṣ^{i}r* (supporter).

Lesson 27: al-Ṭāriq Part 2

Verse 11

وَٱلسَّمَآءِ ذَاتِ ٱلرَّجۡعِ

By the sky, [which is the] possessor of rain
Transliteration: w^{a}-al-s^{a}mā^{ʾi} dhāt^{i} al-r^{a}j^{ʿi}
Pronunciation: w^{a}s-s^{a}-mā-^{ʾi} dhā-t^{i}r-r^{a}j-^{ʿi}

W^{a}-al-s^{a}mā^{ʾi} (by the sky) *dhāt^{i} al-r^{a}j^{ʿi}* (possessor of rain).

The phrase *dhāt^{i} al-r^{a}jʿ* literally means "possessor of return". Metaphorically *r^{a}jʿ* is used to refer to rain, since it comes and goes and repeats.

Verse 12

وَٱلۡأَرۡضِ ذَاتِ ٱلصَّدۡعِ

And the earth, possessor of cracks
Transliteration: w^{a}-al-arḍ^{i} dhāt^{i} al-ṣ^{a}d^{ʿi}
Pronunciation: w^{a}l-ar-ḍ^{i} dhā-t^{i}ṣ-ṣ^{a}d-^{ʿi}

W^{a}-al-arḍ^{i} (and the earth) *dhāt^{i} al-ṣ^{a}d^{ʿi}* (possessor of cracks).

Since the previous verse was about rain, this verse is considered to refer to the earth cracking open to let plants out. While *al-ṣ^{a}d^{ʿi}* ("the crack") is singular, in the context it is used as a general term, so it is more correct to translate it as "cracks" in English.

Verse 13

إِنَّهُۥ لَقَوْلٌ فَصْلٌ

Indeed, truly it is a decisive statement
Transliteration: inn^{a}-h^{u} l^{a}-qawl^{un} f^{a}ṣl
Pronunciation: in-n^{a}-h^{u} l^{a}-qaw-l^{un} f^{a}ṣl

Inn^{a}-h^{u} (Indeed, it [is]) *l^{a}-qawl^{un} f^{a}ṣl* (truly a decisive statement).

The word *f^{a}ṣl* means "season", "decisive moment", "to fully separate two things". The phrase *qawl^{un} f^{a}ṣl* means "decisive statement", a statement that puts an end to an argument.

Verse 14

وَمَا هُوَ بِٱلْهَزْلِ

It is not a jest.
Transliteration: w^{a}-mā h^{u}w^{a} b^{i}-al-h^{a}zl
Pronunciation: w^{a}-mā h^{u}-w^{a} b^{i}l-h^{a}zl

W^{a}-mā (and is not) *h^{u}w^{a}* (it) *b^{i}-al-h^{a}zl* (a jest, in jest).

The word *h^{a}zl* means "jest", "joke", "something meant for amusement". The phrase *mā h^{u}w^{a} b^{i}*... is an empathic way of saying "it is not..."

Verse 15

إِنَّهُمْ يَكِيدُونَ كَيْدًا

Indeed, they are planning a plan
Transliteration: inn^{a}-h^{u}m y^{a}kīdūn^{a} k^{a}yd^{an}

Pronunciation: in-n^{a}-h^{u}m y^{a}-kī-dū-n^{a} k^{a}y-d^{an}

Inn^{a}*-h*^{u}*m* (indeed they) *y*^{a}*kīdūn*^{a} (plan) *k*^{a}*yd*^{an} (a plan).

The verb *y*^{a}*kīdūn*^{a} is the plural of *y*^{a}*kīd*^{u} ("he plans", "he schemes"), which is the present form of *kād*^{a} ("he schemed").

كَادَ يَكِيدُ

The word *k*^{a}*yd* comes from the same root and means "plan", "scheme".

Verse 16

وَأَكِيدُ كَيْدًا

And I plan a plan
Transliteration: w^{a}-akīd^{u} k^{a}ydā
Pronunciation: w^{a}-a-kī-d^{u} k^{a}y-dā

W^{a}*-akīd*^{u} (and I plan) *k*^{a}*ydā* (a plan).

In this verse God says that He too plans just as His enemies plan.

Verse 17

فَمَهِّلِ ٱلْكَٰفِرِينَ أَمْهِلْهُمْ رُوَيْدًۢا

So give the deniers respite; give them respite in a leisurely manner
Transliteration: f^{a}-m^{a}hh^{i}l al-kāf^{i}r^{i}n^{a} amh^{i}l-h^{u}m r^{u}w^{a}ydā
Pronunciation: f^{a}-m^{a}h-h^{i}-l^{i}l-kā-f^{i}-r^{i}-n^{a} am-h^{i}l-h^{u}m r^{u}-w^{a}y-dā

F^{a}*-m*^{a}*hh*^{i}*l* (so give respite [to]) *al-kāf*^{i}*r*^{i}*n*^{a} (the deniers) *amh*^{i}*l-h*^{u}*m* (give them respite) *r*^{u}*w*^{a}*ydā* (in a leisurely manner).

The words *m*^{a}*hh*^{i}*l* and *amh*^{i}*l* are two command forms from the same root that mean "give respite". The word *r*^{u}*w*^{a}*ydā* means "gently", "slowly", "in a leisurely manner".

This page intentionally left blank

Lesson 27 Review

وَٱلسَّمَآءِ ذَاتِ ٱلرَّجۡعِ

W^{a}-al-s^{a}mā^{i} (by the sky) *dhāt^{i} al-r^{a}j^{i}* (possessor of rain).

وَٱلۡأَرۡضِ ذَاتِ ٱلصَّدۡعِ

W^{a}-al-arḍ^{i} (and the earth) *dhāt^{i} al-ṣ^{a}d^{i}* (possessor of cracks).

إِنَّهُۥ لَقَوۡلٞ فَصۡلٞ

Inn^{a}-h^{u} (Indeed, it [is]) *l^{a}-qawl^{un} f^{a}ṣl* (truly a decisive statement).

وَمَا هُوَ بِٱلۡهَزۡلِ

W^{a}-mā (and is not) *h^{u}w^{a}* (it) *b^{i}-al-h^{a}zl* (a jest, in jest).

إِنَّهُمۡ يَكِيدُونَ كَيۡدٗا

Inn^{a}-h^{u}m (indeed they) *y^{a}kīdūn^{a}* (plan) *k^{a}yd^{an}* (a plan).

وَأَكِيدُ كَيۡدٗا

W^{a}-akīd^{u} (and I plan) *k^{a}ydā* (a plan).

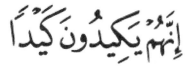

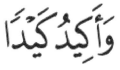

فَمَهِّلِ ٱلْكَٰفِرِينَ أَمْهِلْهُمْ رُوَيْدًۢا

F^{a}*-m*^{a}*hh*^{i}*l* (so give respite [to]) *al-kāf*^{i}*r*^{i}*n*^{a} (the deniers) *amh*^{i}*l-h*^{u}*m* (give them respite) *r*^{u}*w*^{a}*ydā* (in a leisurely manner).

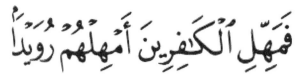

Lesson 28: al-Ḥadīd Part 1

In this lesson we will move on to chapter 57 of the Quran; *al-Ḥadīd* ("Iron").

بِسۡمِ ٱللَّهِ ٱلرَّحۡمَٰنِ ٱلرَّحِيمِ

Verse 1, part 1

سَبَّحَ لِلَّهِ مَا فِي ٱلسَّمَٰوَٰتِ وَٱلۡأَرۡضِۖ

Everything in the heavens and the earth chants exaltation for God
Transliteration: s^{a}bb^{a}ḥa l^{i}llāh^{i} mā fī al-s^{a}māwāt^{i} w^{a}-al-arḍ
Pronunciation: s^{a}b-b^{a}ḥa l^{i}l-lā-h^{i} mā f^{i}s-s^{a}-mā-wā-t^{i} w^{a}l-arḍ

S^{a}bb^{a}ḥa (it chanted exaltation, it exalted) *l^{i}llāh^{i}* (for God) *mā fī* (what is in, everything in) *al-s^{a}māwāt^{i}* (the heavens) *w^{a}-al-arḍ* (and the earth).

Notice the "ll" in *l^{i}llāh* ("for God", "to God") is pronounced as the "l" in "lamp". This is the case whenever there is a *kasra* before *llāh*. But normally, as we have mentioned, the "ll" in *Allāh* is pronounced like the "ll" in "call".

The phrase *mā fī* means "what is in", but from the context sometimes "everything in" is a more correct way of translating it.

Al-s^{a}māwāt literally means "the skies", it is the plural of *al-samā'* ("the sky"). But it is used to mean the present universe's sky and spaces outside of it from the Unseen world, therefore "the heavens" is more fitting.

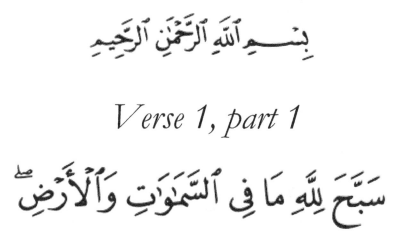

Verse 1, part 2

وَهُوَ ٱلْعَزِيزُ ٱلْحَكِيمُ

And He is the the Mighty, the Wise
Transliteration: w^{a}-h^{u}w^{a} al-^{ʿa}zīz^{u} al-ḥ^{a}kīm
Pronunciation: w^{a}-h^{u}-w^{a}l-^{ʿa}-zī-z^{u}l-ḥ^{a}-kīm

W^{a}-h^{u}w^{a} (and he is) *al-^{a}zīz^{u}* (the Mighty) *al-ḥ^{a}kīm* (the Wise).

Verse 2, part 1

لَهُۥ مُلْكُ ٱلسَّمَٰوَٰتِ وَٱلْأَرْضِ ۖ

To Him belongs the dominion of the heavens and the earth
Transliteration: l^{a}-hū m^{u}lk^{u} al-s^{a}māwāt^{i} w^{a}-al-arḍ
Pronunciation: l^{a}-hū m^{u}l-*k^{u}s*-s^{a}-mā-wā-t^{i} w^{a}l-arḍ

L^{a}-hū (for Him [is]) *m^{u}lk^{u}* (the dominion [of]) *al-s^{a}māwāt^{i} w^{a}-al-arḍ* (the heavens and the earth).

The phrase *l^{a}-hū* means "for him [is]...", "to him belongs".

M^{u}lk means "dominion", "reign", "supreme rule".

Verse 2, part 2

يُحْىِۦ وَيُمِيتُ ۖ وَهُوَ عَلَىٰ كُلِّ شَىْءٍ قَدِيرٌ

He brings to life and causes to die, and He is over all things extremely capable
Transliteration: y^{u}ḥy^{i} w^{a}-y^{u}mīt^{u} w^{a}-h^{u}w^{a} ^{ʿa}lā k^{u}ll^{i} sh^{a}y^{ʾin} q^{a}dīr
Pronunciation: y^{u}ḥ-y^{i} w^{a}-y^{u}-mī-t^{u} w^{a}-h^{u}-w^{a} ^{ʿa}-lā k^{u}l-l^{i} sh^{a}y-^{ʾin} q^{a}-dīr

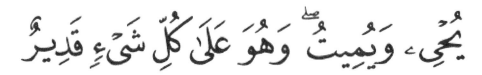

Y^{u}ḥy^{i} (He brings to life) *w^{a}-y^{u}mīt^{u}* (and causes to die) *w^{a}-h^{u}w^{a}* (and he [is]) *^{a}lā* (upon) *k^{u}ll^{i}* (every) *sh^{a}y^{in}* (thing) *q^{a}dīr* (extremely capable).

The verb *y^{u}ḥyī* ("he causes to live", "he brings to life") is the third person present form of *aḥyā* ("he brought to life"). In the Quranic text the final *yā'* of *y^{u}ḥyī* has been removed.

أَحْيَا يُحْيِي

The verb *y^{u}mīt* ("he causes to die") is the third present form of *amāt^{a}* ("he caused it to die", "he caused it to stop living").

أَمَاتَ يُمِيتُ

The phrase *^{a}lā k^{u}ll^{i} sh^{a}y^{in} q^{a}dīr* ("over all things extremely capable") means "capable of all things", "all-powerful".

Verse 3, part 1

هُوَ ٱلْأَوَّلُ وَٱلْءَاخِرُ وَٱلظَّٰهِرُ وَٱلْبَاطِنُ ۖ

He is the First and the Last, the Apparent and the Hidden
Transliteration: h^{u}w^{a} al-aww^{a}l^{u} w^{a}-al-ākh^{i}r^{u} w^{a}-al-ẓāh^{i}r^{u} w^{a}-al-b^{a}ṭ^{i}n
Pronunciation: h^{u}-w^{a}l-aw-w^{a}-l^{u} w^{a}l-ā-kh^{i}-r^{u} *w^{a}ẓ*-ẓā-h^{i}-r^{u} w^{a}l-b^{a}-ṭ^{i}n

H^{u}w^{a} (He [is]) *al-aww^{a}l^{u}* (the First) *w^{a}-al-ākh^{i}r^{u}* (and the Last) *w^{a}-al-ẓāh^{i}r^{u}* (and the Apparent) *w^{a}-al-b^{a}ṭ^{i}n* (and the Hidden).

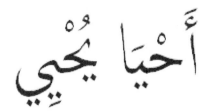

Verse 3, part 2

وَهُوَ بِكُلِّ شَيۡءٍ عَلِيمٌ

And He is about all things extremely knowing
Transliteration: w^{a}-h^{u}w^{a} b^{i}-k^{u}ll^{i} sh^{a}y^{ʾin} ^{ʿa}līm
Pronunciation: w^{a}-h^{u}-w^{a} b^{i}-k^{u}l-l^{i} sh^{a}y-^{ʾin} ^{ʿa}-līm

W^{a}-h^{u}w^{a} (and He is) *b^{i}* (of, about) *k^{u}ll^{i} sh^{a}y^{in}* (everything) *^{a}līm* (extremely knowing).

Verse 4, part 1

هُوَ ٱلَّذِي خَلَقَ ٱلسَّمَٰوَٰتِ وَٱلۡأَرۡضَ فِي سِتَّةِ أَيَّامٖ

He is the One Who created the heavens and the earth in six days
Transliteration: h^{u}w^{a} all^{a}dhī kh^{a}l^{a}q^{a} al-s^{a}māwāt^{i} w^{a}-al-arḍa fī s^{i}tt^{a}t^{i} ayyām
Pronunciation: h^{u}-w^{a} al-l^{a}dhī kh^{a}-l^{a}-q^{a} al-s^{a}-mā-wā-t^{i} w^{a}l-ar-ḍa fī s^{i}t-t^{a}-t^{i} ay-yām

H^{u}w^{a} (He [is]) *all^{a}dhī* (the One Who) *kh^{a}l^{a}q^{a}* (He created) *al-s^{a}māwāt^{i} w^{a}-al-arḍa* (the heavens and the earth) *fī* (in) *s^{i}tt^{a}t^{i}* (six) *ayyām* (days).

Verse 4, part 2

ثُمَّ ٱسۡتَوَىٰ عَلَى ٱلۡعَرۡشِۚ

Then He established Himself upon the Throne
Transliteration: th^{u}mm^{a} ist^{a}wā ^{ʿa}lā al-^{ʿa}rsh
Pronunciation: th^{u}m-m^{a}s-t^{a}-wā ^{ʿa}-l^{a}l-^{ʿa}rsh

Th^{u}mm^{a} (then, next) *ist^{a}wā* (He balanced Himself, He established Himself) *^{a}lā* (upon) *al-^{a}rsh* (the Throne).

The verb *ist^{a}wā* means "he became balanced", "he straightened up", "it became established", "it became equal to".

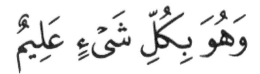

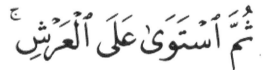

اسْتَوَى يَسْتَوِي اسْتَوِ اسْتِوَاء مُسْتَوٍ

From right to left: it became established; it becomes established; become established!; to become established; one who is established.

Verse 4, part 3

يَعْلَمُ مَا يَلِجُ فِى ٱلْأَرْضِ وَمَا يَخْرُجُ مِنْهَا

He knows what penetrates into the earth and what comes out of her.
Transliteration: y^{a}ʿl^{a}m^{u} mā y^{a}l^{i}j^{u} fī al-arḍ^{i} w^{a}-mā y^{a}khr^{u}j^{u} m^{i}n-hā
Pronunciation: y^{a}ʿ-l^{a}-m^{u} mā y^{a}-l^{i}-j^{u} f^{i}l-ar-ḍ^{i} w^{a}-mā y^{a}kh-r^{u}-j^{u} m^{i}n-hā

Y^{a}ʿl^{a}m^{u} (He knows") *mā* (what) *y^{a}l^{i}j^{u}* (penetrates) *fī* (into) *al-arḍ^{i}* (the earth) *w^{a}-mā* (and what) *y^{a}khr^{u}j^{u}* (comes out) *m^{i}n-hā* (from her).

The verb *y^{a}l^{i}j^{u}* means "it goes into [something] so that it partly or completely disappears", "it inserts itself into [something]", "it penetrates [into]". The past tense form is *w^{a}l^{a}j^{a}* ("it entered [into]").

Verse 4, part 4

وَمَا يَنزِلُ مِنَ ٱلسَّمَآءِ وَمَا يَعْرُجُ فِيهَا ۖ

And what descends from the heaven and what ascends into her
Transliteration: w^{a}-mā y^{a}nz^{i}l^{u} m^{i}n al-s^{a}mā^{ʾi} w^{a}-mā y^{a}ʿr^{u}j^{u} fī-hā
Pronunciation: w^{a}-mā y^{a}n-z^{i}-l^{u} m^{i}-*n^{a}s*-s^{a}-mā-^{ʾi} w^{a}-mā y^{a}ʿ-r^{u}-j^{u} fī-hā

W^{a}-mā (and what) *y^{a}nz^{i}l^{u}* (descends) *m^{i}n* (from) *al-s^{a}mā^{ʾi}* (the heaven, the sky) *w^{a}-mā* (and what) *y^{a}ʿr^{u}j^{u}* (ascends) *fī-hā* (into her).

نَزَلَ يَنْزِلُ انْزِلْ نُزُول نَازِل مَنْزُول

From right to left: he descended; he descends; unz^{u}l ("descend!"); to descend or descent; descender; [thing that was] made to descend.

Y^{a}ʿr^{u}j^{u} ("it goes up", "it ascends") is the present tense form of ^{a}r^{a}j^{a}.

Verse 4, part 5

وَهُوَ مَعَكُمْ أَيْنَ مَا كُنتُمْ ۚ

And He is with you [plural] wherever you [plural] are
Transliteration: w^{a}-h^{u}w^{a} m^{aca}-k^{u}m ayn^{a} mā k^{u}nt^{u}-m
Pronunciation: w^{a}-h^{u}-w^{a} m^{a}-^{ca}-k^{u}m ay-n^{a} mā k^{u}n-t^{u}m

W^{a}-h^{u}w^{a} (and He [is]) m^{a}ʿ^{a}-k^{u}m (with you) ayn^{a} mā (wherever) k^{u}nt^{u}-m (you were).

The word ayn^{a} means "where", it can be used in questions, as follows:

أَيْنَ أَنتَ ؟

"Where are you?"

But the phrase ayn^{a} mā... means "wherever".

Verse 4, part 6

وَٱللَّهُ بِمَا تَعْمَلُونَ بَصِيرٌ

And God is of what you [plural] do seeing
Transliteration: w^{a}-allāh^{u} b^{i}-mā t^{ac}m^{a}lūn^{a} b^{a}ṣīr
Pronunciation: w^{a}l-lā-h^{u} b^{i}-mā t^{ac}-m^{a}-lū-n^{a} b^{a}-ṣīr

W^{a}-allāh^{u} (and God [is]) b^{i}-mā (of what) t^{a}ʿm^{a}lūn^{a} (you do) b^{a}ṣīr (one who sees, [a] seeing [person]).

The word t^{a}ʿm^{a}lūn^{a} ("you do", "you work") is the second person plural of t^{a}ʿm^{a}l^{u} ("you [singular] do", "you work"), which is the present tense form of ^{a}m^{i}l^{a} ("he did", "he worked").

The word *b*^{a}*ṣīr* means “one who sees”, from the verb *b*^{a}*ṣ*^{u}*r*^{a} (“he saw”).

بَصُرَ ، يَبْصُرُ ، بَصَر وَبَصَارَة ، بَصِيْر

From right to left: he saw; he sees; *b*^{a}*ṣ*^{a}*r* and *b*^{a}*ṣār*^{a} (“the act of seeing”, “the ability to see”, “eyesight”, “insight”); one who sees.

This page intentionally left blank

Lesson 28 Review

بِسۡمِ ٱللَّهِ ٱلرَّحۡمَٰنِ ٱلرَّحِيمِ

سَبَّحَ لِلَّهِ مَا فِي ٱلسَّمَٰوَٰتِ وَٱلۡأَرۡضِۖ

S^{a}*bb*^{a}*ḥa* (it chanted exaltation, it exalted) *l*^{i}*llāh*^{i} (for God) *mā fī* (what is in, everything in) *al-s*^{a}*māwāt*^{i} (the heavens) *w*^{a}*-al-arḍ* (and the earth).

وَهُوَ ٱلۡعَزِيزُ ٱلۡحَكِيمُ

W^{a}*-h*^{u}*w*^{a} (and he is) *al-*^{a}*zīz*^{u} (the Mighty) *al-ḥ*^{a}*kīm* (the Wise).

لَهُۥ مُلۡكُ ٱلسَّمَٰوَٰتِ وَٱلۡأَرۡضِۖ

L^{a}*-hū* (for Him [is]) *m*^{u}*lk*^{u} (the dominion [of]) *al-s*^{a}*māwāt*^{i} *w*^{a}*-al-arḍ* (the heavens and the earth).

يُحۡيِۦ وَيُمِيتُۖ وَهُوَ عَلَىٰ كُلِّ شَيۡءٖ قَدِيرٌ

Y^{u}*ḥy*^{i} (He brings to life) *w*^{a}*-y*^{u}*mīt*^{u} (and causes to die) *w*^{a}*-h*^{u}*w*^{a} (and he [is]) ^{a}*lā* (upon) *k*^{u}*ll*^{i} (every) *sh*^{a}*y*^{in} (thing) *q*^{a}*dīr* (extremely capable).

هُوَ ٱلْأَوَّلُ وَٱلْـَٔاخِرُ وَٱلظَّـٰهِرُ وَٱلْبَاطِنُ ۖ

H^{u}w^{a} (He [is]) *al-aww^{a}l^{u}* (the First) *w^{a}-al-ākh^{i}r^{u}* (and the Last) *w^{a}-al-ẓāh^{i}r^{u}* (and the Apparent) *w^{a}-al-b^{a}ṭ^{i}n* (and the Hidden).

وَهُوَ بِكُلِّ شَىْءٍ عَلِيمٌ

W^{a}-h^{u}w^{a} (and He is) *b^{i}* (of, about) *k^{u}ll^{i} sh^{a}y^{in}* (everything) *^{a}līm* (extremely knowing).

هُوَ ٱلَّذِى خَلَقَ ٱلسَّمَـٰوَٰتِ وَٱلْأَرْضَ فِى سِتَّةِ أَيَّامٍ

H^{u}w^{a} (He [is]) *all^{a}dhī* (the One Who) *kh^{a}l^{a}q^{a}* (He created) *al-s^{a}māwāt^{i} w^{a}-al-arḍa* (the heavens and the earth) *fī* (in) *s^{i}tt^{a}t^{i}* (six) *ayyām* (days).

ثُمَّ ٱسْتَوَىٰ عَلَى ٱلْعَرْشِ ۚ

Th^{u}mm^{a} (then, next) *ist^{a}wā* (He balanced Himself, He established Himself) *^{a}lā* (upon) *al-^{a}rsh* (the Throne).

يَعْلَمُ مَا يَلِجُ فِى ٱلْأَرْضِ وَمَا يَخْرُجُ مِنْهَا

Y^{a}ʿl^{a}m^{u} (He knows") *mā* (what) *y^{a}l^{i}j^{u}* (penetrates) *fī* (into) *al-arḍ^{i}* (the earth) *w^{a}-mā* (and what) *y^{a}khr^{u}j^{u}* (comes out) *m^{i}n-hā* (from her).

وَمَا يَنزِلُ مِنَ ٱلسَّمَآءِ وَمَا يَعۡرُجُ فِيهَاۖ

W^{a}*-mā* (and what) *y*^{a}*nz*^{i}*l*^{u} (descends) *m*^{i}*n* (from) *al-s*^{a}*mā*^{i} (the heaven, the sky) *w*^{a}*-mā* (and what) *y*^{a}*ʿr*^{u}*j*^{u} (ascends) *fī-hā* (into her).

وَهُوَ مَعَكُمۡ أَيۡنَ مَا كُنتُمۡۚ

W^{a}*-h*^{u}*w*^{a} (and He [is]) *m*^{aʿa}*-k*^{u}*m* (with you) *ayn*^{a} *mā* (wherever) *k*^{u}*nt*^{u}*-m* (you were).

W^{a}*-h*^{u}*w*^{a} *m*^{aʿa}*-k*^{u}*m* (and He is with you) *ayn*^{a} *mā k*^{u}*nt*^{u}*-m* (wherever you are).

وَٱللَّهُ بِمَا تَعۡمَلُونَ بَصِيرٞ

W^{a}*-allāh*^{u} (and God [is]) *b*^{i}*-mā* (of what) *t*^{a}*ʿm*^{a}*lūn*^{a} (you do) *b*^{a}*ṣīr* (one who sees, [a] seeing [person]).

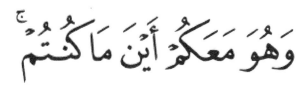

This page intentionally left blank

Lesson 29: al-Ḥadīd Part 2

Verse 5

لَهُۥ مُلْكُ ٱلسَّمَٰوَٰتِ وَٱلْأَرْضِ ۚ وَإِلَى ٱللَّهِ تُرْجَعُ ٱلْأُمُورُ

To Him belongs the dominion of the heavens and the earth, and to God are returned all matters
Transliteration: l^{a}-hū m^{u}lk^{u} al-s^{a}māwāt^{i} w^{a}-al-arḍ^{i} w^{a}-ilā allāh^{i} t^{u}rj^{aʿu} al-umūr
Pronunciation: l^{a}-hū m^{u}l-k^{u}s-s^{a}-mā-wā-t^{i} w^{a}l-ar-ḍ^{i} w^{a}-il^{a}l-lā-h^{i} t^{u}r-j^{a}-^{ʿu}l-u-mūr

L^{a}-hū (for Him [is], to Him [belongs]) *m^{u}lk^{u}* (the dominion [of]) *al-s^{a}māwāt^{i} w^{a}-al-arḍ^{i}* (the heavens and the earth) *w^{a}-ilā* (and to) *allāh^{i}* (God) *t^{u}rj^{aʿu}* (are returned) *al-umūr* (the matters).

The meaning of the verse is that all matters or affairs are under God's control. It can also refer to the fact that all human deeds are returned to Him for judgment.

The verb *t^{u}rj^{aʿu}* ("is returned") is the passive form of *t^{a}rj^{iʿu}* ("he returns"). The word *umūr* ("commands", "matters", "affairs") is the plural of *amr* ("command", "matter", "affair").

Verse 6, part 1

يُولِجُ ٱلَّيْلَ فِى ٱلنَّهَارِ وَيُولِجُ ٱلنَّهَارَ فِى ٱلَّيْلِ ۚ

He causes the night to penetrate into the daytime and the daytime to penetrate into the night
Transliteration: yūl^{i}j^{u} al-l^{a}yl^{a} fī al-n^{a}hār^{i} w^{a}-yūl^{i}j^{u} al-n^{a}hār^{a} fī al-l^{a}yl
Pronunciation: yū-l^{i}-j^{u}l-l^{a}y-l^{a} *f^{i}n*-n^{a}-hā-r^{i} w^{a}-yū-l^{i}-*j^{u}n*-n^{a}-hā-r^{a} fil-l^{a}yl

Yūl^{i}j^{u} (He causes to penetrate) *al-l^{a}yl^{a}* (the night) *fī* (into) *al-n^{a}hār^{i}* (the daytime) *w^{a}-yūl^{i}j^{u}* (and causes to penetrate) *al-n^{a}hār^{a}* (the daytime) *fī* (into) *al-l^{a}yl* (the night).

The verse refers to the way the night merges into the day and the day merges into the night. *yūl^{i}j^{u}* comes from the same root as *y^{a}l^{i}j^{u}* ("it penetrates [into]") in verse 4, part 3. But while the past tense form of *yūl*^{i}*j*^{u} is *awl*^{a}*j*^{a} ("he caused it to penetrate [int]", "he inserted it"), the past tense form of *y*^{a}*l*^{i}*j*^{u} is *w*^{a}*l*^{a}*j*^{a} ("it penetrated into", "it became inserted").

وَلَجَ يَلِجُ ، أَوْلَجَ يُوْلِجُ

Verse 6, part 2

وَهُوَ عَلِيمٌۢ بِذَاتِ ٱلصُّدُورِ

And He is extremely knowing of that which is in the chests
Transliteration: w^{a}-h^{u}w^{a} ^{ʿa}līm^{un} b^{i}-dhāt^{i} al-ṣ^{u}dūr
Pronunciation: w^{a}-h^{u}-w^{a} ^{ʿa}-lī-*m*^{um} b^{i}-dhā-*t*^{i}*ṣ*-ṣ^{u}-dūr

W^{a}*-h*^{u}*w*^{a} (and He [is]) *^{ʿa}līm*^{un} (extremely knowing) *b*^{i}*-dhāt*^{i} *al-ṣ*^{u}*dūr* (of that which accompanies the chests, of that which is in the chests).

The word *^{ʿa}līm* means "extremely knowing", from the word *^{ʿa}l*^{i}*m*^{a} ("he knew"). The form of the word *^{ʿa}līm* is known as *ṣīgh*^{a}*t al-m*^{u}*bāl*^{a}*gh*^{a} ("the hyperbolic form") of *ʿāl*^{i}*m* ("one who knows"). It strengthens its meaning and makes it extreme.

عَالِم عَلِيْم

From right to left: *ʿāl*^{i}*m* ("one who knows"), *^{ʿa}līm* ("one who knows extremely", "one who is extremely knowing").

The phrase *dhāt*^{i} *al-ṣ*^{u}*dūr* is a special expression that means "what is in the chests", i.e. what is in the hearts. Literally *dhāt*^{i} means "possessor of", however in certain special expressions it means "companion of", "associate of". Here it means "companion of the chests", "that which is in the chests", meaning that which accompanies the chests, i.e. the secrets that are in people's hearts.

Verse 7, part 1

ءَامِنُوا۟ بِٱللَّهِ وَرَسُولِهِۦ

Believe in God and His Messenger
Transliteration: ām^{i}nū b^{i}-allāh^{i} w^{a}-r^{a}sūl^{i}-h^{i}
Pronunciation: ā-m^{i}-nū b^{i}l-lā-h^{i} w^{a}-r^{a}-sū-l^{i}-h^{i}

Ām^{i}nū (believe!) *b^{i}-allāh^{i}* (in God) *w^{a}-r^{a}sūl^{i}-h^{i}* (and His Messenger).

The verb *ām^{i}nū* is a command directed at a group, it means "believe!" Its singular form is *ām^{i}n* ("believe! [directed at one person]"). It comes from the verb *ām^{a}n^{a}* ("he believed").

آمَنَ يُؤْمِنُ آمِنْ

آمَنُوا يُؤْمِنُونَ آمِنُوا

Top from right to left: he believed; he believes; believe!

Bottom from right to left: they believed; they believe; believe! [directed at a group].

The word r^{a}sūl means "messenger", "one who is sent by someone to carry a message", from the verb *ars^{a}l^{a}* ("he sent [a message]", "he sent [a messenger]").

Verse 7, part 2

وَأَنفِقُوا۟ مِمَّا جَعَلَكُم مُّسْتَخْلَفِينَ فِيهِ ۖ

And spend of that which He made you stewards of
Transliteration: w^{a}-anf^{i}qū m^{i}-mmā j^{a}ʿ^{a}l^{a}-k^{u}m m^{u}st^{a}khl^{a}fīn^{a} fī-h
Pronunciation: w^{a}-an-f^{i}-qū m^{i}m-mā j^{a}-ʿ^{a}-l^{a}-k^{u}m m^{u}s-t^{a}kh-l^{a}-fī-n^{a} fīh

W^{a}-anf^{i}qū (and spend) *m^{i}-mmā* (of that which) *j^{a}^{a}l^{a}-k^{u}m* (He made you) *m^{u}st^{a}khl^{a}fīn^{a} fī-h* (stewards in it / of it).

God here tells humans that they wealth they have is actually God's wealth that has been entrusted to them. They are its stewards or trustees and they should spend it in God's way.

أَنْفَقَ يُنْفِقُ أَنْفِقْ

أَنْفَقُوا يُنْفِقُونَ أَنْفِقُوا

Top from right to left: he spent; he spends; spend!

Bottom from right to left: they spent; they spend; spend! [directed at a group]

The word *m^{u}st^{a}khl^{a}fīn* is the plural of *m^{u}st^{a}khl^{a}f* ("one who has been made a successor", "steward", "trustee"), from the verb *ist^{a}khl^{a}f^{a}* ("he made him a steward/successor/trustee").

Verse 7, part 3

فَٱلَّذِينَ ءَامَنُوا۟ مِنكُمْ وَأَنفَقُوا۟ لَهُمْ أَجْرٌ كَبِيرٌ

Because those who believed among you and spent for them is a great reward

Transliteration: f^{a}-all^{a}dhīn^{a} ām^{a}nū m^{i}n-k^{u}m w^{a}-anf^{a}qū l^{a}-h^{u}m ajr^{un} k^{a}bīr

Pronunciation: f^{a}l-l^{a}-dhī-n^{a} ā-m^{a}-nū m^{i}n-k^{u}m w^{a}-an-f^{a}-qū l^{a}-h^{u}m aj-r^{un} k^{a}-bīr

F^{a}-all^{a}dhīn^{a} (because those who) *ām^{a}nū* (believed) *m^{i}n-k^{u}m* (of you, among you) *w^{a}-anf^{a}qū* (and spent) *l^{a}-h^{u}m* (for them) *ajr^{un}* (a reward) *k^{a}bīr* (great).

While *f^{a}* usually means "then", "so", here it more correctly means "because" since it is starting the conclusion to the statement that came before it.

Verse 8, part 1

وَمَا لَكُمْ لَا تُؤْمِنُونَ بِٱللَّهِ ۙ وَٱلرَّسُولُ يَدْعُوكُمْ لِتُؤْمِنُوا۟ بِرَبِّكُمْ

What is with you [plural] that you do not believe in God while the Messenger invites you to believe in your Lord?
Transliteration: w^{a}-mā l^{a}-k^{u}m l^{a} t^{u}ʾm^{i}nūn^{a} b^{i}-all^{a}h^{i} w^{a}-al-r^{a}sūl^{u} y^{a}dʿū-k^{u}m l^{i}-t^{u}ʾm^{i}nū b^{i}-r^{a}bb^{i}-k^{u}m
Pronunciation: w^{a}-mā l^{a}-k^{u}m l^{a} t^{u}ʾ-m^{i}-nū-n^{a} b^{i}l-l^{a}-h^{i} *w^{a}r-r^{a}*-sū-l^{u} y^{a}d-ʿū-k^{u}m l^{i}-t^{u}ʾ-m^{i}-nū b^{i}-r^{a}b-b^{i}-k^{u}m

W^{a}-mā l^{a}-k^{u}m (and what is [going on] with you) *l^{a} t^{u}ʾm^{i}nūn^{a}* (you do not believe) *b^{i}-all^{a}h^{i}* (in God) *w^{a}-al-r^{a}sūl^{u} y^{a}dʿū-k^{u}m* (while the Messenger invites you) *l^{i}-t^{u}ʾm^{i}nū b^{i}-r^{a}bb^{i}-k^{u}m* (to believe in your Lord).

The phrase *mā l^{a}-k^{u}m* means "what is [going on] with you?", "what is up with you?", "what is wrong with you?"

The tiny *lā* symbol above *b^{i}-all^{a}h^{i}* tells reciters not to stop at that point because stopping would change the meaning of the verse.

The *w^{a}* in *w^{a}-al-r^{a}sūl^{u}* means "while". It is known as a *wāw al-ḥāl* and is different from the first *w^{a}* in the verse (which is what we commonly see) which is known as a *wāw al-ʿaṭf*. The context determines which *wāw* it is. The *wāw al-ḥāl* is rare, so it is usually safe to assume a *wāw* is *wāw al-ʿaṭf* ("and").

Verse 8, part 2

وَقَدْ أَخَذَ مِيثَٰقَكُمْ إِن كُنتُم مُّؤْمِنِينَ

And truly He has taken your covenant if you are truly believers
Transliteration: w^{a}-q^{a}d akh^{a}dh^{a} mīthāq^{a}-k^{u}m in k^{u}n-t^{u}m m^{u}ʾm^{i}nīn
Pronunciation: w^{a}-q^{a}d a-kh^{a}-dh^{a} mī-thā-q^{a}-k^{u}m in k^{u}n-t^{u}m m^{u}ʾ-m^{i}-nīn

W^{a}-q^{a}d (and truly has) *akh^{a}dh^{a}* (He took) *mīthāq^{a}-k^{u}m* (your covenant) *in k^{u}n-t^{u}m* (if truly you were) *m^{u}ʾm^{i}nīn* (believers).

Verse 9, part 1

هُوَ ٱلَّذِى يُنَزِّلُ عَلَىٰ عَبْدِهِۦٓ ءَايَٰتٍۭ بَيِّنَٰتٍ

He is the One Who sends down upon His servant clear verses
Transliteration: h^{u}w^{a} all^{a}dhī y^{u}nazz^{i}l^{u} ^{ʿa}lā ^{ʿa}bd^{i}-h^{i} āy^{a}t^{in} b^{a}yy^{i}nāt
Pronunciation: h^{u}-w^{a} al-l^{a}-dhī y^{u}-n^{a}z-z^{i}-l^{u} ^{ʿa}-lā ^{ʿa}b-d^{i}-h^{i} ā-y^{a}-*t*^{im} b^{a}y-y^{i}-nāt

H^{u}w^{a} (He [is]) *all^{a}dhī* (the One Who) *y^{u}nazz^{i}l^{u}* (sends down) *^{ʿa}lā* (upon) *^{ʿa}bd^{i}-h^{i}* (His servant) *āy^{a}t^{in}* (verses) *b^{a}yy^{i}nāt* (clear ones).

The word *b^{a}yy^{i}nāt* is the plural of *b^{a}yy^{i}n^{a}*, which means “clear evidence”, “evident”.

بَيِّنَة

Verse 9, part 2

لِّيُخْرِجَكُم مِّنَ ٱلظُّلُمَٰتِ إِلَى ٱلنُّورِ ۚ

To take you out of the darknesses into the light
Transliteration: l^{i}-y^{u}khr^{i}j^{a}-k^{u}m m^{i}n^{a} al-ẓ^{u}l^{u}māt^{i} ilā al-nūr
Pronunciation: l^{i}-y^{u}kh-r^{i}-j^{a}-k^{u}m m^{i}-*n^{a}ẓ*-ẓ^{u}-l^{u}-mā-t^{i} i-*l^{a}n*-nūr

L^{i}-y^{u}khr^{i}j^{a}-k^{u}m (to take you out) *m^{i}n^{a} al-ẓ^{u}l^{u}māt^{i}* (from the darknesses) *ilā al-nūr* (to the light).

The word ẓ^{u}l^{u}māt^{i} is the plural of ẓ^{u}lm^{a} (“darkness”, “the darkness of the night [or a storm, etc.]”):

ظُلْمَة

Verse 9, part 3

وَإِنَّ ٱللَّهَ بِكُمْ لَرَءُوفٌ رَّحِيمٌ

And indeed God toward you is truly Sympathetic, Merciful
Transliteration: w^{a}-inn^{a} allāh^{a} b^{i}-k^{u}m l^{a}-r^{a}ʿūf^{un} r^{a}ḥīm
Pronunciation: w^{a}-in-n^{a}l-lā-h^{a} b^{i}-k^{u}m l^{a}-r^{a}-ʿū-f^{un} r^{a}-ḥīm

W^{a}-inn^{a} (and indeed) *allāh^{a}* (God [is]) *b^{i}-k^{u}m* (with you, toward you) *l^{a}-r^{a}ʿūf^{un}* (truly Sympathetic) *r^{a}ḥīm* (Merciful).

R^{a}ʿūf means "soft-hearted and sympathetic", from the verb *r^{a}ʾ^{u}f^{a}* ("he was sympathetic"):

رَؤُفَ يَرْؤُفُ رَأْفَة رَءُوْف

From right to left: *r^{a}ʾ^{u}f^{a}* ("he sympathized"); *y^{a}r^{a}ʾ^{u}f^{u}* ("he sympathizes"); *r^{a}ʾf^{a}* ("sympathy"); *r^{a}ʿūf* ("one who sympathizes", "sympathetic").

This page intentionally left blank

Lesson 29 Review

لَّهُۥ مُلْكُ ٱلسَّمَٰوَٰتِ وَٱلْأَرْضِ ۚ وَإِلَى ٱللَّهِ تُرْجَعُ ٱلْأُمُورُ

L^{a}*-hū* (for Him [is], to Him [belongs]) *m*^{u}*lk*^{u} (the dominion [of]) *al-s*^{a}*māwāt*^{i} *w*^{a}*-al-arḍ*^{i} (the heavens and the earth) *w*^{a}*-ilā* (and to) *allāh*^{i} (God) *t*^{u}*rj*^{a}^{u} (are returned) *al-umūr* (the matters).

يُولِجُ ٱلَّيْلَ فِى ٱلنَّهَارِ وَيُولِجُ ٱلنَّهَارَ فِى ٱلَّيْلِ ۚ

Yūl^{i}*j*^{u} (He causes to penetrate) *al-l*^{a}*yl*^{a} (the night) *fī* (into) *al-n*^{a}*hār*^{i} (the daytime) *w*^{a}*-yūl*^{i}*j*^{u} (and causes to penetrate) *al-n*^{a}*hār*^{a} (the daytime) *fī* (into) *al-l*^{a}*yl* (the night).

وَهُوَ عَلِيمٌۢ بِذَاتِ ٱلصُّدُورِ

W^{a}*-h*^{u}*w*^{a} (and He [is]) ^{a}*līm*^{un} (extremely knowing) *b*^{i}*-dhāt*^{i} *al-ṣ*^{u}*dūr* (of that which accompanies the chests, of that which is in the chests).

ءَامِنُوا۟ بِٱللَّهِ وَرَسُولِهِۦ

Ām^{i}*nū* (believe!) *b*^{i}*-allāh*^{i} (in God) *w*^{a}*-r*^{a}*sūl*^{i}*-h*^{i} (and His Messenger).

وَأَنفِقُوا۟ مِمَّا جَعَلَكُم مُّسْتَخْلَفِينَ فِيهِ ۖ

W^{a}*-anf*^{i}*qū* (and spend) *m*^{i}*-mmā* (of that which) *j*^{a}^{a}*l*^{a}*-k*^{u}*m* (He made you) *m*^{u}*st*^{a}*khl*^{a}*fīn*^{a} *fī-h* (stewards in it / of it).

فَٱلَّذِينَ ءَامَنُواْ مِنكُمْ وَأَنفَقُواْ لَهُمْ أَجْرٌ كَبِيرٌ

F^{a}*-all*^{a}*dhīn*^{a} (because those who) *ām*^{a}*nū* (believed) *m*^{i}*n-k*^{u}*m* (of you, among you) *w*^{a}*-anf*^{a}*qū* (and spent) *l*^{a}*-h*^{u}*m* (for them) *ajr*^{un} (a reward) *k*^{a}*bīr* (great).

وَمَا لَكُمْ لَا تُؤْمِنُونَ بِٱللَّهِ ۙ وَٱلرَّسُولُ يَدْعُوكُمْ لِتُؤْمِنُواْ بِرَبِّكُمْ

W^{a}*-mā l*^{a}*-k*^{u}*m* (and what is [going on] with you) *l*^{a} *t*^{u}*'m*^{i}*nūn*^{a} (you do not believe) *b*^{i}*-all*^{a}*h*^{i} (in God) *w*^{a}*-al-r*^{a}*sūl*^{u} *y*^{a}*d'ū-k*^{u}*m* (while the Messenger invites you) *l*^{i}*-t*^{u}*'m*^{i}*nū b*^{i}*-r*^{a}*bb*^{i}*-k*^{u}*m* (to believe in your Lord).

وَقَدْ أَخَذَ مِيثَٰقَكُمْ إِن كُنتُم مُّؤْمِنِينَ

W^{a}*-q*^{a}*d* (and truly has) *akh*^{a}*dh*^{a} (He took) *mīthāq*^{a}*-k*^{u}*m* (your covenant) *in k*^{u}*n-t*^{u}*m* (if truly you were) *m*^{u}*'m*^{i}*nīn* (believers).

هُوَ ٱلَّذِى يُنَزِّلُ عَلَىٰ عَبْدِهِۦٓ ءَايَٰتٍۭ بَيِّنَٰتٍ

H^{u}*w*^{a} (He [is]) *all*^{a}*dhī* (the One Who) *y*^{u}*nazz*^{i}*l*^{u} (sends down) ^{a}*lā* (upon) ^{a}*bd*^{i}*-h*^{i} (His servant) *āy*^{a}*t*^{in} (verses) *b*^{a}*yy*^{i}*nāt* (clear ones).

لِّيُخْرِجَكُم مِّنَ ٱلظُّلُمَٰتِ إِلَى ٱلنُّورِ ۚ

L^{i}*-y*^{u}*khr*^{i}*j*^{a}*-k*^{u}*m* (to take you out) *m*^{i}*n*^{a} *al-ẓ*^{u}*l*^{u}*māt*^{i} (from the darknesses) *ilā al-nūr* (to the light).

وَإِنَّ ٱللَّهَ بِكُمْ لَرَءُوفٌ رَّحِيمٌ

W^{a}*-inn*^{a} (and indeed) *allāh*^{a} (God [is]) *b*^{i}*-k*^{u}*m* (with you, toward you) *l*^{a}*-r*^{a}*ʿūf*^{un} (truly Sympathetic) *r*^{a}*ḥīm* (Merciful).

This page intentionally left blank

Lesson 30: al-Ḥadīd Part 3

Verse 10, part 1

وَمَا لَكُمْ أَلَّا تُنفِقُوا۟ فِى سَبِيلِ ٱللَّهِ

And what is [going on] with you [plural] that you do not spend in the way of God
Transliteration: w^{a}-mā l^{a}-k^{u}m al-lā t^{u}nf^{i}qū fī s^{a}bīl^{i} allāh^{i}
Pronunciation: w^{a}-mā l^{a}-k^{u}m al-lā t^{u}n-f^{i}-qū fī s^{a}-bī-l^{i}l-lā-h^{i}

W^{a}-mā l^{a}-k^{u}m (and what is with you) *al-lā* (to not) *t^{u}nf^{i}qū* (you spend) *fī* (in) *s^{a}bīl^{i}* (way [of]) *allāh^{i}* (God).

Verse 10, part 2

وَلِلَّهِ مِيرَٰثُ ٱلسَّمَٰوَٰتِ وَٱلْأَرْضِ ۚ

While to God belongs the inheritance of the heavens and the earth
Transliteration: w^{a}-l^{i}llāh^{i} mīrāth^{u} al-s^{a}māwāt^{i} w^{a}-al-arḍ
Pronunciation: w^{a}-l^{i}l-lā-h^{i} mī-rā-th^{u}s-s^{a}-mā-wā-t^{i} w^{a}l-arḍ

W^{a}-l^{i}llāh^{i} (and for God is, and to God belongs) *mīrāth^{u}* (the inheritance [of]) *al-s^{a}māwāt^{i} w^{a}-al-arḍ* (the heavens and the earth).

The meaning of the verse is that to God belongs all of the wealth of the heavens and the earth.

Verse 10, part 3

لَا يَسْتَوِى مِنكُم مَّنْ أَنفَقَ مِن قَبْلِ ٱلْفَتْحِ وَقَٰتَلَ ۚ

Is not equal among you the one who spent before the conquest [of Mecca] and fought

Transliteration: lā y^{a}st^{a}wī m^{i}n-k^{u}m m^{a}n anf^{a}q^{a} m^{i}n q^{a}bl^{i} al-f^{a}tḥ^{i} w^{a}-qāt^{a}l

Pronunciation: lā y^{a}s-t^{a}-wī m^{i}n-k^{u}m m^{a}n an-f^{a}-q^{a} m^{i}n q^{a}b-l^{i}l-f^{a}t-ḥ^{i} w^{a} qā-t^{a}l

Lā (does not) *y^{a}st^{a}wī* (equals, is equal to) *m^{i}n-k^{u}m* (of you, among you) *m^{a}n* (he who) *anf^{a}q^{a}* (spent) *m^{i}n q^{a}bl^{i}* (before) *al-f^{a}tḥ^{i}* (the conquest) *w^{a}-qāt^{a}l* (and fought).

The word *q^{a}bl* means "before". The phase *m^{i}n q^{a}bl^{i}* also merely means "before".

The verb *qāt^{a}l^{a}* means "he fought" while *q^{a}t^{a}l^{a}* means "he killed".

قَتَلَ يَقْتُلُ اقْتُلْ قَتْلٌ

قَاتَلَ يُقَاتِلُ قَاتِلْ قِتَال

Top from right to left: he killed; he kills; kill!; [the act of] killing / homicide.

Bottom from right to left: he fought; he fights; fight!; fighting / [a] fight.

Verse 10, part 4

أُوْلَٰٓئِكَ أَعْظَمُ دَرَجَةً مِّنَ ٱلَّذِينَ أَنفَقُواْ مِنۢ بَعْدُ وَقَٰتَلُواْۚ

Those are greater in degree than those who spent afterwards and fought

Transliteration: ulā^{ʾi}k^{a} a^{ʿ}ẓ^{a}m^{u} d^{a}r^{a}j^{a}t^{an} m^{i}n all^{a}dhīn^{a} anf^{a}qū m^{i}n b^{aʿ}d^{u} w^{a}-qāt^{a}l^{u}

Pronunciation: u-lā-^{ʾi}-k^{a} a^{ʿ}-ẓ$^{a-}$m^{u} d^{a}-r^{a}-j^{a}-t^{an} m^{i}-n^{a}l-l^{a}-dhī-n^{a} an-f^{a}-qū m^{i}n b^{aʿ}-d^{u} w^{a}-qā-t^{a}-l^{u}

Ulā^{i}k^{a} (those [are]) *a^{ʿ}ẓ^{a}m^{u}* (greater) *d^{a}r^{a}j^{a}t^{an}* (a degree, a rank) *m^{i}n* (than) *all^{a}dhīn^{a}* (those who) *anf^{a}qū* (spent) *m^{i}n b^{a}ʿd^{u}* (afterwards) *w^{a}-qāt^{a}l^{u}* (and fought).

The word *b^{a}ʿd* means "after". The phrase *m^{i}n b^{a}ʿd^{u}* means "after", "afterwards".

Verse 10, part 5

وَكُلًّا وَعَدَ ٱللَّهُ ٱلْحُسْنَىٰ ۚ وَٱللَّهُ بِمَا تَعْمَلُونَ خَبِيرٌ

And [to] all [of them] He has promised the best [reward], and God is cognizant of what you [plural] do

Transliteration: w^{a}-k^{u}ll^{an} w^{aʿa}d^{a} allāh^{u} al-ḥ^{u}snā w^{a}-allāh^{u} b^{i}-mā t^{aʿ}m^{a}lūn^{a} kh^{a}bīr

Pronunciation: w^{a}-k^{u}l-l^{an} w^{a}-^{ʿa}-d^{a}l-lā-h^{u}l-ḥ^{u}s-nā w^{a}l-lā-h^{u} b^{i}-mā t^{aʿ}-m^{a}-lū-n^{a} kh^{a}-bīr

W^{a}-k^{u}ll^{an} (and every, and all) *w$^{a a}$d^{a}* (He promised) *allāh^{u}* (God) *al-ḥ^{u}snā* (the most beautiful, the best) *w^{a}-allāh^{u}* (and God [is]) *b^{i}-mā* (of what) *t^{a}ʿm^{a}lūn^{a}* (you do) *kh^{a}bīr* (cognizant, knowing, aware).

Verse 11, part 1

مَّن ذَا ٱلَّذِى يُقْرِضُ ٱللَّهَ قَرْضًا حَسَنًا

Who is it who lends God a wholesome loan…?

Transliteration: m^{a}n dhā all^{a}dhī y^{u}qr^{i}ḍ^{u} allāh^{a} q^{a}rḍ^{an} ḥ^{a}s^{a}nā

Pronunciation: m^{a}n dh^{a}l-l^{a}-dhī y^{u}q-r^{i}-ḍ^{u}l-lā-h^{a} q^{a}r-ḍ^{an} ḥ^{a}-s^{a}-nā

M^{a}n dhā all^{a}dhī (who is the one who) *y^{u}qr^{i}ḍ^{u}* (lends) *allāh^{a}* (God) *q^{a}rḍ^{an} ḥ^{a}s^{a}nā* (a good loan).

The word *m^{a}n* means "who", *dhā* means "that" and *all^{a}dhī* means "the one". The full phrase means "who is the one who…?", "who is the one that…?"

أَقْرَضَ يُقْرِضُ إِقْرَاض مُقْرِض مُقْرَض

From right to left: he lent; he lends; to lend; lender; lent [thing].

The word *q^{a}rḍ* comes from the same root and means "loan".

The word *ḥasan* means "beautiful", "goodly", "wholesome".

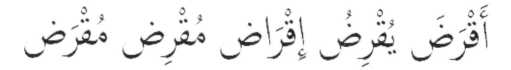

Verse 11, part 2

فَيُضَٰعِفَهُۥ لَهُۥ وَلَهُۥٓ أَجْرٌ كَرِيمٌ

So He multiplies it for him and for him is a generous reward
Transliteration: fa-y^{u}ḍā^{ʿi}f^{u}-h^{u} l^{a}-h^{u} w^{a}-l^{a}-h^{u} ajr^{un} k^{a}rīm
Pronunciation: fa-y^{u}-ḍā-^{ʿi}-f^{u}-h^{u} l^{a}-h^{u} w^{a}-l^{a}-h^{u} aj-r^{un} k^{a}-rīm

Fa-y^{u}ḍā^{ʿi}f^{u}-h^{u} (so He multiplies it) *l^{a}-h^{u}* (for him) *w^{a}-l^{a}-h^{u}* (and for him) *ajr^{un}* (a reward) *k^{a}rīm* (generous).

The verb *y^{u}ḍā^{ʿi}f^{u}* is the third person present form of *ḍāʿafa* ("he doubled it", "he multiplied it").

ضَاعَفَ يُضَاعِفُ مُضَاعَفَة مُضَاعِف

From right to left: he multiplied [it]; he multiplies [it]; multiplication; multiplier.

Verse 12, part 1

يَوْمَ تَرَى ٱلْمُؤْمِنِينَ وَٱلْمُؤْمِنَٰتِ

[On] the day you [singular] see the believers [masculine] and the believers [feminine]
Transliteration: y^{a}wm^{a} t^{a}rā al-m^{uʾ}m^{i}nīn^{a} w^{a}-al-m^{uʾ}m^{i}nāt^{i}
Pronunciation: y^{a}w-m^{a} t^{a}-rā al-m^{uʾ}-m^{i}-nī-n^{a} w^{a}l-m^{uʾ}-m^{i}-nā-t^{i}

Y^{a}wm^{a} ([on] the day) *t^{a}rā* (you see) *al-m^{u}ʾm^{i}nīn^{a}* (the [male] believers) *w^{a}-al-m^{u}ʾm^{i}nāt^{i}* (the [female] believers).

The "on" at the beginning is there due to the context of this verse and the previous one.

Verse 12, part 2

يَسْعَىٰ نُورُهُم بَيْنَ أَيْدِيهِمْ وَبِأَيْمَٰنِهِم

Their light proceeding in front of them and on their right sides
Transliteration: y^{a}s‘ā nūr^{u}-h^{u}m b^{a}yn^{a} aydī-h^{i}m w^{a} b^{i}-aymān^{i}-h^{i}m
Pronunciation: y^{a}s-‘ā nū-r^{u}-h^{u}m b^{a}y-n^{a} ay-dī-h^{i}m w^{a} b^{i}-ay-mā-n^{i}-h^{i}m

Y^{a}s‘ā (it proceeds) *nūr^{u}-h^{u}m* (their light) *b^{a}yn^{a} aydī-h^{i}m* (in front of them) *w^{a} b^{i}-aymān^{i}-h^{i}m* (and on their right sides).

The verb *y^{a}s‘ā* means "it goes forth hurriedly", "it proceeds fast", "it runs".

The phrase *b^{a}yn^{a} aydī-h^{i}m* literally means "between their hands", it is a common Arabic expression that menas "in front of them".

Verse 12, part 3

بُشْرَىٰكُمُ ٱلْيَوْمَ جَنَّٰتٌ تَجْرِى مِن تَحْتِهَا ٱلْأَنْهَٰرُ

Your [plural] good tidings today are gardens under which rivers flow
Transliteration: b^{u}shrā-k^{u}m^{u} al-y^{a}wm^{a} j^{a}nnāt^{un} t^{a}jrī m^{i}n t^{a}ḥt^{i}hā al-anhār
Pronunciation: b^{u}sh-rā-k^{u}-m^{u}l-y^{a}w-m^{a} j^{a}n-nā-t^{un} t^{a}j-rī m^{i}n t^{a}ḥ-t^{i}-h^{a}l-an-hār

B^{u}shrā-k^{u}m^{u} (your good tiding) *al-y^{a}wm^{a}* (today) *j^{a}nnāt^{un}* (gardens) *t^{a}jrī* (they flow) *m^{i}n t^{a}ḥt^{i}hā* (from underneath them) *al-anhār* (the rivers).

The word *b^{u}shrā* means "good news", "good tiding".

Verse 12, part 4

خَٰلِدِينَ فِيهَا ۚ ذَٰلِكَ هُوَ ٱلْفَوْزُ ٱلْعَظِيمُ

Immortal in them. That is the great success

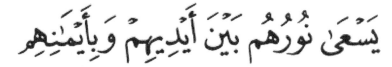

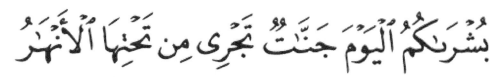

Transliteration: khāl^{i}dīn^{a} fī-hā dhāl^{i}k^{a} h^{u}w^{a} al-f^{a}wz^{u} al-^{ca}ẓīm

Pronunciation: khā-l^{i}-dī-n^{a} fī-hā dhā-l^{i}-k^{a} h^{u}-w^{a} al-f^{a}w-z^{u}l-^{ca}-ẓīm

Khāl^{i}dīn^{a} (immortal [ones]) *fī-hā* (in them, i.e. in the gardens) *dhāl^{i}k^{a} h^{u}w^{a}* (that is) *al-f^{a}wz^{u}* (the success) *al-^{a}ẓīm* (the great).

While *dhāl^{i}k^{a}* means "that [is]", *dhāl^{i}k^{a} h^{u}w^{a}* also means the same, it is just a more emphatic way of saying "that [is]".

Verse 13, part 1

يَوْمَ يَقُولُ ٱلْمُنَٰفِقُونَ وَٱلْمُنَٰفِقَٰتُ لِلَّذِينَ ءَامَنُوا۟

[On] the day the [male] hypocrites and the [female] hypocrites say to those who believed...

Transliteration: y^{a}wm^{a} y^{a}qūl^{u} al-m^{u}nāf^{i}qūn^{a} w^{a}-al-m^{u}nāf^{i}qāt^{u} l^{i}-all^{a}dhīn^{a} ām^{a}nū

Pronunciation: y^{a}w-m^{a} y^{a}-qū-l^{u}l-m^{u}-nā-f^{i}-qū-n^{a} w^{a}l-m^{u}-nā-f^{i}-qā-t^{u} l^{i}l-l^{a}-dhī-n^{a} ā-m^{a}-nū

Y^{a}wm^{a} ([on] the day) *y^{a}qūl^{u}* ([they] say) *al-m^{u}nāf^{i}qūn^{a}* (the [male] hypocrites) *w^{a}-al-m^{u}nāf^{i}qāt^{u}* (the [female] hypocrites) *l^{i}-all^{a}dhīn^{a}* (to those who) *ām^{a}nū* (they believed).

Verse 13, part 2

ٱنظُرُونَا نَقْتَبِسْ مِن نُّورِكُمْ

"Wait for us, we may take some of your light."

Transliteration: unẓ^{u}rūnā n^{a}qt^{a}b^{i}s m^{i}n nūr^{i}-k^{u}m

Pronunciation: un-ẓ^{u}-rū-nā n^{a}q-t^{a}-b^{i}s m^{i}n nū-r^{i}-k^{u}m

Unẓ^{u}rūnā (wait for us) *n^{a}qt^{a}b^{i}s* (we take) *m^{i}n* (from) *nūr^{i}-k^{u}m* (your light).

The phrase *unẓ^{u}rū* ("wait!", "give [us] time!") is the plural command form of *anẓ^{a}r^{a}* ("he gave respite", "he gave time", "he waited").

The verb *n^{a}qt^{a}b^{i}s* is the first person plural of *iqt^{a}b^{a}s^{a}* ("he took something from a larger whole"), for example to take a burning ember from a fire.

اقْتَبَسَ يَقْتَبِسُ اقْتِبَاس

From right to left: he took something from a larger whole; he takes something from a larger whole; to take something from a larger whole (it is also used to mean "quotation", a piece of text taken out from a book, speech, etc.)

Verse 13, part 3

قِيلَ ٱرْجِعُوا۟ وَرَآءَكُمْ فَٱلْتَمِسُوا۟ نُورًا

It was said, "Go back behind you then seek light."
Transliteration: qīl^{a} irj^{iʿ}ū w^{a}rā^{ʾa}-k^{u}m f^{a}-ilt^{a}m^{i}sū nūrā
Pronunciation: qī-l^{a}r-j^{i}-ʿū w^{a}-rā-^{ʾa}-k^{u}m f^{a}l-t^{a}-m^{i}-sū nū-rā

Qīl^{a} (it was said) *irj^{i}ʿū* (return) *w^{a}rā^{a}-k^{u}m* (behind you) *f^{a}-ilt^{a}m^{i}sū* (then seek) *nūrā* (a light).

After the hypocrites demand to have some light, here they are told to go back and seek light. It may be a taunt that tells them to go back to the worldly life and do good deeds so that they may earn some light. But of course, they will not be able to go back.

The verb *ilt^{a}m^{i}sū* is the command form of *ilt^{a}m^{a}s^{a}* ("he sought for it", "he petitioned for it", "he pleaded for it").

الْتَمَسَ يَلْتَمِسُ الْتِمَاس

From right to left: he sought; he seeks; an act of seeking / petition / supplication.

Verse 13, part 4

فَضُرِبَ بَيْنَهُم بِسُورٍ لَّهُۥ بَابٌۢ

So a wall was placed between them that had a door

Transliteration: f^{a}-ḍ^{u}r^{i}b^{a} b^{a}yn^{a}-h^{u}m b^{i}-sūr^{in} l^{a}-h^{u} bāb

Pronunciation: f^{a}-ḍ^{u}-r^{i}-b^{a} b^{a}y-n^{a}-h^{u}m b^{i}-sū-r^{in} l^{a}-h^{u} bāb

F^{a}-ḍ^{u}r^{i}b^{a} (so it was placed) *b^{a}yn^{a}-h^{u}m* (between them) *b^{i}-sūr^{in}* (a wall) *l^{a}-h^{u}* (for it [was]) *bāb* (a door).

The verb *ḍ^{u}r^{i}b^{a}* is the passive form of *ḍ^{a}r^{a}b^{a}* (“he struck”, “he let down”, “he set up”). The word *sūr* means “a wall meant to keep people out”. The usual word for “wall” in Arabic is *j^{i}dār*.

جِدَار

Verse 13, part 5

بَاطِنُهُۥ فِيهِ ٱلرَّحْمَةُ وَظَٰهِرُهُۥ مِن قِبَلِهِ ٱلْعَذَابُ

Its interior contains mercy and its exterior, from its direction [comes] torment

Transliteration: bāṭ^{i}n^{u}-h^{u} fī-h^{i} al-r^{a}ḥm^{a}t^{u} w^{a}-ẓāh^{i}r^{u}-h^{u} m^{i}n q^{i}b^{a}l^{i}-h^{i} al-ʿadhāb

Pronunciation: bā-ṭ^{i}-n^{u}-h^{u} fī-h^{i}r-r^{a}ḥ-m^{a}-t^{u} w^{a}-ẓā-h^{i}-r^{u}-h^{u} m^{i}n q^{i}-b^{a}-l^{i}-h^{i}l-ʿa-dhāb

Bāṭ^{i}n^{u}-h^{u} (its interior) *fī-h^{i}* (in it [is]) *al-r^{a}ḥm^{a}t^{u}* (mercy) *w^{a}-ẓāh^{i}r^{u}-h^{u}* (and its exterior) *m^{i}n q^{i}b^{a}l^{i}-h^{i}* (from its direction [is]) *al-ʿadhāb* (torment).

The word *q^{i}b^{a}l* means “direction”. The phrase *m^{i}n q^{i}b^{a}l* means “from the direction [of]”.

Lesson 30 Review

وَمَا لَكُمْ أَلَّا تُنفِقُوا۟ فِى سَبِيلِ ٱللَّهِ

W^{a}-mā l^{a}-k^{u}m (and what is with you) *al-lā* (to not) *t^{u}nf^{i}qū* (you spend) *fī* (in) *s^{a}bīl^{i}* (way [of]) *allāh^{i}* (God).

وَلِلَّهِ مِيرَٰثُ ٱلسَّمَٰوَٰتِ وَٱلْأَرْضِ ۚ

W^{a}-l^{i}llāh^{i} (and for God is, and to God belongs) *mīrāth^{u}* (the inheritance [of]) *al-s^{a}māwāt^{i} w^{a}-al-arḍ* (the heavens and the earth).

لَا يَسْتَوِى مِنكُم مَّنْ أَنفَقَ مِن قَبْلِ ٱلْفَتْحِ وَقَٰتَلَ ۚ

Lā (does not) *y^{a}st^{a}wī* (equals, is equal to) *m^{i}n-k^{u}m* (of you, among you) *m^{a}n* (he who) *anf^{a}q^{a}* (spent) *m^{i}n q^{a}bl^{i}* (before) *al-f^{a}tḥ^{i}* (the conquest) *w^{a}-qāt^{a}l* (and fought).

أُو۟لَٰٓئِكَ أَعْظَمُ دَرَجَةً مِّنَ ٱلَّذِينَ أَنفَقُوا۟ مِنۢ بَعْدُ وَقَٰتَلُوا۟ ۚ

Ulā^{i}k^{a} (those [are]) *a'ẓ^{a}m^{u}* (greater) *d^{a}r^{a}j^{a}t^{an}* (a degree, a rank) *m^{i}n* (than) *all^{a}dhīn^{a}* (those who) *anf^{a}qū* (spent) *m^{i}n b^{a}'d^{u}* (afterwards) *w^{a}-qāt^{a}l^{u}* (and fought).

وَكُلًّا وَعَدَ ٱللَّهُ ٱلْحُسْنَىٰ ۚ وَٱللَّهُ بِمَا تَعْمَلُونَ خَبِيرٌ

W^{a}-k^{u}ll^{an} (and every, and all) *w^{a}'^{a}d^{a}* (He promised) *allāh^{u}* (God) *al-ḥ^{u}snā* (the most beautiful, the best) *w^{a}-allāh^{u}* (and God [is]) *b^{i}-mā* (of what) *t^{a}'m^{a}lūn^{a}* (you do) *kh^{a}bīr* (cognizant, knowing, aware).

مَّن ذَا ٱلَّذِى يُقْرِضُ ٱللَّهَ قَرْضًا حَسَنًا

M^{a}n dhā all^{a}dhī (who is the one who) *y^{u}qr^{i}ḍ^{u}* (lends) *allāh^{a}* (God) *q^{a}rḍ^{an} ḥ^{a}s^{a}nā* (a good loan).

فَيُضَٰعِفَهُۥ لَهُۥ وَلَهُۥٓ أَجْرٌ كَرِيمٌ

Fa-y^{u}ḍā^{i}f^{u}-h^{u} (so He multiplies it) *l^{a}-h^{u}* (for him) *w^{a}-l^{a}-h^{u}* (and for him) *ajr^{un}* (a reward) *k^{a}rīm* (generous).

يَوْمَ تَرَى ٱلْمُؤْمِنِينَ وَٱلْمُؤْمِنَٰتِ

Y^{a}wm^{a} ([on] the day) *t^{a}rā* (you see) *al-m^{u}ʾm^{i}nīn^{a}* (the [male] believers) *w^{a}-al-m^{u}ʾm^{i}nāt^{i}* (the [female] believers).

يَسْعَىٰ نُورُهُم بَيْنَ أَيْدِيهِمْ وَبِأَيْمَٰنِهِم

Y^{a}sʿā (it proceeds) *nūr^{u}-h^{u}m* (their light) *b^{a}yn^{a} aydī-h^{i}m* (in front of them) *w^{a} b^{i}-aymān^{i}-h^{i}m* (and on their right sides).

بُشْرَىٰكُمُ ٱلْيَوْمَ جَنَّٰتٌ تَجْرِى مِن تَحْتِهَا ٱلْأَنْهَٰرُ

B^{u}shrā-k^{u}m^{u} (your good tiding) *al-y^{a}wm^{a}* (today) *j^{a}nnāt^{un}* (gardens) *t^{a}jrī* (they flow) *m^{i}n t^{a}ḥt^{i}hā* (from underneath them) *al-anhār* (the rivers).

خَٰلِدِينَ فِيهَا ۚ ذَٰلِكَ هُوَ ٱلْفَوْزُ ٱلْعَظِيمُ

Khāl^{i}dīn^{a} (immortal [ones]) *fī-hā* (in them, i.e. in the gardens) *dhāl^{i}k^{a} h^{u}w^{a}* (that is) *al-f^{a}wz^{u}* (the success) *al-^{a}ẓīm* (the great).

يَوْمَ يَقُولُ ٱلْمُنَٰفِقُونَ وَٱلْمُنَٰفِقَٰتُ لِلَّذِينَ ءَامَنُوا۟

Y^{a}wm^{a} ([on] the day) *y^{a}qūl^{u}* ([they] say) *al-m^{u}nāf^{i}qūn^{a}* (the [male] hypocrites) *w^{a}-al-m^{u}nāf^{i}qāt^{u}* (the [female] hypocrites) *l^{i}-all^{a}dhīn^{a}* (to those who) *ām^{a}nū* (they believed).

ٱنظُرُونَا نَقْتَبِسْ مِن نُّورِكُمْ

Unẓ^{u}rūnā (wait for us) *n^{a}qt^{a}b^{i}s* (we take) *m^{i}n* (from) *nūr^{i}-k^{u}m* (your light).

Unẓ^{u}rūnā n^{a}qt^{a}b^{i}s (wait for us to we take) *m^{i}n* (from) *nūr^{i}-k^{u}m* (your light).

قِيلَ ٱرْجِعُوا۟ وَرَآءَكُمْ فَٱلْتَمِسُوا۟ نُورًا

Qīl^{a} (it was said) *irj^{i}ʿū* (return) *w^{a}rā^{a}-k^{u}m* (behind you) *f^{a}-ilt^{a}m^{i}sū* (then seek) *nūrā* (a light).

فَضُرِبَ بَيْنَهُم بِسُورٍ لَّهُۥ بَابٌۢ

F^{a}-ḍ^{u}r^{i}b^{a} (so it was placed) *b^{a}yn^{a}-h^{u}m* (between them) *b^{i}-sūr^{in}* (a wall) *l^{a}-h^{u}* (for it [was]) *bāb* (a door).

F^{a}-ḍ^{u}r^{i}b^{a} b^{a}yn^{a}-h^{u}m b^{i}-sūr^{in} (so a wall was placed between them) *l^{a}-h^{u} bāb* (for it is/was a door, it has/had a door).

بَاطِنُهُۥ فِيهِ ٱلرَّحْمَةُ وَظَٰهِرُهُۥ مِن قِبَلِهِ ٱلْعَذَابُ

Bāṭ^{i}n^{u}-h^{u} (its interior) *fī-h^{i}* (in it [is]) *al-r^{a}ḥm^{a}t^{u}* (mercy) *w^{a}-ẓāh^{i}r^{u}-h^{u}* (and its exterior) *m^{i}n q^{i}b^{a}l^{i}-h^{i}* (from its direction [is]) *al-ʿadhāb* (torment).

This page intentionally left blank

Lesson 31: al-Ḥadīd Part 4

Verse 14, part 1

يُنَادُونَهُمْ أَلَمْ نَكُن مَّعَكُمْ ۖ قَالُوا بَلَىٰ

They call them, “Were we not with you?” They said, “Rather, yes...”
Transliteration: y^{u}nādūn^{a}-h^{u}m a-l^{a}m n^{a}k^{u}n m^{aʿa}-k^{u}m qālū b^{a}lā
Pronunciation: y^{u}-nā-dū-n^{a}-h^{u}m a-l^{a}m n^{a}-k^{u}n m^{a}-^{ʿa}-k^{u}m qā-lū b^{a}-lā

Y^{u}nādūn^{a}-h^{u}m (they call them) *a-l^{a}m n^{a}k^{u}n* (were we not) *m^{aa}-k^{u}m* (with you) *qālū* (they said) *b^{a}lā* (rather, yes).

Above, the hypocrites are calling the believers, who respond to them.

The verb *y^{u}nādūn^{a}* means “they call”, it is the plural third person of *nādā* (“he called”).

نَادَى يُنَادِي نِدَاء

نَادَوا يُنَادُوْن

Top from right to left: he called; he calls; [a] call.

Bottom from right to left: they called; they call.

Bala is a response that means “rather, yes”, “rather, I did”. It negates the statement it responds to, for example:

أَلَم تَأكُل ؟ بَلَا

"Did you not eat?" "Rather, I did."

أَلَسْتُ جَمِيلًا ؟ بَلَا

"Am I not beautiful?" "Rather, yes (i.e. you are beautiful)."

Verse 14, part 2

وَلَٰكِنَّكُمْ فَتَنتُمْ أَنفُسَكُمْ

But you afflicted yourselves [with trials]
Transliteration: w^{a}-lāk^{i}nn^{a}-k^{u}m f^{a}t^{a}nt^{u}-m anf^{u}s^{a}-k^{u}m
Pronunciation: w^{a}-lā-k^{i}n-n^{a}-k^{u}m f^{a}-t^{a}n-t^{u}m an-f^{u}-s^{a}-k^{u}m

W^{a}-lāk^{i}nn^{a}-k^{u}m (but you) *f^{a}t^{a}nt^{u}-m* (you afflicted) *anf^{u}s^{a}-k^{u}m* (yourselves).

The word *lāk^{i}nn^{a}* means "but". The phrase *w^{a}-lāk^{i}nn^{a}* (literally "and but") is also used to mean "but" when the sentence continues from something before. In English "and but" is never used so the correct translation is merely "but".

F^{a}t^{a}nt^{u}-m is the second person plural of *f^{a}t^{a}n^{a}* ("he afflicted [him] with trials and difficulties").

Verse 14, part 3

وَتَرَبَّصْتُمْ وَٱرْتَبْتُمْ وَغَرَّتْكُمُ ٱلْأَمَانِيُّ

But you [plural] waited watchfully, hestitated and wishful thinking deceived you
Transliteration: w^{a}-t^{a}r^{a}bb^{a}ṣt^{u}-m w^{a}-irt^{a}bt^{u}-m w^{a}-gh^{a}rr^{a}t-k^{u}m^{u} al-amānīy
Pronunciation: w^{a}-t^{a}-r^{a}b-b^{a}ṣ-t^{u}m w^{a}r-t^{a}b-t^{u}-m w^{a}-gh^{a}r-r^{a}t-k^{u}-m^{u}l-a-mā-nīy

W^{a}-t^{a}r^{a}bb^{a}ṣt^{u}-m (and you waited watchfully) *w^{a}-irt^{a}bt^{u}-m* (and you hestitated) *w^{a}-gh^{a}rr^{a}t-k^{u}m^{u}* (they deceived you) *al-amānīy* (the worldly hopes, wishful thoughts).

The verb *t^{a}r^{a}bb^{a}ṣt^{u}-m* ("you waited watchfully [for something to happen]") is the second person plural of *t^{a}r^{a}bb^{a}ṣ^{a}*. *Irt^{a}bt^{u}-m* ("you doubted", "you wavered", "you hesitated") is the second person plural of *irt^{a}b^{a}*.

ارْتَابَ يَرْتَابُ ارْتِيَاب مُرْتَاب

From right to left: he hesitated; he hesitates; hesitation; one who hesitates.

The word *amānīy* ("hopes", "wishes", "wishful thinking") is the plural of *umniya* ("hope", "wish", " greedy and deluded worldly desire").

Verse 14, part 4

حَتَّىٰ جَآءَ أَمْرُ ٱللَّهِ وَغَرَّكُم بِٱللَّهِ ٱلْغَرُورُ

Until the command of God came and the deceiver deceived you about God
Transliteration: ḥ^{a}ttā jā'^{a} amr^{u} allāh^{i} w^{a}-gh^{a}rr^{a}-k^{u}m b^{i}-all^{a}h^{i} al-gh^{a}rūr
Pronunciation: ḥ^{a}t-tā jā-'^{a} am-r^{u}l-lā-h^{i} w^{a}-gh^{a}r-r^{a}-k^{u}m b^{i}l-l^{a}-h^{i}l-gh^{a}-rūr

Ḥ^{a}ttā (until) *jā^{a}* ([it] came) *amr^{u}* (the command [of]) *allāh^{i}* (God) *w^{a}-gh^{a}rr^{a}-k^{u}m* (and deceived you) *b^{i}-all^{a}h^{i}* (about God) *al-gh^{a}rūr* (the deceiver).

The "deceiver" mentioned in the verse is thought to refer to Satan.

Verse 15, part 1

فَٱلْيَوْمَ لَا يُؤْخَذُ مِنكُمْ فِدْيَةٌ وَلَا مِنَ ٱلَّذِينَ كَفَرُوا۟ ۚ

So today no ransom will be taken from you and not from those who denied
Transliteration: f^{a}-al-y^{a}wm^{a} lā y^{u}'kh^{a}dh^{u} m^{i}n-k^{u}m f^{i}dy^{a}t^{un} w^{a}-lā m^{i}n all^{a}dhīn^{a} k^{a}f^{a}rū
Pronunciation: f^{a}l-y^{a}w-m^{a} lā y^{u}'-kh^{a}-dh^{u} m^{i}n-k^{u}m f^{i}d-y^{a}-t^{un} w^{a}-lā m^{i}-n^{a}l-l^{a}-dhī-n^{a} k^{a}-f^{a}-rū

F^{a}-al-y^{a}wm^{a} (so today) *lā* (is not) *y^{u}'kh^{a}dh^{u}* (is taken) *m^{i}n-k^{u}m* (from you) *f^{i}dy^{a}t^{un}* (a ransom) *w^{a}-lā* (and not) *m^{i}n* (from) *all^{a}dhīn^{a}* (those who) *k^{a}f^{a}rū* (denied).

While *y^{a}wm* means “day”, *al-y^{a}wm^{a}* can mean “today” in some contexts.

Verse 15, part 2

مَأْوَىٰكُمُ ٱلنَّارُ ۖ هِىَ مَوْلَىٰكُمْ ۖ وَبِئْسَ ٱلْمَصِيرُ

Your refuge is the fire. She is your protector, and what a horrible destination!
Transliteration: ma’wā-k^{u}m^{u} al-nār^{u} h^{i}y^{a} m^{a}wlā-k^{u}m w^{a}-b$^{i’}$s^{a} al-m^{a}ṣīr
Pronunciation: ma’-wā-k^{u}-m^{u}n-nā-r^{u} h^{i}-y^{a} m^{a}w-lā-k^{u}m w^{a}-b$^{i’}$-s^{a}l-m^{a}-ṣīr

Ma’wā-k^{u}m^{u} (your refuge [is]) *al-nār^{u}* (the fire) *h^{i}y^{a}* (she is) *m^{a}wlā-k^{u}m* (your protector) *w^{a}-b^{i}’s^{a} al-m^{a}ṣīr* (and what a horrible destination!).

The fire is called a “refuge” and “protector” as taunts.

The *b^{i}’s^{a}* (“how horrible!”) is used to exclaim about how bad something is.

Verse 16, part 1

أَلَمْ يَأْنِ لِلَّذِينَ ءَامَنُوٓا۟ أَن تَخْشَعَ قُلُوبُهُمْ لِذِكْرِ ٱللَّهِ

Has the time not come for those who believed that their hearts should humbly submit to the remembrance of God?
Transliteration: a-l^{a}m y$^{a’}$n^{i} l^{i}-all^{a}dhīn^{a} ām^{a}nū an t^{a}khsh^{aʿa} q^{u}lūb^{u}-h^{u}m l^{i}-dh^{i}kr^{i} allāh
Pronunciation: a-l^{a}m y$^{a’}$-n^{i} l^{i}l-l^{a}-dhī-n^{a} ā-m^{a}-nū an t^{a}kh-sh^{a}-^{ʿa} qu-lū-b^{u}-h^{u}m l^{i}-dh^{i}k-r^{i}l-lāh

A-l^{a}m (has not) *y^{a}’n^{i}* (its time comes) *l^{i}-all^{a}dhīn^{a} ām^{a}nū* (for those who believed) *an* (that) *t^{a}khsh^{aʿa}* (humbles [itself]) *q^{u}lūb^{u}-h^{u}m* (their hearts) *l^{i}-dh^{i}kr^{i}* (to the remembrance [of]) *allāh* (God).

The word *y^{a}’n^{i}* (“its time comes”) is *ya’nī* in standard Arabic:

أَنَى يَأْنِي

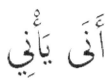

From right to left: its time came; its time comes.

The verb *t^{a}khsh^{a}ʿ* is the feminine third person form of *kh^{a}sh^{a}ʿ^{a}* ("he humbly and fearfully submitted", "he humbled himself"). It is in the feminine because it is used in reference to *q^{u}lūb*, which is feminine due to being plural (the singular *q^{a}lb* ["heart"] is masculine).

Verse 16, part 2

وَمَا نَزَلَ مِنَ ٱلْحَقِّ وَلَا يَكُونُوا۟ كَٱلَّذِينَ أُوتُوا۟ ٱلْكِتَٰبَ مِن قَبْلُ

and that which came down of the truth and not be like those who were given the Book before
Transliteration: w^{a}-mā n^{a}z^{a}l^{a} m^{i}n al-ḥ^{a}qq^{i} w^{a}-lā y^{a}kūn^{u} k^{a}-all^{a}dhīn^{a} ūtū al-k^{i}tāba m^{i}n q^{a}bl
Pronunciation: w^{a}-mā n^{a}-z^{a}-l^{a} m^{i}n al-ḥ^{a}q-q^{i} w^{a}-lā y^{a}-kū-n^{u} k^{a}l-l^{a}-dhī-n^{a} ū-t^{u}l-k^{i}-tā-ba m^{i}n q^{a}bl

W^{a}-mā (and that which) *n^{a}z^{a}l^{a}* (it came down) *m^{i}n* (of) *al-ḥ^{a}qq^{i}* (the truth) *w^{a}-lā* (and not) *y^{a}kūn^{u}* (be) *k^{a}-all^{a}dhīn^{a}* (like those who) *ūtū* (were given) *al-k^{i}tāba* (the Book) *m^{i}n q^{a}bl* (before).

The meaning of this part continues from the previous part.

The word *k^{a}* in *k^{a}-all^{a}dhīn^{a}* means "like". The "Book" refers to past scriptures such as the Torah.

Verse 16, part 3

فَطَالَ عَلَيْهِمُ ٱلْأَمَدُ فَقَسَتْ قُلُوبُهُمْ وَكَثِيرٌ مِّنْهُمْ فَٰسِقُونَ

so the span of time became lengthy upon them so their hearts hardened and many of them are rebellious
Transliteration: f^{a}-ṭāl^{a} ʿ^{a}l^{a}yh^{i}m^{u} al-am^{a}d^{u} f^{a}-q^{a}s^{a}-t q^{u}lūb^{u}-h^{u}m w^{a}-k^{a}thīr^{un} m^{i}n-h^{u}m fās^{i}qūn
Pronunciation: f^{a}-ṭā-l^{a} ʿ^{a}-l^{a}y-h^{i}-m^{u}l-a-m^{a}-d^{u} f^{a}-q^{a}-s^{a}-t q^{u}-lū-b^{u}-h^{u}m w^{a}-k^{a}-thī-r^{un} m^{i}n-h^{u}m fā-s^{i}-qūn

F^{a}-ṭāl^{a} (so it became lengthy) *ʿ^{a}l^{a}yh^{i}m^{u}* (upon them) *al-am^{a}d^{u}* (the span of time) *f^{a}-q^{a}s^{a}-t* (so she hardened) *q^{u}lūb^{u}-h^{u}m* (their hearts) *w^{a}-k^{a}thīr^{un}* (and many) *m^{i}n-h^{u}m* (of them [are]) *fās^{i}qūn* (rebellious ones).

The verb ṭāl^{a} means "it was long" and "it became long", "it became lengthy". The word *am^{a}d* means "duration", "period [of time]", "span [of time]". The phrase *q^{a}s^{a}-t* is the feminine of *q^{a}sā* ("it became hardened"). It is feminine again because it is used in reference to the plural *q^{u}lūb* ("hearts").

Verse 17, part 1

ٱعْلَمُوٓا۟ أَنَّ ٱللَّهَ يُحْىِ ٱلْأَرْضَ بَعْدَ مَوْتِهَا ۚ

Know that God brings to life the earth after her death

Transliteration: iʿl^{a}mū ann^{a} allāh^{a} y^{u}ḥyī al-arḍ^{a} b^{a}ʿd^{a} m^{a}wt^{i}-hā

Pronunciation: iʿ-l^{a}-mū an-n^{a}l-lā-h^{a} y^{u}ḥ-*y^{i}l*-ar-ḍ^{a} b^{a}ʿ-d^{a} m^{a}w-t^{i}-hā

Iʿl^{a}mū (know [directed at a group]) *ann^{a}* (that) *allāh^{a}* (God) *y^{u}ḥyī* (brings to life) *al-arḍ^{a}* (the earth) *b^{a}ʿd^{a}* (after) *m^{a}wt^{i}-hā* (her death).

Verse 17, part 2

قَدْ بَيَّنَّا لَكُمُ ٱلْءَايَٰتِ لَعَلَّكُمْ تَعْقِلُونَ

Truly we have made clear for you the signs so that you may understand

Transliteration: q^{a}d b^{a}yy^{a}n-nā l^{a}k^{u}m^{u} al-āyāt^{i} l^{a}ʿ^{a}ll^{a}-k^{u}m t^{a}ʿq^{i}lūn

Pronunciation: q^{a}d b^{a}y-y^{a}n-nā l^{a}-k^{u}-m^{u}l-ā-yā-t^{i} l^{a}-ʿ^{a}l-l^{a}-k^{u}m t^{a}ʿ-q^{i}-lūn

Q^{a}d (truly have) *b^{a}yy^{a}n-nā* (we made clear) *l^{a}k^{u}m^{u}* (for you) *al-āyāt^{i}* (the signs, the verses) *l^{a}ʿ^{a}ll^{a}-k^{u}m* (so that you may) *t^{a}ʿq^{i}lūn* (understand, comprehend).

The phrase *b^{a}yy^{a}n-nā* ("we have made clear") is made up of *b^{a}yy^{a}n^{a}* and the pronoun *nā*. They are merged together and expressed with a *shadda*.

بَيَّنْ نَا — بَيَّنَّا

The word *l^{a}ʿ^{a}ll^{a}* is a special word that means "so that [you/it] may".

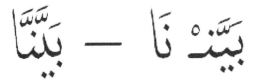

Lesson 31 Review

يُنَادُونَهُمْ أَلَمْ نَكُن مَّعَكُمْ ۖ قَالُوا۟ بَلَىٰ

Y^{u}nādūn^a-h^{u}m (they call them) a-l^{a}m n^{a}k^{u}n (were we not) m^{aa}-k^{u}m (with you) qālū (they said) b^{a}lā (rather, yes).

وَلَـٰكِنَّكُمْ فَتَنتُمْ أَنفُسَكُمْ

W^a-lāk^{i}nn^a-k^{u}m (but you) f^{a}t^{a}nt^u-m (you afflicted) anf^{u}s^a-k^{u}m (yourselves).

وَتَرَبَّصْتُمْ وَٱرْتَبْتُمْ وَغَرَّتْكُمُ ٱلْأَمَانِىُّ

W^a-t^{a}r^{a}bb^{a}ṣt^u-m (and you waited watchfully) w^a-irt^{a}bt^u-m (and you hestitated) w^a-gh^{a}rr^{a}t-k^{u}m^u (they deceived you) al-amānīy (the worldly hopes, wishful thoughts).

حَتَّىٰ جَآءَ أَمْرُ ٱللَّهِ وَغَرَّكُم بِٱللَّهِ ٱلْغَرُورُ

Ḥ^{a}ttā (until) jā^a ([it] came) amr^u (the command [of]) allāh^i (God) w^a-gh^{a}rr^a-k^{u}m (and deceived you) b^i-all^{a}h^i (about God) al-gh^{a}rūr (the deceiver).

فَٱلْيَوْمَ لَا يُؤْخَذُ مِنكُمْ فِدْيَةٌ وَلَا مِنَ ٱلَّذِينَ كَفَرُوا۟ ۚ

F^a-al-y^{a}wm^a (so today) lā (is not) y^u'kh^{a}dh^u (is taken) m^{i}n-k^{u}m (from you) f^{i}dy^{a}t^{un} (a ransom) w^a-lā (and not) m^{i}n (from) all^{a}dhīn^a (those who) k^{a}f^{a}rū (denied).

مَأْوَىٰكُمُ ٱلنَّارُ ۖ هِىَ مَوْلَىٰكُمْ ۖ وَبِئْسَ ٱلْمَصِيرُ

Ma'wā-k^{u}*m*^{u} (your refuge [is]) *al-nār*^{u} (the fire) *h*^{i}*y*^{a} (she is) *m*^{a}*wlā-k*^{u}*m* (your protector) *w*^{a}*-b*^{i}*'s*^{a} *al-m*^{a}*ṣīr* (and what a horrible destination!).

أَلَمْ يَأْنِ لِلَّذِينَ ءَامَنُوٓا۟ أَن تَخْشَعَ قُلُوبُهُمْ لِذِكْرِ ٱللَّهِ

A-l^{a}*m* (has not) *y*^{a}*'n*^{i} (its time comes) *l*^{i}*-all*^{a}*dhīn*^{a} *ām*^{a}*nū* (for those who believed) *an* (that) *t*^{a}*khsh*$^{a\,a}$ (humbles [itself]) *q*^{u}*lūb*^{u}*-h*^{u}*m* (their hearts) *l*^{i}*-dh*^{i}*kr*^{i} (to the remembrance [of]) *allāh* (God).

A-l^{a}*m y*^{a}*'n*^{i} (has its time not come) *l*^{i}*-all*^{a}*dhīn*^{a} *ām*^{a}*nū* (for those who believed) *an t*^{a}*khsh*$^{a\,a}$ *q*^{u}*lūb*^{u}*-h*^{u}*m* (that their hearts [should] humble themselves) *l*^{i}*-dh*^{i}*kr*^{i} (to the remembrance [of]) *allāh* (God).

وَمَا نَزَلَ مِنَ ٱلْحَقِّ وَلَا يَكُونُوا۟ كَٱلَّذِينَ أُوتُوا۟ ٱلْكِتَٰبَ مِن قَبْلُ

W^{a}*-mā* (and that which) *n*^{a}*z*^{a}*l*^{a} (it came down) *m*^{i}*n* (of) *al-ḥ*^{a}*qq*^{i} (the truth) *w*^{a}*-lā* (and not) *y*^{a}*kūn*^{u} (be) *k*^{a}*-all*^{a}*dhīn*^{a} (like those who) *ūtū* (were given) *al-k*^{i}*tāba* (the Book) *m*^{i}*n q*^{a}*bl* (before).

فَطَالَ عَلَيْهِمُ ٱلْأَمَدُ فَقَسَتْ قُلُوبُهُمْ ۖ وَكَثِيرٌ مِّنْهُمْ فَٰسِقُونَ

F^{a}*-ṭāl*^{a} (so it became lengthy) *^{a}l*^{a}*yh*^{i}*m*^{u} (upon them) *al-am*^{a}*d*^{u} (the span of time) *f*^{a}*-q*^{a}*s*^{a}*-t* (so she hardened) *q*^{u}*lūb*^{u}*-h*^{u}*m* (their hearts) *w*^{a}*-k*^{a}*thīr*^{un} (and many) *m*^{i}*n-h*^{u}*m* (of them [are]) *fās*^{i}*qūn* (rebellious ones).

ٱعْلَمُوٓا۟ أَنَّ ٱللَّهَ يُحْىِ ٱلْأَرْضَ بَعْدَ مَوْتِهَا ۚ

I'l^{a}*mū* (know [directed at a group]) *ann*^{a} (that) *allāh*^{a} (God) *y*^{u}*ḥyī* (brings to life) *al-arḍ*^{a} (the earth) *b*^{a}*'d*^{a} (after) *m*^{a}*wt*^{i}*-hā* (her death).

قَدْ بَيَّنَّا لَكُمُ ٱلْـَٔايَـٰتِ لَعَلَّكُمْ تَعْقِلُونَ

Q^{a}*d* (truly have) *b*^{a}*yy*^{a}*n-nā* (we made clear) *l*^{a}*k*^{u}*m*^{u} (for you) *al-āyāt*^{i} (the signs, the verses) *l*^{a}*ʿ*^{a}*ll*^{a}*-k*^{u}*m* (so that you may) *t*^{a}*ʿq*^{i}*lūn* (understand, comprehend).

This page intentionally left blank

Lesson 32: al-Ḥadīd Part 5

Verse 18, part 1

إِنَّ ٱلْمُصَّدِّقِينَ وَٱلْمُصَّدِّقَٰتِ وَأَقْرَضُوا۟ ٱللَّهَ قَرْضًا حَسَنًا

Indeed the [male] givers of charity and the [female] givers of charity and [those who] lent God a wholesome loan

Transliteration: inn^{a} al-m^{u}ṣṣ^{a}dd^{i}qīn^{a} w^{a}-al-m^{u}ṣṣ^{a}dd^{i}qāt^{i} w^{a}-aqr^{a}ḍū allāh^{a} q^{a}rḍ^{an} ḥ^{a}s^{a}nā

Pronunciation: in-n^{a}l-m^{u}ṣ-ṣ^{a}d-d^{i}-qī-n^{a} w^{a}l-m^{u}ṣ-ṣ^{a}d-d^{i}-qā-t^{i} w^{a}-aq-r^{a}-ḍ^{u}l-lā-h^{a} q^{a}r-ḍ^{an} ḥ^{a}-s^{a}-nā

Inn^{a} (indeed) *al-m^{u}ṣṣ^{a}dd^{i}qīn^{a}* (the [male] givers of charity) *w^{a}-al-m^{u}ṣṣ^{a}dd^{i}qāt^{i}* (and the [female] givers of charity) *w^{a}-aqr^{a}ḍū* (and [those who] lent) *allāh^{a}* (God) *q^{a}rḍ^{an}* (a loan) *ḥ^{a}s^{a}nā* (wholesome).

The word *al-m^{u}ṣṣ^{a}dd^{i}qīn^{a}* and *al-m^{u}ṣṣ^{a}dd^{i}qāt^{i}* would be as follows in standard Arabic:

الْمُتَصَدِّقِيْنَ الْمُتَصَدِّقَات

These two words come from the verb *t^{a}ṣ^{a}dd^{a}q^{a}* ("he gave charity").

The phrase *w^{a}-aqr^{a}ḍū* is short for *wa-all^{a}dhīn^{a} aqr^{a}ḍū* ("those who lent").

وَالَّذِيْنَ أَقْرَضُوْا

The *alladhīn^{a}* has been omitted in the Quranic text to create a poetic effect.

Verse 18, part 2

يُضَٰعَفُ لَهُمْ وَلَهُمْ أَجْرٌ كَرِيمٌ

It is multiplied for them and for them is a generous reward
Transliteration: y^{u}ḍā^{ʿa}f^{u} l^{a}-h^{u}m w^{a}-l^{a}-h^{u}m ajr^{un} k^{a}rīm
Pronunciation: y^{u}-ḍā-^{ʿa}-f^{u} l^{a}-h^{u}m w^{a}-l^{a}-h^{u}m aj-r^{un} k^{a}-rīm

Y^{u}ḍā^{a}f^{u} ([it] is multiplied) *l^{a}-h^{u}m* (for them) *w^{a}-l^{a}-h^{u}m* (and for them [is]) *ajr^{un}* (a reward) *k^{a}rīm* (generous).

The verb y^{u}ḍā^{ʿa}f^{u} ("it is multiplied") is the passive form of y^{u}ḍā^{ʿi}f^{u} ("he multiplies").

ضَاعَفَ يُضَاعِفُ

From right to left: he multiplied; he multiplies.

Verse 19, part 1

وَٱلَّذِينَ ءَامَنُوا۟ بِٱللَّهِ وَرُسُلِهِۦٓ أُو۟لَٰٓئِكَ هُمُ ٱلصِّدِّيقُونَ ۖ

And those who believed in God and His Messenger, truly those are the utterly truthful
Transliteration: w^{a}-all^{a}dhīn^{a} ām^{a}nū b^{i}-allāh^{i} w^{a}-r^{u}s^{u}l^{i}-h^{i} ulā^{ʾi}k^{a} h^{u}m^{u} al-ṣ^{i}ddīqūn
Pronunciation: w^{a}l-l^{a}-dhī-n^{a} ā-m^{a}-nū-b^{i}l-lā-h^{i} w^{a}-r^{u}-s^{u}-l^{i}-h^{i} u-lā-^{ʾi}-k^{a} h^{u}-m^{u}ṣ-ṣ^{i}d-dī-qūn

W^{a}-all^{a}dhīn^{a} (and those who) *ām^{a}nū* (believed) *b^{i}-allāh^{i}* (in God) *w^{a}-r^{u}s^{u}l^{i}-h^{i}* (and His Messengers) *ulā^{ʾi}k^{a} h^{u}m^{u}* (truly those are) *al-ṣ^{i}ddīqūn* (the utterly truthful).

The word *ṣ^{i}ddīqūn* is the plural of *ṣ^{i}ddīq* ("utterly truthful"), which can either refer to a person's truthfulness or their strong faith in the truth of God's messages, therefore it may mean "strong affirmers of truth".

The word *ulā^{ʾi}k^{a}* means "those are" while *h^{u}m* also means "those are". When used together they form a more emphatic way of saying "those are", i.e. "truly those are".

Verse 19, part 2

وَٱلشُّهَدَآءُ عِندَ رَبِّهِمْ لَهُمْ أَجْرُهُمْ وَنُورُهُمْ ۖ

And the martyrs [are] with their Lord, for them is their reward and their light
Transliteration: w^{a}-al-sh^{u}h^{a}dā^{ʾu} ^{ʿi}nd^{a} r^{a}bb^{i}-h^{i}m l^{a}-h^{u}m ajr^{u}-h^{u}m w^{a}-nūr^{u}-h^{u}m
Pronunciation: *w*^{a}*sh*-sh^{u}-h^{a}-dā-^{ʾu} ^{ʿi}n-d^{a} r^{a}b-b^{i}-h^{i}m l^{a}-h^{u}m aj-r^{u}-h^{u}m w^{a}-nū-r^{u}-h^{u}m

W^{a}*-al-sh*^{u}*h*^{a}*dā*^{ʾu} (and the martyrs [are]) ^{ʿi}*nd*^{a} (with) *r*^{a}*bb*^{i}*-h*^{i}*m* (their Lord) *l*^{a}*-h*^{u}*m* (for them [is]) *ajr*^{u}*-h*^{u}*m* (their reward) *w*^{a}*-nūr*^{u}*-h*^{u}*m* (and their light).

The word *sh*^{u}*h*^{a}*dā*^{ʾu} ("matyrs", "witnesses") is the plural of *shahīd*.

شَهِيد شُهَدَاء

Verse 19, part 3

وَٱلَّذِينَ كَفَرُوا۟ وَكَذَّبُوا۟ بِـَٔايَٰتِنَآ أُو۟لَٰٓئِكَ أَصْحَٰبُ ٱلْجَحِيمِ

And those who rejected and denied the truth of our signs those are the companions of the violent blaze
Transliteration: w^{a}-all^{a}dhīn^{a} k^{a}f^{a}rū w^{a}-k^{a}dhdh^{a}bū b^{i}-āyāt^{i}n^{a} ulā^{ʾi}k^{a} aṣḥāb^{u} al-j^{a}ḥim
Pronunciation: w^{a}l-l^{a}-dhī-n^{a} k^{a}-f^{a}-rū w^{a}-k^{a}dh-dh^{a}-bū b^{i}-ā-yā-t^{i}-n^{a} u-lā-^{ʾi}-k^{a} aṣ-ḥā-b^{u}l-j^{a}-ḥim

W^{a}*-all*^{a}*dhīn*^{a} (and those who) *k*^{a}*f*^{a}*rū* (rejected) *w*^{a}*-k*^{a}*dhdh*^{a}*bū b*^{i} (denied the truth of) *āyāt*^{i}*n*^{a} (our signs, our verses) *ulā*^{ʾi}*k*^{a} (those [are]) *aṣḥāb*^{u} (companions [of]) *al-j*^{a}*ḥim* (the violent blaze).

The phrase *k*^{a}*dhdh*^{a}*bū b*^{i} means "they denied the truth of". The verb *k*^{a}*f*^{a}*rū* means ("they denied a truth/blessing", "they rejected a truth/blessing"). The word *al-j*^{a}*ḥim* ("the violent blaze") is another way of referring to the Hellfire.

Verse 20, part 1

ٱعْلَمُوٓا۟ أَنَّمَا ٱلْحَيَوٰةُ ٱلدُّنْيَا لَعِبٌ وَلَهْوٌ

Know that truly the life of the world is play and amusement
Transliteration: iʿl^{a}mū ann^a-mā ḥ^{a}yāt^u al-d^{u}nyā l^{aʿi}b^{un} w^a-l^{a}hw
Pronunciation: iʿ-l^a-mū an-n^a-mā ḥ^a-yā-*t^{u}d*-d^{u}n-yā l^a-^{ʿi}-b^{un} w^a-l^{a}hw

Iʿl^{a}mū (know! [directed at a group]) *ann^a-mā* (truly that) *ḥ^{a}yāt^u al-d^{u}nyā* (the life of the world) *l^{aʿi}b^{un}* (play, a game) *w^a l^{a}hw* (and amusement).

The verb *iʿl^{a}mū* is the plural of *iʿl^{a}m* ("know!").

اعْلَم

The phrase *ann^a-mā* ("truly that") is a more empathic form of *ann^a* ("truly that").

Verse 20, part 2

وَزِينَةٌ وَتَفَاخُرٌۢ بَيْنَكُمْ وَتَكَاثُرٌ فِى ٱلْأَمْوَٰلِ وَٱلْأَوْلَٰدِ ۖ

and adornment and boasting between you and a competition in increase in wealth and children
Transliteration: w^a-zīn^{a}t^{un} w^a-t^{a}fākh^{u}r^{un} b^{a}yn^a-k^{u}m w^a-t^{a}kāth^{u}r^{un} fī al-amwāl^i w^a-al-awlād
Pronunciation: w^a-zī-n^a-t^{un} w^a-t^a-fā-kh^u-r^{un} b^{a}y-n^a-k^{u}m w^a-t^a-kā-th^u-r^{un} f^{i}l-am-wā-l^i w^{a}l-aw-lād

W^a-zīn^{a}t^{un} (and adornment) *w^a-t^{a}fākh^{u}r^{un}* (and boasting) *b^{a}yn^a-k^{u}m* (between you) *w^a-t^{a}kāth^{u}r^{un}* (and a competition in increase) *fī* (in) *al-amwāl^i* (wealth, properties) *w^a-al-awlād* (and children).

This part continues describing what the worldly life is.

Verse 20, part 3

كَمَثَلِ غَيْثٍ أَعْجَبَ ٱلْكُفَّارَ نَبَاتُهُۥ

Like the example of a rain whose [resulting] vegetation pleases the rejecters
Transliteration: k^{a}-m^{a}th^{a}l^{i} gh^{a}yth^{in} aʿj^{a}b^{a} al-k^{u}ffār^{u} n^{a}bāt^{u}-h
Pronunciation: k^{a}-m^{a}-th^{a}-l^{i} gh^{a}y-th^{in} aʿ-j^{a}-b^{a}l-k^{u}f-fā-r^{u} n^{a}-bā-t^{u}h

K^{a} (like) *m^{a}th^{a}l^{i}* ([the] example [of]) *gh^{a}yth^{in}* (a rain) *aʿj^{a}b^{a}* (it pleased) *al-k^{u}ffār^{u}* (the rejecters [of truth and blessings]) *n^{a}bāt^{u}-h* (its vegetation).

The word *gh^{a}yth* literally means "rescue", "relief". It is used metaphorically to refer to rain.

Verse 20, part 4

ثُمَّ يَهِيجُ فَتَرَىٰهُ مُصْفَرًّا ثُمَّ يَكُونُ حُطَٰمًا ۖ

then it dries so you see it yellowed then it becomes debris
Transliteration: th^{u}mm^{a} y^{a}hīj^{u} f^{a}-t^{a}rā-h^{u} m^{u}ṣf^{a}rr^{an} th^{u}mm^{a} y^{a}kūn^{u} ḥ^{u}ṭāmā
Pronunciation: th^{u}m-m^{a} y^{a}-hī-j^{u} f^{a}-t^{a}-rā-h^{u} m^{u}ṣ-f^{a}r-r^{an} th^{u}m-m^{a} y^{a}-kū-n^{u} ḥ^{u}-ṭā-mā

Th^{u}mm^{a} (then) *y^{a}hīj^{u}* (it dries) *f^{a}-t^{a}rā-h^{u}* (then you see it) *m^{u}ṣf^{a}rr^{an}* (yellowed) *th^{u}mm^{a}* (then) *y^{a}kūn^{u}* (it is, it will be) *ḥ^{u}ṭāmā* (debris, broken pieces).

Verse 20, part 5

وَفِى ٱلْءَاخِرَةِ عَذَابٌ شَدِيدٌ وَمَغْفِرَةٌ مِّنَ ٱللَّهِ وَرِضْوَٰنٌ

And in the Hereafter is a severe torment and forgiveness from God and [His] pleasure
Transliteration: w^{a}-fī al-ākh^{i}r^{a}t^{i} ʿ^{a}dhāb^{un} sh^{a}dīd^{un} w^{a}-m^{a}ghf^{i}r^{a}t^{un} m^{i}n^{a} allāh^{i} w^{a}-r^{i}ḍwān
Pronunciation: w^{a}-f^{i}l-ā-kh^{i}-r^{a}-t^{i} ʿ^{a}-dhā-b^{un} sh^{a}-dī-*d^{uw}* w^{a}-m^{a}gh-f^{i}-r^{a}-*t^{um}* m^{i}-n^{a}l-lā-h^{i} w^{a}-r^{i}ḍ-wān

W^{a}-fī (and in) *al-ākh^{i}r^{a}t^{i}* (the Hereafter) *^{ʿa}dhāb^{un}* (a torment) *sh^{a}dīd^{un}* (severe) *w^{a}-m^{a}ghf^{i}r^{a}t^{un}* (and a forgiveness) *m^{i}n^{a}* (from) *allāh^{i}* (God) *w^{a}-r^{i}ḍwān* (and [His] pleasure).

The word *r^{i}ḍwān* means "the state of being pleased", from the verb *r^{a}ḍ^{i}y^{a}* ("he was pleased").

Verse 20, part 6

وَمَا ٱلْحَيَوٰةُ ٱلدُّنْيَآ إِلَّا مَتَـٰعُ ٱلْغُرُورِ

And the life of the world is nothing but the goods of delusion
Transliteration: w^{a}-mā al-ḥ^{a}yāt^{u} al-d^{u}nyā illā m^{a}tā^{ʿu} al-gh^{u}rūr
Pronunciation: w^{a}-m^{a}l-ḥ^{a}-yā-*t^{u}d*-d^{u}n-yā il-lā m^{a}-tā-^{ʿu}l-gh^{u}-rūr

W^{a}-mā (and is not) *al-ḥ^{a}yāt^{u} al-d^{u}nyā* (the life of the world) *illā* (except) *m^{a}tā^{ʿu} al-gh^{u}rūr* (goods of delusion).

The word *m^{a}tāʿ* means "goods", "provisions". The word *gh^{u}rūr* means "the state of being deluded", "delusion". The phrase *m^{a}tā^{ʿu} al-gh^{u}rūr* means "goods of delusion", goods that are enjoyed by those who are deluded.

Lesson 32 Review

إِنَّ ٱلْمُصَّدِّقِينَ وَٱلْمُصَّدِّقَـٰتِ وَأَقْرَضُوا۟ ٱللَّهَ قَرْضًا حَسَنًا

Inn^{a} (indeed) *al-m*^{u}*ṣṣ*^{a}*dd*^{i}*qīn*^{a} (the [male] givers of charity) *w*^{a}*-al-m*^{u}*ṣṣ*^{a}*dd*^{i}*qāt*^{i} (and the [female] givers of charity) *w*^{a}*-aqr*^{a}*ḍū* (and [those who] lent) *allāh*^{a} (God) *q*^{a}*rḍ*^{an} (a loan) *ḥ*^{a}*s*^{a}*nā* (wholesome).

يُضَـٰعَفُ لَهُمْ وَلَهُمْ أَجْرٌ كَرِيمٌ

Y^{u}*ḍā*^{a}*f*^{u} ([it] is multiplied) *l*^{a}*-h*^{u}*m* (for them) *w*^{a}*-l*^{a}*-h*^{u}*m* (and for them [is]) *ajr*^{un} (a reward) *k*^{a}*rīm* (generous).

وَٱلَّذِينَ ءَامَنُوا۟ بِٱللَّهِ وَرُسُلِهِۦٓ أُو۟لَـٰٓئِكَ هُمُ ٱلصِّدِّيقُونَ ۖ

W^{a}*-all*^{a}*dhīn*^{a} (and those who) *ām*^{a}*nū* (believed) *b*^{i}*-allāh*^{i} (in God) *w*^{a}*-r*^{u}*s*^{u}*l*^{i}*-h*^{i} (and His Messengers) *ulā*^{i}*k*^{a} *h*^{u}*m*^{u} (truly those are) *al-ṣ*^{i}*ddīqūn* (the utterly truthful).

وَٱلشُّهَدَآءُ عِندَ رَبِّهِمْ لَهُمْ أَجْرُهُمْ وَنُورُهُمْ ۖ

W^{a}*-al-sh*^{u}*h*^{a}*dā*^{u} (and the martyrs [are]) ^{i}*nd*^{a} (with) *r*^{a}*bb*^{i}*-h*^{i}*m* (their Lord) *l*^{a}*-h*^{u}*m* (for them [is]) *ajr*^{u}*-h*^{u}*m* (their reward) *w*^{a}*-nūr*^{u}*-h*^{u}*m* (and their light).

وَٱلَّذِينَ كَفَرُوا۟ وَكَذَّبُوا۟ بِـَٔايَـٰتِنَآ أُو۟لَـٰٓئِكَ أَصْحَـٰبُ ٱلْجَحِيمِ

W^{a}*-all*^{a}*dhīn*^{a} (and those who) *k*^{a}*f*^{a}*rū* (rejected) *w*^{a}*-k*^{a}*dhdh*^{a}*bū b*^{i} (denied the truth of) *āyāt*^{i}*n*^{a} (our signs, our verses) *ulā*^{i}*k*^{a} (those [are]) *aṣḥāb*^{u} (companions [of]) *al-j*^{a}*ḥim* (the violent blaze).

ٱعۡلَمُوٓاْ أَنَّمَا ٱلۡحَيَوٰةُ ٱلدُّنۡيَا لَعِبٞ وَلَهۡوٞ

Iʿlmū (know! [directed at a group]) *ann*^{a}*-mā* (truly that) *ḥ*^{a}*yāt*^{u} *al-d*^{u}*nyā* (the life of the world) *l*^{a}*ʿ*^{i}*b*^{un} (play, a game) *w*^{a} *l*^{a}*hw* (and amusement).

وَزِينَةٞ وَتَفَاخُرُۢ بَيۡنَكُمۡ وَتَكَاثُرٞ فِي ٱلۡأَمۡوَٰلِ وَٱلۡأَوۡلَٰدِۖ

W^{a}*-zīn*^{a}*t*^{un} (and adornment) *w*^{a}*-t*^{a}*fākh*^{u}*r*^{un} (and boasting) *b*^{a}*yn*^{a}*-k*^{u}*m* (between you) *w*^{a}*-t*^{a}*kāth*^{u}*r*^{un} (and a competition in increase) *fī* (in) *al-amwāl*^{i} (wealth, properties) *w*^{a}*-al-awlād* (and children).

كَمَثَلِ غَيۡثٍ أَعۡجَبَ ٱلۡكُفَّارَ نَبَاتُهُۥ

K^{a} (like) *m*^{a}*th*^{a}*l*^{i} ([the] example [of]) *gh*^{a}*yth*^{in} (a rain) *a*^{ʿ}*jb*^{a} (it pleased) *al-k*^{u}*ffār*^{u} (the rejecters [of truth and blessings]) *n*^{a}*bāt*^{u}*-h* (its vegetation).

ثُمَّ يَهِيجُ فَتَرَىٰهُ مُصۡفَرّٗا ثُمَّ يَكُونُ حُطَٰمٗاۖ

Th^{u}*mm*^{a} (then) *y*^{a}*hīj*^{u} (it dries) *f*^{a}*-t*^{a}*rā-h*^{u} (then you see it) *m*^{u}*ṣf*^{a}*rr*^{an} (yellowed) *th*^{u}*mm*^{a} (then) *y*^{a}*kūn*^{u} (it is, it will be) *ḥ*^{u}*ṭāmā* (debris, broken pieces).

وَفِي ٱلۡأٓخِرَةِ عَذَابٞ شَدِيدٞ وَمَغۡفِرَةٞ مِّنَ ٱللَّهِ وَرِضۡوَٰنٞ

W^{a}*-fī* (and in) *al-ākh*^{i}*r*^{a}*t*^{i} (the Hereafter) ^{ʿa}*dhāb*^{un} (a torment) *sh*^{a}*dīd*^{un} (severe) *w*^{a}*-m*^{a}*ghf*^{i}*r*^{a}*t*^{un} (and a forgiveness) *m*^{i}*n*^{a} (from) *allāh*^{i} (God) *w*^{a}*-r*^{i}*ḍwān* (and [His] pleasure).

وَمَا ٱلْحَيَوٰةُ ٱلدُّنْيَآ إِلَّا مَتَٰعُ ٱلْغُرُورِ

W^{a}*-mā* (and is not) *al-ḥ*^{a}*yāt*^{u} *al-d*^{u}*nyā* (the life of the world) *illā* (except) *m*^{a}*tā*^{u} *al-gh*^{u}*rūr* (goods of delusion).

This page intentionally left blank

Lesson 33: al-Ḥadīd Part 6

Verse 21, part 1

سَابِقُوٓا۟ إِلَىٰ مَغْفِرَةٍ مِّن رَّبِّكُمْ

Race each other toward a forgiveness from your Lord
Transliteration: sāb^{i}qū ilā m^{a}ghf^{i}r^{a}t^{in} m^{i}n r^{a}bb^{i}-k^{u}m
Pronunciation: sā-b^{i}-qū ilā m^{a}gh-f^{i}-r^{a}-t^{in} m^{i}n r^{a}b-b^{i}-k^{u}m

Sāb^{i}qū (race [one another, addressed to a group]) *ilā* (toward) *m^{a}ghf^{i}r^{a}t^{in}* (a forgiveness) *m^{i}n r^{a}bb^{i}-k^{u}m* (from your Lord).

The word *sāb^{i}qū* is the plural of *sāb^{i}q* ("race [him]"), from the word *sāb^{a}q^{a}* ("he raced [him]").

سَابَق ، يُسَابِق ، سِبَاق ومُسَابَقَة ، مُسَابِق

From right to left: he raced; he races; race (two forms); racer.

Verse 21, part 2

وَجَنَّةٍ عَرْضُهَا كَعَرْضِ ٱلسَّمَآءِ وَٱلْأَرْضِ

and a garden whose width is like the width of the heavens and the earth
Transliteration: w^{a}-j^{a}nn^{a}t^{in} ^{ʿa}rḍ^{u}-hā k^{a}-^{ʿa}rḍ^{i} al-s^{a}mā^{ʾi} w^{a}-al-arḍ
Pronunciation: w^{a}-j^{a}n-n^{a}-t^{in} ^{ʿa}r-ḍ^{u}-hā k^{a}-^{ʿa}r-*ḍ^{i}s*-s^{a}-mā-^{ʾi} w^{a}l-arḍ

W^{a}-j^{a}nn^{a}t^{in} (and a garden, and a Paradise) *^{a}rḍ^{u}-hā* (her width [is]) *k^{a}-^{a}rḍ^{i}* (like the width [of]) *al-s^{a}mā^{i} w^{a}-al-arḍ* (the heaven and the earth).

Verse 21, part 3

أُعِدَّتْ لِلَّذِينَ ءَامَنُوا۟ بِٱللَّهِ وَرُسُلِهِۦ ۚ

she was prepared for those who believed in God and His Messengers

Transliteration: u^{ʿi}dd^{a}-t l^{i}-all^{a}dhīn^{a} ām^{a}nū b^{i}-all^{a}h^{i} w^{a}-r^{u}s^{u}l^{i}-h

Pronunciation: u-^{ʿi}d-d^{a}t l^{i}l-l^{a}-dhī-n^{a} ā-m^{a}-nū b^{i}l-l^{a}-h^{i} w^{a}-r^{u}-s^{u}-l^{i}h

U^{ʿi}dd^{a}-t (she was prepared) *l^{i}-all^{a}dhīn^{a}* (for those who) *ām^{a}nū* (believed) *b^{i}-all^{a}h^{i}* (in God) *w^{a}-r^{u}s^{u}l^{i}-h* (and His Messengers).

The verb *u^{ʿi}dd^{a}-t* is the passive form of *a^{ʿa}dd^{a}* ("he prepared"). The verse uses "she was..." because it is referring to *j^{a}nn^{a}* from part 2 which is a feminine word.

أَعَدَّ يُعِدُّ إِعْدَاد

From right to left: he prepared; he prepares; preparation.

Verse 21, part 4

ذَٰلِكَ فَضْلُ ٱللَّهِ يُؤْتِيهِ مَن يَشَآءُ ۚ

That is the favor of God, He gives it to whomever He wills

Transliteration: dhāl^{i}ka f^{a}ḍl^{u} allāh^{i} y^{uʿ}tī-h^{i} m^{a}n y^{a}shā'

Pronunciation: dhā-l^{i}-ka f^{a}ḍ-l^{u}l-lā-h^{i} y^{uʿ}-tī-h^{i} m^{a}n y^{a}-shā'

Dhāl^{i}ka (that is) *f^{a}ḍl^{u}* (the favor of) *allāh^{i}* (God) *y^{u}ʿtī-h^{i}* (He gives it [to]) *m^{a}n* (whom) *y^{a}shā'* (He wishes).

Verse 21, part 5

وَٱللَّهُ ذُو ٱلْفَضْلِ ٱلْعَظِيمِ

And God is the possessor of great favor

Transliteration: w^{a}-allāh^{u} dhū al-f^{a}ḍl^{i} al-^{ca}ẓīm

Pronunciation: w^{a}l-lā-h^{u} dh^{u}l-f^{a}ḍ-l^{i}l-^{ca}-ẓīm

W^{a}-allāh^{u} (and God [is]) *dhū* (possessor of) *al-f^{a}ḍl^{i}* (the favor) *al-^{a}ẓīm* (great).

Verse 22, part 1

مَآ أَصَابَ مِن مُّصِيبَةٍ فِي ٱلْأَرْضِ وَلَا فِيٓ أَنفُسِكُمْ

No disaster strikes in the earth nor in yourselves...

Transliteration: mā aṣāb^{a} m^{i}n m^{u}ṣīb^{a}t^{in} fī al-arḍ^{i} w^{a}-lā fī anf^{u}s^{i}-k^{u}m

Pronunciation: mā a-ṣā-b^{a} m^{i}n m^{u}-ṣī-b^{a}-t^{in} f^{i}l-ar-ḍ^{i} w^{a}-lā fī an-f^{u}-s^{i}-k^{u}m

Mā (does not) *aṣāb^{a}* (it struck) *m^{i}n m^{u}ṣīb^{a}t^{in}* ([of any kind] of calamity) *fī* (in) *al-arḍ^{i}* (the earth) *w^{a}-lā* (and not) *fī anf^{u}s^{i}-k^{u}m* (in yourselves).

The word *aṣāb^{a}* means "it struck", "it hit", "it befell". The word *m^{u}ṣīb^{a}* comes from the same root and means "disaster", "calamity". The phrase *m^{i}n m^{u}ṣīb^{a}t^{in}* means something like "of [any kind of] calamity".

Verse 22, part 2

إِلَّا فِي كِتَٰبٍ مِّن قَبْلِ أَن نَّبْرَأَهَآ

except that it is in a book before we bring it into existence

Transliteration: illā fī k^{i}tāb^{in} m^{i}n q^{a}bl^{i} an n^{a}br^{a}'^{a}-ḥā

Pronunciation: il-lā fī k^{i}-tā-b^{in} m^{i}n q^{a}b-l^{i} an n^{a}b-r^{a}-'^{a}-ḥā

Illā (except [that it is]) *fī* (in) *k^{i}tāb^{in}* (a book) *m^{i}n q^{a}bl^{i} an* (before the fact that) *n^{a}br^{a}'^{a}-ḥā* (we bring it about).

The meaning of this part with the previous one is that every disaster that strikes is first written by God before it comes about in the world, meaning that no disaster happens without Him overseeing it and permitting it. The phrase *m^{i}n q^{a}bl^{i} an* means "before the fact that..."

Verse 22, part 3

ذَٰلِكَ عَلَى ٱللَّهِ يَسِيرٌ

That is upon God easy
Transliteration: dhāl^{i}k^{a} ^{ʿa}lā allāh^{i} y^{a}sīr
Pronunciation: dhā-l^{i}-k^{a} ^{ʿa}-l^{a}l-lā-h^{i} y^{a}-sīr

Dhāl^{i}k^{a} (that [is]) *^{ʿa}lā* (upon) *allāh^{i}* (God) *y^{a}sīr* (easy).

Verse 23, part 1

لِّكَيْلَا تَأْسَوْا۟ عَلَىٰ مَا فَاتَكُمْ وَلَا تَفْرَحُوا۟ بِمَآ ءَاتَىٰكُمْ ۗ

So that you [plural] may not grieve over what has escaped you and not exult about what He has given you
Transliteration: l^{i}-k^{a}y-lā t^{aʾ}s^{a}w ^{ʿa}lā mā fāt^{a}-k^{u}m w^{a}-lā t^{a}fr^{a}ḥū b^{i}-mā ātā-k^{u}m
Pronunciation: l^{i}-k^{a}y-lā t^{aʾ}-s^{a}w ^{ʿa}-lā mā fā-t^{a}-k^{u}m w^{a}-lā t^{a}f-r^{a}-ḥū b^{i}-mā ā-tā-k^{u}m

L^{i}-k^{a}y-lā (so that not) *t^{a}ʾs^{a}w* (you grieve) *^{ʿa}lā* (upon) *mā fāt^{a}-k^{u}m* (what escaped you) *w^{a}-lā* (and not) *t^{a}fr^{a}ḥū* (you exult) *b^{i}-mā ātā-k^{u}m* (about what He gave you).

The phrase *l^{i}-k^{a}y-lā* means "so that [you/it/etc.] may not". In standard Arabic it would be written as follows:

لِكَيْ لَا

The verb *t^{a}ʾs^{a}w* ("you grieve") is the second person plural of *asīy^{a}*.

أَسِيَ يَأْسَى

From right to left: he grieved; he grieves.

The word *t*^{a}*fr*^{a}*ḥū* ("you exult [about something]", "you become happy [about something]") is the plural second person form of *t*^{a}*fr*^{a}*ḥ* ("you exult"), whose third person past tense form is *f*^{a}*r*^{i}*ḥ*^{a}.

فَرِحَ يَفْرَحُ فَرَح

From right to left: he exulted; he exults; exultation / happiness.

The symbol at above the last word tells reciters it is recommended for them to pause here before going on.

Verse 23, part 2

وَٱللَّهُ لَا يُحِبُّ كُلَّ مُخْتَالٍ فَخُورٍ

and God does not love each conceited boasting person
Transliteration: w^{a}-allāh^{u} lā y^{u}ḥ^{i}bb^{u} k^{u}ll^{a} m^{u}khtāl^{in} f^{a}khūr
Pronunciation: w^{a}l-lā-h^{u} lā y^{u}-ḥ^{i}b-b^{u} k^{u}l-l^{a} m^{u}kh-tā-l^{in} f^{a}-khūr

W^{a}*-allāh*^{u} (and God) *lā y*^{u}*ḥ*^{i}*bb*^{u} (does not love) *k*^{u}*ll*^{a} (each, every) *m*^{u}*khtāl*^{in} (conceited, self-satisfied) *f*^{a}*khūr* (one who boasts).

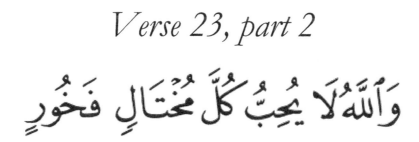

Verse 24, part 1

ٱلَّذِينَ يَبْخَلُونَ وَيَأْمُرُونَ ٱلنَّاسَ بِٱلْبُخْلِ ۗ

Those who withhold [their wealth] and command people toward stinginess

Transliteration: all^{a}dhīn^{a} y^{a}bkh^{a}lūn^{a} w^{a}-y^{a}ʾm^{u}rūn^{a} al-nās^{a} b^{i}-al-b^{u}khl

Pronunciation: al-l^{a}-dhī-n^{a} y^{a}b-kh^{a}-lū-n^{a} w^{a}-y^{a}ʾ-m^{u}-rū-n^{a}n-nā-s^{a} b^{i}l-b^{u}khl

All^{a}dhīn^{a} (those who) *y^{a}bkh^{a}lūn^{a}* (withhold) *w^{a}-y^{a}ʾm^{u}rūn^{a}* (and they command) *al-nās^{a}* (people) *b^{i}-al-b^{u}khl* (with stinginess, toward stinginess).

Verse 24, part 2

وَمَن يَتَوَلَّ فَإِنَّ ٱللَّهَ هُوَ ٱلْغَنِىُّ ٱلْحَمِيدُ

and whoever turns away then indeed God is Needless, Praiseworthy

Transliteration: w^{a}-m^{a}n y^{a}t^{a}w^{a}ll^{a} f^{a}-inn^{a} allāh^{a} h^{u}w^{a} al-gh^{a}nīy^{u} al-ḥ^{a}mīd

Pronunciation: w^{a}-m^{a}n y^{a}-t^{a}-w^{a}l-l^{a} f^{a}-in-n^{a}l-lā-h^{a} h^{u}-w^{a}l-gh^{a}-nī-y^{u}l-ḥ^{a}-mīd

W^{a}-m^{a}n (and whoever) *y^{a}t^{a}w^{a}ll^{a}* (turns away) *f^{a}-inn^{a}* (then indeed) *allāh^{a}* (God) *h^{u}w^{a}* (He [is]) *al-gh^{a}nīy^{u}* (the Needless) *al-ḥ^{a}mīd* (the Praiseworthy).

The *h^{u}w^{a}* serves for emphasis.

Verse 25, part 1

لَقَدْ أَرْسَلْنَا رُسُلَنَا بِٱلْبَيِّنَٰتِ

Truly we sent our Messengers with the clear demonstrations

Transliteration: l^{a}-q^{a}d ars^{a}l-nā r^{u}s^{u}l^{a}-nā b^{i}-al-b^{a}yy^{i}nāt

Pronunciation: l^{a}-q^{a}d ar-s^{a}l-nā r^{u}-s^{u}-l^{a}-nā b^{i}l-b^{a}y-y^{i}-nāt

L^{a}-q^{a}d (truly have) *ars^{a}l-nā* (we sent) *r^{u}s^{u}l^{i}-nā* (our Messengers) *b^{i}-al-b^{a}yy^{i}nāt* (with the clear proofs, with the clear demonstrations).

Verse 25, part 2

وَأَنزَلْنَا مَعَهُمُ ٱلْكِتَٰبَ وَٱلْمِيزَانَ لِيَقُومَ ٱلنَّاسُ بِٱلْقِسْطِ ۖ

And we sent down with them the Book and the balance so that people may establish justice
Transliteration: w^{a}-anz^{a}l-nā m^{aʿa}-h^{u}m al-k^{i}tāb^{a} w^{a}-al-mīzān^{a} l^{i}-y^{a}qūm^{a} al-nās^{a} b^{i}-al-q^{i}sṭ
Pronunciation: w^{a}-an-z^{a}l-nā m^{a}-^{ʿa}-h^{u}m al-k^{i}-tā-b^{a} w^{a}l-mī-zā-n^{a} l^{i}-y^{a}-qū-*m^{a}n*-nā-s^{a} b^{i}l-q^{i}sṭ

W^{a}-anz^{a}l-nā (and we sent down) *m^{aʿa}-h^{u}m* (with them) *al-k^{i}tāb^{a}* (the Book) *w^{a}-al-mīzān^{a}* (the balance) *l^{i}-y^{a}qūm^{a}* (so that they establish) *al-nās^{a}* (the people) *b^{i}-al-q^{i}sṭ* (justice).

Above, *al-mīzān* ("the balance", "the scales") may refer to the knowledge of how to establish justice. The phrase *l^{i}-y^{a}qūm^{a}...b^{i}* means "so that they may..."

Verse 25, part 3

وَأَنزَلْنَا ٱلْحَدِيدَ فِيهِ بَأْسٌ شَدِيدٌ وَمَنَٰفِعُ لِلنَّاسِ

And we sent down iron, in it there is severe [military] capability and benefits for the people
Transliteration: w^{a}-anz^{a}l-nā al-ḥ^{a}dīd^{a} fī-h^{i} b^{aʾ}s^{un} sh^{a}dīd^{un} w^{a}-m^{a}nāf^{iʿu} l^{i}-al-nās
Pronunciation: w^{a}-an-z^{a}l-nā al-ḥ^{a}-dī-d^{a} fī-h^{i} b^{aʾ}-s^{un} sh^{a}-dī-d^{un} w^{a}-m^{a}-nā-f^{i}-^{ʿu} *l^{i}n*-nās

W^{a}-anz^{a}l-nā (and we sent down) *al-ḥ^{a}dīd^{a}* (iron) *fī-h^{i}* (in it [is]) *b^{aʾ}s^{un}* (injury, military power) *sh^{a}dīd^{un}* (severe) *w^{a}-m^{a}nāf^{iʿu}* (and benefits) *l^{i}-al-nās* (for the people).

Verse 25, part 4

وَلِيَعْلَمَ ٱللَّهُ مَن يَنصُرُهُۥ وَرُسُلَهُۥ بِٱلْغَيْبِ ۚ إِنَّ ٱللَّهَ قَوِىٌّ عَزِيزٌ

And so that God may know who supports Him and His Messengers unseen. Indeed God is Strong, Mighty

Transliteration: w^{a}-l^{i}-y^{a}ʿl^{a}m^{a} allāh^{u} m^{a}n y^{a}nṣ^{u}r^{u}-h^{u} w^{a}-rus^{u}l^{u}-h^{u} b^{i}-al-gh^{a}yb inn^{a} allāh^{a} q^{a}wīy^{un} ʿ^{a}zīz

Pronunciation: w^{a}-l^{i}-y^{a}ʿ-l^{a}-m^{a}l-lā-h^{u} m^{a}n y^{a}n-ṣ^{u}-r^{u}-h^{u} w^{a}-ru-s^{u}-l^{u}-h^{u} b^{i}l-gh^{a}yb in-n^{a}l-lā-h^{a} q^{a}-wī-y^{un} ʿ^{a}-zīz

W^{a}-l^{i}-y^{a}ʿl^{a}m^{a} (so that He knows) *allāh^{u}* (God) *m^{a}n* (who) *y^{a}nṣ^{u}r^{u}-h^{u}* (supports Him) *w^{a}-rus^{u}l^{u}-h^{u}* (and His Messengers) *b^{i}-al-gh^{a}yb* (unseen) *inn^{a}* (indeed) *allāh^{a}* (God [is]) *q^{a}wīy^{un}* (Strong) *ʿ^{a}zīz* (Mighty).

The phrase *b^{i}-al-gh^{a}yb* means “in a state of not being seen”, meaning that they support God even though there is apparently no one looking at them and forcing them.

Lesson 33 Review

سَابِقُوٓاْ إِلَىٰ مَغۡفِرَةٖ مِّن رَّبِّكُمۡ

Sāb^{i}*qū* (race [one another, addressed to a group]) *ilā* (toward) *m*^{a}*ghf*^{i}*r*^{a}*t*^{in} (a forgiveness) *m*^{i}*n r*^{a}*bb*^{i}*-k*^{u}*m* (from your Lord).

وَجَنَّةٍ عَرۡضُهَا كَعَرۡضِ ٱلسَّمَآءِ وَٱلۡأَرۡضِ

W^{a}*-j*^{a}*nn*^{a}*t*^{in} (and a garden, and a Paradise) ^{a}*rḍ*^{u}*-hā* (her width [is]) *k*^{a}*-*^{a}*rḍ*^{i} (like the width [of]) *al-s*^{a}*mā*^{i} *w*^{a}*-al-arḍ* (the heaven and the earth).

أُعِدَّتۡ لِلَّذِينَ ءَامَنُواْ بِٱللَّهِ وَرُسُلِهِۦۚ

U^{i}*dd*^{a}*-t* (she was prepared) *l*^{i}*-all*^{a}*dhīn*^{a} (for those who) *ām*^{a}*nū* (believed) *b*^{i}*-all*^{a}*h*^{i} (in God) *w*^{a}*-r*^{u}*s*^{u}*l*^{i}*-h* (and His Messengers).

ذَٰلِكَ فَضۡلُ ٱللَّهِ يُؤۡتِيهِ مَن يَشَآءُۚ

Dhāl^{i}*ka* (that is) *f*^{a}*ḍl*^{u} (the favor of) *allāh*^{i} (God) *y*^{u}*'tī-h*^{i} (He gives it [to]) *m*^{a}*n* (whom) *y*^{a}*shā'* (He wishes).

وَٱللَّهُ ذُو ٱلۡفَضۡلِ ٱلۡعَظِيمِ

W^{a}*-allāh*^{u} (and God [is]) *dhū* (possessor of) *al-f*^{a}*ḍl*^{i} (the favor) *al-*^{a}*ẓīm* (great).

مَآ أَصَابَ مِن مُّصِيبَةٍ فِى ٱلْأَرْضِ وَلَا فِىٓ أَنفُسِكُمْ

Mā (does not) *aṣāb*^{a} (it struck) *m*^{i}*n m*^{u}*ṣīb*^{a}*t*^{in} ([of any kind] of calamity) *fī* (in) *al-arḍ*^{i} (the earth) *w*^{a}*-lā* (and not) *fī anf*^{u}*s*^{i}*-k*^{u}*m* (in yourselves).

إِلَّا فِى كِتَٰبٍ مِّن قَبْلِ أَن نَّبْرَأَهَآ

Illā (except [that it is]) *fī* (in) *k*^{i}*tāb*^{in} (a book) *m*^{i}*n q*^{a}*bl*^{i} *an* (before the fact that) *n*^{a}*br*^{a}^{a}*-ḥā* (we bring it about).

ذَٰلِكَ عَلَى ٱللَّهِ يَسِيرٌ

Dhāl^{i}*k*^{a} (that [is]) ^{a}*lā* (upon) *allāh*^{i} (God) *y*^{a}*sīr* (easy).

لِّكَيْلَا تَأْسَوْا۟ عَلَىٰ مَا فَاتَكُمْ وَلَا تَفْرَحُوا۟ بِمَآ ءَاتَىٰكُمْ ۗ

L^{i}*-k*^{a}*y-lā* (so that not) *t*^{a}*ʾs*^{a}*w* (you grieve) ^{a}*lā* (upon) *mā fāt*^{a}*-k*^{u}*m* (what escaped you) *w*^{a}*-lā* (and not) *t*^{a}*fr*^{a}*ḥū* (you exult) *b*^{i}*-mā ātā-k*^{u}*m* (about what He gave you).

وَٱللَّهُ لَا يُحِبُّ كُلَّ مُخْتَالٍ فَخُورٍ

W^{a}*-allāh*^{u} (and God) *lā y*^{u}*ḥ*^{i}*bb*^{u} (does not love) *k*^{u}*ll*^{a} (each, every) *m*^{u}*khtāl*^{in} (conceited, self-satisfied) *f*^{a}*khūr* (one who boasts).

ٱلَّذِينَ يَبْخَلُونَ وَيَأْمُرُونَ ٱلنَّاسَ بِٱلْبُخْلِ ۗ

All^{a}dhīn^{a} (those who) *y^{a}bkh^{a}lūn^{a}* (withhold) *w^{a}-y^{a}'m^{u}rūn^{a}* (and they command) *al-nās^{a}* (people) *b^{i}-al-b^{u}khl* (with stinginess, toward stinginess).

وَمَن يَتَوَلَّ فَإِنَّ ٱللَّهَ هُوَ ٱلْغَنِىُّ ٱلْحَمِيدُ

W^{a}-m^{a}n (and whoever) *y^{a}t^{a}w^{a}ll^{a}* (turns away) *f^{a}-inn^{a}* (then indeed) *allāh^{a}* (God) *h^{u}w^{a}* (He [is]) *al-gh^{a}nīy^{u}* (the Needless) *al-ḥ^{a}mīd* (the Praiseworthy).

لَقَدْ أَرْسَلْنَا رُسُلَنَا بِٱلْبَيِّنَٰتِ

L^{a}-q^{a}d (truly have) *ars^{a}l-nā* (we sent) *r^{u}s^{u}l^{a}-nā* (our Messengers) *b^{i}-al-b^{a}yy^{i}nāt* (with the clear proofs, with the clear demonstrations).

وَأَنزَلْنَا مَعَهُمُ ٱلْكِتَٰبَ وَٱلْمِيزَانَ لِيَقُومَ ٱلنَّاسُ بِٱلْقِسْطِ ۖ

W^{a}-anz^{a}l-nā (and we sent down) *m$^{a\,a}$-h^{u}m* (with them) *al-k^{i}tāb^{a}* (the Book) *w^{a}-al-mīzān^{a}* (the balance) *l^{i}-y^{a}qūm^{a}* (so that they establish) *al-nās^{a}* (the people) *b^{i}-al-q^{i}sṭ* (justice).

وَأَنزَلْنَا ٱلْحَدِيدَ فِيهِ بَأْسٌ شَدِيدٌ وَمَنَٰفِعُ لِلنَّاسِ

W^{a}-anz^{a}l-nā (and we sent down) *al-ḥ^{a}dīd^{a}* (iron) *fī-h^{i}* (in it [is]) *b^{a}'s^{un}* (injury, military power) *sh^{a}dīd^{un}* (severe) *w^{a}-m^{a}nāf$^{i\,u}$* (and benefits) *l^{i}-al-nās* (for the people).

وَلِيَعْلَمَ ٱللَّهُ مَن يَنصُرُهُۥ وَرُسُلَهُۥ بِٱلْغَيْبِ ۚ إِنَّ ٱللَّهَ قَوِىٌّ عَزِيزٌ

W^{a}*-l*^{i}*-y*^{a}*ʿl*^{a}*m*^{a} (so that He knows) *allāh*^{u} (God) *m*^{a}*n* (who) *y*^{a}*nṣ*^{u}*r*^{u}*-h*^{u} (supports Him) *w*^{a}*-rus*^{u}*l*^{u}*-h*^{u} (and His Messengers) *b*^{i}*-al-gh*^{a}*yb* (unseen) *inn*^{a} (indeed) *allāh*^{a} (God [is]) *q*^{a}*wīy*^{un} (Strong) ^{a}*zīz* (Mighty).

Lesson 34: al-Ḥadīd Part 7

Verse 26, part 1

وَلَقَدْ أَرْسَلْنَا نُوحًا وَإِبْرَٰهِيمَ وَجَعَلْنَا فِى ذُرِّيَّتِهِمَا ٱلنُّبُوَّةَ وَٱلْكِتَٰبَ ۖ

And truly We sent Noah and Abraham and placed within their descendants prophethood and the Book

Transliteration: w^{a}-l^{a}-q^{a}d ars^{a}l-nā nūḥ^{an} w^{a}-ibrāhīm^{a} w^{a}-j^{aca}l-nā fī dh^{u}rrīy^{a}t^{i}-h^{i}mā al-n^{u}b^{u}ww^{a}t^{a} w^{a}-al-k^{i}tāb

Pronunciation: w^{a}-l^{a}-q^{a}d ar-s^{a}l-nā nū-ḥ^{an} w^{a}-ib-rā-hī-m^{a} w^{a}-j^{a}-^{ca}l-nā fī dh^{u}r-rī-y^{a}-t^{i}-h^{i}-m^{a}l-n^{u}-b^{u}w-w^{a}-t^{a} w^{a}l-k^{i}-tāb

W^{a}-l^{a}-q^{a}d (and truly have) *ars^{a}l-nā* (We sent) *nūḥ^{an}* (Noah) *w^{a}-ibrāhīm^{a}* (and Abarahm) *w^{a}-j^{a}^{a}l-nā* (and We placed, and We made) *fī* (in) *dh^{u}rrīy^{a}t^{i}-h^{i}mā* (their descendants) *al-n^{u}b^{u}ww^{a}t^{a}* (prophethood) *w^{a}-al-k^{i}tāb* (and the Book).

The word *dh^{u}rrīy^{a}* means "descendants". The *h^{i}mā* is the dual pronoun; it means "the two of them".

Verse 26, part 2

فَمِنْهُم مُّهْتَدٍ ۖ وَكَثِيرٌ مِّنْهُمْ فَٰسِقُونَ

so from them is [the occasional] one who is guided, and many of them are rebellious

Transliteration: f^{a}-m^{i}n-h^{u}m m^{u}ht^{a}d^{in} w^{a}-k^{a}thīr^{un} m^{i}n-h^{u}m fās^{i}qūn

Pronunciation: f^{a}-m^{i}n-h^{u}m m^{u}h-t^{a}-d^{in} w^{a}-k^{a}-thī-r^{un} m^{i}n-h^{u}m fā-s^{i}-qūn

F^{a}-m^{i}n-h^{u}m (so from them) *m^{u}ht^{a}d^{in}* (a guided one) *w^{a}-k^{a}thīr^{un}* (and many) *m^{i}n-h^{u}m* (of them [are]) *fās^{i}qūn* (rebellious, sinful).

The meaning of the verse is that you will find one here and there among them who is guided, but that most of them are rebellious (against God).

Verse 27, part 1

ثُمَّ قَفَّيْنَا عَلَىٰٓ ءَاثَٰرِهِم بِرُسُلِنَا وَقَفَّيْنَا بِعِيسَى ٱبْنِ مَرْيَمَ

Then we sent our Messengers after their footsteps and sent Jesus son of Mary after [them]
Transliteration: th^{u}mm^{a} q^{a}ff^{a}y-nā ʿ^{a}lā āthār^{i}-h^{i}m b^{i}-r^{u}s^{u}l^{i}-nā w^{a}-q^{a}ff^{a}y-nā b^{i}-ʿīsā ibn^{i} m^{a}ry^{a}m
Pronunciation: th^{u}m-m^{a} q^{a}f-f^{a}y-nā ʿ^{a}lā ā-thā-r^{i}-h^{i}m b^{i}-r^{u}-s^{u}-l^{i}-nā w^{a}-q^{a}f-f^{a}y-nā b^{i}-ʿī-*s*^{a}*b*-n^{i} m^{a}r-y^{a}m

Th^{u}mm^{a} (then, next) *q^{a}ff^{a}y-nā* (we sent after [them]) *ʿ^{a}lā* (upon) *āthār^{i}-h^{i}m* (their footsteps) *b^{i}-r^{u}s^{u}l^{i}-nā* (our Messengers) *w^{a}-q^{a}ff^{a}y-nā* (and we sent after [them]) *b^{i}-ʿīsā* (Jesus) *ibn^{i} m^{a}ry^{a}m* (son of Mary).

The verb *q^{a}ff^{a}y-nā* is the first person plural of *qaffā* ("he sent him after [another person]", "he caused him to follow [another person]"). The phrase *qaffā...b^{i}* has the same meaning.

Verse 27, part 2

وَءَاتَيْنَٰهُ ٱلْإِنجِيلَ وَجَعَلْنَا فِى قُلُوبِ ٱلَّذِينَ ٱتَّبَعُوهُ رَأْفَةً

And we gave him the Gospel and placed in the hearts of those who followed him a compassion
Transliteration: w^{a}-āt^{a}y-nā-h^{u} al-injīl^{a} w^{a}-j^{a}ʿ^{a}lnā fī q^{u}lūb^{i} all^{a}dhīn^{a} itt^{a}b^{a}ʿū-h^{u} r^{a}ʾf^{a}t^{an}
Pronunciation: w^{a}-ā-t^{a}y-nā-h^{u}l-in-jī-l^{a} w^{a}-j^{a}-ʿ^{a}l-nā fī q^{u}-lū-b^{i}l-l^{a}-dhī-n^{a}t-t^{a}b^{a}-ʿū-h^{u} r^{a}ʾ-f^{a}-t^{an}

W^{a}-āt^{a}y-nā-h^{u} (and We gave him) *al-injīl^{a}* (the Gospel) *w^{a}-j^{a}ʿ^{a}lnā* (and We placed) *fī* (in) *q^{u}lūb^{i}* (the hearts [of]) *all^{a}dhīn^{a}* (those who) *itt^{a}b^{a}ʿū-h^{u}* (followed him) *r^{a}ʾf^{a}t^{an}* (a compassion).

Verse 27, part 3

وَرَحْمَةً وَرَهْبَانِيَّةً ٱبْتَدَعُوهَا مَا كَتَبْنَٰهَا عَلَيْهِمْ

and a mercy and a monasticism they invented, we did not prescribe it upon them
Transliteration: w^{a}-r^{a}ḥm^{a}t^{an} w^{a}-r^{a}hbānīy^{a}t^{an} ibt^{a}d^{a}ʿū-hā mā k^{a}t^{a}bnā-hā ʿ^{a}l^{a}y-h^{i}m
Pronunciation: w^{a}-r^{a}ḥ-m^{a}-t^{an} w^{a}-r^{a}h-bā-nī-y^{a}-t^{an} ib-t^{a}-d^{a}-ʿū-hā mā k^{a}-t^{a}b-nā-hā ʿ^{a}-l^{a}y-h^{i}m

W^{a}-r^{a}ḥm^{a}t^{an} (and a mercy) *w^{a}-r^{a}hbānīy^{a}t^{an}* (and a monasticism) *ibt^{a}d^{a}ʿū-hā* (they invented it) *mā k^{a}t^{a}bnā-hā* (we did not prescribe it) *ʿ^{a}l^{a}y-h^{i}m* (upon them).

The word *k^{a}t^{a}bnā* literally means "we wrote". But when it is followed by *ʿalā* ("upon") it means "we prescribed", "we made it obligatory".

Verse 27, part 4

فَمَا رَعَوْهَا حَقَّ رِعَايَتِهَا ۖ فَآتَيْنَا الَّذِينَ آمَنُوا مِنْهُمْ أَجْرَهُمْ ۖ وَكَثِيرٌ مِّنْهُمْ فَاسِقُونَ

but they did not observe it its rightful observance, so we gave those who believed of them their reward, and many of them are rebellious

Transliteration: f^{a}-mā r$^{a‘a}$w-hā ḥ^{a}qq^{a} r$^{i‘}$āy^{a}t^{i}-hā f^{a}-āt^{a}y-nā all^{a}dhīn^{a} ām^{a}nū m^{i}n-h^{u}m ajr^{a}-h^{u}m w^{a}-k^{a}thīr^{un} m^{i}n-h^{u}m fās^{i}qūn

Pronunciation: f^{a}-mā r^{a}-$^{‘a}$w-hā ḥ^{a}q-q^{a} r^{i}-‘ā-y^{a}-t^{i}-hā f^{a}-ā-t^{a}y-nā al-l^{a}-dhī-n^{a} ā-m^{a}-nū m^{i}n-h^{u}m aj-r^{a}-h^{u}m w^{a}-k^{a}-thī-r^{un} m^{i}n-h^{u}m fā-s^{i}-qūn

F^{a}-mā (but not) *r$^{a‘a}$w-hā* (they observed it) *ḥ^{a}qq^{a}* (due, rightful) *r$^{i‘}$āy^{a}t^{i}-hā* (its observance) *f^{a}-āt^{a}y-nā* (so We gave) *all^{a}dhīn^{a} ām^{a}nū* (those who believed) *m^{i}n-h^{u}m* (of them) *ajr^{a}-h^{u}m* (their reward) *w^{a}-k^{a}thīr^{un}* (and many) *m^{i}n-h^{u}m* (of them [are]) *fās^{i}qūn* (rebellious ones).

Verse 28, part 1

يَا أَيُّهَا الَّذِينَ آمَنُوا اتَّقُوا اللَّهَ وَآمِنُوا بِرَسُولِهِ

O those who believed, fear God and believe in His Messenger

Transliteration: yā-^{ʾa}yy^{u}ḥā all^{a}dhīn^{a} ām^{a}nū itt^{a}qū allāh^{a} w^{a}-ām^{i}nū b^{i}-r^{a}sūl^{i}-h

Pronunciation: yā-^{ʾa}y-y^{u}-ḥ^{a}l-l^{a}-dhī-n^{a} ā-m^{a}-*n^{u}t*-t^{a}-q^{u}l-lā-h^{a} w^{a}-ā-m^{i}-nū b^{i}-r^{a}-sū-l^{i}h

Yā-^{a}yy^{u}ḥā all^{a}dhīn^{a} (O those who...) *ām^{a}nū* (they believed) *itt^{a}qū* (fear) *allāh^{a}* (God) *w^{a}-ām^{i}nū* (and believe) *b^{i}-r^{a}sūl^{i}-h* (in His Messenger).

Verse 28, part 2

يُؤْتِكُمْ كِفْلَيْنِ مِن رَّحْمَتِهِ

He will give you two shares of His mercy

Transliteration: y^{u}’t^{i}-k^{u}m k^{i}fl^{a}yn^{i} m^{i}n r^{a}ḥm^{a}t^{i}-h
Pronunciation: y^{u}’-t^{i}-k^{u}m k^{i}f-l^{a}y-n^{i} m^{i}n r^{a}ḥ-m^{a}-t^{i}h

Y^{u}’t^{i}-k^{u}m (He gives you) *k^{i}fl^{a}yn^{i}* (two shares) *m^{i}n* (of) *r^{a}ḥm^{a}t^{i}-h* (His mercy).

The word *k^{i}fl^{a}yn* is the dual of *k^{i}fl* (“portion”, “share”).

Verse 28, part 2

وَيَجۡعَل لَّكُمۡ نُورٗا تَمۡشُونَ بِهِۦ

And He will assign for you [plural] a light which you will walk with
Transliteration: w^{a}-y^{a}j^{a}‘^{a}l l^{a}-k^{u}m nūr^{an} t^{a}mshūn^{a} b^{i}-h
Pronunciation: w^{a}-y^{a}j-‘^{a}l l^{a}-k^{u}m nū-r^{an} t^{a}m-shū-n^{a} b^{i}h

W^{a}-y^{a}j^{a}l (and He assigns, and He places) *l^{a}-k^{u}m* (for you) *nūr^{an}* (a light) *t^{a}mshūn^{a}* (you walk) *b^{i}-h* (with it, by it).

Verse 28, part 3

وَيَغۡفِرۡ لَكُمۡۚ وَٱللَّهُ غَفُورٞ رَّحِيمٞ

and He will forgive you, and God is the Forgiving, the Merciful
Transliteration: w^{a}-y^{a}ghf^{i}r l^{a}-k^{u}m w^{a}-allāh^{u} gh^{a}fūr^{un} r^{a}ḥīm
Pronunciation: w^{a}-y^{a}gh-f^{i}r l^{a}-k^{u}m w^{a}l-lā-h^{u} gh^{a}-fū-r^{un} r^{a}-ḥīm

W^{a}-y^{a}ghf^{i}r l^{a}-k^{u}m (and He forgives you) *w^{a}-allāh^{u}* (and God [is]) *gh^{a}fūr^{un}* (Forgiving) *r^{a}ḥīm* (Merciful).

The phrase *y^{a}ghf^{i}r l^{a}-k^{u}m* means “He forgives you”, it is the third person present tense of *gh^{a}f^{a}r^{a} li* (“He forgave”).

Verse 29, part 1

لِّئَلَّا يَعْلَمَ أَهْلُ ٱلْكِتَٰبِ

So that the People of the Book may know...
Transliteration: l^{i}-allā y^{aʿ}l^{a}m^{a} ahl^{u} al-k^{i}tāb^{i}
Pronunciation: l^{i}-al-lā y^{aʿ}-l^{a}-m^{a} ah-l^{u}l-k^{i}-tā-b^{i}

L^{i}-allā y^{a}ʿl^{a}m^{a} (so that they know) *ahl^{u} al-k^{i}tāb^{i}* (the People of the Book).

The phrase *l^{i}-allā* is short for *li-an lā*. It literally means "so that [it/they/etc] may not", "so that [it/they/etc] will not", but here it is used to mean the opposite; "so that [it/they/etc] may". This use of something to mean its opposite is used for grabbing attention. The phrase *ahl^{u} al-k^{i}tāb* means "the People of the Book". It refers to Jews, Christians and others belonging to the Abrahaic religions.

Verse 29, part 2

أَلَّا يَقْدِرُونَ عَلَىٰ شَىْءٍ مِّن فَضْلِ ٱللَّهِ ۙ وَأَنَّ ٱلْفَضْلَ بِيَدِ ٱللَّهِ

That they do not have power over any of God's favor and that favor is in God's hand
Transliteration: allā y^{a}qd^{i}rūn^{a} ʿ^{a}lā sh^{a}y^{ʾin} m^{i}n f^{a}ḍl^{i} allāh^{i} w^{a}-ann^{a} al-f^{a}ḍl^{a} b^{i}-y^{a}d^{i} allāh
Pronunciation: al-lā y^{a}q-d^{i}-rū-n^{a} ʿ^{a}-lā sh^{a}y-^{ʾin} m^{i}n f^{a}ḍ-l^{i}l-lā-h^{i} w^{a}-an-n^{a}l-f^{a}ḍ-l^{a} b^{i}-y^{a}-d^{i}l-lāh

Allā (that not) *y^{a}qd^{i}rūn^{a}* (they have power) *ʿ^{a}lā* (over) *sh^{a}y^{in}* (anything) *m^{i}n* (of) *f^{a}ḍl^{i}* (the favor [of]) *allāh^{i}* (God) *w^{a}-ann^{a}* (and that) *al-f^{a}ḍl^{a}* (favor [is]) *b^{i}-y^{a}d^{i}* (in that hand [of]) *allāh* (God).

The meaning of this part with the previous one is that the People of the Book have no power over God's favor. The Jews claimed that the favor of prophethood was bestowed upon them and exclusive to them, but God took that favor away and gave it to Muhammad who was a non-Jew. Here God affirms His power to place His favors wherever He wants.

Verse 29, part 3

يُؤْتِيهِ مَن يَشَآءُ ۚ وَٱللَّهُ ذُو ٱلْفَضْلِ ٱلْعَظِيمِ

He gives it [i.e. His favor] to whomever He wills, and God is the possessor of great favor
Transliteration: y^{u}'tī-h^{i} m^{a}n y^{a}shā' w^{a}-allāh^{u} dhū al-faḍl^{i} al-ʿaẓīm
Pronunciation: y^{u}'-tī-h^{i} m^{a}n y^{a}-shā' w^{a}l-lā-h^{u} dh^{u}l-faḍ-l^{i}l-ʿa-ẓīm

Y^{u}'tī-h^{i} (He gives it [to]) *m^{a}n* (whomever) *y^{a}shā'* (He wills) *w^{a}-allāh^{u}* (and God [is]) *dhū al-faḍl^{i}* (possessor of the favor) *al-ʿaẓīm* (the great).

Lesson 34 Review

وَلَقَدْ أَرْسَلْنَا نُوحًا وَإِبْرَٰهِيمَ وَجَعَلْنَا فِى ذُرِّيَّتِهِمَا ٱلنُّبُوَّةَ وَٱلْكِتَٰبَ ۖ

W^{a}-l^{a}-q^{a}d (and truly have) *ars^{a}l-nā* (We sent) *nūḥ^{an}* (Noah) *w^{a}-ibrāhīm^{a}* (and Abarahm) *w^{a}-j^{a}ʿ^{a}l-nā* (and We placed, and We made) *fī* (in) *dh^{u}rrīy^{a}t^{i}-h^{i}mā* (their descendants) *al-n^{u}b^{u}ww^{a}t^{a}* (prophethood) *w^{a}-al-k^{i}tāb* (and the Book).

فَمِنْهُم مُّهْتَدٍ ۖ وَكَثِيرٌ مِّنْهُمْ فَٰسِقُونَ

F^{a}-m^{i}n-h^{u}m (so from them) *m^{u}ht^{a}d^{in}* (a guided one) *w^{a}-k^{a}thīr^{un}* (and many) *m^{i}n-h^{u}m* (of them [are]) *fās^{i}qūn* (rebellious, sinful).

ثُمَّ قَفَّيْنَا عَلَىٰٓ ءَاثَٰرِهِم بِرُسُلِنَا وَقَفَّيْنَا بِعِيسَى ٱبْنِ مَرْيَمَ

Th^{u}mm^{a} (then, next) *q^{a}ff^{a}y-nā* (we sent after [them]) *ʿ^{a}lā* (upon) *āthār^{i}-h^{i}m* (their footsteps) *b^{i}-r^{u}s^{u}l^{i}-nā* (our Messengers) *w^{a}-q^{a}ff^{a}y-nā* (and we sent after [them]) *b^{i}-ʿīsā* (Jesus) *ibn^{i} m^{a}ry^{a}m* (son of Mary).

وَءَاتَيْنَٰهُ ٱلْإِنجِيلَ وَجَعَلْنَا فِى قُلُوبِ ٱلَّذِينَ ٱتَّبَعُوهُ رَأْفَةً

W^{a}-āt^{a}y-nā-h^{u} (and We gave him) *al-injīl^{a}* (the Gospel) *w^{a}-j^{a}ʿ^{a}lnā* (and We placed) *fī* (in) *q^{u}lūb^{i}* (the hearts [of]) *all^{a}dhīn^{a}* (those who) *itt^{a}b^{a}ʿū-h^{u}* (followed him) *r^{a}ʾf^{a}t^{an}* (a compassion).

وَرَحْمَةً وَرَهْبَانِيَّةً ٱبْتَدَعُوهَا مَا كَتَبْنَٰهَا عَلَيْهِمْ

W^{a}-r^{a}ḥm^{a}t^{an} (and a mercy) *w^{a}-r^{a}hbānīy^{a}t^{an}* (and a monasticism) *ibt^{a}d^{a}ʿū-hā* (they invented it) *mā k^{a}t^{a}bnā-hā* (we did not prescribe it) *ʿ^{a}l^{a}y-h^{i}m* (upon them).

فَمَا رَعَوْهَا حَقَّ رِعَايَتِهَا ۖ فَـَٔاتَيْنَا ٱلَّذِينَ ءَامَنُوا۟ مِنْهُمْ أَجْرَهُمْ ۖ وَكَثِيرٌ مِّنْهُمْ فَـٰسِقُونَ

F^{a}*-mā* (but not) *r*$^{a\,a}$*w-hā* (they observed it) *ḥ*^{a}*qq*^{a} (due, rightful) *r*^{i}*ʿāy*^{a}*t*^{i}*-hā* (its observance) *f*^{a}*-āt*^{a}*y-nā* (so We gave) *all*^{a}*dhīn*^{a} *ām*^{a}*nū* (those who believed) *m*^{i}*n-h*^{u}*m* (of them) *ajr*^{a}*-h*^{u}*m* (their reward) *w*^{a}*-k*^{a}*thīr*^{un} (and many) *m*^{i}*n-h*^{u}*m* (of them [are]) *fās*^{i}*qūn* (rebellious ones).

يَـٰٓأَيُّهَا ٱلَّذِينَ ءَامَنُوا۟ ٱتَّقُوا۟ ٱللَّهَ وَءَامِنُوا۟ بِرَسُولِهِۦ

Yā-^{a}*yy*^{u}*hā all*^{a}*dhīn*^{a} (O those who...) *ām*^{a}*nū* (they believed) *itt*^{a}*qū* (fear) *allāh*^{a} (God) *w*^{a}*-ām*^{i}*nū* (and believe) *b*^{i}*-r*^{a}*sūl*^{i}*-h* (in His Messenger).

يُؤْتِكُمْ كِفْلَيْنِ مِن رَّحْمَتِهِۦ

Y^{u}*ʾt*^{i}*-k*^{u}*m* (He gives you) *k*^{i}*fl*^{a}*yn*^{i} (two shares) *m*^{i}*n* (of) *r*^{a}*ḥm*^{a}*t*^{i}*-h* (His mercy).

وَيَجْعَل لَّكُمْ نُورًا تَمْشُونَ بِهِۦ

W^{a}*-y*^{a}*j*^{a}*l* (and He assigns, and He places) *l*^{a}*-k*^{u}*m* (for you) *nūr*^{an} (a light) *t*^{a}*mshūn*^{a} (you walk) *b*^{i}*-h* (with it, by it).

وَيَغْفِرْ لَكُمْ ۚ وَٱللَّهُ غَفُورٌ رَّحِيمٌ

W^{a}*-y*^{a}*ghf*^{i}*r l*^{a}*-k*^{u}*m* (and He forgives you) *w*^{a}*-allāh*^{u} (and God [is]) *gh*^{a}*fūr*^{un} (Forgiving) *r*^{a}*ḥīm* (Merciful).

لِّئَلَّا يَعۡلَمَ أَهۡلُ ٱلۡكِتَٰبِ

L^{i}-allā y^{a}ʿl^{a}m^{a} (so that they know) *ahl^{u} al-k^{i}tāb^{i}* (the People of the Book).

أَلَّا يَقۡدِرُونَ عَلَىٰ شَيۡءٖ مِّن فَضۡلِ ٱللَّهِ ۙ وَأَنَّ ٱلۡفَضۡلَ بِيَدِ ٱللَّهِ

Allā (that not) *y^{a}qd^{i}rūn^{a}* (they have power) *^{a}lā* (over) *sh^{a}y^{in}* (anything) *m^{i}n* (of) *f^{a}ḍl^{i}* (the favor [of]) *allāh^{i}* (God) *w^{a}-ann^{a}* (and that) *al-f^{a}ḍl^{a}* (favor [is]) *b^{i}-y^{a}d^{i}* (in that hand [of]) *allāh* (God).

يُؤۡتِيهِ مَن يَشَآءُ ۚ وَٱللَّهُ ذُو ٱلۡفَضۡلِ ٱلۡعَظِيمِ

Y^{u}ʾtī-h^{i} (He gives it [to]) *m^{a}n* (whomever) *y^{a}shāʾ* (He wills) *w^{a}-allāh^{u}* (and God [is]) *dhū al-faḍl^{i}* (possessor of the favor) *al-ʿaẓīm* (the great).

This page intentionally left blank

Lesson 35: al-Insān Part 1

In this lesson we will cover chapter 76 of the Quran which is titled *al-Insān* ("The Human").

بِسْمِ ٱللَّهِ ٱلرَّحْمَٰنِ ٱلرَّحِيمِ

Verse 1

هَلْ أَتَىٰ عَلَى ٱلْإِنسَٰنِ حِينٌ مِّنَ ٱلدَّهْرِ لَمْ يَكُن شَيْـًٔا مَّذْكُورًا

Has a period of time come upon the human [when] he was not a mentioned thing?
Transliteration: h^{a}l atā ^{ʿa}lā al-insān^{i} ḥīn^{un} m^{i}n^{a} al-d^{a}hr^{i} l^{a}m y^{a}k^{u}n sh^{a}y^{ʾan} m^{a}dhkūrā
Pronunciation: h^{a}l atā ^{ʿa}lā al-insān^{i} ḥīn^{un} m^{i}n^{a} al-d^{a}hr^{i} l^{a}m y^{a}k^{u}n sh^{a}y^{ʾan} m^{a}dhkūrā

H^{a}l (has it...?, is it true that...?) *atā* (it came) *^{a}lā* (upon) *al-insān^{i}* (the human) *ḥīn^{un}* (a period [of time], a point [in time]) *m^{i}n^{a}* (of) *al-d^{a}hr^{i}* (time, eternity) *l^{a}m* (not) *y^{a}k^{u}n* (was) *sh^{a}y^{an}* (a thing) *m^{a}dhkūrā* (remembered).

This verse asks humans the rhetorical question if there was ever a time they were not something that was not mentioned. It is reminding humans that there was a time when they did not even exist.

Verse 2

إِنَّا خَلَقْنَا ٱلْإِنسَٰنَ مِن نُّطْفَةٍ أَمْشَاجٍ نَّبْتَلِيهِ فَجَعَلْنَٰهُ سَمِيعًۢا بَصِيرًا

Indeed We created the human from a sperm-drop mixture [so that] we [may] test him so we made him hearing and seeing.
Transliteration: innā kh^{a}l^{a}q-nā al-insān^{a} m^{i}n n^{u}ṭf^{a}t^{in} amshāj^{in} n^{a}bt^{a}lī-h^{i} f^{a}-j^{aʿa}lnā-h^{u} s^{a}mī^{ʿan} b^{a}ṣ^{i}rā
Pronunciation: in-nā kh^{a}-l^{a}q-n^{a}l-in-sā-n^{a} m^{i}n n^{u}ṭ-f^{a}-t^{in} am-shā-j^{in} n^{a}b-t^{a}-lī-h^{i} f^{a}-j^{a}-^{ʿa}l-nā-h^{u} s^{a}-mī-^{ʿan} b^{a}-ṣ^{i}-rā

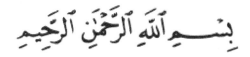

Innā (indeed We) kh^{a}l^{a}q-nā (We created) al-insān^{a} (the human) m^{i}n (from) n^{u}ṭf^{a}t^{in} (a sperm-drop) amshāj^{in} (mixed) n^{a}bt^{a}lī-h^{i} (We test him) f^{a}-j^{aʿa}lnā-h^{u} (so We made him) s^{a}mī^{ʿan} (hearing [i.e. able to hear]) b^{a}ṣ^{i}rā (seeing).

Verse 3

إِنَّا هَدَيْنَٰهُ ٱلسَّبِيلَ إِمَّا شَاكِرًا وَإِمَّا كَفُورًا

Indeed We guided him to the way, whether grateful or ungrateful
Transliteration: innā h^{a}d^{a}ynā-h^{u} al-s^{a}bīl^{a} immā shāk^{i}r^{an} wa-immā k^{a}fūrā
Pronunciation: in-nā h^{a}-d^{a}y-nā-h^{u}s-s^{a}-bī-l^{a} im-mā shā-k^{i}-r^{an} wa-im-mā k^{a}-fū-rā

Innā (indeed We) *h^{a}d^{a}ynā-h^{u}* (guided him [to]) *al-s^{a}bīl^{a}* (the way) *immā* (whether) *shāk^{i}r^{an}* (grateful) *wa-immā k^{a}fūrā* (or whether ungrateful).

Verse 4

إِنَّآ أَعْتَدْنَا لِلْكَٰفِرِينَ سَلَٰسِلَا۟ وَأَغْلَٰلًا وَسَعِيرًا

Indeed We have prepared for the deniers chains, shackles and a blaze
Transliteartion: innā a^{ʿ}t^{a}d-nā l^{i}-al-kāf^{i}rīn^{a} s^{a}lās^{i}l^{a} w^{a}-aghlāl^{an} w^{a}-s^{aʿ}īrā
Pronunciation: in-nā a^{ʿ}-t^{a}d-nā l^{i}l-kā-f^{i}-rī-n^{a} s^{a}-lā-s^{i}-l^{a} w^{a}-agh-lā-*l^{aw}* w^{a}-s^{a}-ʿī-rā

Innā (indeed we) *aʿt^{a}d-nā* (we prepared) *l^{i}-al-kāf^{i}rīn^{a}* (for the deniers) *s^{a}lās^{i}l^{a}* (chains) *w^{a}-aghlāl^{an}* (shackles) *w^{a}-s^{a}ʿīrā* (and a blaze).

While *s^{a}lās^{i}l^{a}* appears to have an *alif* at the end, it is not pronounced in the common reading of the Quran.

Verse 5

إِنَّ ٱلْأَبْرَارَ يَشْرَبُونَ مِن كَأْسٍ كَانَ مِزَاجُهَا كَافُورًا

Indeed the righteous drink of a cup its mixture is of camphor
Transliteartion: inn^{a} al-abrār^{a} y^{a}shr^{a}būn^{a} m^{i}n k^{aʾ}s^{in} kān^{a} m^{i}zāj^{u}-hā kāfūrā
Pronunciation: in-n^{a}l-ab-rā-r^{a} y^{a}sh-r^{a}-bū-n^{a} m^{i}n k^{aʾ}-s^{in} kā-n^{a} m^{i}-zā-j^{u}-hā kā-fū-rā

Inn^{a} (indeed) *al-abrār^{a}* (the righteous) *y^{a}shr^{a}būn^{a}* (they drink) *m^{i}n* (from) *k^{aʾ}s^{in}* (a cup) *kān^{a}* (is/was) *m^{i}zāj^{u}-hā* (its mixture) *kāfūrā* (camphor).

Verse 6

عَيْنًا يَشْرَبُ بِهَا عِبَادُ ٱللَّهِ يُفَجِّرُونَهَا تَفْجِيرًا

A spring the servants of God drink by [which] they make gush forth abundantly.
Transliteration: ^{ʿa}yn^{an} y^{a}shr^{a}b^{u} b^{i}-hā ^{ʿi}b^{a}d^{u} allāh^{i} y^{u}f^{a}jj^{i}rūn^{a}-hā t^{a}fjīrā
Pronunciation: ^{ʿa}y-n^{an} y^{a}sh-r^{a}-b^{u} b^{i}-hā ^{ʿi}-b^{a}-d^{u}l-lā-h^{i} y^{u}-f^{a}j-j^{i}-rū-n^{a}-hā t^{a}f-jī-rā

^{ʿa}yn^{an} (a spring) *y^{a}shr^{a}b^{u}* (drinks) *b^{i}-hā* (by it) *^{ʿi}b^{a}d^{u}* (the servants [of]) *allāh^{i}* (God) *y^{u}f^{a}jj^{i}rūn^{a}-hā* (they cause it to gush forth) *t^{a}fjīrā* (an extreme gushing forth).

The word *^{ʿa}yn* means both "eye" and "spring" (a place where water comes out of the ground).

Verse 7

يُوفُونَ بِٱلنَّذْرِ وَيَخَافُونَ يَوْمًا كَانَ شَرُّهُۥ مُسْتَطِيرًا

They fulfill their vows and fear a day whose evil will be widespread
Transliteration: yūfūn^{a} b^{i}-al-n^{a}dhr^{i} w^{a}-y^{a}khāfūn^{a} y^{a}wm^{an} kān^{a} sh^{a}rr^{u}-h^{u} m^{u}st^{a}ṭīrā
Pronunciation: yū-fū-n^{a} b^{i}n-n^{a}dh-r^{i} w^{a}-y^{a}-khā-fū-n^{a} y^{a}w-m^{an} kā-n^{a} sh^{a}r-r^{u}-h^{u} m^{u}s-t^{a}-ṭī-rā

Yūfūn^{a} (they fulfill) *b^{i}-al-n^{a}dhr^{i}* (their vows) *w^{a}-y^{a}khāfūn^{a}* (and they fear) *y^{a}wm^{an}* (a day) *kān^{a}* (is/was) *sh^{a}rr^{u}-h^{u}* (its evil) *m^{u}st^{a}ṭīrā* (widespread).

Verse 8

وَيُطْعِمُونَ ٱلطَّعَامَ عَلَىٰ حُبِّهِۦ مِسْكِينًا وَيَتِيمًا وَأَسِيرًا

They feed food despite their love for it to the poor, the orphan and the prisoner
Transliteration: w^{a}-y^{u}ṭ^{ʿi}mūna al-ṭ^{aʿ}ām^{a} ^{ʿa}lā ḥ^{u}bb^{i}-h^{i} m^{i}skīn^{an} w^{a}-y^{a}tīm^{an} w^{a}-asīrā
Pronunciation: w^{a}-y^{u}ṭ-^{ʿi}-mū-naṭ-ṭ^{a}-ʿā-m^{a} ^{ʿa}-lā ḥ^{u}b-b^{i}-h^{i} m^{i}s-kī-n^{an} w^{a}-y^{a}-tī-m^{an} w^{a}-a-sī-rā

W^{a}-y^{u}ṭ^{ʿi}mūna (and they feed) *al-ṭ^{a}ʿām^{a}* (food) *^{ʿa}lā ḥ^{u}bb^{i}-h^{i}* (despite its love) *m^{i}skīn^{an}* (a needy person) *w^{a}-y^{a}tīm^{an}* (an orphan) *w^{a}-asīrā* (and a prisoner).

The phrase *^{ʿa}lā ḥ^{u}bb^{i}* means “despite their love for it”. It means that these people give away food even though they need it themselves. According to some exegetes the phrase could also mean “out of His love”, i.e. they give away food out of love for God. The question is what the pronoun *h^{i}* in *^{ʿa}lā ḥ^{u}bb^{i}-h^{i}* refers to. It could either refer to the aforementioned food, or to God.

Verse 9

إِنَّمَا نُطْعِمُكُمْ لِوَجْهِ ٱللَّهِ لَا نُرِيدُ مِنكُمْ جَزَآءً وَلَا شُكُورًا

Indeed we feed you only for the [sake of the] Countenance of God, we do not want from you a reward or thanks
Transliteration: inn^{a}-mā n^{u}ṭ^{ʿi}m^{u}-k^{u}m l^{i}-w^{a}jh^{i} allāh^{i} lā n^{u}rīd^{u} m^{i}n-k^{u}m j^{a}zā^{ʾan} w^{a}-lā sh^{u}kūrā
Pronunciation: in-n^{a}-mā n^{u}ṭ-^{ʿi}-m^{u}-k^{u}m l^{i}-w^{a}j-h^{i}l-lā-h^{i} lā n^{u}-rī-d^{u} m^{i}n-k^{u}m j^{a}-zā-^{ʾan} w^{a}-lā sh^{u}-kū-rā

Inn^{a}-mā (indeed only) *n^{u}ṭ^{ʿi}m^{u}-k^{u}m* (we feed you) *l^{i}-w^{a}jh^{i}* (for the Countenance [of]) *allāh^{i}* (God) lā (do not) *n^{u}rīd^{u}* (we want) *m^{i}n-k^{u}m* (from you) *j^{a}zā^{ʾan}* (a reward) *w^{a}-lā* (and no) *sh^{u}kūrā* (thanks).

The phrase *inn^{a}-mā* means “Indeed it is a fact that...only”

Verse 10

إِنَّا نَخَافُ مِن رَّبِّنَا يَوْمًا عَبُوسًا قَمْطَرِيرًا

Indeed we fear from our Lord a day grim and distressful

Transliteration: innā n^{a}khāf^{u} m^{i}n r^{a}bb^{i}-nā y^{a}wm^{an} ^{ʿa}būs^{an} q^{a}mṭ^{a}rīrā

Pronunciation: in-nā n^{a}-khā-f^{u} m^{i}n r^{a}b-b^{i}-nā y^{a}w-m^{an} ^{ʿa}-bū-s^{an} q^{a}m-ṭ^{a}-rī-rā

Innā (indeed we) *n^{a}khāf^{u}* (we fear) *m^{i}n* (from) *r^{a}bb^{i}-nā* (our Lord) *y^{a}wm^{an}* (a day) *^{ʿa}būs^{an}* (grim, austere) *q^{a}mṭ^{a}rīrā* (distressful).

This page intentionally left blank

Lesson 35 Review

بِسْمِ ٱللَّهِ ٱلرَّحْمَٰنِ ٱلرَّحِيمِ

هَلْ أَتَىٰ عَلَى ٱلْإِنسَٰنِ حِينٌ مِّنَ ٱلدَّهْرِ لَمْ يَكُن شَيْـًٔا مَّذْكُورًا

H^{a}l (has it...?, is it true that...?) *atā* (it came) *^{a}lā* (upon) *al-insān^{i}* (the human) *ḥīn^{un}* (a period [of time], a point [in time]) *m^{i}n^{a}* (of) *al-d^{a}hr^{i}* (time, eternity) *l^{a}m* (not) *y^{a}k^{u}n* (was) *sh^{a}y^{ʾan}* (a thing) *m^{a}dhkūrā* (remembered).

إِنَّا خَلَقْنَا ٱلْإِنسَٰنَ مِن نُّطْفَةٍ أَمْشَاجٍ نَّبْتَلِيهِ فَجَعَلْنَٰهُ سَمِيعًۢا بَصِيرًا

Innā (indeed We) kh^{a}l^{a}q-nā (We created) al-insān^{a} (the human) m^{i}n (from) n^{u}ṭf^{a}t^{in} (a sperm-drop) amshāj^{in} (mixed) n^{a}bt^{a}lī-h^{i} (We test him) f^{a}-j^{aʿa}lnā-h^{u} (so We made him) s^{a}mī^{ʿan} (hearing [i.e. able to hear]) b^{a}ṣ^{i}rā (seeing).

إِنَّا هَدَيْنَٰهُ ٱلسَّبِيلَ إِمَّا شَاكِرًا وَإِمَّا كَفُورًا

Innā (indeed We) *h^{a}d^{a}ynā-h^{u}* (guided him [to]) *al-s^{a}bīl^{a}* (the way) *immā* (whether) *shāk^{i}r^{an}* (grateful) *wa-immā k^{a}fūrā* (or whether ungrateful).

إِنَّآ أَعْتَدْنَا لِلْكَٰفِرِينَ سَلَٰسِلَا۟ وَأَغْلَٰلًا وَسَعِيرًا

Innā (indeed we) *aʿt^{a}d-nā* (we prepared) *l^{i}-al-kāf^{i}rīn^{a}* (for the deniers) *s^{a}lās^{i}l^{a}* (chains) *w^{a}-aghlāl^{an}* (shackles) *w^{a}-s^{a}ʿīrā* (and a blaze).

إِنَّ ٱلْأَبْرَارَ يَشْرَبُونَ مِن كَأْسٍ كَانَ مِزَاجُهَا كَافُورًا

Inn^{a} (indeed) *al-abrār*^{a} (the righteous) *y*^{a}*shr*^{a}*būn*^{a} (they drink) *m*^{i}*n* (from) *k*^{a}*ʾs*^{in} (a cup) *kān*^{a} (is/was) *m*^{i}*zāj*^{u}*-hā* (its mixture) *kāfūrā* (camphor).

عَيْنًا يَشْرَبُ بِهَا عِبَادُ ٱللَّهِ يُفَجِّرُونَهَا تَفْجِيرًا

^{a}*yn*^{an} (a spring) *y*^{a}*shr*^{a}*b*^{u} (drinks) *b*^{i}*-hā* (by it) ^{i}*b*^{a}*d*^{u} (the servants [of]) *allāh*^{i} (God) *y*^{u}*f*^{a}*jj*^{i}*rūn*^{a}*-hā* (they cause it to gush forth) *t*^{a}*fjīrā* (an extreme gushing forth).

يُوفُونَ بِٱلنَّذْرِ وَيَخَافُونَ يَوْمًا كَانَ شَرُّهُۥ مُسْتَطِيرًا

Yūfūn^{a} (they fulfill) *b*^{i}*-al-n*^{a}*dhr*^{i} (their vows) *w*^{a}*-y*^{a}*khāfūn*^{a} (and they fear) *y*^{a}*wm*^{an} (a day) *kān*^{a} (is/was) *sh*^{a}*rr*^{u}*-h*^{u} (its evil) *m*^{u}*st*^{a}*ṭīrā* (widespread).

وَيُطْعِمُونَ ٱلطَّعَامَ عَلَىٰ حُبِّهِۦ مِسْكِينًا وَيَتِيمًا وَأَسِيرًا

W^{a}*-y*^{u}*ṭ*^{i}*mūna* (and they feed) *al-ṭ*^{a}*ʿām*^{a} (food) ^{a}*lā ḥ*^{u}*bb*^{i}*-h*^{i} (despite its love) *m*^{i}*skīn*^{an} (a needy person) *w*^{a}*-y*^{a}*tīm*^{an} (an orphan) *w*^{a}*-asīrā* (and a prisoner).

إِنَّمَا نُطْعِمُكُمْ لِوَجْهِ ٱللَّهِ لَا نُرِيدُ مِنكُمْ جَزَآءً وَلَا شُكُورًا

Inn^{a}*-mā* (indeed only) *n*^{u}*ṭ*^{i}*m*^{u}*-k*^{u}*m* (we feed you) *l*^{i}*-w*^{a}*jh*^{i} (for the Countenance [of]) *allāh*^{i} (God) lā (do not) *n*^{u}*rīd*^{u} (we want) *m*^{i}*n-k*^{u}*m* (from you) *j*^{a}*zā*^{an} (a reward) *w*^{a}*-lā* (and no) *sh*^{u}*kūrā* (thanks).

إِنَّا نَخَافُ مِن رَّبِّنَا يَوْمًا عَبُوسًا قَمْطَرِيرًا

Innā (indeed we) *n*^{a}*khāf*^{u} (we fear) *m*^{i}*n* (from) *r*^{a}*bb*^{i}*-nā* (our Lord) *y*^{a}*wm*^{an} (a day) ʿ^{a}*būs*^{an} (grim, austere) *q*^{a}*mṭ*^{a}*rīrā* (distressful).

This page intentionally left blank

Lesson 36: al-Insān Part 2

Verse 11

فَوَقَىٰهُمُ ٱللَّهُ شَرَّ ذَٰلِكَ ٱلْيَوْمِ وَلَقَّىٰهُمْ نَضْرَةً وَسُرُورًا

So God protected them from the evil of that day and granted them radiance and happiness
Transliteration: f^{a}-w^{a}qqā-h^{u}m^{u} allāh^{u} sh^{a}rr^{a} dhāl^{i}k^{a} al-y^{a}wm^{i} w^{a}-l^{a}qqā-h^{u}m n^{a}ḍr^{a}t^{an} w^{a}-s^{u}rūrā
Pronunciation: f^{a}-w^{a}q-qā-h^{u}-m^{u}l-lā-h^{u} sh^{a}r-r^{a} dhā-l^{i}-k^{a}l-y^{a}w-m^{i} w^{a}-l^{a}q-qā-h^{u}m n^{a}ḍ-r^{a}-t^{an} w^{a}-s^{u}-rū-rā

F^{a}-w^{a}qqā-h^{u}m^{u} (so He protected them) *allāh^{u}* (God) *sh^{a}rr^{a}* (the evil) *dhāl^{i}k^{a}* (that) *al-y^{a}wm^{i}* (day) *w^{a}-l^{a}qqā-h^{u}m* (and caused them to meet with, granted them) *n^{a}ḍr^{a}t^{an}* (radiance) *w^{a}-s^{u}rūrā* (and happiness).

Verse 12

وَجَزَىٰهُم بِمَا صَبَرُوا۟ جَنَّةً وَحَرِيرًا

and He rewarded them for their patience with a garden and silk
Transliteration: w^{a}-j^{a}zā-h^{u}m b^{i}-mā ṣ^{a}b^{a}rū j^{a}nn^{a}t^{an} w^{a} ḥ^{a}rīrā
Pronunciation: w^{a}-j^{a}-zā-h^{u}m b^{i}-mā ṣ^{a}-b^{a}-rū j^{a}n-n^{a}-t^{an} w^{a} ḥ^{a}-rī-rā

W^{a}-j^{a}zā-h^{u}m (and He rewarded them with) *b^{i}-mā ṣ^{a}b^{a}rū* (for their patience) *j^{a}nn^{a}t^{an}* (a garden) *w^{a} ḥ^{a}rīrā* (and a silk, and silk).

The phrase *b^{i}-mā ṣ^{a}b^{a}rū* means "for their patience", "for the fact that they were patient".

Verse 13

مُّتَّكِـِٔينَ فِيهَا عَلَى ٱلْأَرَآئِكِ ۖ لَا يَرَوْنَ فِيهَا شَمْسًا وَلَا زَمْهَرِيرًا

reclining upon couches; they see no [burning] sun or [freezing] cold

Transliteration: m^{u}tt^{a}k^{i}ʾīn^{a} fī-hā ^{ca}lā al-arāʾ^{i}k^{i} l^{a} y^{a}r^{a}wn^{a} fī-hā sh^{a}ms^{an} w^{a}-lā z^{a}mh^{a}rīrā

Pronunciation: m^{u}t-t^{a}-k^{i}-ʾī-n^{a} fī-hā ^{ca}-l^{a}l-a-rā-ʾ^{i}-k^{i} l^{a} y^{a}-r^{a}w-n^{a} fī-hā sh^{a}m-s^{an} w^{a}-lā z^{a}m-h^{a}rī-rā

M^{u}tt^{a}k^{i}īn^{a} ([they are] reclining ones) *fī-hā* (in it) *^{a}lā* (upon) *al-arā^{i}k^{i}* (couches) *l^{a} y^{a}r^{a}wn^{a}* (they do not see) *fī-hā* (in it) *sh^{a}ms^{an}* (a sun) *w^{a}-lā* (and not) *z^{a}mh^{a}rīrā* (a freezing cold).

The word *m^{u}tt^{a}k^{i}īn* is the plural of the agent noun (*ism fāʿil*) *m^{u}tt^{a}k^{i}ʾ* ("one who is reclining", "reclining person"). This word comes from the verb *itt^{a}k^{a}ʾ^{a}* ("he reclined", "he leaned onto").

اِتَّكَأَ يَتَّكِئُ اِتِّكَاء مُتَّكِئ

From right to left: he reclined; he reclines; to recline; one who reclines.

The word arāʾ^{i}k ("decorated couches") is the plural of *arīk^{a}*.

أَرِيكَة

Verse 14

وَدَانِيَةً عَلَيْهِمْ ظِلَالُهَا وَذُلِّلَتْ قُطُوفُهَا تَذْلِيلًا

And near above them are its shades and its fruit clusters will be made to hang very low

Transliteration: wa-dān^{i}y^{a}t^{an} ^{ca}l^{a}y-h^{i}m ẓ^{i}lāl^{u}ḥā w^{a}-dh^{u}ll^{i}l^{a}-t q^{u}ṭūf^{u}-hā t^{a}dhlīlā

Pronunciation: wa-dā-n^{i}-y^{a}-t^{an} ^{ca}-l^{a}y-h^{i}m ẓ^{i}-lā-l^{u}-ḥā w^{a}-dh^{u}l-l^{i}-l^{a}t q^{u}-ṭū-f^{u}-hā t^{a}dh-lī-lā

Wa-dān^{i}y^{a}t^{an} (and [are] near, and [are] within reach) *^{a}l^{a}y-h^{i}m* (upon them) *ẓ^{i}lāl^{u}ḥā* (its shades) *w^{a}-dh^{u}ll^{i}l^{a}-t* (and were lowered) *q^{u}ṭūf^{u}-hā* (its fruit clusters) *t^{a}dhlīlā* (an extreme lowering).

The verb *dh^{u}ll^{i}l^{a}-t* means "it was humbled", "it was lowered", while *t^{a}dhlīl* means "to humble". The phrase *dh^{u}ll^{i}l^{a}-t...t^{a}dhlīlā* is an emphatic way of saying something is very humbled or lowered.

Verse 15

وَيُطَافُ عَلَيْهِم بِـَٔانِيَةٍ مِّن فِضَّةٍ وَأَكْوَابٍ كَانَتْ قَوَارِيرَا۠

And will be circulated upon them vessels of silver and cups that are glass
Transliteration: w^{a}-y^{u}ṭāf^{u} ^{ca}l^{a}y-h^{i}m b^{i}-ān^{i}y^{a}t^{in} m^{i}n f^{i}ḍḍ^{a}t^{in} w^{a}-akwāb^{in} kān^{a}t q^{a}wārīrā
Pronunciation: w^{a}-y^{u}-ṭā-f^{u} ^{ca}-l^{a}y-h^{i}m b^{i}-ā-n^{i}-y^{a}-t^{in} m^{i}n f^{i}ḍ-ḍ^{a}-t^{in} w^{a}-ak-wā-b^{in} kā-n^{a}t q^{a}-wā-rī-rā

W^{a}-y^{u}ṭāf^{u} (and is circulated) *^{ca}l^{a}y-h^{i}m* (upon them) *b^{i}-ān^{i}y^{a}t^{in}* (with vessels) *m^{i}n* (of) *f^{i}ḍḍ^{a}t^{in}* (silver) *w^{a}-akwāb^{in}* (and cups) *kān^{a}t* (that were) *q^{a}wārīrā* (glass, crystal).

The word ān^{i}y^{a} is the plural of *inā'* ("container", "vessel").

إِنَاء

The word *akwāb* is the plural of *kūb* ("cup").

كُوْب

The word *q^{a}wārīr* is the plural of *qārūr^{a}* ("glass", "crystal").

قَارُوْرَة

The round symbol at the end of the verse tells reciters to not pronounce the *alif* if they continue their recitation to the next verse without pausing.

Verse 16

قَوَارِيرَا۠ مِن فِضَّةٍ قَدَّرُوهَا تَقْدِيرًا

Glasses of silver, they measured with accurate measuring
Transliteration: q^{a}wārīr^{a} m^{i}n f^{i}ḍḍ^{a}t^{in} q^{a}dd^{a}rū-hā t^{a}qdīrā
Pronunciation: q^{a}-wā-rī-r^{a} m^{i}n f^{i}ḍ-ḍ^{a}-t^{in} q^{a}d-d^{a}-rū-hā t^{a}q-dī-rā

Q^{a}wārīr^{a} (glasses, crystals) *m^{i}n* (of) *f^{i}ḍḍ^{a}t^{in}* (silver) *q^{a}dd^{a}rū-hā* (they measured it) *t^{a}qdīrā* (a measuring).

Since *q^{a}wārīr* refers to a type of glass or crystal, "glasses of silver" may refer to a type of glass that has silver mixed with it. The mentioned measure may refer to the amount of drink in the vessel being perfectly measured to satisfy.

Verse 17

وَيُسْقَوْنَ فِيهَا كَأْسًا كَانَ مِزَاجُهَا زَنجَبِيلًا

And in it they are watered [with] a cup [of wine] whose mixture is ginger
Transliteration: wa-y^{u}sq^{a}wn^{a} fī-hā k^{a}ʾs^{an} kān^{a} m^{i}zāj^{u}-hā z^{a}nj^{a}bīlā
Pronunciation: wa-y^{u}s-q^{a}w-n^{a} fī-hā k^{a}ʾ-s^{an} kā-n^{a} m^{i}-zā-j^{u}-hā z^{a}n-j^{a}-bī-lā

Wa-y^{u}sq^{a}wn^{a} (and they are fed liquid) *fī-hā* (in it, i.e. in the garden) *k^{a}ʾs^{an}* (a cup) *kān^{a}* (it was) *m^{i}zāj^{u}-hā* (its mixture) *z^{a}nj^{a}bīlā* (ginger).

The verb *y^{u}sq^{a}wn^{a}* is the plural passive form of *saqā* ("he watered", "he fed someone a liquid").

سَقَى يَسْقِي

From right to left: he fed liquid [to someone]; he feeds liquid [to someone].

The word *z^{a}nj^{a}bīl* ("ginger") may either refer to actual ginger (thus the wine is ginger-flavored), or it may be the name of a spring in Paradise.

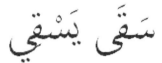

Verse 18

عَيْنًا فِيهَا تُسَمَّىٰ سَلْسَبِيلًا

A spring in it named Salsabīl
Transliteration: ʿ^{a}yn^{an} fī-hā t^{u}s^{a}mmā s^{a}ls^{a}bīlā
Pronunciation: ʿ^{a}y-n^{an} fī-hā t^{u}-s^{a}m-mā s^{a}l-s^{a}-bī-lā

ʿ^{a}yn^{an} (a spring) *fī-hā* (in it) *t^{u}s^{a}mmā* (it is named) *s^{a}ls^{a}bīlā*.

Verse 19

وَيَطُوفُ عَلَيْهِمْ وِلْدَانٌ مُّخَلَّدُونَ إِذَا رَأَيْتَهُمْ حَسِبْتَهُمْ لُؤْلُؤًا مَّنثُورًا

And circulate upon them immortal children; if you saw them you would think them scattered pearls
Transliteration: w^{a}-y^{a}ṭūf^{u} ʿ^{a}l^{a}y-h^{i}m w^{i}ldān^{un} m^{u}kh^{a}ll^{a}dūn^{a} idhā r^{aʾa}yt^{a}-h^{u}m ḥ^{a}s^{i}bt^{a}-h^{u}m l^{uʾ}l^{uʾan} m^{a}nthūrā
Pronunciation: w^{a}-y^{a}-ṭū-f^{u} ʿ^{a}-l^{a}y-h^{i}m w^{i}l-dā-n^{un} m^{u}-kh^{a}l-l^{a}-dū-n^{a} i-dhā r^{a}-^{ʾa}y-t^{a}-h^{u}m ḥ^{a}-s^{i}b-t^{a}-h^{u}m l^{uʾ}-l^{u}-^{ʾan} m^{a}n-thū-rā

W^{a}-y^{a}ṭūf^{u} (and circulate) *ʿ^{a}l^{a}y-h^{i}m* (upon them) *w^{i}ldān^{un}* (children) *m^{u}kh^{a}ll^{a}dūn^{a}* (immortalized) *idhā* (if) *r^{aʾa}yt^{a}-h^{u}m* (you saw them) *ḥ^{a}s^{i}bt^{a}-h^{u}m* (you thought them, you considered them, you assumed them to be) *l^{uʾ}l^{uʾan}* (pearls) *m^{a}nthūrā* (scattered).

The word *w^{i}ldān* ("children") is the plural of *w^{a}līd* ("child", "offspring", literally "begotten [thing]"). While *w^{i}ldān* is generally interpreted as "boys", the gender is not specifically determined by the word. But in verse 52:24 the Quran refers to these same children as *gh^{i}lmān* ("boys").

Verse 20

وَإِذَا رَأَيْتَ ثَمَّ رَأَيْتَ نَعِيمًا وَمُلْكًا كَبِيرًا

And if you saw in that direction, you will see a bliss and a great kingdom

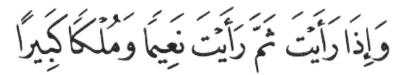

Transliteration: w^{a}-idhā r^{aʾa}yt^{a} th^{a}mm^{a} r^{aʾa}yt^{a} n^{aʿ}īm^{an} w^{a}-m^{u}lk^{an} k^{a}bīrā

Pronunciation: w^{a}-i-dhā r^{a}-^{ʾa}y-t^{a} th^{a}m-m^{a} r^{a}-^{ʾa}yt^{a} n^{a}-^{ʿ}ī-m^{an} w^{a}-m^{u}l-k^{an} k^{a}-bīrā

W^{a}-idhā (and if) *r$^{a\,ʾa}$yt^{a}* (you saw) *th^{a}mm^{a}* (in that direction) *r$^{a\,ʾa}$yt^{a}* (you saw) *n$^{a\,ʿ}$īm^{an}* (blessings, bliss) *w^{a}-m^{u}lk^{an}* (and a kingdom) *k^{a}bīrā* (large, great).

The word *th^{a}mm^{a}* means "in that direction", "toward that direction".

Lesson 36 Review

فَوَقَىٰهُمُ ٱللَّهُ شَرَّ ذَٰلِكَ ٱلْيَوْمِ وَلَقَّىٰهُمْ نَضْرَةً وَسُرُورًا

F^{a}-w^{a}qqā-h^{u}m^{u} (so He protected them) *allāh^{u}* (God) *sh^{a}rr^{a}* (the evil) *dhāl^{i}k^{a}* (that) *al-y^{a}wm^{i}* (day) *w^{a}-l^{a}qqā-h^{u}m* (and caused them to meet with, granted them) *n^{a}ḍr^{a}t^{an}* (radiance) *w^{a}-s^{u}rūrā* (and happiness).

وَجَزَىٰهُم بِمَا صَبَرُوا۟ جَنَّةً وَحَرِيرًا

W^{a}-j^{a}zā-h^{u}m (and He rewarded them with) *b^{i}-mā ṣ^{a}b^{a}rū* (for their patience) *j^{a}nn^{a}t^{an}* (a garden) *w^{a} ḥ^{a}rīrā* (and a silk, and silk).

مُّتَّكِـِٔينَ فِيهَا عَلَى ٱلْأَرَآئِكِ ۖ لَا يَرَوْنَ فِيهَا شَمْسًا وَلَا زَمْهَرِيرًا

M^{u}tt^{a}k^{i}īn^{a} ([they are] reclining ones) *fī-hā* (in it) *^{a}lā* (upon) *al-arā^{i}k^{i}* (couches) *l^{a} y^{a}r^{a}wn^{a}* (they do not see) *fī-hā* (in it) *sh^{a}ms^{an}* (a sun) *w^{a}-lā* (and not) *z^{a}mh^{a}rīrā* (a freezing cold).

وَدَانِيَةً عَلَيْهِمْ ظِلَـٰلُهَا وَذُلِّلَتْ قُطُوفُهَا تَذْلِيلًا

Wa-dān^{i}y^{a}t^{an} (and [are] near, and [are] within reach) *^{a}l^{a}y-h^{i}m* (upon them) *ẓ^{i}lāl^{u}ḥā* (its shades) *w^{a}-dh^{u}ll^{i}l^{a}-t* (and were lowered) *q^{u}ṭūf^{u}-hā* (its fruit clusters) *t^{a}dhlīlā* (an extreme lowering).

وَيُطَافُ عَلَيْهِم بِآنِيَةٍ مِّن فِضَّةٍ وَأَكْوَابٍ كَانَتْ قَوَارِيرَا۠

W[a]-y[u]ṭāf[u] (and is circulated) *[a]l[a]y-h[i]m* (upon them) *b[i]-ān[i]y[a]t[in]* (with vessels) *m[i]n* (of) *f[i]ḍḍ[a]t[in]* (silver) *w[a]-akwāb[in]* (and cups) *kān[a]t* (that were) *q[a]wārīrā* (glass, crystal).

قَوَارِيرَا۟ مِن فِضَّةٍ قَدَّرُوهَا تَقْدِيرًا

Q[a]wārīr[a] (glasses, crystals) *m[i]n* (of) *f[i]ḍḍ[a]t[in]* (silver) *q[a]dd[a]rū-hā* (they measured it) *t[a]qdīrā* (a measuring).

وَيُسْقَوْنَ فِيهَا كَأْسًا كَانَ مِزَاجُهَا زَنجَبِيلًا

Wa-y[u]sq[a]wn[a] (and they are fed liquid) *fī-hā* (in it, i.e. in the garden) *k[a]'s[an]* (a cup) *kān[a]* (it was) *m[i]zāj[u]-hā* (its mixture) *z[a]nj[a]bīlā* (ginger).

عَيْنًا فِيهَا تُسَمَّىٰ سَلْسَبِيلًا

[a]yn[an] (a spring) *fī-hā* (in it) *t[u]s[a]mmā* (it is named) *s[a]ls[a]bīlā*.

وَيَطُوفُ عَلَيْهِمْ وِلْدَٰنٌ مُّخَلَّدُونَ إِذَا رَأَيْتَهُمْ حَسِبْتَهُمْ لُؤْلُؤًا مَّنثُورًا

W[a]-y[a]ṭūf[u] (and circulate) *[a]l[a]y-h[i]m* (upon them) *w[i]ldān[un]* (children) *m[u]kh[a]ll[a]dūn[a]* (immortalized) *idhā* (if) *r[a]'[a]yt[a]-h[u]m* (you saw them) *ḥ[a]s[i]bt[a]-h[u]m* (you thought them, you considered them, you assumed them to be) *l[u]'l[u]'[an]* (pearls) *m[a]nthūrā* (scattered).

وَإِذَا رَأَيْتَ ثَمَّ رَأَيْتَ نَعِيمًا وَمُلْكًا كَبِيرًا

W^{a}*-idhā* (and if) *r*$^{a\,ʾa}$*yt*^{a} (you saw) *th*^{a}*mm*^{a} (in that direction) *r*$^{a\,ʾa}$*yt*^{a} (you saw) *n*^{a}*ʿīm*^{an} (blessings, bliss) *w*^{a}*-m*^{u}*lk*^{an} (and a kingdom) *k*^{a}*bīrā* (large, great).

This page intentionally left blank

Lesson 37: al-Insān Part 3

Verse 21, part 1

عَٰلِيَهُمْ ثِيَابُ سُندُسٍ خُضْرٌ وَإِسْتَبْرَقٌ ۖ

Upon them is clothing of fine green silk and heavy brocade
Transliteration: ʿāl^{i}y^{a}-h^{u}m th^{i}yāb^{u} s^{u}nd^{u}s^{in} kh^{u}ḍr^{un} w^{a}-ist^{a}br^{a}q
Pronunciation: ʿā-l^{i}-y^{a}-h^{u}m th^{i}-yā-b^{u} s^{u}n-d^{u}-s^{in} kh^{u}ḍ-r^{un} w^{a}-is-t^{a}b-r^{a}q

ʿāl^{i}y^{a}-h^{u}m (upon them) *th^{i}yāb^{u}* (clothing [of]) *s^{u}nd^{u}s^{in}* (fine silk) *kh^{u}ḍr^{un}* (green) *w^{a}-ist^{a}br^{a}q* (and silk brocade).

The phrase *ʿāl^{i}y^{a}-h^{u}m* has lead to controversy because it literally means "their higher part". Some consider it to be used here as a non-standard variant of *^{a}l^{a}y-h^{i}m* ("upon them").

The word *s^{u}nd^{u}s* means "fine silk", while *ist^{a}br^{a}q* means "silk brocade", a rich silk with raised patterns on it. The word *kh^{u}ḍr* ("green ones") is the plural of *akhḍ^{a}r*, which means "green".

Verse 21, part 2

وَحُلُّوٓا۟ أَسَاوِرَ مِن فِضَّةٍ وَسَقَىٰهُمْ رَبُّهُمْ شَرَابًا طَهُورًا

And they were adorned with bracelets of silver and their Lord watered them with a pure drink
Transliteration: w^{a}-ḥ^{u}llū asāw^{i}r^{a} m^{i}n f^{i}ḍḍ^{a}t^{in} w^{a}-s^{a}qā-h^{u}m r^{a}bb^{u}-h^{u}m sh^{a}rāb^{an} ṭ^{a}hūrā
Pronunciation: w^{a}-ḥ^{u}l-lū a-sā-w^{i}-r^{a} m^{i}n f^{i}ḍ-ḍ^{a}-t^{in} w^{a}-s^{a}-qā-h^{u}m r^{a}b-b^{u}-h^{u}m sh^{a}-rā-b^{an} ṭ^{a}-hū-rā

W^{a}-ḥ^{u}llū (and they were adorned with) *asāw^{i}r^{a}* (bracelets) *m^{i}n* (of) *f^{i}ḍḍ^{a}t^{in}* (silver) *w^{a}-s^{a}qā-h^{u}m* (and He watered them) *r^{a}bb^{u}-h^{u}m* (their Lord) *sh^{a}rāb^{an}* (a drink) *ṭ^{a}hūrā* (pure).

The verb *ḥ^{u}llū* is the plural passive of *ḥ^{a}llā* ("he adorned [with jewelry, etc.]", "he placed decorations on [it]").

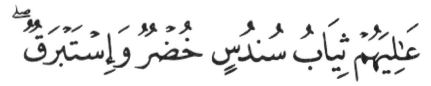

حَلَّى

The word *asāw^{i}r* is the plural of *asw^{i}r^{a}* ("bracelet", "bangle").

أَسْوِرَة

The word *sh^{a}rāb* means "drink", from the verb *sh^{a}r^{i}b^{a}* ("he drank").

شَرِبَ يَشْرَبُ

From right to left: he drank; he drinks.

The word *ṭ^{a}hūr* means "pure", from the verb *ṭ^{a}h^{u}r^{a}* ("it was pure", "it became pure").

طَهُرَ ، يَطْهُرُ ، طَهَارَة وَطُهْر ، طَاهِر وطَهُوْر

From right to left: it was pure; it is pure; purity (two forms); pure (two forms).

Verse 22

إِنَّ هَٰذَا كَانَ لَكُمْ جَزَآءً وَكَانَ سَعْيُكُم مَّشْكُورًا

Indeed this is for you a reward and your effort has been appreciated
Transliteration: inn^{a} hādh^{a} kān^{a} l^{a}-k^{u}m j^{a}zā'^{an} w^{a}-kān^{a} s^{a}'y^{u}-k^{u}m m^{a}shkūrā
Pronunciation: in-n^{a} hā-dh^{a} kā-n^{a} l^{a}-k^{u}m j^{a}-zā-'^{an} w^{a}-kā-n^{a} s^{a}'-y^{u}-k^{u}m m^{a}sh-kū-rā

Inn^{a} (indeed) *hādh^{a}* (this) *kān^{a}* (was) *l^{a}-k^{u}m* (for you) *j^{a}zā'^{an}* (a reward) *w^{a}-kān^{a}* (and was) *s^{a}'y^{u}-k^{u}m* (your effort) *m^{a}shkūrā* (appreciated, thanked).

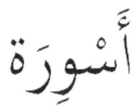

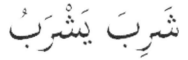

Verse 23

إِنَّا نَحْنُ نَزَّلْنَا عَلَيْكَ ٱلْقُرْءَانَ تَنزِيلًا

Indeed, We have truly sent down the Quran upon you [singular]
Transliteration: innā n^{a}ḥn^{u} n^{a}zz^{a}l-nā ^{ca}l^{a}y-k^{a} al-q^{u}r'ān^{a} t^{a}nzīlā
Pronunciation: in-nā n^{a}ḥ-n^{u} n^{a}z-z^{a}l-nā ^{ca}-l^{a}y-k^{a}l-q^{u}r-'ā-n^{a} t^{a}n-zī-lā

Innā n^{a}ḥn^{u} (indeed we) *n^{a}zz^{a}l-nā* (sent down) *^{ca}l^{a}y-k^{a}* (upon you) *al-q^{u}r'ān^{a}* (the Quran) *t^{a}nzīlā* (a sending down).

The word *innā* means "indeed, we" while *n^{a}ḥn^{u}* also means "we". The additional *n^{a}ḥn^{u}* serves for emphasis. The phrase *n^{a}zz^{a}l-nā...t^{a}nzīlā* literally means "we sent it down...a sending down", it serves for emphasis to repeat the same meaning in this way.

Verse 24

فَٱصْبِرْ لِحُكْمِ رَبِّكَ وَلَا تُطِعْ مِنْهُمْ ءَاثِمًا أَوْ كَفُورًا

So be patient toward the judgment of your Lord and do not obey among them a sinner or rejecter
Transliteration: f^{a}-iṣb^{i}r l^{i}-ḥ^{u}km^{i} r^{a}bb^{i}-k^{a} w^{a}-lā t^{u}ṭ^{ic} m^{i}n-h^{u}m āth^{i}m^{an} aw k^{a}fūrā
Pronunciation: f^{a}ṣ-b^{i}r l^{i}-ḥ^{u}k-m^{i} r^{a}b-b^{i}-k^{a} w^{a}-lā t^{u}-ṭ^{ic} m^{i}n-h^{u}m ā-th^{i}-m^{an} aw k^{a}-fū-rā

F^{a}-iṣb^{i}r (so be patient) *l^{i}* (for, toward) *ḥ^{u}km^{i}* (the judgment [of]) *r^{a}bb^{i}-k^{a}* (your Lord) *w^{a}-lā* (and not) *t^{u}ṭ^{ic}* (you obey) *m^{i}n-h^{u}m* (of them, among them) *āth^{i}m^{an}* (a sinner) *aw k^{a}fūrā* (or a rejecter).

Verse 25

وَٱذْكُرِ ٱسْمَ رَبِّكَ بُكْرَةً وَأَصِيلًا

And remember the Name of your Lord morning and mid-afternoon

Transliteration: w^{a}-udhk^{u}r ism^{a} r^{a}bb^{i}-k^{a} b^{u}kr^{a}t^{an} w^{a}-aṣīlā
Pronunciation: w^{a}dh-k^{u}r is-m^{a} r^{a}b-b^{i}-k^{a} b^{u}k-r^{a}-t^{an} w^{a}-a-ṣī-lā

W^{a}-udhk^{u}r (and remember) *ism^{a}* (the name [of]) *r^{a}bb^{i}-k^{a}* (your Lord) *b^{u}kr^{a}t^{an}* (morning) *w^{a}-aṣīlā* (and mid-afternoon).

The word *b^{u}kr^{a}* literally means "early", "early in the day". The word *aṣīl* refers to the time from the mid-afternoon until sunset.

Verse 26

وَمِنَ ٱلَّيۡلِ فَٱسۡجُدۡ لَهُۥ وَسَبِّحۡهُ لَيۡلٗا طَوِيلًا

And from the night, prostrate to Him and exalt Him a long [part of the] night
Transliteration: w^{a}-m^{i}n^{a} al-l^{a}yl^{i} f^{a}-usj^{u}d l^{a}-h^{u} w^{a}-s^{a}bb^{i}ḥ-h^{u} l^{a}yl^{an} ṭ^{a}wīlā
Pronunciation: w^{a}-m^{i}-n^{a}l-l^{a}y-l^{i} f^{a}s-j^{u}d l^{a}-h^{u} w^{a}-s^{a}b-b^{i}ḥ-h^{u} l^{a}y-l^{an} ṭ^{a}-wī-lā

W^{a}-m^{i}n^{a} (and of) *al-l^{a}yl^{i}* (the night) *f^{a}-usj^{u}d l^{a}-h^{u}* (then prostrate yourself to Him) *w^{a}-s^{a}bb^{i}ḥ-h^{u}* (and exalt Him) *l^{a}yl^{an}* (a night) *ṭ^{a}wīlā* (long).

Verse 27

إِنَّ هَٰٓؤُلَآءِ يُحِبُّونَ ٱلۡعَاجِلَةَ وَيَذَرُونَ وَرَآءَهُمۡ يَوۡمٗا ثَقِيلٗا

Indeed those love the immediate [life] and leave behind them a grave day
Transliteration: inn^{a} hāʾ^{u}lāʾ^{i} y^{u}ḥ^{i}bbūn^{a} al-ʿāj^{i}l^{a}t^{a} w^{a}-y^{a}dh^{a}rūn^{a} w^{a}rāʾ^{a}-h^{u}m y^{a}wm^{an} th^{a}qīlā
Pronunciation: in-n^{a} hā-ʾ^{u}-lā-ʾ^{i} y^{u}-ḥ^{i}b-bū-n^{a}l-ʿā-j^{i}-l^{a}-t^{a} w^{a}-y^{a}-dh^{a}-rū-n^{a} w^{a}-rā-ʾ^{a}-h^{u}m y^{a}w-m^{an} th^{a}-qīlā

Inn^{a} (indeed) *hā^{u}lā^{i}* (those) *y^{u}ḥ^{i}bbūn^{a}* (they love) *al-ʿāj^{i}l^{a}t^{a}* (the immediate) *w^{a}-y^{a}dh^{a}rūn^{a}* (and they leave) *w^{a}rā^{a}-h^{u}m* (behind them) *y^{a}wm^{an} th^{a}qīlā* (a grave day).

The word *th^{a}qīl* litearlly means "heavy". Metaphorically it means "grave", "serious and important".

Verse 28

نَّحْنُ خَلَقْنَٰهُمْ وَشَدَدْنَآ أَسْرَهُمْ ۖ وَإِذَا شِئْنَا بَدَّلْنَآ أَمْثَٰلَهُمْ تَبْدِيلًا

We created them and strengthened their forms, and when We wish we will exchange them for their like

Transliteration: naḥn^{u} kh^{a}l^{a}qnā-h^{u}m w^{a}-sh^{a}d^{a}d-nā asr^{a}-h^{u}m w^{a}-idhā sh^{i}ʾ-nā b^{a}dd^{a}l-nā amthāl^{a}-h^{u}m t^{a}bdīlā

Pronunciation: naḥ-n^{u} kh^{a}-l^{a}q-nā-h^{u}m w^{a}-sh^{a}-d^{a}d-nā as-r^{a}-h^{u}m w^{a}-i-dhā sh^{i}ʾ-nā b^{a}d-d^{a}l-nā am-thā-l^{a}-h^{u}m t^{a}b-dī-lā

Naḥn^{u} (We) *kh*^{a}*l*^{a}*qnā-h*^{u}*m* (We created them) *w*^{a}*-sh*^{a}*d*^{a}*d-nā* (and we strengthened) *asr*^{a}*-h*^{u}*m* (their form) *w*^{a}*-idhā* (and when) *sh*^{i}*ʾ-nā* (We wish, We will) *b*^{a}*dd*^{a}*l-nā* (We exchange) *amthāl*^{a}*-h*^{u}*m* (their likes, their likeness) *t*^{a}*bdīlā* (a [true/real] exchanging).

Verse 29

إِنَّ هَٰذِهِۦ تَذْكِرَةٌ ۖ فَمَن شَآءَ ٱتَّخَذَ إِلَىٰ رَبِّهِۦ سَبِيلًا

Indeed this is a reminder, so whoever wishes takes a path to his Lord

Transliteration: inn^{a} hādh^{i}-h^{i} t^{a}dhk^{i}r^{a}t^{un} f^{a}-m^{a}n shā^{ʾa} itt^{a}kh^{a}dh^{a} ilā r^{a}bb^{i}-h^{i} s^{a}bīlā

Pronunciation: in-n^{a} hā-dh^{i}-h^{i} t^{a}dh-k^{i}-r^{a}-t^{un} f^{a}-m^{a}n shā-^{ʾa}t-t^{a}-kh^{a}-dh^{a} ilā r^{a}b-b^{i}-h^{i} s^{a}-bī-lā

Inn^{a} (indeed) *hādh*^{i}*-h*^{i} (this [is]) *t*^{a}*dhk*^{i}*r*^{a}*t*^{un} (a reminder) *f*^{a}*-m*^{a}*n* (so who) *shā*^{ʾa} (wills, wishes) *itt*^{a}*kh*^{a}*dh*^{a} (takes) *ilā* (to) *r*^{a}*bb*^{i}*-h*^{i} (his Lord) *s*^{a}*bīlā* (a path).

Verse 30

وَمَا تَشَآءُونَ إِلَّآ أَن يَشَآءَ ٱللَّهُ ۚ إِنَّ ٱللَّهَ كَانَ عَلِيمًا حَكِيمًا

And you do not will [anything] unless God wills [it]; indeed God is Knowing, Wise

Transliteration: w^{a}-mā t^{a}shāʾūn^{a} illā an y^{a}shā^{ʾa} allāh^{u} inn^{a} allāh^{a} kān^{a} ʿalīm^{an} ḥ^{a}kīmā

Pronunciation: w^{a}-mā t^{a}-shā-ʾū-n^{a} il-lā an y^{a}-shā-^{ʾa}l-lā-h^{u} in-n^{a}l-lā-h^{a} kā-n^{a} ʿa-lī-m^{an} ḥ^{a}-kī-mā

W^{a}-mā (and not) *t^{a}shā'ūn^{a}* (you will) *illā* (except) *an* (that) *y^{a}shā^{a}* (He wills) *allāh^{u}* (God) *inn^{a}* (indeed) *allāh^{a}* (God) *kān^{a}* (was/is) *'alīm^{an}* (Knowing) *ḥ^{a}kīmā* (Wise, Decisive).

The meaning of this verse is that God is absolutely in charge; no human will can override God's will.

Verse 31

يُدْخِلُ مَن يَشَآءُ فِي رَحْمَتِهِۦ ۚ وَٱلظَّٰلِمِينَ أَعَدَّ لَهُمْ عَذَابًا أَلِيمًۢا

He causes to enter whomever He wills into His mercy, and the wrongdoers—He has prepared for them a painful torment

Transliteration: y^{u}dkh^{i}l^{u} m^{a}n y^{a}shā'^{u} fī r^{a}ḥm^{a}t^{i}-h^{i} w^{a}-al-ẓāl^{i}mīn^{a} a^{ca}dd^{a} l^{a}-h^{u}m ^{ca}dhāb^{an} alīmā

Pronunciation: y^{u}d-kh^{i}-l^{u} m^{a}n y^{a}-shā-'^{u} fī r^{a}ḥ-m^{a}-t^{i}-h^{i} *w^{a}ẓ*-ẓā-l^{i}-mī-n^{a} a-^{ca}d-d^{a} l^{a}-h^{u}m ^{ca}-dhā-b^{an} a-lī-mā

Y^{u}dkh^{i}l^{u} (He causes to enter) *m^{a}n* (whomever) *y^{a}shā^{u}* (He wills) *fī* (in, into) *r^{a}ḥm^{a}t^{i}-h^{i}* (His mercy) *w^{a}-al-ẓāl^{i}mīn^{a}* (and the wrongdoers, and the transgressers) *a^{a}dd^{a}* (He prepared) *l^{a}-h^{u}m* (for them) *^{a}dhāb^{an}* (a torment) *alīmā* (painful).

Lesson 37 Review

عَٰلِيَهُمْ ثِيَابُ سُندُسٍ خُضْرٌ وَإِسْتَبْرَقٌ ۖ

ʿāl^{i}y^{a}-h^{u}m (upon them) *th^{i}yāb^{u}* (clothing [of]) *s^{u}nd^{u}s^{in}* (fine silk) *kh^{u}ḍr^{un}* (green) *w^{a}-ist^{a}br^{a}q* (and silk brocade).

وَحُلُّوٓا۟ أَسَاوِرَ مِن فِضَّةٍ وَسَقَىٰهُمْ رَبُّهُمْ شَرَابًا طَهُورًا

W^{a}-ḥ^{u}llū (and they were adorned with) *asāw^{i}r^{a}* (bracelets) *m^{i}n* (of) *f^{i}ḍḍ^{a}t^{in}* (silver) *w^{a}-s^{a}qā-h^{u}m* (and He watered them) *r^{a}bb^{u}-h^{u}m* (their Lord) *sh^{a}rāb^{an}* (a drink) *ṭ^{a}hūrā* (pure).

إِنَّ هَٰذَا كَانَ لَكُمْ جَزَآءً وَكَانَ سَعْيُكُم مَّشْكُورًا

Inn^{a} (indeed) *hādh^{a}* (this) *kān^{a}* (was) *l^{a}-k^{u}m* (for you) *j^{a}zā^{an}* (a reward) *w^{a}-kān^{a}* (and was) *s^{a}ʿy^{u}-k^{u}m* (your effort) *m^{a}shkūrā* (appreciated, thanked).

إِنَّا نَحْنُ نَزَّلْنَا عَلَيْكَ ٱلْقُرْءَانَ تَنزِيلًا

Innā n^{a}ḥn^{u} (indeed we) *n^{a}zz^{a}l-nā* (sent down) *^{a}l^{a}y-k^{a}* (upon you) *al-q^{u}r'ān^{a}* (the Quran) *t^{a}nzīlā* (a sending down).

فَٱصْبِرْ لِحُكْمِ رَبِّكَ وَلَا تُطِعْ مِنْهُمْ ءَاثِمًا أَوْ كَفُورًا

F^{a}-iṣb^{i}r (so be patient) *l^{i}* (for, toward) *ḥ^{u}km^{i}* (the judgment [of]) *r^{a}bb^{i}-k^{a}* (your Lord) *w^{a}-lā* (and not) *t^{u}ṭ^{i}ʿ* (you obey) *m^{i}n-h^{u}m* (of them, among them) *āth^{i}m^{an}* (a sinner) *aw k^{a}fūrā* (or a rejecter).

وَٱذْكُرِ ٱسْمَ رَبِّكَ بُكْرَةً وَأَصِيلًا

W^{a}-udhk^{u}r (and remember) *ism^{a}* (the name [of]) *r^{a}bb^{i}-k^{a}* (your Lord) *b^{u}kr^{a}t^{an}* (morning) *w^{a}-aṣīlā* (and mid-afternoon).

وَمِنَ ٱلَّيْلِ فَٱسْجُدْ لَهُۥ وَسَبِّحْهُ لَيْلًا طَوِيلًا

W^{a}-m^{i}n^{a} (and of) *al-l^{a}yl^{i}* (the night) *f^{a}-usj^{u}d l^{a}-h^{u}* (then prostrate yourself to Him) *w^{a}-s^{a}bb^{i}ḥ-h^{u}* (and exalt Him) *l^{a}yl^{an}* (a night) *ṭ^{a}wīlā* (long).

إِنَّ هَٰٓؤُلَآءِ يُحِبُّونَ ٱلْعَاجِلَةَ وَيَذَرُونَ وَرَآءَهُمْ يَوْمًا ثَقِيلًا

Inn^{a} (indeed) *hā^{u}lā^{i}* (those) *y^{u}ḥ^{i}bbūn^{a}* (they love) *al-ʿāj^{i}l^{a}t^{a}* (the immediate) *w^{a}-y^{a}dh^{a}rūn^{a}* (and they leave) *w^{a}rā^{a}-h^{u}m* (behind them) *y^{a}wm^{an} th^{a}qīlā* (a grave day).

نَّحْنُ خَلَقْنَٰهُمْ وَشَدَدْنَآ أَسْرَهُمْ ۖ وَإِذَا شِئْنَا بَدَّلْنَآ أَمْثَٰلَهُمْ تَبْدِيلًا

Naḥn^{u} (We) *kh^{a}l^{a}qnā-h^{u}m* (We created them) *w^{a}-sh^{a}d^{a}d-nā* (and we strengthened) *asr^{a}-h^{u}m* (their form) *w^{a}-idhā* (and when) *sh^{i}ʾ-nā* (We wish, We will) *b^{a}dd^{a}l-nā* (We exchange) *amthāl^{a}-h^{u}m* (their likes, their likeness) *t^{a}bdīlā* (a [true/real] exchanging).

إِنَّ هَٰذِهِۦ تَذْكِرَةٌ ۖ فَمَن شَآءَ ٱتَّخَذَ إِلَىٰ رَبِّهِۦ سَبِيلًا

Inn^{a} (indeed) *hādh*^{i}*-h*^{i} (this [is]) *t*^{a}*dhk*^{i}*r*^{a}*t*^{un} (a reminder) *f*^{a}*-m*^{a}*n* (so who) *shā*^{a} (wills, wishes) *itt*^{a}*kh*^{a}*dh*^{a} (takes) *ilā* (to) *r*^{a}*bb*^{i}*-h*^{i} (his Lord) *s*^{a}*bīlā* (a path).

وَمَا تَشَآءُونَ إِلَّآ أَن يَشَآءَ ٱللَّهُ ۚ إِنَّ ٱللَّهَ كَانَ عَلِيمًا حَكِيمًا

W^{a}*-mā* (and not) *t*^{a}*shā'ūn*^{a} (you will) *illā* (except) *an* (that) *y*^{a}*shā*^{a} (He wills) *allāh*^{u} (God) *inn*^{a} (indeed) *allāh*^{a} (God) *kān*^{a} (was/is) *ʿalīm*^{an} (Knowing) *ḥ*^{a}*kīmā* (Wise, Decisive).

يُدْخِلُ مَن يَشَآءُ فِى رَحْمَتِهِۦ ۚ وَٱلظَّٰلِمِينَ أَعَدَّ لَهُمْ عَذَابًا أَلِيمًۢا

Y^{u}*dkh*^{i}*l*^{u} (He causes to enter) *m*^{a}*n* (whomever) *y*^{a}*shā*^{u} (He wills) *fī* (in, into) *r*^{a}*ḥm*^{a}*t*^{i}*-h*^{i} (His mercy) *w*^{a}*-al-ẓāl*^{i}*mīn*^{a} (and the wrongdoers, and the transgressers) *a*^{ʿ}*dd*^{a} (He prepared) *l*^{a}*-h*^{u}*m* (for them) ^{ʿ}*dhāb*^{an} (a torment) *alīmā* (painful).

This page intentionally left blank

Lesson 38: Maryam Part 1

This lesson is on chapter 19 of the Quran, which is titled *Maryam* ("Mary"), referring to Mary mother of Jesus (peace be upon him and his mother).

From this lesson on, we will no longer have separate pronunciations and transliterations underneath the Arabic. This is in order to save safe so that we can fit more verses into the remaining part of the book.

بِسْمِ ٱللَّهِ ٱلرَّحْمَٰنِ ٱلرَّحِيمِ

Verse 1

كٓهيعٓصٓ

kā hā yā ^{ca}yn ṣād

The first verse of this chapter starts with a number of disjoined letters that are pronounced as shown above. These letters do not have a meaning as far as we know. They are like musical tones that grab the listerner's attention.

Verse 2

ذِكْرُ رَحْمَتِ رَبِّكَ عَبْدَهُۥ زَكَرِيَّآ

[This is] the mention of your Lord's mercy toward His servant Zechariah

Dh$_{i}$kr^{u} (the mention [of]) *r^{a}ḥm^{a}t^{i}* (the mercy [of]) *r^{a}bb^{i}-k^{a}* (your Lord [toward]) *^{a}bd^{a}-h^{u}* (His servant) *z^{a}k^{a}rīyā* (Zechariah).

The word *r^{a}ḥm^{a}t^{i}* ("mercy [of]") would be written as follows in standard Arabic:

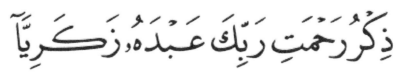

رَحْمَةِ

The phrase *r*^{a}*ḥm*^{a}*t*^{i} *r*^{a}*bb*^{i}*-k*^{a} means "the mercy of your Lord", while the phrase *r*^{a}*ḥm*^{a}*t*^{i} *r*^{a}*bb*^{i}*-k*^{a} ^{a}*bd*^{a}*-h*^{u} means "the mercy of your Lord [toward] His servant" even though there is no explicit "toward" in the statement. It is something gleaned from the phrasing.

Verse 3

إِذْ نَادَىٰ رَبَّهُۥ نِدَآءً خَفِيًّا

When he called his Lord [with a] a secret [act of] calling

Idh (when) *nādā* (he called) *r*^{a}*bb*^{a}*-h*^{u} (his Lord) *n*^{i}*dā*^{an} (an [act of] calling) *kh*^{a}*fiyā* (secret).

Verse 4, part 1

قَالَ رَبِّ إِنِّي وَهَنَ ٱلْعَظْمُ مِنِّي وَٱشْتَعَلَ ٱلرَّأْسُ شَيْبًا

He said, "My Lord, indeed the bones have weakened from me and my head has become kindled with grayness..."

Qāl^{a} (he said) *r*^{a}*bb*^{i} (my Lord) *in-nī* (indeed I) *w*^{a}*h*^{a}*n*^{a} ([they] weakened) *al-*^{a}*ẓm*^{u} (the bones) *m*^{i}*n-nī* (from me) *w*^{a}*-isht*^{a}^{a}*l*^{a} (and it became kindled, and it got set on fire) *al-r*^{a}*'s*^{u} (the head) *sh*^{a}*ybā* (grayness).

The word *r*^{a}*bb*^{i} would be written as *rabb-ī* in standard Arabic.

رَبِّي

In the Quran the ending *yā'* is removed for poetic effect.

The word *isht*$^{a\,a}$*l*^{a} means "it became kindled", "it started to burn". The phrase *isht*$^{a\,a}$*l*^{a} *sh*^{a}*yb*^{an} "it became kindled with grayness" is a highly poetic express that means "the hairs went gray" (i.e. the person became old).

Verse 4, part 2

وَلَمْ أَكُنْ بِدُعَآئِكَ رَبِّ شَقِيًّا

"and I have never been, in my supplication to you, unanswered."

W^{a}*-l*^{a}*m ak*^{u}*n* (and I was not) *b*^{i}*-d*^{u}*ʿā*^{i}*-k*^{a} (by Your supplication, i.e. by my supplication to You) *r*^{a}*bb*^{i} (my Lord) *sh*^{a}*qīyā* (wretched, here meaning one whose supplication is ignored and unanswered).

The verb *ak*^{u}*n* is the present tense form of *k*^{u}*nt*^{u} ("I was"). But *l*^{a}*m* turns iti into the past tense, so *l*^{a}*m ak*^{u}*n* means "I was not").

كُنْتُ، أَكُونُ، لَم أَكُنْ

ذَهَبْتُ، أَذْهَبُ، لَم أَذْهَبْ

Top from right to left: I was; I am; I was not.

Bottom from right to left: I went, I go; I did not go.

Notice the way *wāw* in *akūn*^{u} (first line, middle) is removed when the word is preceded by *l*^{a}*m* (first line, left). This is due to a rule of Arabic grammar that applies to words that have a vowel letter as their second letter. Here the word is *kān*^{a} (when you look at it in the past tense), which has an *alif* as its second letter. Below is a different word that follows the same pattern:

مَاتَ، أَمُوتُ، لَمْ أَمُتْ

From right to left: he died; I die; I did not die.

Verse 5, part 1

وَإِنِّي خِفْتُ ٱلْمَوَٰلِيَ مِن وَرَآءِى

"And indeed I feared the cousins from behind me..."

W^a-innī (and indeed I) *kh^{i}f-t^u* (I feared) *al-m^{a}wāl^{i}y^a* (the cousins, the allies) *m^{i}n* (from) *w^{a}rā'-ī* (behind me).

The word *m^{a}wālī* is the plural of *m^{a}wlā* ("servant", "slave", "master", "ally", "close relative"). Here *m^{a}wālī* is thought to refer to paternal cousins. Here Zechariah is referring to his nation (the Children of Israel) as his cousins and says that he fears for their fate if they are left without a prophet to guide them after his death.

Verse 5, part 2

وَكَانَتِ ٱمْرَأَتِى عَاقِرًا فَهَبْ لِى مِن لَّدُنكَ وَلِيًّا

"and my wife was barren so grant me from Yourself a close ally.

W^a-kān^a-t (and she was) *imr^a^{a}t-ī* (my woman) *'āq^{i}r^{an}* (barren, infertile) *f^a-h^{a}b l-ī* (so grant to me, so bestow upon me) *m^{i}n l^{a}d^{u}n-k^a* (from yourself) *w^{a}līyā* (a close ally).

The phrase *m^{i}n l^{a}d^{u}n-ka* means "from yourself". The word *l^{a}d^{u}n* implies that the thing mentioned is with the person mentioned, as in:

أَخَذْتُ كِتَابًا مِنْ لَدُنْ أَحْمَدَ

"I took a book from Ahmad", literally "I took a book that was with Ahmad", "I took a book from the possession of Ahmad".

Verse 6

يَرِثُنِي وَيَرِثُ مِنْ ءَالِ يَعْقُوبَ ۖ وَٱجْعَلْهُ رَبِّ رَضِيًّا

"He will inherit me and inherit from the family of Jacob, and make him, my Lord, pleasing [to You].

Y^{a}r^{i}th^{u}-nī (he inherits me) *w^{a}-y^{a}r^{i}th^{u}* (and he inherits) *m^{i}n* (from) *āl^{i}* (the family of, the household of) *y^{a}ʿqūb^{a}* (Jacob) *w^{a}-ij^{a}l-h^{u}* (and make him) *r^{a}bb^{i}* (my Lord) *r^{a}ḍīyā* (pleasing).

Y^{a}r^{i}th^{u} means "he inherits", i.e. "he becomes the inheritor [of someone or something]".

Verse 7

يَٰزَكَرِيَّآ إِنَّا نُبَشِّرُكَ بِغُلَٰمٍ ٱسْمُهُۥ يَحْيَىٰ لَمْ نَجْعَل لَّهُۥ مِن قَبْلُ سَمِيًّا

"O Zechariah, indeed We give you the good tidings of a boy whose name is John—we never made for him before that a named one."

Yā-z^{a}k^{a}rīyā (O Zechariah!) *in-nā* (indeed we) *n^{u}b^{a}shsh^{i}r^{u}-k^{a}* (we give you glad tidings) *b^{i}-gh^{u}lām^{in}* (by a boy, about a boy) *ism^{u}-h^{u}* (his name [is]) *y^{a}ḥyā* (John) *l^{a}m n^{a}j^{a}l* (we did not make, we did not assign) *l^{a}-h^{u}* (for him) *m^{i}n q^{a}bl^{u}* (before) *s^{a}mīyā* (a named [person]).

Here God responds to Zechariah's prayer by giving him the good news of a boy that will be born to him whose name was never before used by anyone.

Verse 8

قَالَ رَبِّ أَنَّىٰ يَكُونُ لِى غُلَٰمٌ وَكَانَتِ ٱمْرَأَتِى عَاقِرًا وَقَدْ بَلَغْتُ مِنَ ٱلْكِبَرِ عِتِيًّا

He said, "My Lord, how can there be for me a boy while my wife was barren and I have reached of old age an extreme?

Qāl^{a} (he said) *r^{a}bb^{i}* (my Lord) *annā* (how can) *y^{a}kūn^{u}* (there is, there be) *l-ī* (for me) *gh^{u}lām^{un}* (a boy) *w^{a}-kān^{a}-t* (and she was) *imr^{a}^{a}tī* (my woman) *ʿāq^{i}r^{an}* (barren) *w^{a}-q^{a}d* (and have) *b^{a}l^{a}ght^{u}* (I reached) *m^{i}n* (from) *al-k^{i}b^{a}r^{i}* (oldness, old age) *^{i}tīyā* (an extreme).

The word ʿ^{i}*tī* is the gerund (*maṣdar*) of ʿ^{a}*tā* ("he transgressed", "he went to an extreme").

عَتَىٰ

Verse 9

قَالَ كَذَٰلِكَ قَالَ رَبُّكَ هُوَ عَلَيَّ هَيِّنٌ وَقَدْ خَلَقْتُكَ مِن قَبْلُ وَلَمْ تَكُ شَيْـًٔا

He said, "Thus [it will be]; your Lord said 'It is easy on me and I created you from before while you were nothing.'"

Qāl^{a} (he said) *k*^{a}*-dhālik*^{a} (thus, like that) *qāl*^{a} (he said) *r*^{a}*bb*^{u}*-k*^{a} (your Lord) *h*^{u}*w*^{a} (it [is]) ʿ^{a}*l*^{a}*y-y*^{a} (upon me) *h*^{a}*yy*^{i}*n*^{un} (easy) *w*^{a}*-q*^{a}*d* (and have) *kh*^{a}*l*^{a}*q-t*^{u}*-k*^{a} (I created you) *m*^{i}*n* (from) *q*^{a}*bl*^{u} (before) *w*^{a} (while) *l*^{a}*m* *t*^{a}*k*^{u} (you were not) *sh*^{a}*y*ʾ^{an} (a thing).

The word *t*^{a}*k*^{u} is a short form of *t*^{a}*k*^{u}*n*.

The speaker here may be an angel who says that God said such and such.

Lesson 38 Review

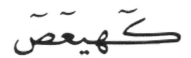

بِسْمِ ٱللَّهِ ٱلرَّحْمَٰنِ ٱلرَّحِيمِ

كٓهيعٓصٓ

kā hā yā ^{ca}yn ṣād

ذِكْرُ رَحْمَتِ رَبِّكَ عَبْدَهُۥ زَكَرِيَّآ

Dh$_{i}$*kr*^{u} (the mention [of]) *r*^{a}*ḥm*^{a}*t*^{i} (the mercy [of]) *r*^{a}*bb*^{i}*-k*^{a} (your Lord [toward]) ^{a}*bd*^{a}*-h*^{u} (His servant) *z*^{a}*k*^{a}*rīyā* (Zechariah).

إِذْ نَادَىٰ رَبَّهُۥ نِدَآءً خَفِيًّا

Idh (when) *nādā* (he called) *r*^{a}*bb*^{a}*-h*^{u} (his Lord) *n*^{i}*dā*^{an} (an [act of] calling) *kh*^{a}*fiyā* (secret).

قَالَ رَبِّ إِنِّي وَهَنَ ٱلْعَظْمُ مِنِّي وَٱشْتَعَلَ ٱلرَّأْسُ شَيْبًا

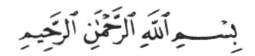

Qāl^{a} (he said) *r*^{a}*bb*^{i} (my Lord) *in-nī* (indeed I) *w*^{a}*h*^{a}*n*^{a} ([they] weakened) *al-*^{a}*ẓm*^{u} (the bones) *m*^{i}*n-nī* (from me) *w*^{a}*-isht*^{a}^{a}*l*^{a} (and it became kindled, and it got set on fire) *al-r*^{a}*'s*^{u} (the head) *sh*^{a}*ybā* (grayness).

وَلَمْ أَكُنۢ بِدُعَآئِكَ رَبِّ شَقِيًّا

W^{a}*-l*^{a}*m ak*^{u}*n* (and I was not) *b*^{i}*-d*^{u}*ʿā*^{i}*-k*^{a} (by Your supplication, i.e. by my supplication to You) *r*^{a}*bb*^{i} (my Lord) *sh*^{a}*qīyā* (wretched, here meaning one whose supplication is ignored and unanswered).

وَإِنِّى خِفْتُ ٱلْمَوَٰلِىَ مِن وَرَآءِى

W^{a}*-innī* (and indeed I) *kh*^{i}*f-t*^{u} (I feared) *al-m*^{a}*wāl*^{i}*y*^{a} (the cousins, the allies) *m*^{i}*n* (from) *w*^{a}*rā'-ī* (behind me).

وَكَانَتِ ٱمْرَأَتِى عَاقِرًا فَهَبْ لِى مِن لَّدُنكَ وَلِيًّا

W^{a}*-kān*^{a}*-t* (and she was) *imr*^{a}^{a}*t-ī* (my woman) *ʿāq*^{i}*r*^{an} (barren, infertile) *f*^{a}*-h*^{a}*b l-ī* (so grant to me, so bestow upon me) *m*^{i}*n l*^{a}*d*^{u}*n-k*^{a} (from yourself) *w*^{a}*līyā* (a close ally).

يَرِثُنِى وَيَرِثُ مِنْ ءَالِ يَعْقُوبَ ۖ وَٱجْعَلْهُ رَبِّ رَضِيًّا

Y^{a}*r*^{i}*th*^{u}*-nī* (he inherits me) *w*^{a}*-y*^{a}*r*^{i}*th*^{u} (and he inherits) *m*^{i}*n* (from) *āl*^{i} (the family of, the household of) *y*^{a}*ʿqūb*^{a} (Jacob) *w*^{a}*-ijʿ*^{a}*l-h*^{u} (and make him) *r*^{a}*bb*^{i} (my Lord) *r*^{a}*ḍīyā* (pleasing).

يَٰزَكَرِيَّآ إِنَّا نُبَشِّرُكَ بِغُلَٰمٍ ٱسْمُهُۥ يَحْيَىٰ لَمْ نَجْعَل لَّهُۥ مِن قَبْلُ سَمِيًّا

Yā-z^{a}*k*^{a}*rīyā* (O Zechariah!) *in-nā* (indeed we) *n*^{u}*b*^{a}*shsh*^{i}*r*^{u}*-k*^{a} (we give you glad tidings) *b*^{i}*-gh*^{u}*lām*^{in} (by a boy, about a boy) *ism*^{u}*-h*^{u} (his name [is]) *y*^{a}*ḥyā* (John) *l*^{a}*m n*^{a}*jʿ*^{a}*l* (we did not make, we did not assign) *l*^{a}*-h*^{u} (for him) *m*^{i}*n q*^{a}*bl*^{u} (before) *s*^{a}*mīyā* (a named [person]).

قَالَ رَبِّ أَنَّىٰ يَكُونُ لِي غُلَٰمٌ وَكَانَتِ ٱمۡرَأَتِي عَاقِرٗا وَقَدۡ بَلَغۡتُ مِنَ ٱلۡكِبَرِ عِتِيّٗا

Qāl^{a} (he said) *r*^{a}*bb*^{i} (my Lord) *annā* (how can) *y*^{a}*kūn*^{u} (there is, there be) *l-ī* (for me) *gh*^{u}*lām*^{un} (a boy) *w*^{a}*-kān*^{a}*-t* (and she was) *imr*^{a}^{a}*tī* (my woman) *ʿāq*^{i}*r*^{an} (barren) *w*^{a}*-q*^{a}*d* (and have) *b*^{a}*l*^{a}*ght*^{u} (I reached) *m*^{i}*n* (from) *al-k*^{i}*b*^{a}*r*^{i} (oldness, old age) ^{ʿi}*tīyā* (an extreme).

قَالَ كَذَٰلِكَ قَالَ رَبُّكَ هُوَ عَلَيَّ هَيِّنٞ وَقَدۡ خَلَقۡتُكَ مِن قَبۡلُ وَلَمۡ تَكُ شَيۡـٔٗا

Qāl^{a} (he said) *k*^{a}*-dhālik*^{a} (thus, like that) *qāl*^{a} (he said) *r*^{a}*bb*^{u}*-k*^{a} (your Lord) *h*^{u}*w*^{a} (it [is]) ^{ʿa}*l*^{a}*y-y*^{a} (upon me) *h*^{a}*yy*^{i}*n*^{un} (easy) *w*^{a}*-q*^{a}*d* (and have) *kh*^{a}*l*^{a}*q-t*^{u}*-k*^{a} (I created you) *m*^{i}*n* (from) *q*^{a}*bl*^{u} (before) *w*^{a} (while) *l*^{a}*m t*^{a}*k*^{u} (you were not) *sh*^{a}*y*^{ʾan} (a thing).

This page intentionally left blank

Lesson 39: Maryam Part 2

Verse 10

قَالَ رَبِّ ٱجْعَل لِّىٓ ءَايَةً ۚ قَالَ ءَايَتُكَ أَلَّا تُكَلِّمَ ٱلنَّاسَ ثَلَٰثَ لَيَالٍ سَوِيًّا

He said, "My Lord, assign for me a sign." He said, "Your sign is that you will not speak to people for three nights, [being] sound".

Qāl^{a} (he said) *r*^{a}*bb*^{i} (my Lord) *ij*^{a}*l* (make, assign) *l-ī* (for me) *āy*^{a}*t*^{an} (a sign) *qāl*^{a} (he said) *āy*^{a}*t*^{u}*-k*^{a} (your sign [is]) *allā* (to not) *t*^{u}*k*^{a}*ll*^{i}*m*^{a} (you talk to) *al-nās*^{a} (the people) *th*^{a}*lāth*^{a} (three) *l*^{a}*yāl*^{in} (nights) *s*^{a}*wīyā* ([while being] sound).

The word *s*^{a}*wī* at the end means that Zechariah will not be speaking to people despite being sound and not suffering from an illness that causes you to be unable to speak. It may also refer to the nights, meaning they will be three sound and complete nights.

Verse 11

فَخَرَجَ عَلَىٰ قَوْمِهِۦ مِنَ ٱلْمِحْرَابِ فَأَوْحَىٰٓ إِلَيْهِمْ أَن سَبِّحُوا۟ بُكْرَةً وَعَشِيًّا

He went out to his people from the prayer chamber then signalled to them that "Exalt [God] morning and evening."

F^{a}*-kh*^{a}*r*^{a}*j*^{a} (so he went out) ^{a}*lā* (upon) *q*^{a}*wm*^{i}*-h*^{i} (his people) *m*^{i}*n* (from) *al-m*^{i}*ḥrāb*^{i} (the prayer chamber) *f*^{a}*-awḥā* (so he signaled) *il*^{a}*y-h*^{i}*m* (to them) *an* (that) *s*^{a}*bb*^{i}*-ḥū* (exalt [God]) *b*^{u}*kr*^{a}*t*^{an} (morning) *w*^{a}*-*^{a}*shīyā* (and evening).

The word *awḥā* means "he signaled", "he inspired". It is also used in the Quran to refer to God revealing his Revelation to prophets. ^{a}*shī* refers to the time of day from sunset until the night becomes completely dark about an hour and a half later. The word *'ishā'* comes from the same root and refers to the same time period. The *'ishā'* prayer is the last of the five daily prayers in Islam and is prayed at the very end of ^{a}*shī* when the night has become completely dark.

Verse 12

يَٰيَحۡيَىٰ خُذِ ٱلۡكِتَٰبَ بِقُوَّةٖۖ وَءَاتَيۡنَٰهُ ٱلۡحُكۡمَ صَبِيّٗا

"O John! Grasp the Book with strength!" and we gave him wise judgment as a child

Yā-y^{a}*ḥyā* (O John) *kh*^{u}*dh* (take, grasp) *al-k*^{i}*tāb*^{a} (the Book, i.e. the scripture) *b*^{i}*-q*^{u}*ww*^{a}*t*^{in} (with strength) *w*^{a}*-āt*^{a}*ynā-h*^{u} (and we gave him) *al-ḥ*^{u}*km*^{a} (judgment, wise judgment) *ṣabīyā* ([as] a child).

Verse 13

وَحَنَانٗا مِّن لَّدُنَّا وَزَكَوٰةٗۖ وَكَانَ تَقِيّٗا

And [we gave Him] an affection form us, and a purity, and he was God-fearing

W^{a}*-ḥ*^{a}*nān*^{an} (and an affection) *m*^{i}*n l*^{a}*d*^{u}*n-nā* (from us) *w*^{a}*-z*^{a}*kāt*^{an} (and a purity) *w*^{a}*-kān*^{a} (and he was) *t*^{a}*qīyā* (God-fearing).

Verse 14

وَبَرَّۢا بِوَٰلِدَيۡهِ وَلَمۡ يَكُن جَبَّارًا عَصِيّٗا

And dutiful to his parents, and he was not a disobedient tyrant

W^{a}*-b*^{a}*rr*^{an} (and a dutiful one) *b*^{i}*-wāl*^{i}*d*^{a}*y-h*^{i} (toward his parents) *w*^{a}*-l*^{a}*m* (and not) *y*^{a}*k*^{u}*n* (he is) *j*^{a}*bbār*^{an} (a tyrant) ^{a}*ṣīyā* (disobedient).

Verse 15

وَسَلَٰمٌ عَلَيْهِ يَوْمَ وُلِدَ وَيَوْمَ يَمُوتُ وَيَوْمَ يُبْعَثُ حَيًّا

And peace be upon him the day he was born, the day he will die, and the day he is raised back to life

W^{a}-s^{a}lām^{un} (and a peace [is/will be/be], and a salutation [is/will be/be]) *^{a}l^{a}y-h^{i}* (upon him) *y^{a}wm^{a}* (the day) *w^{u}l^{i}d^{a}* (he was born) *w^{a}-y^{a}wm^{a}* (and the day) *y^{a}mūt^{u}* (he dies) *w^{a}-y^{a}wm^{a}* (and the day) *y^{u}b^{a}th^{u}* (he is raised, he is revivified) *ḥ^{a}yyā* (alive).

Verse 16

وَٱذْكُرْ فِى ٱلْكِتَٰبِ مَرْيَمَ إِذِ ٱنتَبَذَتْ مِنْ أَهْلِهَا مَكَانًا شَرْقِيًّا

And remember in the Book Mary, when she withdrew, from her family, to an easterly place

W^{a}-udhk^{u}r (and remember) *fī* (in) *al-k^{i}tāb^{i}* (the Book) *m^{a}ry^{a}m^{a}* (Mary) *idh* (in) *int^{a}b^{a}dh^{a}-t* (she withdrew to) *min* (from) *ahl^{i}-hā* (her family) *m^{a}kān^{a}n* (a place) *sh^{a}rqīyā* (easterly, i.e. located in the east or east-facing).

Verse 17

فَٱتَّخَذَتْ مِن دُونِهِمْ حِجَابًا فَأَرْسَلْنَآ إِلَيْهَا رُوحَنَا فَتَمَثَّلَ لَهَا بَشَرًا سَوِيًّا

So she took up, away from them, a screen. So we sent to her Our Spirit so he assumed toward her the likeness of a proper human

F^{a}-itt^{a}kh^{a}dh^{a}-t (so she took up, so she adopted) *m^{i}n dūn^{i}-h^{i}m* (apart from them) *ḥ^{i}jāb^{an}* (a screen) *f^{a}-ars^{a}lnā* (so we sent) *il^{a}y-hā* (to her) *rūḥ^{a}-nā* (Our Spirit) *f^{a}-t^{a}m^{a}thth^{a}l^{a}* (so he adopted the likeness [of]) *l^{a}-hā* (for her) *b^{a}sh^{a}r^{an}* (a human) *s^{a}wīyā* (proper, sound).

Verse 18

قَالَتْ إِنِّىٓ أَعُوذُ بِٱلرَّحْمَٰنِ مِنكَ إِن كُنتَ تَقِيًّا

She said, "Indeed I seek protection with the most Gracious from you, if you are God-fearing."

Qāl^{a}-t (she said) *in-nī* (indeed I) *aʿūdh^{u}* (I seek protection) *b^{i}-al-r^{a}ḥmān^{i}* (with the most Gracious, by the most Gracious) *m^{i}n-k^{a}* (from you) *in* (if) *k^{u}n-t^{a}* (you are) *t^{a}qīyā* (God-fearing).

Verse 19

قَالَ إِنَّمَآ أَنَا۠ رَسُولُ رَبِّكِ لِأَهَبَ لَكِ غُلَٰمًا زَكِيًّا

He said, "Indeed I am only the messenger of your Lord, to grant you a pure boy."

Qāla (he said) *inn^{a}-mā an^{a}* (indeed I am only) *r^{a}sūl^{u}* (the messenger [of]) *r^{a}bb^{i}-k^{i}* (your Lord) *l^{i}-ah^{a}b^{a}* (to bestow, to grant) *l^{a}-k^{i}* (to you) *gh^{u}lām^{an}* (a boy) *z^{a}kīyā* (pure).

The phrases *r^{a}bb^{i}-k^{i}* and *l^{a}-k^{i}* both have the ending *yā'* removed for poetic effect.

Verse 20

قَالَتْ أَنَّىٰ يَكُونُ لِى غُلَٰمٌ وَلَمْ يَمْسَسْنِى بَشَرٌ وَلَمْ أَكُ بَغِيًّا

She said, "How can there be for me a boy while no human has touched me and I was not an unchaste [woman]?

Qāl^{a}-t (she said) *annā* (how can) *y^{a}kūn^{u}* (there will be) *l-ī* (for me) *gh^{u}lām^{un}* (a boy) *w^{a}-l^{a}m* (while did not) *y^{a}ms^{a}s-nī* (touch me) *b^{a}sh^{a}r^{un}* (a human) *w^{a}-l^{a}m* (and was not) *ak^{u}* (I was) *b^{a}ghīyā* (an unchaste woman, a harlot).

Lesson 39 Review

قَالَ رَبِّ ٱجْعَل لِّيٓ ءَايَةً ۚ قَالَ ءَايَتُكَ أَلَّا تُكَلِّمَ ٱلنَّاسَ ثَلَٰثَ لَيَالٍ سَوِيًّا

Qāl^{a} (he said) *r*^{a}*bb*^{i} (my Lord) *ij*^{a}*l* (make, assign) *l-ī* (for me) *āy*^{a}*t*^{an} (a sign) *qāl*^{a} (he said) *āy*^{a}*t*^{u}*-k*^{a} (your sign [is]) *allā* (to not) *t*^{u}*k*^{a}*ll*^{i}*m*^{a} (you talk to) *al-nās*^{a} (the people) *th*^{a}*lāth*^{a} (three) *l*^{a}*yāl*^{in} (nights) *s*^{a}*wīyā* ([while being] sound).

فَخَرَجَ عَلَىٰ قَوْمِهِۦ مِنَ ٱلْمِحْرَابِ فَأَوْحَىٰٓ إِلَيْهِمْ أَن سَبِّحُوا۟ بُكْرَةً وَعَشِيًّا

F^{a}*-kh*^{a}*r*^{a}*j*^{a} (so he went out) ^{a}*lā* (upon) *q*^{a}*wm*^{i}*-h*^{i} (his people) *m*^{i}*n* (from) *al-m*^{i}*ḥrāb*^{i} (the prayer chamber) *f*^{a}*-awḥā* (so he signaled) *il*^{a}*y-h*^{i}*m* (to them) *an* (that) *s*^{a}*bb*^{i}*-ḥū* (exalt [God]) *b*^{u}*kr*^{a}*t*^{an} (morning) *w*^{a}*-*^{a}*shīyā* (and evening).

يَٰيَحْيَىٰ خُذِ ٱلْكِتَٰبَ بِقُوَّةٍ ۖ وَءَاتَيْنَٰهُ ٱلْحُكْمَ صَبِيًّا

Yā-y^{a}*ḥyā* (O John) *kh*^{u}*dh* (take, grasp) *al-k*^{i}*tāb*^{a} (the Book, i.e. the scripture) *b*^{i}*-q*^{u}*ww*^{a}*t*^{in} (with strength) *w*^{a}*-āt*^{a}*ynā-h*^{u} (and we gave him) *al-ḥ*^{u}*km*^{a} (judgment, wise judgment) *ṣabīyā* ([as] a child).

وَحَنَانًا مِّن لَّدُنَّا وَزَكَوٰةً ۖ وَكَانَ تَقِيًّا

W^{a}*-ḥ*^{a}*nān*^{an} (and an affection) *m*^{i}*n l*^{a}*d*^{u}*n-nā* (from us) *w*^{a}*-z*^{a}*kāt*^{an} (and a purity) *w*^{a}*-kān*^{a} (and he was) *t*^{a}*qīyā* (God-fearing).

وَبَرًّا بِوَٰلِدَيْهِ وَلَمْ يَكُن جَبَّارًا عَصِيًّا

W^{a}*-b*^{a}*rr*^{an} (and a dutiful one) *b*^{i}*-wāl*^{i}*d*^{a}*y-h*^{i} (toward his parents) *w*^{a}*-l*^{a}*m* (and not) *y*^{a}*k*^{u}*n* (he is) *j*^{a}*bbār*^{an} (a tyrant) ^{a}*ṣīyā* (disobedient).

وَسَلَٰمٌ عَلَيْهِ يَوْمَ وُلِدَ وَيَوْمَ يَمُوتُ وَيَوْمَ يُبْعَثُ حَيًّا

W^{a}*-s*^{a}*lām*^{un} (and a peace [is/will be/be], and a salutation [is/will be/be]) ^{a}*l*^{a}*y-h*^{i} (upon him) *y*^{a}*wm*^{a} (the day) *w*^{u}*l*^{i}*d*^{a} (he was born) *w*^{a}*-y*^{a}*wm*^{a} (and the day) *y*^{a}*mūt*^{u} (he dies) *w*^{a}*-y*^{a}*wm*^{a} (and the day) *y*^{u}*b*^{a}*th*^{u} (he is raised, he is revivified) *ḥ*^{a}*yyā* (alive).

Lesson 40: Maryam Part 3

Verse 21, part 1

قَالَ كَذَٰلِكِ قَالَ رَبُّكِ هُوَ عَلَيَّ هَيِّنٌ ۖ

He said, "[It is] thus. Your Lord said, 'It is easy for me...'"

Qāl^{a} (he said) *k*^{a}*-dhāl*^{i}*k*^{i} (thus, like that) *qāl*^{a} (He said) *r*^{a}*bb*^{u}*-k*^{i} (your Lord) *h*^{u}*w*^{a} (it [is]) ^{a}*l*^{a}*y-y*^{a} (on me) *h*^{a}*yy*^{i}*n*^{un} (easy).

Verse 21, part 2

وَلِنَجْعَلَهُۥٓ ءَايَةً لِّلنَّاسِ وَرَحْمَةً مِّنَّا ۚ وَكَانَ أَمْرًا مَّقْضِيًّا

"and to make him a sign for the people and a mercy from us. It is a matter decreed."

W^{a} (and) *l*^{i} (to) *n*^{a}*j*^{a}*l*^{a}*-h*^{u} (we make him) *āy*^{a}*t*^{an} (a sign) *l*^{i}*-al-nās*^{i} (for the people) *w*^{a}*-raḥm*^{a}*t*^{an} (and a mercy) *m*^{i}*n-nā* (from us) *w*^{a}*-kān*^{a} (and it was) *amr*^{an} (a matter) *m*^{a}*qḍīyā* (decreed).

قَضَى، يَقْضِي، اقْضِ، قَضَاء وقَضْي، قَاضِي،

مَقْضِي

From right to left: he decreed; he decrees; decree!; to decree (two forms); decreer (also means judge); that which has been decreed.

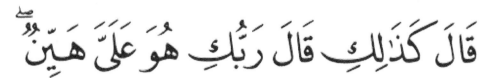

Verse 22

فَحَمَلَتْهُ فَٱنتَبَذَتْ بِهِۦ مَكَانًا قَصِيًّا

So she carried him then withdrew, with him, to a remote place

F^{a}-ḥ^{a}m^{a}l^{a}-t-h^{u} (so she carried him) *f^{a}-int^{a}b^{a}dh^{a}-t* (so she withdrew to) *b^{i}-h^{i}* (with him) *m^{a}kān^{an}* (a place) *q^{a}ṣīyā* (remote).

Verse 23, part 1

فَأَجَآءَهَا ٱلْمَخَاضُ إِلَىٰ جِذْعِ ٱلنَّخْلَةِ

So the pains of childbirth drove her to the trunk of the date-palm

Fa-ajā^{a}-hā (so it drove her, so it caused her to go) *al-m^{a}khāḍu* (the pains of childbirth) *ilā* (to) *j^{a}z^{i}* (the trunk [of]) *al-n^{a}khl^{a}t^{i}* (the date-palm).

Verse 23, part 2

قَالَتْ يَٰلَيْتَنِى مِتُّ قَبْلَ هَٰذَا وَكُنتُ نَسْيًا مَّنسِيًّا

She said, "Oh I wish I had died before this and I was abandoned, forgotten."

Qāl^{a}-t (she said) *yā-l^{a}yt^{a}-nī* (Oh I wish I had) *m^{i}t-t^{u}* (I died) *q^{a}bl^{a}* (before) *hādhā* (this) *w^{a}-k^{u}n-t^{u}* (and I was) *n^{a}sy^{an}* (an abandoned and thrown away thing) *m^{a}nsīyā* (a forgotten thing).

Verse 24

فَنَادَىٰهَا مِن تَحۡتِهَآ أَلَّا تَحۡزَنِي قَدۡ جَعَلَ رَبُّكِ تَحۡتَكِ سَرِيّٗا

So he called her from below her that “Do not grieve, your Lord truly has placed beneath you a stream.”

F^{a}*-nādā-hā* (so he called her) *m*^{i}*n t*^{a}*ḥt*^{i}*-hā* (from beneath her) *al-lā* (that do not) *t*^{a}*ḥz*^{a}*-nī* (you grieve) *q*^{a}*d* (truly has) *j*^{a}*ʿ*^{a}*l*^{a} (He placed) *r*^{a}*bb*^{u}*-k*^{i} (your Lord) *t*^{a}*ḥt*^{a}*k*^{i} (beneath you) *s*^{a}*rīyā* (a stream).

Verse 25

وَهُزِّيٓ إِلَيۡكِ بِجِذۡعِ ٱلنَّخۡلَةِ تُسَٰقِطۡ عَلَيۡكِ رُطَبٗا جَنِيّٗا

And shake toward you the trunk of the date-palm, it will drop upon you fresh, ripe dates

W^{a}*-h*^{u}*zz-ī* (and shake) *il*^{a}*y-k*^{i} (toward you) *b*^{i}*-j*^{i}*dh*^{i} (the trunk) *al-n*^{a}*khl*^{a}*t*^{i} (the date-palm) *t*^{u}*sāq*^{i}*ṭ* (it drops) *ʿ*^{a}*l*^{a}*y-k*^{i} (on you) *r*^{u}*ṭ*^{a}*b*^{an} (fresh dates) *j*^{a}*nīyā* (ripe).

Verse 26, part 1

فَكُلِي وَٱشۡرَبِي وَقَرِّي عَيۡنٗاۖ فَإِمَّا تَرَيِنَّ مِنَ ٱلۡبَشَرِ أَحَدٗا

“So eat, drink, and gain consolation. And if you see from humanity anyone...”

F^{a}*-k*^{u}*l-ī* (so eat) *w*^{a}*-ishr*^{a}*b-ī* (and drink) *w*^{a}*-q*^{a}*rr-ī ʿ*^{a}*yn*^{an} (and gain consolation) *f*^{a}*-immā* (and if) *t*^{a}*r*^{a}*y*^{i}*nn*^{a} (you see) *m*^{i}*n*^{a} (from) *al-b*^{a}*sh*^{a}*r*^{i} (humans, humanity) *aḥ*^{a}*dā* (a one, anyone).

The phrase *q*^{a}*rr-ī ʿ*^{a}*yn*^{an} literally means “let your eyes become cool”, “cool your eyes”. It is a phrase that means to gain consolation by observing someone you love. Here she is being asked to interact with the infant in order to console herself with the love she will feel for it.

The word *t*^{a}*r*^{a}*y*^{i}*nn*^{a} is originally *t*^{a}*r*^{a}*yn*^{a} with the *nūn* of emphasis (something we have not seen before) added to its end:

تَرَيْنَ + نَ = تَرَيِنَّ

Below is another example of the use of the emphatic *nūn*:

تَذْهَبَ + نَ = تَذْهَبَنَّ

Verse 26, part 2

فَقُولِىٓ إِنِّى نَذَرْتُ لِلرَّحْمَٰنِ صَوْمًا فَلَنْ أُكَلِّمَ ٱلْيَوْمَ إِنسِيًّا

Then say, "Indeed I have vowed to the Most Gracious a fast, so I will not speak with any human today."

F^{a}*-qūl-ī* (then say) *in-nī* (indeed I) *n*^{a}*dh*^{a}*r-t*^{u} (I vowed) *l*^{i}*-al-r*^{a}*ḥmān*^{i} (to the Most Gracious) *ṣawm*^{an} (a fast [from speaking]) *f*^{a}*-l*^{a}*n* (so will not) *uk*^{a}*ll*^{i}*m*^{a} (I speak with) *al-y*^{a}*wm*^{a} (today) *insīyā* (one of humankind).

Verse 27

فَأَتَتْ بِهِۦ قَوْمَهَا تَحْمِلُهُۥ ۖ قَالُوا۟ يَٰمَرْيَمُ لَقَدْ جِئْتِ شَيْـًۭٔا فَرِيًّۭا

So she brought him to her people, carrying him. They said, "O Mary, you have truly brought a tremendous thing."

F^{a}*-at*^{a}*-t b*^{i}*-h*^{i} (so she brought him) *q*^{a}*wm*^{a}*-hā* ([to] her people) *t*^{a}*ḥm*^{i}*l*^{u}*-h*^{u} (she carries him) *qālū* (they said) *y*^{a}*-m*^{a}*ry*^{a}*m*^{u} (O Mary) *l*^{a}*-q*^{a}*d* (truly have) *j*^{i}*'t*^{i} (you have brought) *sh*^{a}*y*^{an} (a thing) *f*^{a}*rīyā* (tremendous).

The word *q*^{a}*wm* means "kinsfolk", "[one's] people", "nation".

Verse 28

يَٰٓأُخۡتَ هَٰرُونَ مَا كَانَ أَبُوكِ ٱمۡرَأَ سَوۡءٖ وَمَا كَانَتۡ أُمُّكِ بَغِيّٗا

"O sister of Aaron, your father was not a man of evil nor was your mother an unchatse woman."

Yā-ukht^{a} (O sister [of]) *hārūn*^{a} (Aaron) *mā kān*^{a} (was not) *abū-k*^{i} (your father) *imr*$^{a\,a}$ (a man [of]) *sū*^{in} (evil) *w*^{a}*-mā kān*^{a}*-t* (and was not) *umm*^{i}*-k*^{i} (your mother) *b*^{a}*ghīyā* (an unchaste woman).

Verse 29

فَأَشَارَتۡ إِلَيۡهِۖ قَالُواْ كَيۡفَ نُكَلِّمُ مَن كَانَ فِي ٱلۡمَهۡدِ صَبِيّٗا

So she pointed to him. They said, "How do we speak with one who is a child, in the cradle?"

F^{a}*-ashār*^{a}*-t* (so she pointed) *il*^{a}*y-h*^{i} (to him) *qālū* (they said) *k*^{a}*yf*^{a} (how do) *n*^{u}*k*^{a}*ll*^{i}*m*^{u} (we speak with) *m*^{a}*n* (one who) *kān*^{a} (was) *fī* (in) *al-m*^{a}*hd*^{i} (the cradle) *ṣ*^{a}*bīyā* (a child).

This page intentionally left blank

Lesson 40 Review

وَٱذۡكُرۡ فِي ٱلۡكِتَٰبِ مَرۡيَمَ إِذِ ٱنتَبَذَتۡ مِنۡ أَهۡلِهَا مَكَانٗا شَرۡقِيّٗا

W^{a}*-udhk*^{u}*r* (and remember) *fī* (in) *al-k*^{i}*tāb*^{i} (the Book) *m*^{a}*ry*^{a}*m*^{a} (Mary) *idh* (in) *int*^{a}*b*^{a}*dh*^{a}*-t* (she withdrew to) *min* (from) *ahl*^{i}*-hā* (her family) *m*^{a}*kān*^{a}*n* (a place) *sh*^{a}*rqīyā* (easterly, i.e. located in the east or east-facing).

فَٱتَّخَذَتۡ مِن دُونِهِمۡ حِجَابٗا فَأَرۡسَلۡنَآ إِلَيۡهَا رُوحَنَا فَتَمَثَّلَ لَهَا بَشَرٗا سَوِيّٗا

F^{a}*-itt*^{a}*kh*^{a}*dh*^{a}*-t* (so she took up, so she adopted) *m*^{i}*n dūn*^{i}*-h*^{i}*m* (apart from them) *ḥ*^{i}*jāb*^{an} (a screen) *f*^{a}*-ars*^{a}*lnā* (so we sent) *il*^{a}*y-hā* (to her) *rūḥ*^{a}*-nā* (Our Spirit) *f*^{a}*-t*^{a}*m*^{a}*thth*^{a}*l*^{a} (so he adopted the likeness [of]) *l*^{a}*-hā* (for her) *b*^{a}*sh*^{a}*r*^{an} (a human) *s*^{a}*wīyā* (proper, sound).

قَالَتۡ إِنِّيٓ أَعُوذُ بِٱلرَّحۡمَٰنِ مِنكَ إِن كُنتَ تَقِيّٗا

Qāl^{a}*-t* (she said) *in-nī* (indeed I) *a'ūdh*^{u} (I seek protection) *b*^{i}*-al-r*^{a}*ḥmān*^{i} (with the most Gracious, by the most Gracious) *m*^{i}*n-k*^{a} (from you) *in* (if) *k*^{u}*n-t*^{a} (you are) *t*^{a}*qīyā* (God-fearing).

قَالَ إِنَّمَآ أَنَا۠ رَسُولُ رَبِّكِ لِأَهَبَ لَكِ غُلَٰمٗا زَكِيّٗا

Qāla (he said) *inn*^{a}*-mā an*^{a} (indeed I am only) *r*^{a}*sūl*^{u} (the messenger [of]) *r*^{a}*bb*^{i}*-k*^{i} (your Lord) *l*^{i}*-ah*^{a}*b*^{a} (to bestow, to grant) *l*^{a}*-k*^{i} (to you) *gh*^{u}*lām*^{an} (a boy) *z*^{a}*kīyā* (pure).

قَالَتْ أَنَّىٰ يَكُونُ لِى غُلَٰمٌ وَلَمْ يَمْسَسْنِى بَشَرٌ وَلَمْ أَكُ بَغِيًّا

Qāl^{a}-t (she said) *annā* (how can) *y^{a}kūn^{u}* (there will be) *l-ī* (for me) *gh^{u}lām^{un}* (a boy) *w^{a}-l^{a}m* (while did not) *y^{a}ms^{a}s-nī* (touch me) *b^{a}sh^{a}r^{un}* (a human) *w^{a}-l^{a}m* (and was not) *ak^{u}* (I was) *b^{a}ghīyā* (an unchaste woman, a harlot).

قَالَ كَذَٰلِكِ قَالَ رَبُّكِ هُوَ عَلَىَّ هَيِّنٌ ۖ

Qāl^{a} (he said) *k^{a}-dhāl^{i}k^{i}* (thus, like that) *qāl^{a}* (He said) *r^{a}bb^{u}-k^{i}* (your Lord) *h^{u}w^{a}* (it [is]) *^{ʿa}l^{a}y-y^{a}* (on me) *h^{a}yy^{i}n^{un}* (easy).

وَلِنَجْعَلَهُۥٓ ءَايَةً لِّلنَّاسِ وَرَحْمَةً مِّنَّا ۚ وَكَانَ أَمْرًا مَّقْضِيًّا

W^{a} (and) *l^{i}* (to) *n^{a}j^{a}l^{a}-h^{u}* (we make him) *āy^{a}t^{an}* (a sign) *l^{i}-al-nās^{i}* (for the people) *w^{a}-raḥm^{a}t^{an}* (and a mercy) *m^{i}n-nā* (from us) *w^{a}-kān^{a}* (and it was) *amr^{an}* (a matter) *m^{a}qḍīyā* (decreed).

فَحَمَلَتْهُ فَٱنتَبَذَتْ بِهِۦ مَكَانًا قَصِيًّا

F^{a}-ḥ^{a}m^{a}l^{a}-t-h^{u} (so she carried him) *f^{a}-int^{a}b^{a}dh^{a}-t* (so she withdrew to) *b^{i}-h^{i}* (with him) *m^{a}kān^{an}* (a place) *q^{a}ṣīyā* (remote).

فَأَجَآءَهَا ٱلْمَخَاضُ إِلَىٰ جِذْعِ ٱلنَّخْلَةِ

Fa-ajā^{a}-hā (so it drove her, so it caused her to go) *al-m^{a}khāḍu* (the pains of childbirth) *ilā* (to) *j^{a}z^{i}* (the trunk [of]) *al-n^{a}khl^{a}t^{i}* (the date-palm).

قَالَتْ يَٰلَيْتَنِي مِتُّ قَبْلَ هَٰذَا وَكُنتُ نَسْيًا مَّنسِيًّا

Qāl^{a}-t (she said) *yā-l^{a}yt^{a}-nī* (Oh I wish I had) *m^{i}t-t^{u}* (I died) *q^{a}bl^{a}* (before) *hādhā* (this) *w^{a}-k^{u}n-t^{u}* (and I was) *n^{a}sy^{an}* (an abandoned and thrown away thing) *m^{a}nsīyā* (a forgotten thing).

فَنَادَىٰهَا مِن تَحْتِهَآ أَلَّا تَحْزَنِي قَدْ جَعَلَ رَبُّكِ تَحْتَكِ سَرِيًّا

F^{a}-nādā-hā (so he called her) *m^{i}n t^{a}ḥt^{i}-hā* (from beneath her) *al-lā* (that do not) *t^{a}ḥz^{a}-nī* (you grieve) *q^{a}d* (truly has) *j^{a}^{a}l^{a}* (He placed) *r^{a}bb^{u}-k^{i}* (your Lord) *t^{a}ḥt^{a}k^{i}* (beneath you) *s^{a}rīyā* (a stream).

وَهُزِّيٓ إِلَيْكِ بِجِذْعِ ٱلنَّخْلَةِ تُسَٰقِطْ عَلَيْكِ رُطَبًا جَنِيًّا

W^{a}-h^{u}zz-ī (and shake) *il^{a}y-k^{i}* (toward you) *b^{i}-j^{i}dh^{i}* (the trunk) *al-n^{a}khl^{a}t^{i}* (the date-palm) *t^{u}sāq^{i}ṭ* (it drops) *^{a}l^{a}y-k^{i}* (on you) *r^{u}ṭ^{a}b^{an}* (fresh dates) *j^{a}nīyā* (ripe).

فَكُلِي وَٱشْرَبِي وَقَرِّي عَيْنًا ۖ فَإِمَّا تَرَيِنَّ مِنَ ٱلْبَشَرِ أَحَدًا

F^{a}-k^{u}l-ī (so eat) *w^{a}-ishr^{a}b-ī* (and drink) *w^{a}-q^{a}rr-ī* *^{a}yn^{an}* (and gain consolation) *f^{a}-immā* (and if) *t^{a}r^{a}y^{i}nn^{a}* (you see) *m^{i}n^{a}* (from) *al-b^{a}sh^{a}r^{i}* (humans, humanity) *aḥ^{a}dā* (a one, anyone).

فَقُولِيٓ إِنِّي نَذَرْتُ لِلرَّحْمَٰنِ صَوْمًا فَلَنْ أُكَلِّمَ ٱلْيَوْمَ إِنسِيًّا

F^{a}-qūl-ī (then say) *in-nī* (indeed I) *n^{a}dh^{a}r-t^{u}* (I vowed) *l^{i}-al-r^{a}ḥmān^{i}* (to the Most Gracious) *ṣawm^{an}* (a fast [from speaking]) *f^{a}-l^{a}n* (so will not) *uk^{a}ll^{i}m^{a}* (I speak with) *al-y^{a}wm^{a}* (today) *insīyā* (one of humankind).

فَأَتَتْ بِهِۦ قَوْمَهَا تَحْمِلُهُۥ ۖ قَالُوا۟ يَٰمَرْيَمُ لَقَدْ جِئْتِ شَيْـًۭٔا فَرِيًّۭا

F^{a}-at^{a}-t b^{i}-h^{i} (so she brought him) *q^{a}wm^{a}-hā* ([to] her people) *t^{a}ḥm^{i}l^{u}-h^{u}* (she carries him) *qālū* (they said) *y^{a}-m^{a}ry^{a}m^{u}* (O Mary) *l^{a}-q^{a}d* (truly have) *j^{i}ʾt^{i}* (you have brought) *sh^{a}y^{an}* (a thing) *f^{a}rīyā* (tremendous).

يَٰٓأُخْتَ هَٰرُونَ مَا كَانَ أَبُوكِ ٱمْرَأَ سَوْءٍۢ وَمَا كَانَتْ أُمُّكِ بَغِيًّۭا

Yā-ukht^{a} (O sister [of]) *hārūn^{a}* (Aaron) *mā kān^{a}* (was not) *abū-k^{i}* (your father) *imr^{a}ʾ^{a}* (a man [of]) *sū^{in}* (evil) *w^{a}-mā kān^{a}-t* (and was not) *umm^{i}-k^{i}* (your mother) *b^{a}ghīyā* (an unchaste woman).

فَأَشَارَتْ إِلَيْهِ ۖ قَالُوا۟ كَيْفَ نُكَلِّمُ مَن كَانَ فِى ٱلْمَهْدِ صَبِيًّۭا

F^{a}-ashār^{a}-t (so she pointed) *il^{a}y-h^{i}* (to him) *qālū* (they said) *k^{a}yf^{a}* (how do) *n^{u}k^{a}ll^{i}m^{u}* (we speak with) *m^{a}n* (one who) *kān^{a}* (was) *fī* (in) *al-m^{a}hd^{i}* (the cradle) *ṣ^{a}bīyā* (a child).

Lesson 41: Maryam Part 4

Verse 30

قَالَ إِنِّي عَبْدُ ٱللَّهِ ءَاتَىٰنِيَ ٱلْكِتَٰبَ وَجَعَلَنِي نَبِيًّا

He [the infant Jesus] said, “Indeed I am the servant of God. He has given me the Book and made me a prophet.”

Qāl^{a} (he said) *in-nī* (indeed I [am]) ʿ^{a}*bd*^{u} (the servant [of]) *allāh*^{i} (God) *ātān*^{i} (He gave me) *al-k*^{i}*tāb*^{a} (the Book) *w*^{a}*-j*^{a}ʿ^{a}*l*^{a}*-nī* (and He made me) *n*^{a}*bīyā* (a prophet).

Verse 31

وَجَعَلَنِي مُبَارَكًا أَيْنَ مَا كُنتُ وَأَوْصَٰنِي بِٱلصَّلَوٰةِ وَٱلزَّكَوٰةِ مَا دُمْتُ حَيًّا

And He made me blessed wherever I am and enjoined on me the prayer and the zakah as long as I remain alive

W^{a}*-j*^{a}ʿ^{a}*l*^{a}*-nī* (and He made me) *m*^{u}*bār*^{a}*k*^{an} (a blessed [one]) *ayn*^{a} *mā* (wherever) *k*^{u}*n-t*^{u} (I was) *w*^{a}*-awṣā-nī* (and He enjoined on me) *b*^{i}*-al-ṣ*^{a}*lāt*^{i} (the prayer) *w*^{a}*-al-z*^{a}*kāt*^{i} (the zakah) *mā d*^{u}*m-t*^{u} (as long as I remain) *ḥ*^{a}*yyā* (alive).

The phrase *d*^{u}*m-t*^{u} means “I remained”. The phrase *mā d*^{u}*m-t*^{u} means “as long as I remained”, “while I remained”.

Verse 32

وَبَرًّۢا بِوَٰلِدَتِي وَلَمْ يَجْعَلْنِي جَبَّارًا شَقِيًّا

And dutiful to my mother and He did not make me a wretched tyrant

W^{a}-b^{a}rr^{an} (and a dutiful one) *b^{i}-wāl^{i}d^{a}-tī* (to my mother) *w^{a}-lam* (and did not) *yaj'al-nī* (He made me) *jabbāran* (a tyrant) *shaqīyā* (a wretched one).

Verse 33

وَٱلسَّلَٰمُ عَلَيَّ يَوۡمَ وُلِدتُّ وَيَوۡمَ أَمُوتُ وَيَوۡمَ أُبۡعَثُ حَيّٗا

And peace is on me the day I was born, the day I die and the die I will be raised back to life

W^{a}-al-s^{a}lām^{u} (and peace [is]) *^{a}l^{a}y-y^{a}* (upon me) *y^{a}wm^{a}* (the day) *w^{u}l^{i}d-t^{u}* (I was born) *w^{a}-y^{a}wm^{a}* (and the day) *amū-t^{u}* (I die) *w^{a}-y^{a}wm^{a}* (and the day) *ub^{a}th^{u}* (I am raised back) *ḥ^{a}yyā* (alive).

Verse 34

ذَٰلِكَ عِيسَى ٱبۡنُ مَرۡيَمَۖ قَوۡلَ ٱلۡحَقِّ ٱلَّذِي فِيهِ يَمۡتَرُونَ

That is Jesus son of Mary, the word of truth about which they dispute

Dhāl^{i}k^{a} (that is) *'īsā ibn^{i} m^{a}ry^{a}m^{a}* (Jesus son of Mary) *q^{a}wl^{a}* (the word [of]) *al-ḥ^{a}qq^{i}* (the truth) *all^{a}dhī* (which) *fī-h^{i}* (in it) *y^{a}mt^{a}rūn* (they dispute).

Verse 35, part 1

مَا كَانَ لِلَّهِ أَن يَتَّخِذَ مِن وَلَدٖۖ سُبۡحَٰنَهُۥٓۚ

It is not befitting for God to take a son, exalted and pure is He [above such a thing]!

Mā kān^{a} (it was not) *l^{i}-llāh^{i}* (for God) *an* (to) *y^{a}tt^{a}kh^{i}dh^{a}* (take) *w^{a}l^{a}d^{in}* (a son) *s^{u}bḥān^{a}h* (exalted and pure is He!).

Verse 35, part 2

إِذَا قَضَىٰٓ أَمْرًا فَإِنَّمَا يَقُولُ لَهُۥ كُن فَيَكُونُ

If He decrees a matter, truly He only says to it "Be!" and it is.

Idhā (if) *q*^{a}*ḍā* (He decreed) *amr*^{an} (a matter) *f*^{a}*-inn*^{a}*-mā* (then truly [He] only) *y*^{a}*qūl*^{u} (He says) *l*^{a}*-h*^{u} (to it) *k*^{u}*n* (be!) *f*^{a}*-y*^{a}*kūn* (and it is).

Verse 36

وَإِنَّ ٱللَّهَ رَبِّى وَرَبُّكُمْ فَٱعْبُدُوهُ ۚ هَٰذَا صِرَٰطٌ مُّسْتَقِيمٌ

[Jesus said,] "And indeed God is my Lord and your [plural] Lord so worship Him, this is a straight path

W^{a}*-inn*^{a} (and indeed) *allāh*^{a} (God [is]) *r*^{a}*bb-ī* (my Lord) *w*^{a}*-r*^{a}*bb*^{u}*-k*^{u}*m* (and your Lord) *f*^{a}*-uʿb*^{u}*d*^{u}*-h*^{u} (so worship him) *hādhā* (this [is]) *ṣ*^{i}*rāt*^{un} (a path) *m*^{u}*st*^{a}*qīm* (straight).

Verse 37

فَٱخْتَلَفَ ٱلْأَحْزَابُ مِنۢ بَيْنِهِمْ ۖ فَوَيْلٌ لِّلَّذِينَ كَفَرُوا۟ مِن مَّشْهَدِ يَوْمٍ عَظِيمٍ

So the factions differed between themselves. So woe to those who denied from the scene of a tremendous day

F^{a}*-ikht*^{a}*l*^{a}*f*^{a} (so they differed, so they disagreed) *l-aḥzāb*^{u} (the factions, the parties) *m*^{i}*n* (from) *b*^{a}*yn*^{i}*-h*^{i}*m* (between them) *f*^{a}*-w*^{a}*yl*^{un} (so woe) *li-all*^{a}*dhīn*^{a} (to those who) *k*^{a}*f*^{a}*rū* (denied) *m*^{i}*n* (from) *m*^{a}*shh*^{a}*d*^{i} (the scene [of]) *y*^{a}*wm*^{in} (a day) *ʿaḍīm* (tremendous, great).

Verse 38

أَسۡمِعۡ بِهِمۡ وَأَبۡصِرۡ يَوۡمَ يَأۡتُونَنَاۖ لَٰكِنِ ٱلظَّٰلِمُونَ ٱلۡيَوۡمَ فِي ضَلَٰلٖ مُّبِينٖ

How hearing and how seeing the day they come to us! But the wrongdoers today are in a clear error

Asmiʿ b^{i}-h^{i}m (how hearing!) *w^{a} abṣ^{i}r* (and how seeing!) *y^{a}wm^{a}* (the day) *y^{a}ʿtūn^{a}-nā* (they come to us) *lāk^{i}n^{i}* (but) *al-ẓāl^{i}m^{u}n^{a}* (the wrongdoers, the oppressors) *al-y^{a}wm^{a}* (today [are]) *fī* (in) *ḍ^{a}lāl^{in}* (error, misguidance) *m^{u}bīn* (clear).

The word *asmiʿ* means "more hearing", "most hearing". The phrase *asmiʿ b^{i}* is an exclamation that means "how hearing!" (i.e. how able to hear they are!). The same applies to *abṣ^{i}r b^{i}*.

Verse 39

وَأَنذِرۡهُمۡ يَوۡمَ ٱلۡحَسۡرَةِ إِذۡ قُضِيَ ٱلۡأَمۡرُ وَهُمۡ فِي غَفۡلَةٖ وَهُمۡ لَا يُؤۡمِنُونَ

And warn them about the day of regret when the matter is decreed, while they are in obliviousness and while they do not believe

W^{a}-andh^{i}r-h^{u}m (and warn them about) *y^{a}wm^{a}* (the day [of]) *al-ḥ^{a}sr^{a}t^{i}* (grief) *idh* (when) *q^{u}ḍ^{i}y^{a}* (it was decreed) *al-amr^{u}* (the matter) *w^{a}-h^{u}m* (while they [are]) *fī* (in) *gh^{a}fl^{a}t^{in}* (obliviousness) *w^{a}-h^{u}m* (and they) *lā y^{u}ʿm^{i}nūn* (do not believe).

Lesson 41 Review

قَالَ إِنِّي عَبْدُ ٱللَّهِ ءَاتَىٰنِيَ ٱلْكِتَٰبَ وَجَعَلَنِي نَبِيًّا

Qāl^{a} (he said) *in-nī* (indeed I [am]) *ʿ*^{a}*bd*^{u} (the servant [of]) *allāh*^{i} (God) *ātān*^{i} (He gave me) *al-k*^{i}*tāb*^{a} (the Book) *w*^{a}*-j*^{a}*ʿ*^{a}*l*^{a}*-nī* (and He made me) *n*^{a}*bīyā* (a prophet).

وَجَعَلَنِي مُبَارَكًا أَيْنَ مَا كُنتُ وَأَوْصَٰنِي بِٱلصَّلَوٰةِ وَٱلزَّكَوٰةِ مَا دُمْتُ حَيًّا

W^{a}*-j*^{a}*ʿ*^{a}*l*^{a}*-nī* (and He made me) *m*^{u}*bār*^{a}*k*^{an} (a blessed [one]) *ayn*^{a} *mā* (wherever) *k*^{u}*n-t*^{u} (I was) *w*^{a}*-awṣā-nī* (and He enjoined on me) *b*^{i}*-al-ṣ*^{a}*lāt*^{i} (the prayer) *w*^{a}*-al-z*^{a}*kāt*^{i} (the zakah) *mā d*^{u}*m-t*^{u} (as long as I remain) *ḥ*^{a}*yyā* (alive).

وَبَرًّۢا بِوَٰلِدَتِي وَلَمْ يَجْعَلْنِي جَبَّارًا شَقِيًّا

W^{a}*-b*^{a}*rr*^{an} (and a dutiful one) *b*^{i}*-wāl*^{i}*d*^{a}*-tī* (to my mother) *w*^{a}*-lam* (and did not) *yajʿal-nī* (He made me) *jabbāran* (a tyrant) *shaqīyā* (a wretched one).

وَٱلسَّلَٰمُ عَلَيَّ يَوْمَ وُلِدتُّ وَيَوْمَ أَمُوتُ وَيَوْمَ أُبْعَثُ حَيًّا

W^{a}*-al-s*^{a}*lām*^{u} (and peace [is]) *ʿ*^{a}*l*^{a}*y-y*^{a} (upon me) *y*^{a}*wm*^{a} (the day) *w*^{u}*l*^{i}*d-t*^{u} (I was born) *w*^{a}*-y*^{a}*wm*^{a} (and the day) *amū-t*^{u} (I die) *w*^{a}*-y*^{a}*wm*^{a} (and the day) *ubʿ*^{a}*th*^{u} (I am raised back) *ḥ*^{a}*yyā* (alive).

ذَٰلِكَ عِيسَى ٱبۡنُ مَرۡيَمَۖ قَوۡلَ ٱلۡحَقِّ ٱلَّذِي فِيهِ يَمۡتَرُونَ

Dhāl^{i}k^{a} (that is) *ʿīsā ibn^{i} m^{a}ry^{a}m^{a}* (Jesus son of Mary) *q^{a}wl^{a}* (the word [of]) *al-ḥ^{a}qq^{i}* (the truth) *all^{a}dhī* (which) *fī-h^{i}* (in it) *y^{a}mt^{a}rūn* (they dispute).

مَا كَانَ لِلَّهِ أَن يَتَّخِذَ مِن وَلَدٖۖ سُبۡحَٰنَهُۥٓۚ

Mā kān^{a} (it was not) *l^{i}-llāh^{i}* (for God) *an* (to) *y^{a}tt^{a}kh^{i}dh^{a}* (take) *w^{a}l^{a}d^{in}* (a son) *s^{u}bḥān^{a}h* (exalted and pure is He!).

إِذَا قَضَىٰٓ أَمۡرٗا فَإِنَّمَا يَقُولُ لَهُۥ كُن فَيَكُونُ

Idhā (if) *q^{a}ḍā* (He decreed) *amr^{an}* (a matter) *f^{a}-inn^{a}-mā* (then truly [He] only) *y^{a}qūl^{u}* (He says) *l^{a}-h^{u}* (to it) *k^{u}n* (be!) *f^{a}-y^{a}kūn* (and it is).

وَإِنَّ ٱللَّهَ رَبِّي وَرَبُّكُمۡ فَٱعۡبُدُوهُۚ هَٰذَا صِرَٰطٞ مُّسۡتَقِيمٞ

W^{a}-inn^{a} (and indeed) *allāh^{a}* (God [is]) *r^{a}bb-ī* (my Lord) *w^{a}-r^{a}bb^{u}-k^{u}m* (and your Lord) *f^{a}-uʿb^{u}d^{u}-h^{u}* (so worship him) *hādhā* (this [is]) *ṣ^{i}rāt^{un}* (a path) *m^{u}st^{a}qīm* (straight).

فَٱخۡتَلَفَ ٱلۡأَحۡزَابُ مِنۢ بَيۡنِهِمۡۖ فَوَيۡلٞ لِّلَّذِينَ كَفَرُواْ مِن مَّشۡهَدِ يَوۡمٍ عَظِيمٍ

F^{a}-ikht^{a}l^{a}f^{a} (so they differed, so they disagreed) *l-aḥzāb^{u}* (the factions, the parties) *m^{i}n* (from) *b^{a}yn^{i}-h^{i}m* (between them) *f^{a}-w^{a}yl^{un}* (so woe) *li-all^{a}dhīn^{a}* (to those who) *k^{a}f^{a}rū* (denied) *m^{i}n* (from) *m^{a}shh^{a}d^{i}* (the scene [of]) *y^{a}wm^{in}* (a day) *ʿaḍīm* (tremendous, great).

أَسْمِعْ بِهِمْ وَأَبْصِرْ يَوْمَ يَأْتُونَنَا ۖ لَٰكِنِ ٱلظَّٰلِمُونَ ٱلْيَوْمَ فِى ضَلَٰلٍ مُّبِينٍ

Asmiʿ b^{i}*-h*^{i}*m* (how hearing!) *w*^{a} *abṣ*^{i}*r* (and how seeing!) *y*^{a}*wm*^{a} (the day) *y*^{a}*ʾtūn*^{a}*-nā* (they come to us) *lāk*^{i}*n*^{i} (but) *al-ẓāl*^{i}*m*^{u}*n*^{a} (the wrongdoers, the oppressors) *al-y*^{a}*wm*^{a} (today [are]) *fī* (in) *ḍ*^{a}*lāl*^{in} (error, misguidance) *m*^{u}*bīn* (clear).

وَأَنذِرْهُمْ يَوْمَ ٱلْحَسْرَةِ إِذْ قُضِىَ ٱلْأَمْرُ وَهُمْ فِى غَفْلَةٍ وَهُمْ لَا يُؤْمِنُونَ

W^{a}*-andh*^{i}*r-h*^{u}*m* (and warn them about) *y*^{a}*wm*^{a} (the day [of]) *al-ḥ*^{a}*sr*^{a}*t*^{i} (grief) *idh* (when) *q*^{u}*ḍ*^{i}*y*^{a} (it was decreed) *al-amr*^{u} (the matter) *w*^{a}*-h*^{u}*m* (while they [are]) *fī* (in) *gh*^{a}*fl*^{a}*t*^{in} (obliviousness) *w*^{a}*-h*^{u}*m* (and they) *lā y*^{u}*ʾm*^{i}*nūn* (do not believe).

This page intentionally left blank

Lesson 42: Maryam Part 5

Verse 40

إِنَّا نَحْنُ نَرِثُ ٱلْأَرْضَ وَمَنْ عَلَيْهَا وَإِلَيْنَا يُرْجَعُونَ

Indeed we inherit the earth and those on it and to us they return

Innā (indeed we) *n^{a}ḥn^{u}* (we) *n^{a}r^{i}th^{u}* (we inherit) *al-arḍ^{a}* (the earth) *w^{a}-m^{a}n* (and [those] who [are]) *^{a}l^{a}y-hā* (on it) *w^{a}-il^{a}y-nā* (and to us) *y^{u}rj^{a}ʿūn* (they return).

Verse 41

وَٱذْكُرْ فِى ٱلْكِتَٰبِ إِبْرَٰهِيمَ ۚ إِنَّهُۥ كَانَ صِدِّيقًا نَّبِيًّا

And mention in the Book Abraham; indeed he was a man of truth, a prophet

Wa-udhk^{u}r (and mention) *fī al-k^{i}tāb^{i}* (in the Book) *ibrāhīm^{a}* (Abrahm) *inn^{a}-h^{u}* (indeed he) *kān^{a}* (was) *ṣ^{i}ddīq^{an}* (a man of truth) *n^{a}bīyā* (a prophet).

Verse 42

إِذْ قَالَ لِأَبِيهِ يَٰٓأَبَتِ لِمَ تَعْبُدُ مَا لَا يَسْمَعُ وَلَا يُبْصِرُ وَلَا يُغْنِى عَنكَ شَيْـًٔا

When he said to his father, "O my father, why do you worship that which does not hear, does not see and does not benefit you at all?"

Idh qāl^{a} (when he said) *l^{i}-abīh^{i}* (to his father) *yā ab^{a}t^{i}* (O my father) *l^{i}-m^{a}* (for what) *t^{a}ʿb^{u}d^{u}* (you worship) *mā lā* (what does not) *y^{a}sm^{a}ʿ^{u}* (hears) *w^{a}-lā* (and does not) *y^{u}bṣ^{i}r^{u}* (sees) *w^{a}-lā y^{u}ghnī ^{a}nk^{a}* (and does not benefit you) *sh^{a}y'ā* (anything).

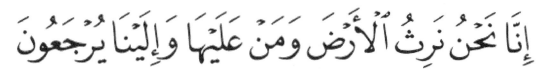

The verb *y*^{u}*ghnī* means “it makes him needless”, “it makes him rich”, while the phrase *y*^{u}*ghnī* ^{ʿa}*n* means “it benefits him”.

Verse 43

يَٰٓأَبَتِ إِنِّي قَدۡ جَآءَنِي مِنَ ٱلۡعِلۡمِ مَا لَمۡ يَأۡتِكَ فَٱتَّبِعۡنِيٓ أَهۡدِكَ صِرَٰطٗا سَوِيّٗا

“O my father, indeed it has come to me of knowledge what has not come to you so follow me, I will guide you to a proper path.”

Yā ab^{a}*t*^{i} (O my father) *in-nī* (indeed I) *q*^{a}*d jā*^{ʾa}*-nī* (it has come to me) *m*^{i}*n*^{a} (from) *al-*^{ʿ}*lm*^{i} (knowledge) *mā l*^{a}*m* (that which did not) *y*^{a}*ʾt*^{i}*-k*^{a} (it comes to you) *f*^{a}*-itt*^{a}*b*^{iʿ}*-nī* (so follow me) *ahd*^{i}*-k*^{a} (I guide you [to]) *ṣ*^{i}*r*^{a}*ṭ*^{an} (a path) *s*^{a}*wīyā* (proper, sound).

Verse 44

يَٰٓأَبَتِ لَا تَعۡبُدِ ٱلشَّيۡطَٰنَۖ إِنَّ ٱلشَّيۡطَٰنَ كَانَ لِلرَّحۡمَٰنِ عَصِيّٗا

“O my father, do not worship Satan. Indeed Satan is toward the Most Gracious disobedient.”

Yā-ab^{a}*t*^{i} (O my father) *l*^{a} (do not) *t*^{a}*b*^{u}*d*^{i} (you worship) *al-sh*^{a}*yṭ*^{a}*n* (Satan, the devil) *inn*^{a} (indeed) *al-sh*^{a}*yṭ*^{a}*n*^{a} (Satan, the devil) *kān*^{a} (was) *l*^{i}*-al-r*^{a}*ḥmān*^{i} (to the most Gracious) ^{ʿa}*ṣīyā* (disobedient).

Verse 45

يَٰٓأَبَتِ إِنِّيٓ أَخَافُ أَن يَمَسَّكَ عَذَابٞ مِّنَ ٱلرَّحۡمَٰنِ فَتَكُونَ لِلشَّيۡطَٰنِ وَلِيّٗا

“O my father, I fear that a torment may touch you from the Most Gracious so that you will be a companion to Satan.”

Yā-ab^{a}*t*^{i} (O my father) *in-nī* (indeed I) *akhāf*^{u} (I fear) *an* (that) *y*^{a}*m*^{a}*ss*^{a}*-k*^{a} (it touches you) *ʿadhāb*^{un} (a torment) *m*^{i}*n*^{a} *al-r*^{a}*ḥmān*^{i} (from the Most Gracious) *f*^{a}*-t*^{a}*kūn*^{a} (so that you are, so that you will be) *l*^{i}*-al-sh*^{a}*yṭān*^{i} (to Satan) *w*^{a}*līyā* (a companion, a close ally).

Verse 46

قَالَ أَرَاغِبٌ أَنتَ عَنْ ءَالِهَتِى يَـٰٓإِبْرَٰهِيمُ ۖ لَئِن لَّمْ تَنتَهِ لَأَرْجُمَنَّكَ ۖ وَٱهْجُرْنِى مَلِيًّا

Are you desireless toward my gods O Abraham? If you do not stop truly I will stone you, and leave me for a long time.

Qāl^{a} (he said) *a-rāgh*^{i}*b*^{un} (are you desirious) *ant*^{a} (you) *ʿ*^{a}*n* (away [from]) *āl*^{i}*h*^{a}*t-ī* (my gods) *yā ibrāhīm* (O Abraham) *l*^{a}*-in* (truly if) *l*^{a}*m* (do not) *t*^{a}*nt*^{a}*h*^{i} (you stop) *l*^{a}*-arj*^{u}*m*^{a}*nn*^{a}*-k*^{a} (I will truly stone you) *w*^{a}*-uhj*^{u}*r-nī* (and leave me) *m*^{a}*līyā* (prolongedly).

The word *rāgh*^{i}*b* means "one who desires". But the phrase *rāgh*^{i}*b*^{un}*…ʿ*^{a}*n* means "desirious away [from]", meaning undesirious. The word *arj*^{u}*m*^{a}*nn*^{a} ("I truly stone") is *arj*^{u}*m*^{a} ("I stone") with the emphatic *nūn* added to it.

Verse 47

قَالَ سَلَـٰمٌ عَلَيْكَ ۖ سَأَسْتَغْفِرُ لَكَ رَبِّىٓ ۖ إِنَّهُۥ كَانَ بِى حَفِيًّا

He said, "Peace be upon you. I will seek forgiveness for you from my Lord, He was toward me gracious."

Qāl^{a} (he said) *s*^{a}*lām*^{un} (peace [be]) *ʿ*^{a}*l*^{a}*y-k*^{a} (upon you) *s*^{a}*-ast*^{a}*ghf*^{i}*r*^{u} (I will seek forgiveness [from]) *l*^{a}*-k*^{a} (for you) *r*^{a}*bb-ī* (my Lord) *inn*^{a}*-h*^{u} (indeed He) *kān*^{a} (was) *b-ī* (to me) *ḥ*^{a}*fīyā* (a gracious One).

Verse 48

وَأَعْتَزِلُكُمْ وَمَا تَدْعُونَ مِن دُونِ ٱللَّهِ وَأَدْعُوا۟ رَبِّى عَسَىٰٓ أَلَّآ أَكُونَ بِدُعَآءِ رَبِّى شَقِيًّا

"And I leave you and what you call besides God and I call my Lord, perhaps I will not be regarding my prayer to my Lord wretched."

W^{a}*-aʿt*^{a}*z*^{i}*l*^{u}*-k*^{u}*m* (and I leave you, and I cut off myself from you) *w*^{a}*-mā* (and what) *t*^{a}*dʿūn*^{a} (you call) *m*^{i}*n dūn*^{i} (apart from, besides, without) *allāh*^{i} (God) *w*^{a}*-adʿū* (and I call) *r*^{a}*bb-ī* (my Lord) *ʿ*^{a}*sā* (perhaps) *allā* (that will not) *akūn*^{a} (I am, I [will] be) *b*^{i}*-d*^{u}*ʿā*^{i} (regarding my prayer [to]) *r*^{a}*bb-ī* (my Lord) *sh*^{a}*qīyā* (wretched).

Here Abrahm says he will leave them so that perhaps his prayers will not go unanswered. Since in the previous verse he said he would pray for his father to be forgiven, here he may be saying that by abandoning these people, he hopes his prayer for his father's forgiveness will be accepted.

Verse 49

فَلَمَّا ٱعۡتَزَلَهُمۡ وَمَا يَعۡبُدُونَ مِن دُونِ ٱللَّهِ وَهَبۡنَا لَهُۥٓ إِسۡحَٰقَ وَيَعۡقُوبَۖ وَكُلًّا جَعَلۡنَا نَبِيًّا

So when he left them and what they worship besides God We gave to him Isaac and Jacob, and each we made a prophet.

F^{a}*-l*^{a}*mmā* (so when, so once) *iʿt*^{a}*z*^{a}*la-h*^{u}*m* (he left them, he cut off himself from them) *w*^{a}*-mā* (and what) *y*^{a}*ʿb*^{u}*dūn*^{a} (they worship) *m*^{i}*n dūn*^{i} (without, apart from) *allāh*^{i} (God) *w*^{a}*h*^{a}*b-nā* (we granted, we bestowed) *l*^{a}*-hū* (to him) *isḥāqā* (Isaac) *w*^{a}*-yaʿqūb*^{a} (and Jacob) *w*^{a}*-k*^{u}*ll*^{an} (and each, and everyone) *j*^{a}*ʿ*^{a}*l-nā* (we made) *n*^{a}*bīyā* (a prophet).

Verse 50

وَوَهَبۡنَا لَهُم مِّن رَّحۡمَتِنَا وَجَعَلۡنَا لَهُمۡ لِسَانَ صِدۡقٍ عَلِيًّا

And We granted them of our mercy and made for them a reputation of high honor

W^{a}*-w*^{a}*h*^{a}*b-nā* (and We granted) *l*^{a}*-h*^{u}*m* (to them) *m*^{i}*n* (from) *r*^{a}*ḥm*^{a}*t*^{i}*-nā* (Our mercy) *w*^{a}*-j*^{a}*ʿ*^{a}*l-nā* (and We made) *l*^{a}*-h*^{u}*m* (for them) *l*^{i}*sān*^{a} *ṣ*^{i}*dq*^{in} ^{a}*līyā* (a true reputation of high honor).

The word *l*^{i}*sān* means "tongue", *ṣ*^{i}*dq* means "truthfulness" and ^{a}*lī* means "high", "exalted". The phrase *l*^{i}*sān*^{a} *ṣ*^{i}*dq*^{in} means "a truthful mention", "a true reputation".

Lesson 42 Review

إِنَّا نَحْنُ نَرِثُ ٱلْأَرْضَ وَمَنْ عَلَيْهَا وَإِلَيْنَا يُرْجَعُونَ

Innā (indeed we) *n*^{a}*ḥn*^{u} (we) *n*^{a}*r*^{i}*th*^{u} (we inherit) *al-arḍ*^{a} (the earth) *w*^{a}*-m*^{a}*n* (and [those] who [are]) *ʿ*^{a}*l*^{a}*y-hā* (on it) *w*^{a}*-il*^{a}*y-nā* (and to us) *y*^{u}*rj*^{a}*ʿūn* (they return).

وَٱذْكُرْ فِى ٱلْكِتَٰبِ إِبْرَٰهِيمَ ۚ إِنَّهُۥ كَانَ صِدِّيقًا نَّبِيًّا

Wa-udhk^{u}*r* (and mention) *fī al-k*^{i}*tāb*^{i} (in the Book) *ibrāhīm*^{a} (Abrahm) *inn*^{a}*-h*^{u} (indeed he) *kān*^{a} (was) *ṣ*^{i}*ddīq*^{an} (a man of truth) *n*^{a}*bīyā* (a prophet).

إِذْ قَالَ لِأَبِيهِ يَٰٓأَبَتِ لِمَ تَعْبُدُ مَا لَا يَسْمَعُ وَلَا يُبْصِرُ وَلَا يُغْنِى عَنكَ شَيْـًٔا

Idh qāl^{a} (when he said) *l*^{i}*-abīh*^{i} (to his father) *yā ab*^{a}*t*^{i} (O my father) *l*^{i}*-m*^{a} (for what) *t*^{a}*ʿb*^{u}*d*^{u} (you worship) *mā lā* (what does not) *y*^{a}*sm*^{aʿu} (hears) *w*^{a}*-lā* (and does not) *y*^{u}*bṣ*^{i}*r*^{u} (sees) *w*^{a}*-lā y*^{u}*ghnī ʿ*^{a}*nk*^{a} (and does not benefit you) *sh*^{a}*y'ā* (anything).

يَٰٓأَبَتِ إِنِّى قَدْ جَآءَنِى مِنَ ٱلْعِلْمِ مَا لَمْ يَأْتِكَ فَٱتَّبِعْنِىٓ أَهْدِكَ صِرَٰطًا سَوِيًّا

Yā ab^{a}*t*^{i} (O my father) *in-nī* (indeed I) *q*^{a}*d jā*^{a}*-nī* (it has come to me) *m*^{i}*n*^{a} (from) *al-ʿ*^{i}*lm*^{i} (knowledge) *mā l*^{a}*m* (that which did not) *y*^{a}*'t*^{i}*-k*^{a} (it comes to you) *f*^{a}*-itt*^{a}*b*^{i}*ʿ-nī* (so follow me) *ahd*^{i}*-k*^{a} (I guide you [to]) *ṣ*^{i}*r*^{a}*ṭ*^{an} (a path) *s*^{a}*wīyā* (proper, sound).

يَٰٓأَبَتِ لَا تَعۡبُدِ ٱلشَّيۡطَٰنَۖ إِنَّ ٱلشَّيۡطَٰنَ كَانَ لِلرَّحۡمَٰنِ عَصِيّٗا

Yā-ab^{a}*t*^{i} (O my father) *l*^{a} (do not) *t*^{a}*ʿb*^{u}*d*^{i} (you worship) *al-sh*^{a}*yṭ*^{a}*n* (Satan, the devil) *inn*^{a} (indeed) *al-sh*^{a}*yṭ*^{a}*n*^{a} (Satan, the devil) *kān*^{a} (was) *l*^{i}*-al-r*^{a}*ḥmān*^{i} (to the most Gracious) *ʿ*^{a}*ṣīyā* (disobedient).

يَٰٓأَبَتِ إِنِّيٓ أَخَافُ أَن يَمَسَّكَ عَذَابٞ مِّنَ ٱلرَّحۡمَٰنِ فَتَكُونَ لِلشَّيۡطَٰنِ وَلِيّٗا

Yā-ab^{a}*t*^{i} (O my father) *in-nī* (indeed I) *akhāf*^{u} (I fear) *an* (that) *y*^{a}*m*^{a}*ss*^{a}*-k*^{a} (it touches you) *ʿadhāb*^{un} (a torment) *m*^{i}*n*^{a} *al-r*^{a}*ḥmān*^{i} (from the Most Gracious) *f*^{a}*-t*^{a}*kūn*^{a} (so that you are, so that you will be) *l*^{i}*-al-sh*^{a}*yṭān*^{i} (to Satan) *w*^{a}*līyā* (a companion, a close ally).

قَالَ أَرَاغِبٌ أَنتَ عَنۡ ءَالِهَتِي يَٰٓإِبۡرَٰهِيمُۖ لَئِن لَّمۡ تَنتَهِ لَأَرۡجُمَنَّكَۖ وَٱهۡجُرۡنِي مَلِيّٗا

Qāl^{a} (he said) *a-rāgh*^{i}*b*^{un} (are you desirious) *ant*^{a} (you) *ʿ*^{a}*n* (away [from]) *āl*^{i}*h*^{a}*t-ī* (my gods) *yā ibrāhīm* (O Abraham) *l*^{a}*-in* (truly if) *l*^{a}*m* (do not) *t*^{a}*nt*^{a}*h*^{i} (you stop) *l*^{a}*-arj*^{u}*m*^{a}*nn*^{a}*-k*^{a} (I will truly stone you) *w*^{a}*-uhj*^{u}*r-nī* (and leave me) *m*^{a}*līyā* (prolongedly).

قَالَ سَلَٰمٌ عَلَيۡكَۖ سَأَسۡتَغۡفِرُ لَكَ رَبِّيٓۖ إِنَّهُۥ كَانَ بِي حَفِيّٗا

Qāl^{a} (he said) *s*^{a}*lām*^{un} (peace [be]) *ʿ*^{a}*l*^{a}*y-k*^{a} (upon you) *s*^{a}*-ast*^{a}*ghf*^{i}*r*^{u} (I will seek forgiveness [from]) *l*^{a}*-k*^{a} (for you) *r*^{a}*bb-ī* (my Lord) *inn*^{a}*-h*^{u} (indeed He) *kān*^{a} (was) *b-ī* (to me) *ḥ*^{a}*fīyā* (a gracious One).

وَأَعۡتَزِلُكُمۡ وَمَا تَدۡعُونَ مِن دُونِ ٱللَّهِ وَأَدۡعُواْ رَبِّي عَسَىٰٓ أَلَّآ أَكُونَ بِدُعَآءِ رَبِّي شَقِيّٗا

W^{a}*-aʿt*^{a}*z*^{i}*l*^{u}*-k*^{u}*m* (and I leave you, and I cut off myself from you) *w*^{a}*-mā* (and what) *t*^{a}*dʿūn*^{a} (you call) *m*^{i}*n dūn*^{i} (apart from, besides, without) *allāh*^{i} (God) *w*^{a}*-adʿū* (and I call) *r*^{a}*bb-ī* (my Lord) *ʿ*^{a}*sā* (perhaps) *allā* (that will not) *akūn*^{a} (I am, I [will] be) *b*^{i}*-d*^{u}*ʿā*^{i} (regarding my prayer [to]) *r*^{a}*bb-ī* (my Lord) *sh*^{a}*qīyā* (wretched).

فَلَمَّا ٱعْتَزَلَهُمْ وَمَا يَعْبُدُونَ مِن دُونِ ٱللَّهِ وَهَبْنَا لَهُۥٓ إِسْحَٰقَ وَيَعْقُوبَ ۖ وَكُلًّا جَعَلْنَا نَبِيًّا

F^{a}*-l*^{a}*mmā* (so when, so once) *iʿt*^{a}*z*^{a}*la-h*^{u}*m* (he left them, he cut off himself from them) *w*^{a}*-mā* (and what) *y*^{a}*ʿb*^{u}*dūn*^{a} (they worship) *m*^{i}*n dūn*^{i} (without, apart from) *allāh*^{i} (God) *w*^{a}*h*^{a}*b-nā* (we granted, we bestowed) *l*^{a}*-hū* (to him) *isḥāqā* (Isaac) *w*^{a}*-yaʿqūb*^{a} (and Jacob) *w*^{a}*-k*^{u}*ll*^{an} (and each, and everyone) *j*^{a}*ʿ*^{a}*l-nā* (we made) *n*^{a}*bīyā* (a prophet).

وَوَهَبْنَا لَهُم مِّن رَّحْمَتِنَا وَجَعَلْنَا لَهُمْ لِسَانَ صِدْقٍ عَلِيًّا

W^{a}*-w*^{a}*h*^{a}*b-nā* (and We granted) *l*^{a}*-h*^{u}*m* (to them) *m*^{i}*n* (from) *r*^{a}*ḥm*^{a}*t*^{i}*-nā* (Our mercy) *w*^{a}*-j*^{a}*ʿ*^{a}*l-nā* (and We made) *l*^{a}*-h*^{u}*m* (for them) *l*^{i}*sān*^{a} *ṣ*^{i}*dq*^{in} *ʿ*^{a}*līyā* (a true reputation of high honor).

This page intentionally left blank

Lesson 43: Maryam Part 6

Verse 51

وَٱذْكُرْ فِى ٱلْكِتَٰبِ مُوسَىٰٓ ۚ إِنَّهُۥ كَانَ مُخْلَصًا وَكَانَ رَسُولًا نَّبِيًّا

And mention in the Book Moses; indeed he was chosen and was a messenger who was a prophet.

W^{a}-udhk^{u}r (and mention) *fī* (in) *al-k^{i}tāb^{i}* (the Book) *mūsā* (Moses) *inn^{a}-h^{u}* (indeed he) *kān^{a}* (he was) *m^{u}khl^{a}ṣ^{an}* (chosen) *w^{a}-kān^{a}* (and he was) *r^{a}sūl^{an}* (a messenger [who was]) *n^{a}bīyā* (a prophet).

Verse 52

وَنَٰدَيْنَٰهُ مِن جَانِبِ ٱلطُّورِ ٱلْأَيْمَنِ وَقَرَّبْنَٰهُ نَجِيًّا

And We called him from the side of the mountain on the right and We brought him near, [as] a confidant [in us]

W^{a}-nād^{a}ynā-h^{u} (and We called him) *m^{i}n* (from) *jān^{i}b^{i}* (the side [of]) *al-ṭūr^{i}* (the mountain) *al-aym^{a}n^{i}* (on the right) *w^{a}-q^{a}rr^{a}bnā-h^{u}* (and We brough him near) *n^{a}jīyā* (a confidant, one who holds secret and intimate conversation [with another person]).

While the phrase *jān^{i}b^{i} al-ṭūr^{i} al-aym^{a}n^{i}* literally appears to mean "on the right side of the mountain", Quran exegetes say the mountain had no right side and that the "right" here refers to the right side of Moses.

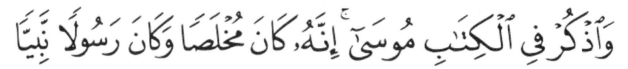

Verse 53

وَوَهَبْنَا لَهُۥ مِن رَّحْمَتِنَآ أَخَاهُ هَٰرُونَ نَبِيًّا

And We granted him from Our mercy his brother Aaron [as] a prophet

W^{a}-w^{a}h^{a}b-nā (and we granted) *l^{a}-h^{u}* (to him) *m^{i}n* (from) *r^{a}ḥm^{a}t^{i}-nā* (Our mercy) *akhā-h^{u}* (his brother) *hārūn^{a}* (Aaron) *n^{a}bīyā* ([as] a prophet).

Verse 54

وَٱذْكُرْ فِى ٱلْكِتَٰبِ إِسْمَٰعِيلَ ۚ إِنَّهُۥ كَانَ صَادِقَ ٱلْوَعْدِ وَكَانَ رَسُولًا نَّبِيًّا

And mention in the Book Ishmael; indeed he was true to his promises and was messenger who was a prophet

W^{a}-udhk^{u}r (and mention) *fī al-k^{i}tāb^{i}* (in the Book) *ismāʿīl* (Ishmael) *inn^{a}-h^{u}* (indeed he) *kān^{a}* (he was) *ṣad^{i}q^{a}* (truthful [to]) *al-w^{a}ʿd^{i}* (the promise) *w^{a}-kān^{a}* (and he was) *r^{a}sūl^{an}* (a messenger [who was]) *n^{a}bīyā* (a prophet).

The word *ṣad^{i}q* means "truthful", while the phrase *ṣad^{i}q^{a} al-w^{a}ʿd* means "one who keeps his promises", "one who is true to his promises".

Verse 55

وَكَانَ يَأْمُرُ أَهْلَهُۥ بِٱلصَّلَوٰةِ وَٱلزَّكَوٰةِ وَكَانَ عِندَ رَبِّهِۦ مَرْضِيًّا

And he used to enjoin on his family the prayer and zakah and was, to his God, pleasing

W^{a}-kān^{a} (and he was, and he used to) *y^{a}ʾm^{u}r^{u}* (he commands, he enjoins) *ahl^{a}-h^{u}* (his family) *b^{i}-al-ṣ^{a}lāt^{i}* (with the prayer) *w^{a}-al-z^{a}kāt^{i}* (and the zakah) *w^{a}-kān^{a}* (and was) *^{i}nd^{a}* (by, with) *r^{a}bb^{i}-h^{i}* (his Lord) *m^{a}rḍīyā* (pleasing).

Verse 56

وَٱذْكُرْ فِى ٱلْكِتَٰبِ إِدْرِيسَ ۚ إِنَّهُۥ كَانَ صِدِّيقًا نَّبِيًّا

And mention in the Book Idrīs; indeed he was a man of truth who was a prophet

Wa-udhk^{u}*r* (and mention) *fī al-k*^{i}*tāb*^{i} (in the book) *idrīs* (Idrīs) *inn*^{a}*-h*^{u} (indeed he) *kān*^{a} (was) *ṣ*^{i}*ddīq*^{an} (a man of truth) *n*^{a}*bīyā* (a prophet).

Verse 57

وَرَفَعْنَٰهُ مَكَانًا عَلِيًّا

And We raised him to an exalted place

W^{a}*-r*^{a}*fa'nā-h*^{u} (and We raised him) *m*^{a}*kān*^{an} (a place, a station) ^{a}*līyā* (high, exalted).

Verse 58, part 1

أُو۟لَٰٓئِكَ ٱلَّذِينَ أَنْعَمَ ٱللَّهُ عَلَيْهِم مِّنَ ٱلنَّبِيِّـۧنَ مِن ذُرِّيَّةِ ءَادَمَ

Those are the ones upon whom God bestowed favor from the prophets of the descendants of Adam

Ulā'ik^{a} (those [are]) *all*^{a}*dhīn*^{a} (the ones who) *an*^{a}*m*^{a} (He bestowed His favor) *allāh*^{u} (God) ^{a}*l*^{a}*y-h*^{i}*m* (upon them) *m*^{i}*n* (from) *al-n*^{a}*bīyīn*^{a} (the prophets) *m*^{i}*n* (from) *dh*^{u}*rrīy*^{a}*t*^{i} (the descendants [of]) *ād*^{a}*m*^{a} (Adam).

Verse 58, part 2

وَمِمَّنْ حَمَلْنَا مَعَ نُوحٍ وَمِن ذُرِّيَّةِ إِبْرَٰهِيمَ وَإِسْرَٰٓءِيلَ

And of those whom We carried with Noah and of the descendants of Abraham and Israel

W^{a}*-m*^{i}*m-m*^{a}*n* (and from those whom) *ḥ*^{a}*m*^{a}*l-nā* (we carried) *ma*^{a} (with) *nūḥ*^{in} (Noah) *w*^{a}*-m*^{i}*n* (and from) *dh*^{u}*rrīy*^{a}*t*^{i} (the descendants [of]) *ibrāhīm*^{a} (Abraham) *w*^{a}*-isrā'īl*^{a} (and Israel).

The phrase *m*^{i}*m-m*^{a}*n* is *m*^{i}*n* and *m*^{a}*n* combined together.

Israel is another name for the prophet Jacob son of Isaac son of Abraham. The Jewish people are called the Children of Israel in the Quran because they are all descended from Jacob's twelve sons.

Verse 58, part 3

وَمِمَّنْ هَدَيْنَا وَٱجْتَبَيْنَآ إِذَا تُتْلَىٰ عَلَيْهِمْ ءَايَٰتُ ٱلرَّحْمَٰنِ خَرُّوا۟ سُجَّدًا وَبُكِيًّا

And from those whom We guided and We chose; when the verses of the Most Gracious were recited upon them they fell prostrating themselves and weaping

W^{a}*-m*^{i}*m-m*^{a}*n* (and of those whom) *h*^{a}*d*^{a}*y-nā* (We guided) *w*^{a}*-ijt*^{a}*b*^{a}*y-nā* (We chose, we selected and preferred) *idhā* (when) *t*^{u}*tlā* (it is recited) *^{a}l*^{a}*y-h*^{i}*m* (on them) *āy*^{a}*t*^{u} (the verses [of]) *al-r*^{a}*ḥmān*^{i} (the Most Gracious) *kh*^{a}*rrū* (the fell) *s*^{u}*jj*^{a}*d*^{an} (in a state of prostration) *w*^{a}*-b*^{u}*kīyā* (in a state of weaping).

The vertical line tells readers that as an optional act of worship they may prostrate themselves at the end of reading or reciting the verse.

Verse 59

فَخَلَفَ مِنۢ بَعْدِهِمْ خَلْفٌ أَضَاعُوا۟ ٱلصَّلَوٰةَ وَٱتَّبَعُوا۟ ٱلشَّهَوَٰتِ ۖ فَسَوْفَ يَلْقَوْنَ غَيًّا

So they succeeded them successors who neglected the prayer and followed their base desires; soon they will meet evil

F^{a}*-kh*^{a}*l*^{a}*f*^{a} (so they succeeded) *m*^{i}*n b*^{a}*ʿd*^{i} (after) *h*^{i}*m* (them) *kh*^{a}*lf*^{an} (a succession, a group of successors) *aḍāʿū* (they lost, they neglected) *al-ṣ*^{a}*lāt*^{a} (the prayer) *w*^{a}*-itt*^{a}*baʿū* (and they followed) *al-sh*^{a}*h*^{a}*wāt*^{i} (the base desires) *f*^{a}*-s*^{a}*wf*^{a} (so are going to) *y*^{a}*lq*^{a}*wn*^{a} (they meet) *gh*^{a}*yyā* (evil, corruption, an evil fate, the Hellfire).

This page intentionally left blank

Lesson 43 Review

وَٱذْكُرْ فِى ٱلْكِتَٰبِ مُوسَىٰٓ ۚ إِنَّهُۥ كَانَ مُخْلَصًا وَكَانَ رَسُولًا نَّبِيًّا

W^{a}*-udhk*^{u}*r* (and mention) *fī* (in) *al-k*^{i}*tāb*^{i} (the Book) *mūsā* (Moses) *inn*^{a}*-h*^{u} (indeed he) *kān*^{a} (he was) *m*^{u}*khl*^{a}*ṣ*^{an} (chosen) *w*^{a}*-kān*^{a} (and he was) *r*^{a}*sūl*^{an} (a messenger [who was]) *n*^{a}*bīyā* (a prophet).

وَنَٰدَيْنَٰهُ مِن جَانِبِ ٱلطُّورِ ٱلْأَيْمَنِ وَقَرَّبْنَٰهُ نَجِيًّا

W^{a}*-nād*^{a}*ynā-h*^{u} (and We called him) *m*^{i}*n* (from) *jān*^{i}*b*^{i} (the side [of]) *al-ṭūr*^{i} (the mountain) *al-aym*^{a}*n*^{i} (on the right) *w*^{a}*-q*^{a}*rr*^{a}*bnā-h*^{u} (and We brough him near) *n*^{a}*jīyā* (a confidant, one who holds secret and intimate conversation [with another person]).

وَوَهَبْنَا لَهُۥ مِن رَّحْمَتِنَآ أَخَاهُ هَٰرُونَ نَبِيًّا

W^{a}*-w*^{a}*h*^{a}*b-nā* (and we granted) *l*^{a}*-h*^{u} (to him) *m*^{i}*n* (from) *r*^{a}*ḥm*^{a}*t*^{i}*-nā* (Our mercy) *akhā-h*^{u} (his brother) *hārūn*^{a} (Aaron) *n*^{a}*bīyā* ([as] a prophet).

وَٱذْكُرْ فِى ٱلْكِتَٰبِ إِسْمَٰعِيلَ ۚ إِنَّهُۥ كَانَ صَادِقَ ٱلْوَعْدِ وَكَانَ رَسُولًا نَّبِيًّا

W^{a}*-udhk*^{u}*r* (and mention) *fī al-k*^{i}*tāb*^{i} (in the Book) *ismāʿīl* (Ishmael) *inn*^{a}*-h*^{u} (indeed he) *kān*^{a} (he was) *ṣad*^{i}*q*^{a} (truthful [to]) *al-w*^{a}*ʿd*^{i} (the promise) *w*^{a}*-kān*^{a} (and he was) *r*^{a}*sūl*^{an} (a messenger [who was]) *n*^{a}*bīyā* (a prophet).

وَكَانَ يَأْمُرُ أَهْلَهُۥ بِٱلصَّلَوٰةِ وَٱلزَّكَوٰةِ وَكَانَ عِندَ رَبِّهِۦ مَرْضِيًّا

W^{a}-kān^{a} (and he was, and he used to) *y^{a}'m^{u}r^{u}* (he commands, he enjoins) *ahl^{a}-h^{u}* (his family) *b^{i}-al-ṣ^{a}lāt^{i}* (with the prayer) *w^{a}-al-z^{a}kāt^{i}* (and the zakah) *w^{a}-kān^{a}* (and was) *^{i}nd^{a}* (by, with) *r^{a}bb^{i}-h^{i}* (his Lord) *m^{a}rḍīyā* (pleasing).

وَٱذۡكُرۡ فِي ٱلۡكِتَٰبِ إِدۡرِيسَۚ إِنَّهُۥ كَانَ صِدِّيقٗا نَّبِيّٗا

Wa-udhk^{u}r (and mention) *fī al-k^{i}tāb^{i}* (in the book) *idrīs* (Idrīs) *inn^{a}-h^{u}* (indeed he) *kān^{a}* (was) *ṣ^{i}ddīq^{an}* (a man of truth) *n^{a}bīyā* (a prophet).

وَرَفَعۡنَٰهُ مَكَانًا عَلِيًّا

W^{a}-r^{a}fa'nā-h^{u} (and We raised him) *m^{a}kān^{an}* (a place, a station) *^{a}līyā* (high, exalted).

أُوْلَٰٓئِكَ ٱلَّذِينَ أَنۡعَمَ ٱللَّهُ عَلَيۡهِم مِّنَ ٱلنَّبِيِّـۧنَ مِن ذُرِّيَّةِ ءَادَمَ

Ulā'ik^{a} (those [are]) *all^{a}dhīn^{a}* (the ones who) *an^{a}m^{a}* (He bestowed His favor) *allāh^{u}* (God) *^{a}l^{a}y-h^{i}m* (upon them) *m^{i}n* (from) *al-n^{a}bīyīn^{a}* (the prophets) *m^{i}n* (from) *dh^{u}rrīy^{a}t^{i}* (the descendants [of]) *ād^{a}m^{a}* (Adam).

وَمِمَّنۡ حَمَلۡنَا مَعَ نُوحٖ وَمِن ذُرِّيَّةِ إِبۡرَٰهِيمَ وَإِسۡرَٰٓءِيلَ

W^{a}-m^{i}m-m^{a}n (and from those whom) *ḥ^{a}m^{a}l-nā* (we carried) *ma^{a}* (with) *nūḥ^{in}* (Noah) *w^{a}-m^{i}n* (and from) *dh^{u}rrīy^{a}t^{i}* (the descendants [of]) *ibrāhīm^{a}* (Abraham) *w^{a}-isrā'īl^{a}* (and Israel).

وَمِمَّنۡ هَدَيۡنَا وَٱجۡتَبَيۡنَآۚ إِذَا تُتۡلَىٰ عَلَيۡهِمۡ ءَايَٰتُ ٱلرَّحۡمَٰنِ خَرُّواْۤ سُجَّدٗاۤ وَبُكِيّٗا

W^{a}-m^{i}m-m^{a}n (and of those whom) *h^{a}d^{a}y-nā* (We guided) *w^{a}-ijt^{a}b^{a}y-nā* (We chose, we selected and preferred) *idhā* (when) *t^{u}tlā* (it is recited) *^{a}l^{a}y-h^{i}m* (on them) *āy^{a}t^{u}* (the verses [of]) *al-r^{a}ḥmān^{i}* (the Most Gracious) *kh^{a}rrū* (the fell) *s^{u}jj^{a}d^{an}* (in a state of prostration) *w^{a}-b^{u}kīyā* (in a state of weaping).

فَخَلَفَ مِنۢ بَعۡدِهِمۡ خَلۡفٌ أَضَاعُواْ ٱلصَّلَوٰةَ وَٱتَّبَعُواْ ٱلشَّهَوَٰتِۖ فَسَوۡفَ يَلۡقَوۡنَ غَيًّا

F^{a}-kh^{a}l^{a}f^{a} (so they succeeded) *m^{i}n b^{a}ʿd^{i}* (after) *h^{i}m* (them) *kh^{a}lf^{un}* (a succession, a group of successors) *aḍāʿū* (they lost, they neglected) *al-ṣ^{a}lāt^{a}* (the prayer) *w^{a}-itt^{a}baʿū* (and they followed) *al-sh^{a}h^{a}wāt^{i}* (the base desires) *f^{a}-s^{a}wf^{a}* (so are going to) *y^{a}lq^{a}wn^{a}* (they meet) *gh^{a}yyā* (evil, corruption, an evil fate, the Hellfire).

This page intentionally left blank

Lesson 44: Maryam Part 7

Verse 60

إِلَّا مَن تَابَ وَءَامَنَ وَعَمِلَ صَٰلِحًا فَأُوْلَٰٓئِكَ يَدْخُلُونَ ٱلْجَنَّةَ وَلَا يُظْلَمُونَ شَيْـًٔا

Except one who repents, believes and does good deeds; so those enter Paradise and are not wronged in any way

Illā (except) *m*^{a}*n* (one [who]) *tāb*^{a} (he repented) *w*^{a}*-*ʿ^{a}*m*^{i}*l*^{a} (he did, he performed) *ṣāliḥ*^{an} (a good one, good deeds) *f*^{a}*-ulā*^{i}*k*^{a} (so those) *y*^{a}*dkh*^{u}*lūn*^{a} (they enter) *al-j*^{a}*nn*^{a}*t*^{a} (Paradise) *w*^{a}*-lā* (and do not) *y*^{u}*ẓl*^{a}*mūn*^{a} (they get wronged) *sh*^{a}*y'ā* (anything, in any way).

Verse 61

جَنَّٰتِ عَدْنٍ ٱلَّتِى وَعَدَ ٱلرَّحْمَٰنُ عِبَادَهُۥ بِٱلْغَيْبِ ۚ إِنَّهُۥ كَانَ وَعْدُهُۥ مَأْتِيًّا

Gardens of perptual residence which the Most Gracious promised to His servants unseen; indeed His promise is one which comes

J^{a}*nnāt*^{i} (Gardens [of]) ʿ^{a}*dn*^{in} (perpetual residence) *all*^{a}*tī* (which) *w*^{a}ʿ^{a}*d*^{a} (He promised) *al-r*^{a}*ḥmān*^{u} (the Most Gracious) ʿ^{i}*b*^{a}*d*^{a}*-h*^{u} (His servants) *b*^{i}*-al-gh*^{a}*yb* (unseen [while unseen]) *inn*^{a}*-h*^{u} (indeed He) *kān*^{a} (was) *w*^{a}ʿ*d*^{u}*-h*^{u} (His promise) *m*^{a}ʾ*tīyā* (one that comes).

Verse 62

لَّا يَسْمَعُونَ فِيهَا لَغْوًا إِلَّا سَلَٰمًا ۖ وَلَهُمْ رِزْقُهُمْ فِيهَا بُكْرَةً وَعَشِيًّا

They hear not in it bad speech except [words of] peace; and for them is their provision morning and evening

Lā (do not) *y*^{a}*sm*^{a}*ʿūn*^{a} (they hear) *fī-hā* (in it) *l*^{a}*ghw*^{an} (bad speech, ill speech, vain talk) *illā* (except) *s*^{a}*lām*^{an} (peace) *w*^{a}*-l*^{a}*-h*^{u}*m* (and for them [is]) *r*^{i}*zq*^{u}*-h*^{u}*m* (their provision) *fī-hā* (in it) *b*^{u}*kr*^{a}*t*^{an} (morning) *w*^{a}*-*^{a}*shīyā* (and evening).

Verse 63

تِلْكَ ٱلْجَنَّةُ ٱلَّتِى نُورِثُ مِنْ عِبَادِنَا مَن كَانَ تَقِيًّا

That is the Paradise which we cause [some] of our servants to inherit; the ones who are God-fearing

T^{i}*lk*^{a} (that [is]) *al-j*^{a}*nn*^{a}*t*^{i} (the Paradise) *all*^{a}*tī* (the one which) *nūr*^{i}*th*^{u} (we cause to inherit) *m*^{i}*n* (of) *ʿibād*^{i}*-nā* (our servants) *m*^{a}*n* (who) *kān*^{a} (was) *t*^{a}*qīyā* (God-fearing).

Verse 64, part 1

وَمَا نَتَنَزَّلُ إِلَّا بِأَمْرِ رَبِّكَ ۖ

"And we do not come down except by the command of your Lord..."

W^{a}*-mā* (and do not) *n*^{a}*t*^{a}*n*^{a}*zz*^{a}*l*^{u} (we descend, we come down) *illā* (except) *b*^{i}*-amr*^{i} (with the command [of], by the command [of]) *r*^{a}*bb*^{i}*-k* (your Lord).

Here the speaker is an angel, considered to be the angel Gabriel.

Verse 64, part 2

لَهُۥ مَا بَيْنَ أَيْدِينَا وَمَا خَلْفَنَا وَمَا بَيْنَ ذَٰلِكَ ۚ وَمَا كَانَ رَبُّكَ نَسِيًّا

"for Him is what is before us, what is behind us, and what is between that." And your Lord is not forgetful

L^{a}*-h*^{u} (for Him [is]) *mā* (what [is]) *b*^{a}*yn*^{a} (between) *aydīnā* (our hands) *w*^{a}*-mā* (and what [is]) *kh*^{a}*lf*^{a}*nā* (behind us) *w*^{a}*-mā* (and what [is]) *b*^{a}*yn*^{a} (between) *dhāl*^{i}*k*^{a} (that) *w*^{a}*-mā* (and not) *kān*^{a} (He was) *r*^{a}*bb*^{u}*-k*^{a} (your Lord) *n*^{a}*sīyā* (a forgetful One).

Verse 65, part 1

رَبُّ ٱلسَّمَٰوَٰتِ وَٱلْأَرْضِ وَمَا بَيْنَهُمَا

The Lord of the heavens and the earth and what is between them

R^{a}*bb*^{u} (the Lord [of]) *al-s*^{a}*māwāt*^{i} (the heavens) *w*^{a}*-al-arḍ*^{i} (and the earth) *w*^{a}*-mā* (and what [is]) *b*^{a}*yn*^{a} (between) *dhāl*^{i}*k*^{a} (that).

Verse 65, part 2

فَٱعْبُدْهُ وَٱصْطَبِرْ لِعِبَٰدَتِهِۦ ۚ هَلْ تَعْلَمُ لَهُۥ سَمِيًّا

So worship him and be patient for His worship. Do you know anyone who shares His name?

F^{a}*-u'b*^{u}*d-h*^{u} (so worship Him) *w*^{a}*-iṣt*^{a}*b*^{i}*r* (and be patient) *l*^{i}*-'ibād*^{a}*t*^{i}*-h*^{i} (for His worship) *h*^{a}*l* (do) *t*^{a}*'l*^{a}*m*^{u} (you know) *l*^{a}*-h*^{u} (for Him) *s*^{a}*mīyā* (a named one).

This page intentionally left blank

Lesson 44 Review

إِلَّا مَن تَابَ وَءَامَنَ وَعَمِلَ صَٰلِحًا فَأُوْلَٰٓئِكَ يَدْخُلُونَ ٱلْجَنَّةَ وَلَا يُظْلَمُونَ شَيْـًٔا

Illā (except) *m^{a}n* (one [who]) *tāb^{a}* (he repented) *w^{a}-^{a}m^{i}l^{a}* (he did, he performed) *ṣāliḥ^{an}* (a good one, good deeds) *f^{a}-ulā^{i}k^{a}* (so those) *y^{a}dkh^{u}lūn^{a}* (they enter) *al-j^{a}nn^{a}t^{a}* (Paradise) *w^{a}-lā* (and do not) *y^{u}ẓl^{a}mūn^{a}* (they get wronged) *sh^{a}y'ā* (anything, in any way).

جَنَّٰتِ عَدْنٍ ٱلَّتِى وَعَدَ ٱلرَّحْمَٰنُ عِبَادَهُۥ بِٱلْغَيْبِ ۚ إِنَّهُۥ كَانَ وَعْدُهُۥ مَأْتِيًّا

J^{a}nnāt^{i} (Gardens [of]) *^{a}dn^{in}* (perpetual residence) *all^{a}tī* (which) *w^{a}^{a}d^{a}* (He promised) *al-r^{a}ḥmān^{u}* (the Most Gracious) *^{i}b^{a}d^{a}-h^{u}* (His servants) *b^{i}-al-gh^{a}yb* (unseen [while unseen]) *inn^{a}-h^{u}* (indeed He) *kān^{a}* (was) *w^{a}ʿd^{u}-h^{u}* (His promise) *m^{a}'tīyā* (one that comes).

لَّا يَسْمَعُونَ فِيهَا لَغْوًا إِلَّا سَلَٰمًا ۖ وَلَهُمْ رِزْقُهُمْ فِيهَا بُكْرَةً وَعَشِيًّا

Lā (do not) *y^{a}sm^{a}ʿūn^{a}* (they hear) *fī-hā* (in it) *l^{a}ghw^{an}* (bad speech, ill speech, vain talk) *illā* (except) *s^{a}lām^{an}* (peace) *w^{a}-l^{a}-h^{u}m* (and for them [is]) *r^{i}zq^{u}-h^{u}m* (their provision) *fī-hā* (in it) *b^{u}kr^{a}t^{an}* (morning) *w^{a}-^{a}shīyā* (and evening).

تِلْكَ ٱلْجَنَّةُ ٱلَّتِى نُورِثُ مِنْ عِبَادِنَا مَن كَانَ تَقِيًّا

T^{i}lk^{a} (that [is]) *al-j^{a}nn^{a}t^{i}* (the Paradise) *all^{a}tī* (the one which) *nūr^{i}th^{u}* (we cause to inherit) *m^{i}n* (of) *ʿibād^{i}-nā* (our servants) *m^{a}n* (who) *kān^{a}* (was) *t^{a}qīyā* (God-fearing).

وَمَا نَتَنَزَّلُ إِلَّا بِأَمْرِ رَبِّكَ ۖ

W^{a}*-mā* (and do not) *n*^{a}*t*^{a}*n*^{a}*zz*^{a}*l*^{u} (we descend, we come down) *illā* (except) *b*^{i}*-amr*^{i} (with the command [of], by the command [of]) *r*^{a}*bb*^{i}*-k* (your Lord).

لَهُۥ مَا بَيْنَ أَيْدِينَا وَمَا خَلْفَنَا وَمَا بَيْنَ ذَٰلِكَ ۚ وَمَا كَانَ رَبُّكَ نَسِيًّا

L^{a}*-h*^{u} (for Him [is]) *mā* (what [is]) *b*^{a}*yn*^{a} (between) *aydīnā* (our hands) *w*^{a}*-mā* (and what [is]) *kh*^{a}*lf*^{a}*nā* (behind us) *w*^{a}*-mā* (and what [is]) *b*^{a}*yn*^{a} (between) *dhāl*^{i}*k*^{a} (that) *w*^{a}*-mā* (and not) *kān*^{a} (He was) *r*^{a}*bb*^{u}*-k*^{a} (your Lord) *n*^{a}*sīyā* (a forgetful One).

رَّبُّ ٱلسَّمَٰوَٰتِ وَٱلْأَرْضِ وَمَا بَيْنَهُمَا

R^{a}*bb*^{u} (the Lord [of]) *al-s*^{a}*māwāt*^{i} (the heavens) *w*^{a}*-al-arḍ*^{i} (and the earth) *w*^{a}*-mā* (and what [is]) *b*^{a}*yn*^{a} (between) *dhāl*^{i}*k*^{a} (that).

فَٱعْبُدْهُ وَٱصْطَبِرْ لِعِبَٰدَتِهِۦ ۚ هَلْ تَعْلَمُ لَهُۥ سَمِيًّا

F^{a}*-uʿb*^{u}*d-h*^{u} (so worship Him) *w*^{a}*-iṣt*^{a}*b*^{i}*r* (and be patient) *l*^{i}*-ʿibād*^{a}*t*^{i}*-h*^{i} (for His worship) *h*^{a}*l* (do) *t*^{a}*ʿl*^{a}*m*^{u} (you know) *l*^{a}*-h*^{u} (for Him) *s*^{a}*mīyā* (a named one).

Lesson 45: Maryam Part 8

Verse 66

وَيَقُولُ ٱلْإِنسَٰنُ أَءِذَا مَا مِتُّ لَسَوْفَ أُخْرَجُ حَيًّا

And the human says, "When I die, will I be brought out alive?"

W^{a}*-y*^{a}*qūl*^{u} (and he says) *al-insān*^{u} (the human) *a-idhā mā* (will I when) *m*^{i}*t-t*^{u} (I died) *l*^{a}*-s*^{a}*wf*^{a} (truly will be) *ukhr*^{a}*j*^{u} (I am brought out) *ḥ*^{a}*yyā* (alive).

Verse 67

أَوَلَا يَذْكُرُ ٱلْإِنسَٰنُ أَنَّا خَلَقْنَٰهُ مِن قَبْلُ وَلَمْ يَكُ شَيْـًٔا

And does he not remember that We created him before when he was not a thing?

A-w^{a}*-lā* (and does not...?) *y*^{a}*dhk*^{u}*r*^{u} (he remembers) *al-insān*^{u} (the human) *an-nā* (that We) *kh*^{a}*l*^{a}*qnā-h*^{u} (we created him) *m*^{i}*n q*^{a}*bl*^{u} (before) *w*^{a}*-l*^{a}*m* (and not) *y*^{a}*k*^{u} (he was) *sh*^{a}*y'ā* (a thing).

Verse 68

فَوَرَبِّكَ لَنَحْشُرَنَّهُمْ وَٱلشَّيَٰطِينَ ثُمَّ لَنُحْضِرَنَّهُمْ حَوْلَ جَهَنَّمَ جِثِيًّا

So by your Lord, we surely truly gather them and the devils then we will surely bring them into prescence around Hell bent upon their knees

F^{a} (then) *w*^{a} (by) *r*^{a}*bb*^{i}*-k*^{a} (your Lord) *l*^{a}*-n*^{a}*ḥsh*^{u}*r*^{a}*nn*^{a}*-h*^{u}*m* (We will surely gather them) *w*^{a}*-al-sh*^{a}*yāṭīn*^{a} (and the devils) *th*^{u}*mm*^{a} *l*^{a}*-n*^{a}*ḥḍ*^{u}*r*^{a}*nn*^{a}*-h*^{u}*m* (We will surely bring them into prescence, we will bring them before [something]) *ḥ*^{a}*wl*^{a} (around) *j*^{a}*h*^{a}*nn*^{a}*m*^{a} (Hell) *jithīyā* (bent on knees).

Verse 69

ثُمَّ لَنَنزِعَنَّ مِن كُلِّ شِيعَةٍ أَيُّهُمْ أَشَدُّ عَلَى ٱلرَّحْمَٰنِ عِتِيًّا

Then We will surely extract from each faction which of them is the most extreme in insolence upon the Most Gracious

Th^{u}mm^a (then) *l^a-n^{a}nz^{a} ^{a}nn^a* (We will surely extract, We will surely remove) *m^{i}n* (from) *k^{u}ll^i* (each) *shī^{a}t^{in}* (faction, sect) *ayy^u-h^{u}m* (which one of them) *ash^{a}dd^u* (the most servere) *^{a}lā* (upon) *al-r^{a}ḥmān^i* (the Most Gracious) *^{i}tīyā* ([in] insolence, [in] disobedience).

Verse 70

ثُمَّ لَنَحْنُ أَعْلَمُ بِٱلَّذِينَ هُمْ أَوْلَىٰ بِهَا صِلِيًّا

Then We are most knowing about those who are most worthy of burning by it

Th^{u}mm^a (then) *l^a-n^{a}ḥn^u* (we surely [are]) *a^{ʿ}l^{a}m^u* (most knowing) *b^i-all^{a}dhīn^a* (about those) *h^{u}m* (they [are]) *awlā* (worthiest) *b^i-hā* (by it) *ṣ^{i}līyā* (to burn, the act of experiencing burn).

Verse 71

وَإِن مِّنكُمْ إِلَّا وَارِدُهَا ۚ كَانَ عَلَىٰ رَبِّكَ حَتْمًا مَّقْضِيًّا

And there is none of you except that he is one who enters it, that is upon your Lord an inevitability decreed

W^a-in (and [there is] none) *m^{i}n-k^{u}m* (of you) *illā* (except [that]) *wār^{i}d^u-hā* (one who enters it) *kān^a* (it was) *^{a}lā* (on) *r^{a}bb^i-k^a* (your Lord) *ḥ^{a}tm^{an}* (a matter of inevitability) *m^{a}qḍīyā* (a decreed thing).

Verse 72

ثُمَّ نُنَجِّى ٱلَّذِينَ ٱتَّقَوا۟ وَّنَذَرُ ٱلظَّٰلِمِينَ فِيهَا جِثِيًّا

Then We save those who feared [God] and We leave the wrongdoers in it bent on their knees

Th^{u}*mm*^{a} (then) *n*^{u}*n*^{a}*jjī* (We save) *all*^{a}*dhīn*^{a} (those who) *itt*^{a}*q*^{a}*w* (they feared [God]) *w*^{a}*-n*^{a}*dh*^{a}*r*^{u} (and We leave) *al-ẓāl*^{i}*m*^{i}*n*^{a} (the wrongdoers) *fī-hā* (in it) *j*^{i}*thīyā* (bent on their knees).

Verse 73, part 1

وَإِذَا تُتْلَىٰ عَلَيْهِمْ ءَايَٰتُنَا بَيِّنَٰتٍ قَالَ ٱلَّذِينَ كَفَرُوا۟

And when it is recited upon them our verses, [which are] clear, those who denied say...

W^{a}*-idhā* (and if) *t*^{u}*tlā* (it is recited) ^{a}*l*^{a}*y-h*^{i}*m* (on them) *āyāt*^{u}*-nā* (our verses) *b*^{a}*yy*^{i}*nāt*^{in} (clear ones) *qāl*^{a} (they said) *all*^{a}*dhīn*^{a} (those who) *k*^{a}*f*^{a}*rū* (denied).

Verse 73, part 2

لِلَّذِينَ ءَامَنُوٓا۟ أَىُّ ٱلْفَرِيقَيْنِ خَيْرٌ مَّقَامًا وَأَحْسَنُ نَدِيًّا

to those who believed, "Which of the two groups is best in position and best in association?"

L^{i}*-all*^{a}*dhīn*^{a} (to those who) *ʿām*^{a}*nū* (they believed) *ayy*^{u} (which [of]) *al-f*^{a}*rīq*^{a}*yn*^{i} (the two groups) *kh*^{a}*yr*^{un} ([is] better) *m*^{a}*qām*^{an} ([when it comes to] position) *w*^{a}*-aḥs*^{a}*n*^{u} (and better) *n*^{a}*dīyā* ([when it comes to] association).

Here the rejecters ask which of the two groups (the believers or the rejecters) are better when it comes to status and when it comes to association (friendships and alliances).

Verse 74

وَكَمْ أَهْلَكْنَا قَبْلَهُم مِّن قَرْنٍ هُمْ أَحْسَنُ أَثَٰثًا وَرِءْيًا

And how many generations we destroyed before them who were better in material goods and outward appearance?

W^{a}*-k*^{a}*m* (and how many) *ahl*^{a}*k-nā* (we destroyed) *q*^{a}*bl*^{a}*-h*^{u}*m* (before them) *m*^{i}*n* (of) *q*^{a}*rn*^{in} (a generation) *h*^{u}*m* (they [were]) *aḥs*^{a}*n*^{u} (better) *athāth*^{an} ([in] possessions, [in] equipment) *w*^{a}*-r*$^{a\,i}$*yā* ([in outward] appearance).

Verse 75, part 1

قُلْ مَن كَانَ فِى ٱلضَّلَٰلَةِ فَلْيَمْدُدْ لَهُ ٱلرَّحْمَٰنُ مَدًّا ۚ

Say, "Whoever is in error, then let the Most Gracious extend for him an extension [in wealth and time]..."

Q^{u}*l* (say) *m*^{a}*n* (who, whoever) *kān*^{a} (was) *fī* (in) *al-ḍ*^{a}*lāl*^{a}*t*^{i} (error, misguidance) *f*^{a}*-l*^{i}*-y*^{u}*md*^{i}*d* (then let Him extend) *l*^{a}*-h*^{u} (for him) *al-r*^{a}*ḥmān*^{u} (the Most Gracious) *m*^{a}*ddā* (an extension).

Verse 75, part 2

حَتَّىٰٓ إِذَا رَأَوْا۟ مَا يُوعَدُونَ إِمَّا ٱلْعَذَابَ وَإِمَّا ٱلسَّاعَةَ

Until when they see what they are promised; whether torment or the Hour [of Judgment]...

Ḥ^{a}*ttā* (until) *idhā* (when) *r*$^{a\,a}$*w* (the saw) *mā yū*^{a}*dūn*^{a} (that which they are promised) *imam* (either) *al-*^{a}*dhāb*^{a} (the torment) *w*^{a}*-immā* (and either) *al-sā*^{a}*t*^{a} (the Hour).

Verse 75, part 3

فَسَيَعْلَمُونَ مَنْ هُوَ شَرٌّ مَّكَانًا وَأَضْعَفُ جُندًا

Then they will know who is worse in position and weaker in soldiers

F^{a}-s^{a}-y^{a}ʿl^{a}mūn^{a} (so they know) *m^{a}n h^{u}w^{a}* (who is the one who) *sh^{a}rr^{un}* (worse) *m^{a}kān^{an}* ([in] position) *w^{a}-aḍ^{a}f^{u}* (and weaker) *j^{u}ndā* ([in] soldiers).

Verse 76, part 1

وَيَزِيدُ ٱللَّهُ ٱلَّذِينَ ٱهْتَدَوْا۟ هُدًى ۗ

And God increases those who attained guidance in guidance

W^{a}-y^{a}zīd^{u} (and He increases) *allāh^{u}* (God) *all^{a}dhīn^{a}* (those who) *iht^{a}d^{a}w* (they attained guidance) *h^{u}dā* ([in] guidance).

Verse 76, part 2

وَٱلْبَٰقِيَٰتُ ٱلصَّٰلِحَٰتُ خَيْرٌ عِندَ رَبِّكَ ثَوَابًا وَخَيْرٌ مَّرَدًّا

and the enduring good deeds are better by your Lord in reward and better in returns

W^{a}-al-bāq^{i}yāt^{u} (and the enduring) *al-ṣ^{a}l^{i}ḥāt^{u}* (good deeds) *kh^{a}yr^{un}* ([are] better) *^{i}nd^{a}* (with, by, from the perspective of) *r^{a}bb^{i}-k^{a}* (your Lord) *th^{a}w^{a}b^{an}* ([in] reward) *w^{a}-kh^{a}yr^{un}* (and better) *m^{a}r^{a}ddā* ([in] returns, [in] benefits, [in] profits).

This page intentionally left blank

Lesson 45 Review

وَيَقُولُ ٱلْإِنسَٰنُ أَءِذَا مَا مِتُّ لَسَوْفَ أُخْرَجُ حَيًّا

W^{a}-y^{a}qūl^{u} (and he says) *al-insān^{u}* (the human) *a-idhā mā* (will I when) *m^{i}t-t^{u}* (I died) *l^{a}-s^{a}wf^{a}* (truly will be) *ukhr^{a}j^{u}* (I am brought out) *ḥ^{a}yyā* (alive).

أَوَلَا يَذْكُرُ ٱلْإِنسَٰنُ أَنَّا خَلَقْنَٰهُ مِن قَبْلُ وَلَمْ يَكُ شَيْـًٔا

A-w^{a}-lā (and does not...?) *y^{a}dhk^{u}r^{u}* (he remembers) *al-insān^{u}* (the human) *an-nā* (that We) *kh^{a}l^{a}qnā-h^{u}* (we created him) *m^{i}n q^{a}bl^{u}* (before) *w^{a}-l^{a}m* (and not) *y^{a}k^{u}* (he was) *sh^{a}y'ā* (a thing).

فَوَرَبِّكَ لَنَحْشُرَنَّهُمْ وَٱلشَّيَٰطِينَ ثُمَّ لَنُحْضِرَنَّهُمْ حَوْلَ جَهَنَّمَ جِثِيًّا

F^{a} (then) *w^{a}* (by) *r^{a}bb^{i}-k^{a}* (your Lord) *l^{a}-n^{a}ḥsh^{u}r^{a}nn^{a}-h^{u}m* (We will surely gather them) *w^{a}-al-sh^{a}yāṭīn^{a}* (and the devils) *th^{u}mm^{a} l^{a}-n^{a}ḥḍ^{u}r^{a}nn^{a}-h^{u}m* (We will surely bring them into prescence, we will bring them before [something]) *ḥ^{a}wl^{a}* (around) *j^{a}h^{a}nn^{a}m^{a}* (Hell) *jithīyā* (bent on knees).

ثُمَّ لَنَنزِعَنَّ مِن كُلِّ شِيعَةٍ أَيُّهُمْ أَشَدُّ عَلَى ٱلرَّحْمَٰنِ عِتِيًّا

Th^{u}mm^{a} (then) *l^{a}-n^{a}nz^{a}^{a}nn^{a}* (We will surely extract, We will surely remove) *m^{i}n* (from) *k^{u}ll^{i}* (each) *shī^{a}t^{in}* (faction, sect) *ayy^{u}-h^{u}m* (which one of them) *ash^{a}dd^{u}* (the most servere) *^{a}lā* (upon) *al-r^{a}ḥmān^{i}* (the Most Gracious) *^{i}tīyā* ([in] insolence, [in] disobedience).

ثُمَّ لَنَحْنُ أَعْلَمُ بِٱلَّذِينَ هُمْ أَوْلَىٰ بِهَا صِلِيًّا

Th^{u}mm^{a} (then) *l^{a}-n^{a}ḥn^{u}* (we surely [are]) *aʿl^{a}m^{u}* (most knowing) *b^{i}-all^{a}dhīn^{a}* (about those) *h^{u}m* (they [are]) *awlā* (worthiest) *b^{i}-hā* (by it) *ṣ^{i}līyā* (to burn, the act of experiencing burn).

وَإِن مِّنكُمْ إِلَّا وَارِدُهَا ۚ كَانَ عَلَىٰ رَبِّكَ حَتْمًا مَّقْضِيًّا

W^{a}-in (and [there is] none) *m^{i}n-k^{u}m* (of you) *illā* (except [that]) *wār^{i}d^{u}-hā* (one who enters it) *kān^{a}* (it was) *ʿ^{a}lā* (on) *r^{a}bb^{i}-k^{a}* (your Lord) *ḥ^{a}tm^{an}* (a matter of inevitability) *m^{a}qḍīyā* (a decreed thing).

ثُمَّ نُنَجِّي ٱلَّذِينَ ٱتَّقَوا۟ وَّنَذَرُ ٱلظَّٰلِمِينَ فِيهَا جِثِيًّا

Th^{u}mm^{a} (then) *n^{u}n^{a}jjī* (We save) *all^{a}dhīn^{a}* (those who) *itt^{a}q^{a}w* (they feared [God]) *w^{a}-n^{a}dh^{a}r^{u}* (and We leave) *al-ẓāl^{i}m^{i}n^{a}* (the wrongdoers) *fī-hā* (in it) *j^{i}thīyā* (bent on their knees).

وَإِذَا تُتْلَىٰ عَلَيْهِمْ ءَايَٰتُنَا بَيِّنَٰتٍ قَالَ ٱلَّذِينَ كَفَرُوا۟

W^{a}-idhā (and if) *t^{u}tlā* (it is recited) *ʿ^{a}l^{a}y-h^{i}m* (on them) *āyāt^{u}-nā* (our verses) *b^{a}yy^{i}nāt^{in}* (clear ones) *qāl^{a}* (they said) *all^{a}dhīn^{a}* (those who) *k^{a}f^{a}rū* (denied).

لِلَّذِينَ ءَامَنُوٓا۟ أَىُّ ٱلْفَرِيقَيْنِ خَيْرٌ مَّقَامًا وَأَحْسَنُ نَدِيًّا

L^{i}-all^{a}dhīn^{a} (to those who) *ʿām^{a}nū* (they believed) *ayy^{u}* (which [of]) *al-f^{a}rīq^{a}yn^{i}* (the two groups) *kh^{a}yr^{un}* ([is] better) *m^{a}qām^{an}* ([when it comes to] position) *w^{a}-aḥs^{a}n^{u}* (and better) *n^{a}dīyā* ([when it comes to] association).

وَكَمْ أَهْلَكْنَا قَبْلَهُم مِّن قَرْنٍ هُمْ أَحْسَنُ أَثَٰثًا وَرِءْيًا

W^{a}-k^{a}m (and how many) *ahl^{a}k-nā* (we destroyed) *q^{a}bl^{a}-h^{u}m* (before them) *m^{i}n* (of) *q^{a}rn^{in}* (a generation) *h^{u}m* (they [were]) *aḥs^{a}n^{u}* (better) *athāth^{an}* ([in] possessions, [in] equipment) *w^{a}-r$^{a\,i}$yā* ([in outward] appearance).

قُلْ مَن كَانَ فِى ٱلضَّلَٰلَةِ فَلْيَمْدُدْ لَهُ ٱلرَّحْمَٰنُ مَدًّا ۚ

Q^{u}l (say) *m^{a}n* (who, whoever) *kān^{a}* (was) *fī* (in) *al-ḍ^{a}lāl^{a}t^{i}* (error, misguidance) *f^{a}-l^{i}-y^{u}md^{i}d* (then let Him extend) *l^{a}-h^{u}* (for him) *al-r^{a}ḥmān^{u}* (the Most Gracious) *m^{a}ddā* (an extension).

حَتَّىٰٓ إِذَا رَأَوْا۟ مَا يُوعَدُونَ إِمَّا ٱلْعَذَابَ وَإِمَّا ٱلسَّاعَةَ

Ḥ^{a}ttā (until) *idhā* (when) *r$^{a\,a}$w* (the saw) *mā yū^{a}dūn^{a}* (that which they are promised) *imam* (either) *al-^{a}dhāb^{a}* (the torment) *w^{a}-immā* (and either) *al-sā^{a}t^{a}* (the Hour).

فَسَيَعْلَمُونَ مَنْ هُوَ شَرٌّ مَّكَانًا وَأَضْعَفُ جُندًا

F^{a}-s^{a}-y^{a}ʿl^{a}mūn^{a} (so they know) *m^{a}n h^{u}w^{a}* (who is the one who) *sh^{a}rr^{un}* (worse) *m^{a}kān^{an}* ([in] position) *w^{a}-aḍ^{a}ʿf^{u}* (and weaker) *j^{u}ndā* ([in] soldiers).

وَيَزِيدُ ٱللَّهُ ٱلَّذِينَ ٱهْتَدَوْا۟ هُدًى ۗ

W^{a}*-y*^{a}*zīd*^{u} (and He increases) *allāh*^{u} (God) *all*^{a}*dhīn*^{a} (those who) *iht*^{a}*d*^{a}*w* (they attained guidance) *h*^{u}*dā* ([in] guidance).

وَٱلْبَـٰقِيَـٰتُ ٱلصَّـٰلِحَـٰتُ خَيْرٌ عِندَ رَبِّكَ ثَوَابًا وَخَيْرٌ مَّرَدًّا

W^{a}*-al-bāq*^{i}*yāt*^{u} (and the enduring) *al-ṣ*^{a}*l*^{i}*ḥāt*^{u} (good deeds) *kh*^{a}*yr*^{un} ([are] better) ^{i}*nd*^{a} (with, by, from the perspective of) *r*^{a}*bb*^{i}*-k*^{a} (your Lord) *th*^{a}*w*^{a}*b*^{an} ([in] reward) *w*^{a}*-kh*^{a}*yr*^{un} (and better) *m*^{a}*r*^{a}*ddā* ([in] returns, [in] benefits, [in] profits).

Lesson 46: Maryam Part 9

Verse 77, part 1

أَفَرَءَيْتَ ٱلَّذِى كَفَرَ بِـَٔايَـٰتِنَا

Have you then seen the one who rejected our verses...?

A-f^{a}*-r*^{a}^{a}*yt*^{a} (so have you seen) *all*^{a}*dhī* (the one who) *k*^{a}*f*^{a}*r*^{a} (rejected, denied) *b*^{i}*-āyāt*^{i}*nā* (our verses).

The phrase *k*^{a}*f*^{a}*r*^{a} *b*^{i} means "he rejected [a truth or blessing]". It means to display disbelief and ingratitude despite knowing the truth of a fact or blessing.

Verse 77, part 2

وَقَالَ لَأُوتَيَنَّ مَالًا وَوَلَدًا

And he said, "I will surely be given wealth and children."

W^{a}*-qāl*^{a} (and he said) *l*^{a}*-ūt*^{a}*y*^{a}*nn*^{a} (surely I will be given) *māl*^{an} (wealth) *w*^{a}*-w*^{a}*l*^{a}*dā* (children).

Verse 78

أَطَّلَعَ ٱلْغَيْبَ أَمِ ٱتَّخَذَ عِندَ ٱلرَّحْمَـٰنِ عَهْدًا

Has he inspected the Unseen or has he taken from the Most Gracious a promise?

Aṭṭ^{a}*la*^{a} (has he inspected, has he perused) *al-gh*^{a}*yb*^{a} (the Unseen) *am*^{i} (or [has he]) *itt*^{a}*kh*^{a}*dh*^{a} (he took) ^{i}*nd*^{a} (with, by) *al-r*^{a}*ḥmān*^{i} (the Most Gracious) ^{a}*hdā* (a promise, a pact).

Verse 79

كَلَّا سَنَكْتُبُ مَا يَقُولُ وَنَمُدُّ لَهُۥ مِنَ ٱلْعَذَابِ مَدًّا

No! But we will write what he says and will extend for him of torment and extension

K^{a}llā (No! But) *s^a-n^{a}kt^{u}b^u* (we will write) *mā* (what) *y^{a}qūl^u* (he says) *w^a-n^{a}m^{u}dd^u* (and we extend) *l^a-h^u* (for him) *m^{i}n* (from) *al-^{a}dhāb^i* (torment) *m^{a}ddā* (an extension).

Verse 80

وَنَرِثُهُۥ مَا يَقُولُ وَيَأْتِينَا فَرْدًا

We will inherit from him what he says and he will come to us alone

W^a-n^{a}r^{i}th^u-h^u (and we inherit him) *mā* (what) *y^{a}qūl^u* (he says) *w^a-y^a'tīnā* (and hecomes to us) *f^{a}rdā* (as an individual, alone).

Verse 81

وَٱتَّخَذُوا۟ مِن دُونِ ٱللَّهِ ءَالِهَةً لِّيَكُونُوا۟ لَهُمْ عِزًّا

They took gods apart from God to be for them a source of glory

W^a-itt^{a}kh^{a}dhū (and they took, and they assigned to themselves) *m^{i}n dūn^i* (apart from, without) *allāh^i* (God) *āl^{i}h^{a}t^{an}* (gods) *l^i* (in order [for them]) *y^{a}kūnū* (to be) *l^a-h^{u}m* (for them) *^{i}zzā* (a [source of] glory).

Verse 82

كَلَّاۚ سَيَكۡفُرُونَ بِعِبَادَتِهِمۡ وَيَكُونُونَ عَلَيۡهِمۡ ضِدًّا

No! But they will reject their worship and will be against them helpers

K^{a}llā (No! But) *s^{a}-y^{a}kf^{u}rūn^{a}* (they will reject) *b^{i}-ʿ^{i}bād^{a}t^{i}-h^{i}m* (their worship) *w^{a}-y^{a}kūnūn^{a}* (and will be) *^{a}l^{a}y-h^{i}m* (against them) *ḍ^{i}ddā* (helpers).

The meaning of the verse is that the statues they worshiped will reject their worship (God will cause the statues to talk) on the Day of Judgment and will help the cause of God against the pagans by bearing witness that they were not gods and that they reject such worship.

Verse 83

أَلَمۡ تَرَ أَنَّآ أَرۡسَلۡنَا ٱلشَّيَٰطِينَ عَلَى ٱلۡكَٰفِرِينَ تَؤُزُّهُمۡ أَزّٗا

Have you not seen that indeed we sent the devils upon the rejecters, constantly inciting them?

A-l^{a}m (did not) *t^{a}r^{a}* (you saw) *an-nā* (indeed We) *ars^{a}l-nā* (we sent) *al-sh^{a}yāṭīn^{a}* (the devils) *^{a}lā* (upon) *al-kāf^{i}rīn^{a}* (the rejecters) *t^{a} ^{u}zz^{u}-h^{u}m* (they incite them) *azzā* (an inciting).

Verse 84

فَلَا تَعۡجَلۡ عَلَيۡهِمۡۖ إِنَّمَا نَعُدُّ لَهُمۡ عَدّٗا

So make no haste against them; we indeed only count for them a number

F^{a}-lā (so do not) *t^{a}ʿ^{a}jl* (you make haste) *^{a}l^{a}y-h^{i}m* (against them) *inn^{a}-mā* (indeed only) *n^{a} ^{a}dd^{u}* (we count) *l^{a}-h^{u}m* (for them) *^{a}ddā* (a number, a sum).

The meaning of this verse is that God is counting for them the number of days (etc.) until they meet their judgment.

Verse 85

يَوْمَ نَحْشُرُ ٱلْمُتَّقِينَ إِلَى ٱلرَّحْمَٰنِ وَفْدًا

[On] the day we gather the God-fearing ones to the Most Gracious as a delegation

Y^{a}wm^{a} (the day) *n^{a}ḥsh^{u}r^{u}* (we gather) *al-m^{u}tt^{a}qīn^{a}* (the God-fearing ones) *ilā* (to) *al-r^{a}ḥmān^{i}* (the Most Gracious) *w^{a}fdā* ([as] a delegation).

Verse 86

وَنَسُوقُ ٱلْمُجْرِمِينَ إِلَىٰ جَهَنَّمَ وِرْدًا

And we drive the criminals to Hell as a thirsty herd

W^{a}-n^{a}sūq^{u} (and we drive) *al-m^{u}jr^{i}mīn^{a}* (the criminals) *ilā* (to) *j^{a}h^{a}nn^{a}m^{a}* (Hell) *w^{i}rdā* ([as] a thirsty herd, [in] a state of thirst).

Verse 87

لَّا يَمْلِكُونَ ٱلشَّفَٰعَةَ إِلَّا مَنِ ٱتَّخَذَ عِندَ ٱلرَّحْمَٰنِ عَهْدًا

They do not possess the power of intercession except one who has taken a promise from the Most Gracious

L^{a} y^{a}ml^{i}kūn^{a} (they do not possess) *al-sh^{a}fāʿ^{a}t^{a}* (the power of intercession) *illā* (except) *m^{a}n* (one who) *itt^{a}kh^{a}dh^{a}* (he took) *ʿ^{i}nd^{a}* (with, from) *al-r^{a}ḥmān^{i}* (the Most Gracious) *ʿ^{a}hdā* (a promise, a pact).

Verse 88

وَقَالُوا۟ ٱتَّخَذَ ٱلرَّحْمَٰنُ وَلَدًا

And they said, "The Most Gracious has taken a child [as a son]."

W^{a}*-qālū* (and they said) *itt*^{a}*kh*^{a}*dh*^{a} (He took) *al-r*^{a}*ḥmān*^{u} (the Most Gracious) *w*^{a}*l*^{a}*dā* (a child).

Verse 89

لَّقَدْ جِئْتُمْ شَيْـًٔا إِدًّا

You have truly brought forth an atrocious thing

L^{a}*-q*^{a}*d* (truly have) *j*^{i}*'t*^{u}*m* (you brought) *sh*^{a}*y*^{a}*n* (a thing) *iddā* (atrocious, monstrous).

This page intentionally left blank

Lesson 46 Review

أَفَرَءَيْتَ ٱلَّذِى كَفَرَ بِـَٔايَـٰتِنَا

A-f^{a}-r^{a}^{a}yt^{a} (so have you seen) *all^{a}dhī* (the one who) *k^{a}f^{a}r^{a}* (rejected, denied) *b^{i}-āyāt^{i}nā* (our verses).

وَقَالَ لَأُوتَيَنَّ مَالًا وَوَلَدًا

W^{a}-qāl^{a} (and he said) *l^{a}-ūt^{a}y^{a}nn^{a}* (surely I will be given) *māl^{an}* (wealth) *w^{a}-w^{a}l^{a}dā* (children).

أَطَّلَعَ ٱلْغَيْبَ أَمِ ٱتَّخَذَ عِندَ ٱلرَّحْمَـٰنِ عَهْدًا

Aṭṭ^{a}la^{a} (has he inspected, has he perused) *al-gh^{a}yb^{a}* (the Unseen) *am^{i}* (or [has he]) *itt^{a}kh^{a}dh^{a}* (he took) *^{i}nd^{a}* (with, by) *al-r^{a}ḥmān^{i}* (the Most Gracious) *^{a}hdā* (a promise, a pact).

كَلَّا ۚ سَنَكْتُبُ مَا يَقُولُ وَنَمُدُّ لَهُۥ مِنَ ٱلْعَذَابِ مَدًّا

K^{a}llā (No! But) *s^{a}-n^{a}kt^{u}b^{u}* (we will write) *mā* (what) *y^{a}qūl^{u}* (he says) *w^{a}-n^{a}m^{u}dd^{u}* (and we extend) *l^{a}-h^{u}* (for him) *m^{i}n* (from) *al-^{a}dhāb^{i}* (torment) *m^{a}ddā* (an extension).

وَنَرِثُهُۥ مَا يَقُولُ وَيَأْتِينَا فَرْدًا

W^{a}-n^{a}r^{i}th^{u}-h^{u} (and we inherit him) *mā* (what) *y^{a}qūl^{u}* (he says) *w^{a}-y^{a}'tīnā* (and hecomes to us) *f^{a}rdā* (as an individual, alone).

وَٱتَّخَذُوا۟ مِن دُونِ ٱللَّهِ ءَالِهَةً لِّيَكُونُوا۟ لَهُمْ عِزًّا

W^{a}-itt^{a}kh^{a}dhū (and they took, and they assigned to themselves) *m^{i}n dūn^{i}* (apart from, without) *allāh^{i}* (God) *āl^{i}h^{a}t^{an}* (gods) *l^{i}* (in order [for them]) *y^{a}kūnū* (to be) *l^{a}-h^{u}m* (for them) *^{i}zzā* (a [source of] glory).

كَلَّا ۚ سَيَكْفُرُونَ بِعِبَادَتِهِمْ وَيَكُونُونَ عَلَيْهِمْ ضِدًّا

K^{a}llā (No! But) *s^{a}-y^{a}kf^{u}rūn^{a}* (they will reject) *b^{i}-^{i}bād^{a}t^{i}-h^{i}m* (their worship) *w^{a}-y^{a}kūnūn^{a}* (and will be) *^{a}l^{a}y-h^{i}m* (against them) *ḍ^{i}ddā* (helpers).

أَلَمْ تَرَ أَنَّآ أَرْسَلْنَا ٱلشَّيَٰطِينَ عَلَى ٱلْكَٰفِرِينَ تَؤُزُّهُمْ أَزًّا

A-l^{a}m (did not) *t^{a}r^{a}* (you saw) *an-nā* (indeed We) *ars^{a}l-nā* (we sent) *al-sh^{a}yāṭīn^{a}* (the devils) *^{a}lā* (upon) *al-kāf^{i}rīn^{a}* (the rejecters) *t^{a}^{u}zz^{u}-h^{u}m* (they incite them) *azzā* (an inciting).

فَلَا تَعْجَلْ عَلَيْهِمْ ۖ إِنَّمَا نَعُدُّ لَهُمْ عَدًّا

F^{a}-lā (so do not) *t^{a}ʿj^{a}l* (you make haste) *^{a}l^{a}y-h^{i}m* (against them) *inn^{a}-mā* (indeed only) *n^{a}^{u}dd^{u}* (we count) *l^{a}-h^{u}m* (for them) *^{a}ddā* (a number, a sum).

يَوْمَ نَحْشُرُ ٱلْمُتَّقِينَ إِلَى ٱلرَّحْمَٰنِ وَفْدًا

Y^{a}*wm*^{a} (the day) *n*^{a}*ḥsh*^{u}*r*^{u} (we gather) *al-m*^{u}*tt*^{a}*qīn*^{a} (the God-fearing ones) *ilā* (to) *al-r*^{a}*ḥmān*^{i} (the Most Gracious) *w*^{a}*fdā* ([as] a delegation).

وَنَسُوقُ ٱلْمُجْرِمِينَ إِلَىٰ جَهَنَّمَ وِرْدًا

W^{a}*-n*^{a}*sūq*^{u} (and we drive) *al-m*^{u}*jr*^{i}*mīn*^{a} (the criminals) *ilā* (to) *j*^{a}*h*^{a}*nn*^{a}*m*^{a} (Hell) *w*^{i}*rdā* ([as] a thirsty herd, [in] a state of thirst).

لَّا يَمْلِكُونَ ٱلشَّفَٰعَةَ إِلَّا مَنِ ٱتَّخَذَ عِندَ ٱلرَّحْمَٰنِ عَهْدًا

L^{a} *y*^{a}*ml*^{i}*kūn*^{a} (they do not possess) *al-sh*^{a}*fāʿt*^{a} (the power of intercession) *illā* (except) *m*^{a}*n* (one who) *itt*^{a}*kh*^{a}*dh*^{a} (he took) ^{ʿi}*nd*^{a} (with, from) *al-r*^{a}*ḥmān*^{i} (the Most Gracious) ^{ʿa}*hdā* (a promise, a pact).

وَقَالُوا۟ ٱتَّخَذَ ٱلرَّحْمَٰنُ وَلَدًا

W^{a}*-qālū* (and they said) *itt*^{a}*kh*^{a}*dh*^{a} (He took) *al-r*^{a}*ḥmān*^{u} (the Most Gracious) *w*^{a}*l*^{i}*dā* (a child).

لَّقَدْ جِئْتُمْ شَيْـًٔا إِدًّا

L^{a}*-q*^{a}*d* (truly have) *j*^{iʾ}*t*^{u}*m* (you brought) *sh*^{a}*y*^{ʾa}*n* (a thing) *iddā* (atrocious, monstrous).

This page intentionally left blank

Lesson 47: Maryam Part 10

Verse 90, part 1

تَكَادُ ٱلسَّمَٰوَٰتُ يَتَفَطَّرْنَ مِنْهُ

The heavens almost repture from it...

T^{a}*kād*^{u} ([it is / they are] about to) *al-s*^{a}*māwāt*^{u} (the heavens) *y*^{a}*t*^{a}*f*^{a}*ṭṭ*^{a}*rn*^{a} (they burst, they repture) *m*^{i}*n-h*^{u} (from it).

Verse 90, part 2

وَتَنشَقُّ ٱلْأَرْضُ وَتَخِرُّ ٱلْجِبَالُ هَدًّا

And the earth [almost] splits asunder and the mountains collapse in devastation

W^{a}*-t*^{a}*nsh*^{a}*qq*^{u} (and splits asunder) *al-arḍ*^{u} (the earth) *w*^{a}*-t*^{a}*kh*^{i}*rr*^{u} (and they collapse) *al-j*^{i}*bāl*^{u} (the mountains) *h*^{a}*ddā* ([in] ruins, [in] devastation).

Verse 91

أَن دَعَوْا۟ لِلرَّحْمَٰنِ وَلَدًا

That they invoke a child for the Most Gracious

An (that) *d*^{a}^{a}*w* (they called) *l*^{i}*-al-r*^{a}*ḥmān*^{i} (for the Most Gracious) *w*^{a}*l*^{a}*dā* (a child).

Verse 92

وَمَا يَنۢبَغِى لِلرَّحۡمَٰنِ أَن يَتَّخِذَ وَلَدًا

And it is not befitting for the Most Gracious to take a child

W^{a}-mā (and not) *y^{a}nb^{a}ghī* (it befits) *l^{i}-al-r^{a}ḥmān^{i}* (for the Most Gracious) *an* (that) *y^{a}tt^{a}kh^{i}dh^{a}* (he takes) *y^{a}l^{a}dā* (a child).

Verse 93

إِن كُلُّ مَن فِى ٱلسَّمَٰوَٰتِ وَٱلۡأَرۡضِ إِلَّآ ءَاتِى ٱلرَّحۡمَٰنِ عَبۡدًا

There is none in the heavens and the earth except that he comes to the Most Gracious as a servant

In ([there is] not) *k^{u}ll^{u}* (any) *m^{a}n* (who [is]) *fī* (in) *al-s^{a}māwāt^{i}* (the heavens) *w^{a}-al-arḍ^{i}* (and the earth) *illā* (except) *ātī* (he comes [to]) *al-r^{a}ḥmān^{i}* (the Most Gracious) *ʿabdā* ([as] a servant).

Verse 94

لَّقَدۡ أَحۡصَىٰهُمۡ وَعَدَّهُمۡ عَدًّا

He has enumerated them and counted them with a [proper] counting

L^{a}-q^{a}d (he truly has) *aḥṣā-h^{u}m* (enumerated them) *w^{a}-^{a}dd^{a}-h^{u}m* (and counted them) *^{a}ddā* ([with] a [proper] counting).

Verse 95

وَكُلُّهُمْ ءَاتِيهِ يَوْمَ ٱلْقِيَـٰمَةِ فَرْدًا

And each of them comes to Him on the Day of Judgment alone

W^{a}-k^{u}ll^{u}-h^{u}m (and all of them, and each of them) *ātī-h^{i}* (he comes to Him) *y^{a}wm^{a}* (the day [of]) *al-q^{i}yām^{a}t^{i}* (judgment) *f^{a}rdā* (alone, singly).

Verse 96

إِنَّ ٱلَّذِينَ ءَامَنُوا۟ وَعَمِلُوا۟ ٱلصَّـٰلِحَـٰتِ سَيَجْعَلُ لَهُمُ ٱلرَّحْمَـٰنُ وُدًّا

Indeed, those who believed and did good deeds—the Most Gracious will appoint for them love

Inn^{a} (indeed) *all^{a}dhīn^{a}* (those who) *ām^{a}nū* (they believed) *w^{a}-^{a}m^{i}lū* (the did, they performed) *al-ṣāl^{i}ḥāt^{i}* (good deeds) *s^{a}-y^{a}j^{a}l^{u}* (He will appoint, He will make) *l^{a}-h^{u}m* (for them) *al-r^{a}ḥmān^{u}* (the Most Gracious) *w^{u}ddā* (love, affection).

Verse 97

فَإِنَّمَا يَسَّرْنَـٰهُ بِلِسَانِكَ لِتُبَشِّرَ بِهِ ٱلْمُتَّقِينَ وَتُنذِرَ بِهِۦ قَوْمًا لُّدًّا

Indeed We have only made it easy in your tongue in order to give good tidings to the God-fearing and to warn with it a hostile people

F^{a}-inn^{a}-mā (indeed we have only) *y^{a}ss^{a}rnā-h^{u}* (we made it easy) *b^{i}-l^{i}sān^{i}-k^{a}* (with your tongue, in your tongue) *l^{i}-t^{u}b^{a}shsh^{i}r^{a}* (to give good tidings [to]) *b^{i}-h^{i}* (with it) *al-m^{u}tt^{a}qīn^{a}* (the God-fearing ones) *w^{a}-t^{u}ndh^{i}r^{a}* (and warn) *b^{i}-h^{i}* (with it) *q^{a}wm^{an}* (a people) *l^{u}ddā* (hostile).

Verse 98

وَكَمْ أَهْلَكْنَا قَبْلَهُم مِّن قَرْنٍ هَلْ تُحِسُّ مِنْهُم مِّنْ أَحَدٍ أَوْ تَسْمَعُ لَهُمْ رِكْزًا

And how many a generation we destroyed before them—do you sense from them anyone or do you hear from them a faint sound?

W^{a}-$k^{a}m$ (and how many) $ahl^{a}k$-*nā* (we destroyed) $q^{a}bl^{a}$-$h^{u}m$ (before them) $m^{i}n$ $q^{a}rn^{in}$ (a generation) $h^{a}l$ (do...?) $t^{u}\text{ḥ}^{i}ss^{u}$ (you sense) $m^{i}n$-$h^{u}m$ (from them) $m^{i}n$ $a\text{ḥ}^{a}d^{in}$ (any one) *aw* (or) $t^{a}sm^{a\,u}$ (you hear) l^{a}-$h^{u}m$ (to them, from them) $r^{i}kz\bar{a}$ (a faint sound, a whisper).

Lesson 47 Review

تَكَادُ ٱلسَّمَٰوَٰتُ يَتَفَطَّرْنَ مِنْهُ

T^{a}*kād*^{u} ([it is / they are] about to) *al-s*^{a}*māwāt*^{u} (the heavens) *y*^{a}*t*^{a}*f*^{a}*ṭṭ*^{a}*rn*^{a} (they burst, they repture) *m*^{i}*n-h*^{u} (from it).

وَتَنشَقُّ ٱلْأَرْضُ وَتَخِرُّ ٱلْجِبَالُ هَدًّا

W^{a}*-t*^{a}*nsh*^{a}*qq*^{u} (and splits asunder) *al-arḍ*^{u} (the earth) *w*^{a}*-t*^{a}*kh*^{i}*rr*^{u} (and they collapse) *al-j*^{i}*bāl*^{u} (the mountains) *h*^{a}*ddā* ([in] ruins, [in] devastation).

أَن دَعَوْا۟ لِلرَّحْمَٰنِ وَلَدًا

An (that) *d*^{a}^{a}*w* (they called) *l*^{i}*-al-r*^{a}*ḥmān*^{i} (for the Most Gracious) *w*^{a}*l*^{a}*dā* (a child).

وَمَا يَنۢبَغِى لِلرَّحْمَٰنِ أَن يَتَّخِذَ وَلَدًا

W^{a}*-mā* (and not) *y*^{a}*nb*^{a}*ghī* (it befits) *l*^{i}*-al-r*^{a}*ḥmān*^{i} (for the Most Gracious) *an* (that) *y*^{a}*tt*^{a}*kh*^{i}*dh*^{a} (he takes) *y*^{a}*l*^{a}*dā* (a child).

إِن كُلُّ مَن فِي ٱلسَّمَٰوَٰتِ وَٱلْأَرْضِ إِلَّآ ءَاتِي ٱلرَّحْمَٰنِ عَبْدًا

In ([there is] not) *k*^{u}*ll*^{u} (any) *m*^{a}*n* (who [is]) *fī* (in) *al-s*^{a}*māwāt*^{i} (the heavens) *w*^{a}*-al-arḍ*^{i} (and the earth) *illā* (except) *ātī* (he comes [to]) *al-r*^{a}*ḥmān*^{i} (the Most Gracious) *ʿabdā* ([as] a servant).

لَّقَدْ أَحْصَىٰهُمْ وَعَدَّهُمْ عَدًّا

L^{a}*-q*^{a}*d* (he truly has) *aḥṣā-h*^{u}*m* (enumerated them) *w*^{a}*-*^{a}*dd*^{a}*-h*^{u}*m* (and counted them) ^{a}*ddā* ([with] a [proper] counting).

وَكُلُّهُمْ ءَاتِيهِ يَوْمَ ٱلْقِيَٰمَةِ فَرْدًا

W^{a}*-k*^{u}*ll*^{u}*-h*^{u}*m* (and all of them, and each of them) *ātī-h*^{i} (he comes to Him) *y*^{a}*wm*^{a} (the day [of]) *al-q*^{i}*yām*^{a}*t*^{i} (judgment) *f*^{a}*rdā* (alone, singly).

إِنَّ ٱلَّذِينَ ءَامَنُوا۟ وَعَمِلُوا۟ ٱلصَّٰلِحَٰتِ سَيَجْعَلُ لَهُمُ ٱلرَّحْمَٰنُ وُدًّا

Inn^{a} (indeed) *all*^{a}*dhīn*^{a} (those who) *ām*^{a}*nū* (they believed) *w*^{a}*-*^{a}*m*^{i}*lū* (the did, they performed) *al-ṣāl*^{i}*ḥāt*^{i} (good deeds) *s*^{a}*-y*^{a}*j*^{a}*l*^{u} (He will appoint, He will make) *l*^{a}*-h*^{u}*m* (for them) *al-r*^{a}*ḥmān*^{u} (the Most Gracious) *w*^{u}*ddā* (love, affection).

فَإِنَّمَا يَسَّرْنَٰهُ بِلِسَانِكَ لِتُبَشِّرَ بِهِ ٱلْمُتَّقِينَ وَتُنذِرَ بِهِۦ قَوْمًا لُّدًّا

F^{a}*-inn*^{a}*-mā* (indeed we have only) *y*^{a}*ss*^{a}*rnā-h*^{u} (we made it easy) *b*^{i}*-l*^{i}*sān*^{i}*-k*^{a} (with your tongue, in your tongue) *l*^{i}*-t*^{u}*b*^{a}*shsh*^{i}*r*^{a} (to give good tidings [to]) *b*^{i}*-h*^{i} (with it) *al-m*^{u}*tt*^{a}*qīn*^{a} (the God-fearing ones) *w*^{a}*-t*^{u}*ndh*^{i}*r*^{a} (and warn) *b*^{i}*-h*^{i} (with it) *q*^{a}*wm*^{an} (a people) *l*^{u}*ddā* (hostile).

وَكَمْ أَهْلَكْنَا قَبْلَهُم مِّن قَرْنٍ هَلْ تُحِسُّ مِنْهُم مِّنْ أَحَدٍ أَوْ تَسْمَعُ لَهُمْ رِكْزًا

W^{a}*-k*^{a}*m* (and how many) *ahl*^{a}*k-nā* (we destroyed) *q*^{a}*bl*^{a}*-h*^{u}*m* (before them) *m*^{i}*n q*^{a}*rn*^{in} (a generation) *h*^{a}*l* (do...?) *t*^{u}*ḥ*^{i}*ss*^{u} (you sense) *m*^{i}*n-h*^{u}*m* (from them) *m*^{i}*n aḥ*^{a}*d*^{in} (any one) *aw* (or) *t*^{a}*sm*$^{a\,u}$ (you hear) *l*^{a}*-h*^{u}*m* (to them, from them) *r*^{i}*kzā* (a faint sound, a whisper).

This page intentionally left blank

Lesson 48: al-Furqān Part 1

In this lesson we will cover chapter 25 of the Quran; al-Furqān ("The Criterion").

Verse 1

تَبَارَكَ ٱلَّذِى نَزَّلَ ٱلْفُرْقَانَ عَلَىٰ عَبْدِهِۦ لِيَكُونَ لِلْعَـٰلَمِينَ نَذِيرًا

Blessed is the One who sent down the Criterion upon His servant to be a warner to the worlds

T^{a}bār^{a}k^{a} (is blessed) *all^{a}dhī* (the One who) *n^{a}zz^{a}l^{a}* (He sent down) *al-f^{u}rqān^{a}* (the Criterion) *^{a}lā* (upon) *^{a}bd^{i}-h^{i}* (His servant) *l^{i}-y^{a}kūn^{a}* ([in order for him] to be) *l^{i}-al-ʿāl^{a}mīn^{a}* (for the worlds, for the inhabitants of the worlds) *n^{a}dhīrā* (a warner).

Verse 2, part 1

ٱلَّذِى لَهُۥ مُلْكُ ٱلسَّمَـٰوَٰتِ وَٱلْأَرْضِ وَلَمْ يَتَّخِذْ وَلَدًا

The One for whom is the dominion of the heavens and the earth and did not take a child [as a son]

All^{a}dhī (the One who) *l^{a}-h^{u}* (for Him [is]) *m^{u}lk^{u}* (the dominion [of]) *al-s^{a}māwāt^{i}* (the heavens) *w^{a}-al-arḍ^{i}* (the earth) *w^{a}-l^{a}m* (and did not) *y^{a}tt^{a}kh^{i}dh* (He takes) *w^{a}l^{a}dā* (a child).

Verse 2, part 2

وَلَمْ يَكُن لَّهُۥ شَرِيكٌ فِى ٱلْمُلْكِ وَخَلَقَ كُلَّ شَىْءٍ فَقَدَّرَهُۥ تَقْدِيرًا

and there was not for Him a partner in dominion and created everything so He determined it with a [precise] determination

W^{a}-l^{a}m (and not) *y^{a}k^{u}n* (was) *l^{a}-h^{u}* (for Him) *sh^{a}rīk^{un}* (a partner) *fī* (in) *al-m^{u}lk^{i}* (the dominion) *w^{a}-kh^{a}l^{a}q^{a}* (and created) *k^{u}ll^{a}* (every) *sh^{a}y^{in}* (thing) *f^{a}-q^{a}dd^{a}r^{a}-h^{u}* (so He determined it) *t^{a}qdīrā* ([with] a [precise] determination).

Verse 3, part 1

وَٱتَّخَذُوا۟ مِن دُونِهِۦٓ ءَالِهَةً لَّا يَخْلُقُونَ شَيْـًٔا

And they took apart from gods—they do not create a thing

W^{a}*-itt*^{a}*kh*^{a}*dhū* (they took, they took up) *m*^{i}*n dūn*^{i}*-h*^{i} (apart from Him) *āl*^{i}*h*^{a}*t*^{an} (gods) *lā* (do not) *y*^{a}*khl*^{u}*qūn*^{a} (they create) *sh*^{a}*y*$^{'an}$ (a thing).

Verse 3, part 2

وَهُمْ يُخْلَقُونَ وَلَا يَمْلِكُونَ لِأَنفُسِهِمْ ضَرًّا وَلَا نَفْعًا

and they are created and they do not possess for themselves a harm or benefit

W^{a}*-h*^{u}*m* (and they) *y*^{u}*khl*^{a}*qūn*^{a} (they are created) *w*^{a}*-lā* (and not) *y*^{a}*ml*^{i}*kūn*^{a} (they possess) *li-anf*^{u}*s*^{i}*-h*^{i}*m* (for themselves) *ḍ*^{a}*rr*^{an} (a harm) *w*^{a}*-lā n*^{a}*f*$^{'an}$ (a benefit).

Verse 3, part 3

وَلَا يَمْلِكُونَ مَوْتًا وَلَا حَيَوٰةً وَلَا نُشُورًا

and they possess no death, no life and no resurrection

W^{a}*-lā y*^{a}*ml*^{i}*kūn*^{a} (and they do not possess) *m*^{a}*wt*^{an} (a death) *w*^{a}*-lā* (and not) *ḥ*^{a}*yāt*^{an} (a life) *w*^{a}*-l*^{a} *n*^{u}*shūrā* (and no resurrection).

Verse 4, part 1

وَقَالَ ٱلَّذِينَ كَفَرُوٓا۟ إِنْ هَٰذَآ إِلَّآ إِفْكٌ ٱفْتَرَىٰهُ

And those who rejected said, "This is only a lie he has made up..."

W^{a}*-qāl*^{a} (and said) *all*^{a}*dhīn*^{a} (those who) *k*^{a}*f*^{a}*rū* (they rejected) *in hādhā* (this is not) *illā* (except) *ifk*^{un} (a lie, a made up thing) *ift*^{a}*rā-h*^{u} (he made it up).

Verse 4, part 2

وَأَعَانَهُۥ عَلَيْهِ قَوْمٌ ءَاخَرُونَ ۖ فَقَدْ جَآءُو ظُلْمًا وَزُورًا

"...and another people have helped him on it." Then they have truly brought an injustice and a falsity.

W^{a}*-a'ān*^{a}*-h*^{u} (and they helpd him) ^{a}*l*^{a}*y-h*^{i} (on it) *q*^{a}*wm*^{un} (a people) *ākh*^{a}*rūn* (a different [group], another) *f*^{a}*-q*^{a}*d* (then truly have) *jā'ū* (they brought, they put forward) *ẓ*^{u}*lm*^{an} (an injustice, a transgression) *w*^{a}*-zūrā* (a falsity, a lie).

Verse 5, part 1

وَقَالُوٓا۟ أَسَٰطِيرُ ٱلْأَوَّلِينَ ٱكْتَتَبَهَا

And they said, "[This is] the legends of the ancients he has written down..."

W^{a}*-qālū* (and they said) *asāṭīr*^{u} (tales [of], legends [of]) *al-aww*^{a}*līn*^{a} (the ancients, literaly "the first ones") *ikt*^{a}*t*^{a}*b*^{a}*-hā* (he wrote them down).

Verse 5, part 2

فَهِىَ تُمْلَىٰ عَلَيْهِ بُكْرَةً وَأَصِيلًا

"...so it is dictated to him morning and late afternoon."

F^{a}*-h*^{i}*y*^{a} (so it [is]) *t*^{u}*mlā* ([it is] dictated) ^{a}*ʿl*^{a}*y-h*^{i} (on him) *b*^{u}*kr*^{a}*t*^{an} (morning) *w*^{a}*-aṣīlā* (and late afternoon).

Verse 6, part 1

قُلْ أَنزَلَهُ ٱلَّذِى يَعْلَمُ ٱلسِّرَّ فِى ٱلسَّمَٰوَٰتِ وَٱلْأَرْضِ ۚ

Say, "The one who knows the secret in the heavens and the earth sent it down."

Q^{u}*l* (say) *anz*^{a}*l*^{a}*-h*^{u} (He sent it down) *all*^{a}*dhī* (the One who) *y*^{a}*ʿl*^{a}*m*^{u} (He knows) *al-s*^{i}*rr*^{a} (the secret) *fī* (in) *al-s*^{a}*māwāt*^{i} *w*^{a}*-al-arḍ* (the heavens and the earth).

Verse 6, part 2

إِنَّهُۥ كَانَ غَفُورًا رَّحِيمًا

Indeed He is Forgiving, Merciful

Inn^{a}*-h*^{u} (indeed He) *kān*^{a} (He was) *gh*^{a}*fūr*^{an} (a Forgiving One) *r*^{a}*ḥīmā* (a Merciful One).

Verse 7, part 1

وَقَالُوا۟ مَالِ هَٰذَا ٱلرَّسُولِ يَأْكُلُ ٱلطَّعَامَ

And they said, "What is [wrong] with this messenger—he eats food..."

W^{a}-qālū (and they said) mā-l^{i} (what is with) hādhā (this) al-r^{a}sūli (messenger) y^{a}'k^{u}l^{u} (he eats) al-ṭ^{a}ʿām^{a} (food).

Verse 7, part 2

وَيَمْشِى فِى ٱلْأَسْوَاقِ ۙ لَوْلَآ أُنزِلَ إِلَيْهِ مَلَكٌ فَيَكُونَ مَعَهُۥ نَذِيرًا

"...and he walks in the markets. Why is an angel not sent down to him so that he will be with him a warner?"

W^{a}-y^{a}mshī (and he walks) fī al-aswāq^{i} (in the markets) l^{a}w-lā (why not) unz^{i}l^{a} (was sent down) il^{a}y-h^{i} (to him) m^{a}l^{a}k^{un} (an angel) f^{a}-y^{a}kūn^{a} (so he will be) m^{a}ʿ^{a}-h^{u} (with him) n^{a}dhīrā (a warner).

Verse 8, part 1

أَوْ يُلْقَىٰٓ إِلَيْهِ كَنزٌ أَوْ تَكُونُ لَهُۥ جَنَّةٌ يَأْكُلُ مِنْهَا ۚ

"Or is thrown [down] to him a treasure or there will be for him a [miraculous] garden he eats from."

Aw (or) y^{u}lqā (is thrown) il^{a}y-h^{i} (upon him) k^{a}nz^{un} (a treasure) aw (or) t^{a}kūn^{u} (there is, there will be) l^{a}-h^{u} (for him) j^{a}nn^{a}t^{un} (a garden) y^{a}'k^{u}l^{u} (he eats) m^{i}n-hā (from it).

Verse 8, part 2

وَقَالَ ٱلظَّٰلِمُونَ إِن تَتَّبِعُونَ إِلَّا رَجُلًا مَّسْحُورًا

And the wrong doers said, “You follow none except a bewitched man.”

W^{a}*-qāl*^{a} (and said) *al-ẓāl*^{i}*m*^{u}*n*^{a} (the wrongdoers) *in* (not) *t*^{a}*tt*^{a}*b*^{i}*ʿūn*^{a} (you follow) *illā* (except) *r*^{a}*j*^{u}*l*^{an} (a man) *m*^{a}*sḥūrā* (bewitched, under the influence of magic).

Verse 9, part 1

ٱنظُرْ كَيْفَ ضَرَبُوا۟ لَكَ ٱلْأَمْثَٰلَ

Loo how they coin comparisons for you

Unẓ^{u}*r* (look) *k*^{a}*yf*^{a} (how) *ḍ*^{a}*r*^{a}*bū* (they coined) *l*^{a}*-k*^{a} (for you) *al-amthāl*^{a} (comparisons, similitudes, examples).

The verb *ḍ*^{a}*r*^{a}*b*^{a} literally means “he struck”. It is also used in the context of coin-making to mean that a coin was made by coin press. The phrase *ḍ*^{a}*r*^{a}*b*^{a} *al-amthāl*^{a} (“he coined comparisons”) means he mentioned comparisons for a thing, or examples that are meant to be compared with something.

Verse 9, part 2

فَضَلُّوا۟ فَلَا يَسْتَطِيعُونَ سَبِيلًا

So they went astray so they are unable to [find] a way

F^{a}*-ḍ*^{a}*llū* (so they went astray, so they lost the way) *f*^{a}*-lā* (so do not) *y*^{a}*st*^{a}*ṭīʿūn*^{a} (they are able) *s*^{a}*bīlā* ([to find] a way).

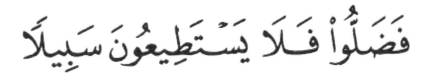

Verse 10, part 1

تَبَارَكَ ٱلَّذِىٓ إِن شَآءَ جَعَلَ لَكَ خَيْرًا مِّن ذَٰلِكَ

Blessed is the One Who, if He willed, [would have] appointed for you better than that

T^{a}*bār*^{a}*k*^{a} (is blessed) *all*^{a}*dhī* (the One who) *in* (if) *shā*^{a} (He willed, He wished) *j*^{a}^{a}*l*^{a} (He made, He appointed) *l*^{a}*-k*^{a} (for you) *kh*^{a}*yr*^{an} (better) *m*^{i}*n* (than) *dhāl*^{i}*k* (that).

Verse 10, part 2

جَنَّـٰتٍ تَجْرِى مِن تَحْتِهَا ٱلْأَنْهَـٰرُ وَيَجْعَل لَّكَ قُصُورًا

Gardens underneath which flow rivels, and He would have made for you palaces

J^{a}*nnāt*^{in} (gardens) *t*^{a}*jrī* (they run, they flow) *m*^{i}*n* (from) *t*^{a}*ḥt*^{i}*-hā* (underneath it) *al-anhār*^{u} (rivers) *w*^{a}*-y*^{a}*j*^{a}*l* (and He appoints, and He makes) *l*^{a}*-k*^{a} (for you) *q*^{u}*ṣūrā* (palaces).

This page intentionally left blank

Lesson 48 Review

تَبَارَكَ ٱلَّذِى نَزَّلَ ٱلْفُرْقَانَ عَلَىٰ عَبْدِهِۦ لِيَكُونَ لِلْعَـٰلَمِينَ نَذِيرًا

Tabāraka (is blessed) *alladhī* (the One who) *nazzala* (He sent down) *al-furqāna* (the Criterion) *ʿalā* (upon) *ʿabdi-hi* (His servant) *li-yakūna* ([in order for him] to be) *li-al-ʿālamīna* (for the worlds, for the inhabitants of the worlds) *nadhīrā* (a warner).

ٱلَّذِى لَهُۥ مُلْكُ ٱلسَّمَـٰوَٰتِ وَٱلْأَرْضِ وَلَمْ يَتَّخِذْ وَلَدًا

Alladhī (the One who) *la-hu* (for Him [is]) *mulku* (the dominion [of]) *al-samāwāti* (the heavens) *wa-al-arḍi* (the earth) *wa-lam* (and did not) *yattakhidh* (He takes) *waladā* (a child).

وَلَمْ يَكُن لَّهُۥ شَرِيكٌ فِى ٱلْمُلْكِ وَخَلَقَ كُلَّ شَىْءٍ فَقَدَّرَهُۥ تَقْدِيرًا

Wa-lam (and not) *yakun* (was) *la-hu* (for Him) *sharīkun* (a partner) *fī* (in) *al-mulki* (the dominion) *wa-khalaqa* (and created) *kulla* (every) *shayin* (thing) *fa-qaddara-hu* (so He determined it) *taqdīrā* ([with] a [precise] determination).

وَٱتَّخَذُوا۟ مِن دُونِهِۦٓ ءَالِهَةً لَّا يَخْلُقُونَ شَيْـًٔا

Wa-ittakhadhū (they took, they took up) *min dūni-hi* (apart from Him) *ālihatan* (gods) *lā* (do not) *yakhluqūna* (they create) *shayan* (a thing).

وَهُمْ يُخْلَقُونَ وَلَا يَمْلِكُونَ لِأَنفُسِهِمْ ضَرًّا وَلَا نَفْعًا

W^{a}-h^{u}m (and they) *y^{u}khl^{a}qūn^{a}* (they are created) *w^{a}-lā* (and not) *y^{a}ml^{i}kūn^{a}* (they possess) *li-anf^{u}s^{i}-h^{i}m* (for themselves) *ḍ^{a}rr^{an}* (a harm) *w^{a}-lā n^{a}f^{an}* (a benefit).

وَلَا يَمْلِكُونَ مَوْتًا وَلَا حَيَوٰةً وَلَا نُشُورًا

W^{a}-lā y^{a}ml^{i}kūn^{a} (and they do not possess) *m^{a}wt^{an}* (a death) *w^{a}-lā* (and not) *ḥ^{a}yāt^{an}* (a life) *w^{a}-l^{a} n^{u}shūrā* (and no resurrection).

وَقَالَ ٱلَّذِينَ كَفَرُوٓا۟ إِنْ هَٰذَآ إِلَّآ إِفْكٌ ٱفْتَرَىٰهُ

W^{a}-qāl^{a} (and said) *all^{a}dhīn^{a}* (those who) *k^{a}f^{a}rū* (they rejected) *in hādhā* (this is not) *illā* (except) *ifk^{un}* (a lie, a made up thing) *ift^{a}rā-h^{u}* (he made it up).

وَأَعَانَهُۥ عَلَيْهِ قَوْمٌ ءَاخَرُونَ ۖ فَقَدْ جَآءُو ظُلْمًا وَزُورًا

W^{a}-a'ān^{a}-h^{u} (and they helpd him) *^{a}l^{a}y-h^{i}* (on it) *q^{a}wm^{un}* (a people) *ākh^{a}rūn* (a different [group], another) *f^{a}-q^{a}d* (then truly have) *jā'ū* (they brought, they put forward) *ẓ^{u}lm^{an}* (an injustice, a transgression) *w^{a}-zūrā* (a falsity, a lie).

وَقَالُوٓا۟ أَسَٰطِيرُ ٱلْأَوَّلِينَ ٱكْتَتَبَهَا

W^{a}-qālū (and they said) *asāṭīr^{u}* (tales [of], legends [of]) *al-aww^{a}līn^{a}* (the ancients, literaly "the first ones") *ikt^{a}t^{a}b^{a}-hā* (he wrote them down).

فَهِىَ تُمْلَىٰ عَلَيْهِ بُكْرَةً وَأَصِيلًا

F^{a}-h^{i}y^{a} (so it [is]) *t^{u}mlā* ([it is] dictated) *^{a}l^{a}y-h^{i}* (on him) *b^{u}kr^{a}t^{an}* (morning) *w^{a}-aṣīlā* (and late afternoon).

قُلْ أَنزَلَهُ ٱلَّذِى يَعْلَمُ ٱلسِّرَّ فِى ٱلسَّمَٰوَٰتِ وَٱلْأَرْضِ ۚ

Q^{u}l (say) *anz^{a}l^{a}-h^{u}* (He sent it down) *all^{a}dhī* (the One who) *y^{a}ʿl^{a}m^{u}* (He knows) *al-s^{i}rr^{a}* (the secret) *fī* (in) *al-s^{a}māwāt^{i}* *w^{a}-al-arḍ* (the heavens and the earth).

إِنَّهُۥ كَانَ غَفُورًا رَّحِيمًا

Inn^{a}-h^{u} (indeed He) *kān^{a}* (He was) *gh^{a}fūr^{an}* (a Forgiving One) *r^{a}ḥīmā* (a Merciful One).

وَقَالُوا۟ مَالِ هَٰذَا ٱلرَّسُولِ يَأْكُلُ ٱلطَّعَامَ

W^{a}-qālū (and they said) *mā-l^{i}* (what is with) *hādhā* (this) *al-r^{a}sūli* (messenger) *y^{a}ʾk^{u}l^{u}* (he eats) *al-ṭ^{a}ʿām^{a}* (food).

وَيَمْشِى فِى ٱلْأَسْوَاقِ ۙ لَوْلَآ أُنزِلَ إِلَيْهِ مَلَكٌ فَيَكُونَ مَعَهُۥ نَذِيرًا

W^{a}-y^{a}mshī (and he walks) *fī al-aswāq^{i}* (in the markets) *l^{a}w-lā* (why not) *unz^{i}l^{a}* (was sent down) *il^{a}y-h^{i}* (to him) *m^{a}l^{a}k^{un}* (an angel) *f^{a}-y^{a}kūn^{a}* (so he will be) *m^{a}ʿ^{a}-h^{u}* (with him) *n^{a}dhīrā* (a warner).

أَوْ يُلْقَىٰٓ إِلَيْهِ كَنزٌ أَوْ تَكُونُ لَهُۥ جَنَّةٌ يَأْكُلُ مِنْهَا

Aw (or) *y^{u}lqā* (is thrown) *il^{a}y-h^{i}* (upon him) *k^{a}nz^{un}* (a treasure) *aw* (or) *t^{a}kūn^{u}* (there is, there will be) *l^{a}-h^{u}* (for him) *j^{a}nn^{a}t^{un}* (a garden) *y^{a}ʾk^{u}l^{u}* (he eats) *m^{i}n-hā* (from it).

وَقَالَ ٱلظَّٰلِمُونَ إِن تَتَّبِعُونَ إِلَّا رَجُلًا مَّسْحُورًا

W^{a}-qāl^{a} (and said) *al-ẓāl^{i}m^{u}n^{a}* (the wrongdoers) *in* (not) *t^{a}tt^{a}b^{i}ʿūn^{a}* (you follow) *illā* (except) *r^{a}j^{u}l^{an}* (a man) *m^{a}sḥūrā* (bewitched, under the influence of magic).

ٱنظُرْ كَيْفَ ضَرَبُوا۟ لَكَ ٱلْأَمْثَٰلَ

Unẓ^{u}r (look) *k^{a}yf^{a}* (how) *ḍ^{a}r^{a}bū* (they coined) *l^{a}-k^{a}* (for you) *al-amthāl^{a}* (comparisons, similitudes, examples).

فَضَلُّوا۟ فَلَا يَسْتَطِيعُونَ سَبِيلًا

F^{a}-ḍ^{a}llū (so they went astray, so they lost the way) *f^{a}-lā* (so do not) *y^{a}st^{a}ṭīʿūn^{a}* (they are able) *s^{a}bīlā* ([to find] a way).

تَبَارَكَ ٱلَّذِىٓ إِن شَآءَ جَعَلَ لَكَ خَيْرًا مِّن ذَٰلِكَ

T^{a}bār^{a}k^{a} (is blessed) *all^{a}dhī* (the One who) *in* (if) *shā^{a}* (He willed, He wished) *j^{a}ʿ^{a}l^{a}* (He made, He appointed) *l^{a}-k^{a}* (for you) *kh^{a}yr^{an}* (better) *m^{i}n* (than) *dhāl^{i}k* (that).

جَنَّٰتٍ تَجْرِى مِن تَحْتِهَا ٱلْأَنْهَٰرُ وَيَجْعَل لَّكَ قُصُورًا

J^{a}*nnāt*^{in} (gardens) *t*^{a}*jrī* (they run, they flow) *m*^{i}*n* (from) *t*^{a}*ḥt*^{i}*-hā* (underneath it) *al-anhār*^{u} (rivers) *w*^{a}*-y*^{a}*j*^{a}*l* (and He appoints, and He makes) *l*^{a}*-k*^{a} (for you) *q*^{u}*ṣūrā* (palaces).

This page intentionally left blank

Lesson 49: al-Furqān Part 2

Verse 11

بَلْ كَذَّبُوا۟ بِٱلسَّاعَةِ ۖ وَأَعْتَدْنَا لِمَن كَذَّبَ بِٱلسَّاعَةِ سَعِيرًا

Rather, they denied the Hour, and We have prepared for the one who denies the Hour a blaze

B^{a}l (rather, but) *k^{a}dhdh^{a}bū b^i* (they denied) *al-sā^{a}t^i* (the Hour) *w^a-aʿt^{a}d-nā* (and we prepared) *l^i-m^{a}n* (for the one who) *k^{a}dhdh^{a}b^a b^i* (he denied) *al-sā^{a}t^i* (the Hour) *s^{a}ʿīrā* (a blaze).

Verse 12

إِذَا رَأَتْهُم مِّن مَّكَانٍۭ بَعِيدٍ سَمِعُوا۟ لَهَا تَغَيُّظًا وَزَفِيرًا

When it [i.e. the Hellfire] sees them from a distant place--they hear from it a fury and roaring

Idhā (when) *r$^{a\,a}$t-h^{u}m* (it sees them) *m^{i}n* (from) *m^{a}kān^{in}* (a place) *baʿīd^{in}* (distant) *s^{a}m^{i}ʿū* (they heard) *l^a-hā* (for it, belonging to it) *t^{a}gh^{a}yy^{u}ẓ^{an}* (fury, craclking) *w^a-z^{a}fīrā* (roaring).

Verse 13

وَإِذَآ أُلْقُوا۟ مِنْهَا مَكَانًا ضَيِّقًا مُّقَرَّنِينَ دَعَوْا۟ هُنَالِكَ ثُبُورًا

And when they are thrown into a narrow place of it, in chains, they will pray there for destruction

W^a-idhā (and when) *ulqū* (they are thrown) *m^{i}n-hā* (from it) *m^{a}kān^{an}* (a place) *ḍ^{a}yy^{i}q^{an}* (narrow) *m^{u}q^{a}rr^{a}nīn^a* ([bound] in chains) *d$^{a\,a}$w* (they call for, they pray for) *h^{u}nālik^a* (there) *th^{u}būrā* (destruction).

Verse 14

لَّا تَدۡعُواْ ٱلۡيَوۡمَ ثُبُورٗا وَٰحِدٗا وَٱدۡعُواْ ثُبُورٗا كَثِيرٗا

Do not call today for one destruction, call for many destructions!

Lā (do not) *t*^{a}*d‘ū* (you call [for]) *al-y*^{a}*wm*^{a} (today) *th*^{u}*būr*^{an} (destruction) *wāḥ*^{i}*d*^{an} (one) *w*^{a}*-ud‘ū* (and call, but call [for]) *th*^{u}*būr*^{an} (destruction) *k*^{a}*thīrā* (many).

Verse 15, part 1

قُلۡ أَذَٰلِكَ خَيۡرٌ أَمۡ جَنَّةُ ٱلۡخُلۡدِ ٱلَّتِي وُعِدَ ٱلۡمُتَّقُونَۚ

Say, "Is that better or the garden of eternity which the God-fearing have been promised?"

Q^{u}*l* (say) *a-dhāl*^{i}*k*^{a} (is that) *kh*^{a}*yr*^{un} (better) *am* (or) *j*^{a}*nn*^{a}*t*^{u} (the garden [of]) *al-kh*^{u}*ld*^{i} (immortality, eternity, perpetuity) *all*^{a}*tī* (that which) *w*^{u}*‘*^{i}*d*^{a} (were promised) *al-m*^{u}*tt*^{a}*qūn* (the God-fearing ones).

Verse 15, part 2

كَانَتۡ لَهُمۡ جَزَآءٗ وَمَصِيرٗا

It will be for them a reward and a destination

Kān^{a}*-t* (it was) *l*^{a}*-h*^{u}*m* (for them) *j*^{a}*zā’*^{an} (a reward) *w*^{a}*-m*^{a}*ṣīrā* (and a destination).

Even though the literal meaning of the statement is in the past tense, we know from the context that it is speaking of a future event, for this reason in the translation we write "It will be..." rather than "It was..."

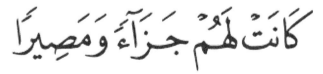

Verse 16, part 1

لَهُمْ فِيهَا مَا يَشَآءُونَ خَٰلِدِينَ

For them is what they wish for, abiding eternally

L^{a}*-h*^{u}*m* (for them [is]) *fī-hā* (in it) *mā* (what) *y*^{a}*shā'ūn*^{a} (they wish for, they will) *khāl*^{i}*dīn* (immortal ones, ones who abide eternally).

Verse 16, part 2

كَانَ عَلَىٰ رَبِّكَ وَعْدًا مَّسْـُٔولًا

It is upon your Lord a promise that one is held responsible for

Kān^{a} (it was) ^{a}*lā* (upon) *r*^{a}*bb*^{i}*-k*^{a} (your Lord) *w*^{a}*'d*^{an} (a promise) *m*^{a}*s'ūlā* (a thing that is asked about, a thing that one is held responsible for).

The phrase *w*^{a}*'d*^{an} *m*^{a}*s'ūlā* means "a promise that the promiser is held responsible for", "a promise that must be fulfilled". Since the promise is from God, the meaning is that this is a promise that God has made obligatory upon Himself to fulfill.

Verse 17, part 1

وَيَوْمَ يَحْشُرُهُمْ وَمَا يَعْبُدُونَ مِن دُونِ ٱللَّهِ

And the day He gathres them and what they worship apart from God

W^{a}*-y*^{a}*wm*^{a} (and the day, and [on] the day) *y*^{a}*ḥsh*^{u}*r*^{u} (He gathers them) *-h*^{u}*m* (them) *w*^{a}*-mā* (and what) *ya'b*^{u}*dūn*^{a} (they worship) *m*^{i}*n dūn*^{i} (apart from) *allāh* (God).

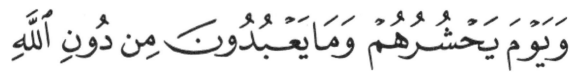

Verse 17, part 2

فَيَقُولُ ءَأَنتُمْ أَضْلَلْتُمْ عِبَادِى هَٰٓؤُلَآءِ أَمْ هُمْ ضَلُّوا۟ ٱلسَّبِيلَ

So He says, "Did you mislead those my servants or did they [themselves] lose the way?

Fa-y^{a}*qūl*^{u} (so He says) *a-ant*^{u}*m* (did you [plural]) *aḍl*^{a}*l-tum* (cause to be misled, cause to be misguided, cause to fall into error) ^{i}*bādī* (my servants) *hā*^{u}*lā*^{i} (those) *am* (or) *h*^{u}*m* (they) *ḍ*^{a}*llū* (became misled [from], strayed [from]) *al-s*^{a}*bīl* (the way).

Verse 18, part 1

قَالُوا۟ سُبْحَٰنَكَ مَا كَانَ يَنۢبَغِى لَنَآ أَن نَّتَّخِذَ مِن دُونِكَ مِنْ أَوْلِيَآءَ

They said, "Exalted are You! It was not for us to take besides You any allies..."

Qālū (they said) *s*^{u}*bḥān*^{a}*-k*^{a} (exalted are You!) *mā* (not) *kān*^{a} (it was) *y*^{a}*nb*^{a}*ghī* (it is befitting, it is rightful) *l*^{a}*-nā* (for us) *an* (to) *n*^{a}*tt*^{a}*kh*^{i}*dh*^{a} (take) *m*^{i}*n dūn*^{i}*-k*^{a} (apart from You, besides You) *awl*^{i}*yā'* (allies, protectors).

Verse 18, part 2

وَلَٰكِن مَّتَّعْتَهُمْ وَءَابَآءَهُمْ حَتَّىٰ نَسُوا۟ ٱلذِّكْرَ وَكَانُوا۟ قَوْمًۢا بُورًا

"...but you provided comforts for them and their fathers until they forgot the message and became a ruined people."

W^{a}*-lāk*^{i}*n* (but) *m*^{a}*tt*^{a}*ʿt*^{a}*-h*^{u}*m* (You provided them with comforts, You provisioned them) *w*^{a}*-ābā*^{a}*-h*^{u}*m* (and their fathers) *ḥ*^{a}*ttā* (until) *n*^{a}*s*^{a}*w* (they forgot) *al-dh*^{i}*kr*^{a} (the message, the remembrance) *w*^{a}*-kānū* (and they were) *q*^{a}*wm*^{an} (a people) *būrā* (ruined).

Verse 19, part 1

فَقَدْ كَذَّبُوكُم بِمَا تَقُولُونَ فَمَا تَسْتَطِيعُونَ صَرْفًا وَلَا نَصْرًا

So surely they have denied you in what you say, so you are unable to avert [the punishment] or [find] help

F^{a}-q^{a}d (so surely has) *k^{a}dhdh^{a}bū-k^{u}m* (they denied you, they called you liars) *b^{i}-mā* (in what) *t^{a}qūl^{u}n^{a}* (you say) *f^{a}-mā* (so not) *t^{a}st^{a}ṭīʿūn^{a}* (you are able) *ṣ^{a}rf^{an}* (to avert) *w^{a}-lā* (and not) *n^{a}ṣrā* (to [find] help).

Verse 19, part 2

وَمَن يَظْلِم مِّنكُمْ نُذِقْهُ عَذَابًا كَبِيرًا

and whoever does wrong of you—We will make him taste a great torment

W^{a}-m^{a}n (and who, and whoever) *y^{a}ḍl^{i}m* (does wrong, wrongs, transgresses) *m^{i}n-k^{u}m* (of you) *n^{u}dh^{i}q-h^{u}* (we make him taste) *^{a}dhāb^{an}* (a torment) *k^{a}bīrā* (great).

This page intentionally left blank

Lesson 49 Review

بَلْ كَذَّبُوا۟ بِٱلسَّاعَةِ ۖ وَأَعْتَدْنَا لِمَن كَذَّبَ بِٱلسَّاعَةِ سَعِيرًا

B^{a}l (rather, but) *k^{a}dhdh^{a}bū b^{i}* (they denied) *al-sā^{a}t^{i}* (the Hour) *w^{a}-aʿt^{a}d-nā* (and we prepared) *l^{i}-m^{a}n* (for the one who) *k^{a}dhdh^{a}b^{a} b^{i}* (he denied) *al-sā^{a}t^{i}* (the Hour) *s^{a}ʿīrā* (a blaze).

إِذَا رَأَتْهُم مِّن مَّكَانٍۭ بَعِيدٍ سَمِعُوا۟ لَهَا تَغَيُّظًا وَزَفِيرًا

Idhā (when) *r^{a}^{a}t-h^{u}m* (it sees them) *m^{i}n* (from) *m^{a}kān^{in}* (a place) *baʿīd^{in}* (distant) *s^{a}m^{i}ʿū* (they heard) *l^{a}-hā* (for it, belonging to it) *t^{a}gh^{a}yy^{u}ẓ^{an}* (fury, craclking) *w^{a}-z^{a}fīrā* (roaring).

وَإِذَآ أُلْقُوا۟ مِنْهَا مَكَانًا ضَيِّقًا مُّقَرَّنِينَ دَعَوْا۟ هُنَالِكَ ثُبُورًا

W^{a}-idhā (and when) *ulqū* (they are thrown) *m^{i}n-hā* (from it) *m^{a}kān^{an}* (a place) *ḍ^{a}yy^{i}q^{an}* (narrow) *m^{u}q^{a}rr^{a}nīn^{a}* ([bound] in chains) *d^{a}^{a}w* (they call for, they pray for) *h^{u}nālik^{a}* (there) *th^{u}būrā* (destruction).

لَّا تَدْعُوا۟ ٱلْيَوْمَ ثُبُورًا وَٰحِدًا وَٱدْعُوا۟ ثُبُورًا كَثِيرًا

Lā (do not) *t^{a}dʿū* (you call [for]) *al-y^{a}wm^{a}* (today) *th^{u}būr^{an}* (destruction) *wāḥ^{i}d^{an}* (one) *w^{a}-udʿū* (and call, but call [for]) *th^{u}būr^{an}* (destruction) *k^{a}thīrā* (many).

قُلْ أَذَٰلِكَ خَيْرٌ أَمْ جَنَّةُ ٱلْخُلْدِ ٱلَّتِى وُعِدَ ٱلْمُتَّقُونَ ۚ

Q^{u}*l* (say) *a-dhāl*^{i}*k*^{a} (is that) *kh*^{a}*yr*^{un} (better) *am* (or) *j*^{a}*nn*^{a}*t*^{u} (the garden [of]) *al-kh*^{u}*ld*^{i} (immortality, eternity, perpetuity) *all*^{a}*tī* (that which) *w*^{u}*ʿ*^{i}*d*^{a} (were promised) *al-m*^{u}*tt*^{a}*qūn* (the God-fearing ones).

كَانَتْ لَهُمْ جَزَآءً وَمَصِيرًا

Kān^{a}*-t* (it was) *l*^{a}*-h*^{u}*m* (for them) *j*^{a}*zāʾ*^{an} (a reward) *w*^{a}*-m*^{a}*ṣīrā* (and a destination).

لَّهُمْ فِيهَا مَا يَشَآءُونَ خَٰلِدِينَ

L^{a}*-h*^{u}*m* (for them [is]) *fī-hā* (in it) *mā* (what) *y*^{a}*shāʾūn*^{a} (they wish for, they will) *khāl*^{i}*dīn* (immortal ones, ones who abide eternally).

كَانَ عَلَىٰ رَبِّكَ وَعْدًا مَّسْـُٔولًا

Kān^{a} (it was) *ʿ*^{a}*lā* (upon) *r*^{a}*bb*^{i}*-k*^{a} (your Lord) *w*^{a}*ʿd*^{an} (a promise) *m*^{a}*sʾūlā* (a thing that is asked about, a thing that one is held responsible for).

وَيَوْمَ يَحْشُرُهُمْ وَمَا يَعْبُدُونَ مِن دُونِ ٱللَّهِ

W^{a}*-y*^{a}*wm*^{a} (and the day, and [on] the day) *y*^{a}*ḥsh*^{u}*r*^{u} (He gathers them) *-h*^{u}*m* (them) *w*^{a}*-mā* (and what) *yaʿb*^{u}*dūn*^{a} (they worship) *m*^{i}*n dūn*^{i} (apart from) *allāh* (God).

فَيَقُولُ ءَأَنتُمْ أَضْلَلْتُمْ عِبَادِى هَٰٓؤُلَآءِ أَمْ هُمْ ضَلُّوا۟ ٱلسَّبِيلَ

Fa-y^{a}qūl^{u} (so He says) *a-ant^{u}m* (did you [plural]) *aḍl^{a}l-tum* (cause to be misled, cause to be misguided, cause to fall into error) *ʿ^{i}bādī* (my servants) *hā^{u}lā^{i}* (those) *am* (or) *h^{u}m* (they) *ḍ^{a}llū* (became misled [from], strayed [from]) *al-s^{a}bīl* (the way).

قَالُوا۟ سُبْحَٰنَكَ مَا كَانَ يَنۢبَغِى لَنَآ أَن نَّتَّخِذَ مِن دُونِكَ مِنْ أَوْلِيَآءَ

Qālū (they said) *s^{u}bḥān^{a}-k^{a}* (exalted are You!) *mā* (not) *kān^{a}* (it was) *y^{a}nb^{a}ghī* (it is befitting, it is rightful) *l^{a}-nā* (for us) *an* (to) *n^{a}tt^{a}kh^{i}dh^{a}* (take) *m^{i}n dūn^{i}-k^{a}* (apart from You, besides You) *awl^{i}yā’* (allies, protectors).

وَلَٰكِن مَّتَّعْتَهُمْ وَءَابَآءَهُمْ حَتَّىٰ نَسُوا۟ ٱلذِّكْرَ وَكَانُوا۟ قَوْمًۢا بُورًا

W^{a}-lāk^{i}n (but) *m^{a}tt^{a}ʿt^{a}-h^{u}m* (You provided them with comforts, You provisioned them) *w^{a}-ābā^{a}-h^{u}m* (and their fathers) *ḥ^{a}ttā* (until) *n^{a}s^{a}w* (they forgot) *al-dh^{i}kr^{a}* (the message, the remembrance) *w^{a}-kānū* (and they were) *q^{a}wm^{an}* (a people) *būrā* (ruined).

فَقَدْ كَذَّبُوكُم بِمَا تَقُولُونَ فَمَا تَسْتَطِيعُونَ صَرْفًا وَلَا نَصْرًا

F^{a}-q^{a}d (so surely has) *k^{a}dhdh^{a}bū-k^{u}m* (they denied you, they called you liars) *b^{i}-mā* (in what) *t^{a}qūl^{u}n^{a}* (you say) *f^{a}-mā* (so not) *t^{a}st^{a}ṭīʿūn^{a}* (you are able) *ṣ^{a}rf^{an}* (to avert) *w^{a}-lā* (and not) *n^{a}ṣrā* (to [find] help).

وَمَن يَظْلِم مِّنكُمْ نُذِقْهُ عَذَابًا كَبِيرًا

W^{a}-m^{a}n (and who, and whoever) *y^{a}ḍl^{i}m* (does wrong, wrongs, transgresses) *m^{i}n-k^{u}m* (of you) *n^{u}dh^{i}q-h^{u}* (we make him taste) *ʿ^{a}dhāb^{an}* (a torment) *k^{a}bīrā* (great).

This page intentionally left blank

Lesson 50: al-Furqān Part 3

Verse 20, part 1

وَمَآ أَرۡسَلۡنَا قَبۡلَكَ مِنَ ٱلۡمُرۡسَلِينَ إِلَّآ إِنَّهُمۡ لَيَأۡكُلُونَ ٱلطَّعَامَ

And we did not send before you of messengers except that they eat food

W^{a}*-mā* (and did not) *ars*^{a}*l-nā* (we sent) *q*^{a}*bl*^{a}*-k*^{a} (before you) *m*^{i}*n* (of) *al-m*^{u}*rs*^{a}*līn*^{a} (messengers, sent ones) *illā* (except [that]) *inn*^{a}*-h*^{u}*m* (indeed they are) *l*^{a}*-y*^{a}*'k*^{u}*lūn*^{a} (they truly eat) *al-ṭ*^{a}*ʿām*^{a} (food).

Verse 20, part 2

وَيَمۡشُونَ فِي ٱلۡأَسۡوَاقِۗ

And they walk in the markets

W^{a}*-y*^{a}*mshūn*^{a} (and they walk) *fī* (in) *al-aswāq* (the markets).

Verse 20, part 3

وَجَعَلۡنَا بَعۡضَكُمۡ لِبَعۡضٖ فِتۡنَةً أَتَصۡبِرُونَۗ وَكَانَ رَبُّكَ بَصِيرٗا

And we have made some of you [a cause of] trials for others—will you be patient? And your Lord is Seeing

W^{a}*-j*^{a}*ʿ*^{a}*l-nā* (and we made, and we assigned) *b*^{a}*ʿḍ*^{u}*-k*^{u}*m* (some of you) *l*^{i}*-b*^{a}*ʿḍ*^{in} (for some of you) *f*^{i}*tn*^{a}*t*^{an} (a trial) *a-t*^{a}*ṣb*^{i}*rūn*^{a} (do you endure patiently?) *w*^{a}*-kān*^{a} (and was) *r*^{a}*bb*^{u}*-k*^{a} (your Lord) *b*^{a}*ṣīrā* (Seeing, One Who sees).

Verse 21, part 1

وَقَالَ ٱلَّذِينَ لَا يَرْجُونَ لِقَآءَنَا لَوْلَآ أُنزِلَ عَلَيْنَا ٱلْمَلَٰٓئِكَةُ

And those who do not wish meeting Us said, "Why are angels not sent down upon us...?"

W^{a}-qāl^{a} (and said) *all^{a}dhīn^{a}* (those who) *lā* (do not) *y^{a}rjūn^{a}* (they wish for, they desire) *l^{i}qā^{a}-nā* (Our meeting, meeting Us) *l^{a}wlā* (why not) *unz^{i}l^{a}* (were sent down) *^{a}l^{a}y-nā* (upon us) *al-m^{a}lā^{i}k^{a}* (the angels).

Verse 21, part 2

أَوْ نَرَىٰ رَبَّنَا ۗ لَقَدِ ٱسْتَكْبَرُوا۟ فِىٓ أَنفُسِهِمْ وَعَتَوْ عُتُوًّا كَبِيرًا

"...or [why do we not] see our Lord?" Truly they have become arrogant in their selves and have acted insolently with great insolence

Aw (or) *n^{a}rā* (we see) *r^{a}bb^{a}-nā* (our Lord) *l^{a}-q^{a}d* (truly have) *ist^{a}kb^{a}rū* (they acted arrogantly) *fī* (in) *anf^{a}s^{i}-h^{i}m* (their own selves, their souls) *w^{a}-^{a}t^{a}w* (and they acted insolently) *^{u}tūw^{an}* ([with] an insolence) *k^{a}bīrā* (great).

Verse 22

يَوْمَ يَرَوْنَ ٱلْمَلَٰٓئِكَةَ لَا بُشْرَىٰ يَوْمَئِذٍ لِّلْمُجْرِمِينَ وَيَقُولُونَ حِجْرًا مَّحْجُورًا

The day they see the angels, there is no good tiding on that day for the criminals and they say "A forbidden barrier!"

Y^{a}wm^{a} (the day) *y^{a}r^{a}wn^{a}* (they see) *al-m^{a}lā^{i}k^{a}t^{a}* (the angels) *lā* (no) *b^{u}shrā* (good tidings) *y^{a}wm^{a}^{i}dh^{in}* (on that day) *l^{i}-al-m^{u}jr^{i}mīn^{a}* (for the criminals) *w^{a}-y^{a}qūlūn^{a}* (and they say) *ḥ^{i}jr^{an}* (a barrier) *māḥjūrā* (forbidden).

Verse 23

وَقَدِمْنَآ إِلَىٰ مَا عَمِلُواْ مِنْ عَمَلٍ فَجَعَلْنَٰهُ هَبَآءً مَّنثُورًا

and We shall proceed to the deeds they have done and scatter them like dust

W^{a}*-q*^{a}*d*^{i}*m-nā* (and We came, and We proceeded) *ilā* (to) *mā* (what) ^{a}*m*^{i}*lū* (they did, they worked) *m*^{i}*n* (of) ^{a}*m*^{a}*l*^{in} (a deed, a work) *f*^{a}*-j*^{a} ^{a}*lnā-h*^{u} (so We made it) *h*^{a}*bā*^{an} (dust) *m*^{a}*nthūrā* (scattered).

Verse 24

أَصْحَٰبُ ٱلْجَنَّةِ يَوْمَئِذٍ خَيْرٌ مُّسْتَقَرًّا وَأَحْسَنُ مَقِيلًا

The companions of the Garden will have a better home on that Day, and a more beautiful resting place

Aṣḥāb^{u} (the companions [of]) *al-j*^{a}*nn*^{a}*t*^{i} (the Garden) *y*^{a}*wm*^{a} ^{i}*dh*^{in} (on that day) *kh*^{a}*yr*^{un} ([will have] a better) *m*^{u}*st*^{a}*q*^{a}*rr*^{an} (abode, home) *w*^{a}*-aḥs*^{a}*n*^{u} (and more beautiful) *m*^{a}*qīlā* (a resting place).

Verse 25

وَيَوْمَ تَشَقَّقُ ٱلسَّمَآءُ بِٱلْغَمَٰمِ وَنُزِّلَ ٱلْمَلَٰٓئِكَةُ تَنزِيلًا

A day when the heaven with the clouds will be rent asunder and the angels will be sent down, a grand descent

W^{a}*-y*^{a}*wm*^{a} (and the day) *t*^{a}*sh*^{a}*qq*^{a}*q*^{u} (splits, is rent asunder) *al-s*^{a}*mā*^{u} (the heaven) *b*^{i}*-algh*^{a}*mām*^{i} (with the clouds) *w*^{a}*-n*^{u}*zz*^{i}*l*^{a} (and were sent down) *al-m*^{a}*lā*^{i}*k*^{a}*t*^{u} (the angels) *t*^{a}*nzīlā* (a [grand] sending down, a [grand] descent).

Verse 26

ٱلْمُلْكُ يَوْمَئِذٍ ٱلْحَقُّ لِلرَّحْمَٰنِ ۚ وَكَانَ يَوْمًا عَلَى ٱلْكَٰفِرِينَ عَسِيرًا

True sovereignty, that day, is for the Most Gracious. And it will be upon the disbelievers a difficult Day

Al-m^{u}lk^{u} (the sovereignty) *y^{a}wm^{i}dh^{in}* (on that day) *al-ḥ^{a}qq^{u}* (true) *l^{i}-al-r^{a}ḥmān^{i}* (for the Most Gracious) *w^{a}-kān^{a}* (and it was) *y^{a}wm^{an}* (a day) *ʿ^{a}lā* (upon) *al-kāf^{i}rīn^{a}* (the rejecters) *ʿ^{a}sīrā* (difficult).

Verse 27

وَيَوْمَ يَعَضُّ ٱلظَّالِمُ عَلَىٰ يَدَيْهِ يَقُولُ يَٰلَيْتَنِى ٱتَّخَذْتُ مَعَ ٱلرَّسُولِ سَبِيلًا

The day the evildoer will bite his own hand and say, "If only I had taken the same path as the Messenger..."

W^{a}-y^{a}wm^{a} (and the day) *y^{a}ʿ^{a}ḍḍ^{u}* (he bites) *al-ẓāl^{i}m^{u}* (the wrongdoer, the transgresser) *ʿ^{a}lā* (upon) *y^{a}d^{a}y-h^{i}* (his [two] hands) *y^{a}qūl^{u}* (he says) *y^{a}l^{a}yt^{a}-nī* (Oh I wish I..., if only I) *itt^{a}kh^{a}dh-t^{u}* (I took) *m^{a}ʿ^{a}* (with) *al-r^{a}sūl^{i}* (the Messenger) *s^{a}bīlā* (a path).

Verse 28

يَٰوَيْلَتَىٰ لَيْتَنِى لَمْ أَتَّخِذْ فُلَانًا خَلِيلًا

"Oh, woe to me! I wish I had not taken that one as a friend..."

Yā-w^{a}yl^{a}tā (Oh woe to me!) *l^{a}yt^{a}-nī* (I wish I, if only I) *l^{a}m* (did not) *att^{a}kh^{i}dh^{a}* (I took, I assigned to myself) *f^{u}lān^{an}* (so and so) *kh^{a}līlā* (a close friend).

Verse 29, part 1

لَّقَدْ أَضَلَّنِى عَنِ ٱلذِّكْرِ بَعْدَ إِذْ جَآءَنِى ۗ

"Truly he led me away from the remembrance after it had come to me."

L^{a}*-q*^{a}*d* (truly has truly did) *aḍ*^{a}*ll*^{a}*-nī* (he misled me) ^{ʿa}*n* (from) *al-dh*^{i}*kr*^{i} (the remembrance) *b*^{aʿ}*d*^{a} (after) *idh* (when) *jā*^{ʾa}*-nī* (it came to me).

Verse 29, part 2

وَكَانَ ٱلشَّيْطَٰنُ لِلْإِنسَٰنِ خَذُولًا

And ever is Satan, to man, a deserter.

W^{a}*-kān*^{a} (and was, and ever is) *al-sh*^{a}*yṭān*^{u} (Satan, the devil) *l*^{i}*-al-insān*^{i} (to the human) *kh*^{a}*dhūlā* (a deserter).

This page intentionally left blank

Lesson 50 Review

وَمَآ أَرْسَلْنَا قَبْلَكَ مِنَ ٱلْمُرْسَلِينَ إِلَّآ إِنَّهُمْ لَيَأْكُلُونَ ٱلطَّعَامَ

W^{a}-mā (and did not) *ars^{a}l-nā* (we sent) *q^{a}bl^{a}-k^{a}* (before you) *m^{i}n* (of) *al-m^{u}rs^{a}līn^{a}* (messengers, sent ones) *illā* (except [that]) *inn^{a}-h^{u}m* (indeed they are) *l^{a}-y^{a}'k^{u}lūn^{a}* (they truly eat) *al-ṭ^{a}ʿām^{a}* (food).

وَيَمْشُونَ فِى ٱلْأَسْوَاقِ ۗ

W^{a}-y^{a}mshūn^{a} (and they walk) *fī* (in) *al-aswāq* (the markets).

وَجَعَلْنَا بَعْضَكُمْ لِبَعْضٍ فِتْنَةً أَتَصْبِرُونَ ۗ وَكَانَ رَبُّكَ بَصِيرًا

W^{a}-j^{a}ʿ^{a}l-nā (and we made, and we assigned) *b^{a}ʿḍ^{u}-k^{u}m* (some of you) *l^{i}-b^{a}ʿḍ^{in}* (for some of you) *f^{i}tn^{a}t^{an}* (a trial) *a-t^{a}ṣb^{i}rūn^{a}* (do you endure patiently?) *w^{a}-kān^{a}* (and was) *r^{a}bb^{u}-k^{a}* (your Lord) *b^{a}ṣīrā* (Seeing, One Who sees).

وَقَالَ ٱلَّذِينَ لَا يَرْجُونَ لِقَآءَنَا لَوْلَآ أُنزِلَ عَلَيْنَا ٱلْمَلَٰٓئِكَةُ

W^{a}-qāl^{a} (and said) *all^{a}dhīn^{a}* (those who) *lā* (do not) *y^{a}rjūn^{a}* (they wish for, they desire) *l^{i}qā^{a}-nā* (Our meeting, meeting Us) *l^{a}wlā* (why not) *unz^{i}l^{a}* (were sent down) *ʿ^{a}l^{a}y-nā* (upon us) *al-m^{a}lā^{i}k^{a}* (the angels).

أَوْ نَرَىٰ رَبَّنَا ۗ لَقَدِ ٱسْتَكْبَرُوا۟ فِىٓ أَنفُسِهِمْ وَعَتَوْ عُتُوًّا كَبِيرًا

Aw (or) *n^{a}rā* (we see) *r^{a}bb^{a}-nā* (our Lord) *l^{a}-q^{a}d* (truly have) *ist^{a}kb^{a}rū* (they acted arrogantly) *fī* (in) *anf^{u}s^{i}-h^{i}m* (their own selves, their souls) *w^{a}-ʿ^{a}t^{a}w* (and they acted insolently) *ʿ^{u}tūw^{an}* ([with] an insolence) *k^{a}bīrā* (great).

يَوْمَ يَرَوْنَ ٱلْمَلَـٰٓئِكَةَ لَا بُشْرَىٰ يَوْمَئِذٍ لِّلْمُجْرِمِينَ وَيَقُولُونَ حِجْرًا مَّحْجُورًا

Y^{a}wm^{a} (the day) *y^{a}r^{a}wn^{a}* (they see) *al-m^{a}lā^{i}k^{a}t^{a}* (the angels) *lā* (no) *b^{u}shrā* (good tidings) *y^{a}wm$^{a\,i}$dh^{in}* (on that day) *l^{i}-al-m^{u}jr^{i}mīn^{a}* (for the criminals) *w^{a}-y^{a}qūlūn^{a}* (and they say) *ḥ^{i}jr^{an}* (a barrier) *māhjūrā* (forbidden).

وَقَدِمْنَآ إِلَىٰ مَا عَمِلُوا۟ مِنْ عَمَلٍ فَجَعَلْنَـٰهُ هَبَآءً مَّنثُورًا

W^{a}-q^{a}d^{i}m-nā (and We came, and We proceeded) *ilā* (to) *mā* (what) *^{a}m^{i}lū* (they did, they worked) *m^{i}n* (of) *^{a}m^{a}l^{in}* (a deed, a work) *f^{a}-j$^{a\,a}$lnā-h^{u}* (so We made it) *h^{a}bā^{an}* (dust) *m^{a}nthūrā* (scattered).

أَصْحَـٰبُ ٱلْجَنَّةِ يَوْمَئِذٍ خَيْرٌ مُّسْتَقَرًّا وَأَحْسَنُ مَقِيلًا

Aṣḥāb^{u} (the companions [of]) *al-j^{a}nn^{a}t^{i}* (the Garden) *y^{a}wm$^{a\,i}$dh^{in}* (on that day) *kh^{a}yr^{un}* ([will have] a better) *m^{u}st^{a}q^{a}rr^{an}* (abode, home) *w^{a}-aḥs^{a}n^{u}* (and more beautiful) *m^{a}qīlā* (a resting place).

وَيَوْمَ تَشَقَّقُ ٱلسَّمَآءُ بِٱلْغَمَـٰمِ وَنُزِّلَ ٱلْمَلَـٰٓئِكَةُ تَنزِيلًا

W^{a}-y^{a}wm^{a} (and the day) *t^{a}sh^{a}qq^{a}q^{u}* (splits, is rent asunder) *al-s^{a}mā^{u}* (the heaven) *b^{i}-algh^{a}mām^{i}* (with the clouds) *w^{a}-n^{u}zz^{i}l^{a}* (and were sent down) *al-m^{a}lā^{i}k^{a}t^{u}* (the angels) *t^{a}nzīlā* (a [grand] sending down, a [grand] descent).

ٱلْمُلْكُ يَوْمَئِذٍ ٱلْحَقُّ لِلرَّحْمَـٰنِ ۚ وَكَانَ يَوْمًا عَلَى ٱلْكَـٰفِرِينَ عَسِيرًا

Al-m^{u}lk^{u} (the sovereignty) *y^{a}wm^{i}dh^{in}* (on that day) *al-ḥ^{a}qq^{u}* (true) *l^{i}-al-r^{a}ḥmān^{i}* (for the Most Gracious) *w^{a}-kān^{a}* (and it was) *y^{a}wm^{an}* (a day) *^{a}lā* (upon) *al-kāf^{i}rīn^{a}* (the rejecters) *^{a}sīrā* (difficult).

وَيَوْمَ يَعَضُّ ٱلظَّالِمُ عَلَىٰ يَدَيْهِ يَقُولُ يَٰلَيْتَنِى ٱتَّخَذْتُ مَعَ ٱلرَّسُولِ سَبِيلًا

W^{a}*-y*^{a}*wm*^{a} (and the day) *y*$^{a\,a}$*ḍḍ*^{u} (he bites) *al-ẓāl*^{i}*m*^{u} (the wrongdoer, the transgresser) ^{a}*lā* (upon) *y*^{a}*d*^{a}*y-h*^{i} (his [two] hands) *y*^{a}*qūl*^{u} (he says) *y*^{a}*l*^{a}*yt*^{a}*-nī* (Oh I wish I..., if only I) *itt*^{a}*kh*^{a}*dh-t*^{u} (I took) *m*$^{a\,a}$ (with) *al-r*^{a}*sūl*^{i} (the Messenger) *s*^{a}*bīlā* (a path).

يَٰوَيْلَتَىٰ لَيْتَنِى لَمْ أَتَّخِذْ فُلَانًا خَلِيلًا

Yā-w^{a}*yl*^{a}*tā* (Oh woe to me!) *l*^{a}*yt*^{a}*-nī* (I wish I, if only I) *l*^{a}*m* (did not) *att*^{a}*kh*^{i}*dh*^{a} (I took, I assigned to myself) *f*^{u}*lān*^{an} (so and so) *kh*^{a}*līlā* (a close friend).

لَّقَدْ أَضَلَّنِى عَنِ ٱلذِّكْرِ بَعْدَ إِذْ جَآءَنِى ۗ

L^{a}*-q*^{a}*d* (truly has truly did) *aḍ*^{a}*ll*^{a}*-nī* (he misled me) ^{a}*n* (from) *al-dh*^{i}*kr*^{i} (the remembrance) *b*^{a}*ʿd*^{a} (after) *idh* (when) *jā*^{a}*-nī* (it came to me).

وَكَانَ ٱلشَّيْطَٰنُ لِلْإِنسَٰنِ خَذُولًا

W^{a}*-kān*^{a} (and was, and ever is) *al-sh*^{a}*yṭān*^{u} (Satan, the devil) *l*^{i}*-al-insān*^{i} (to the human) *kh*^{a}*dhūlā* (a deserter).

This page intentionally left blank

Lesson 51: al-Furqān Part 4

Verse 30

وَقَالَ ٱلرَّسُولُ يَـٰرَبِّ إِنَّ قَوْمِى ٱتَّخَذُوا۟ هَـٰذَا ٱلْقُرْءَانَ مَهْجُورًا

And the Messenger said, “O my Lord, indeed my people have taken this Quran as [a thing] abandoned.”

W^{a}-qāl^{a} (and said) al-r^{a}sūl^{u} (the Messenger) yā-r^{a}bb^{i} (O my Lord) inn^{a} (indeed) q^{a}wm-ī (my people) itt^{a}kh^{a}dhū (they took) hādh^{a} (this) al-q^{u}r’ān^{a} (Quran) m^{a}hjūrā (an abandoned [thing]).

Verse 31

وَكَذَٰلِكَ جَعَلْنَا لِكُلِّ نَبِىٍّ عَدُوًّا مِّنَ ٱلْمُجْرِمِينَ ۗ وَكَفَىٰ بِرَبِّكَ هَادِيًا وَنَصِيرًا

And thus have We made for every prophet an enemy from among the criminals. But sufficient is your Lord as a guide and a helper

W^{a}-k^{a}dhāl^{i}k^{a} (and thus, and in that way) j^{a}ʿ^{a}l-nā (we made, we assigned) l^{i}-k^{u}ll^{i} (for every) n^{a}bīy^{in} (a prophet) ʿ^{a}dūw^{an} (an enemy) m^{i}n^{a} (from, from among) al-m^{u}jr^{i}mīn^{a} (the criminals) w^{a}-k^{a}fā (and is sufficient) b^{i}-r^{a}bb^{i}-k^{a} (your Lord) hād^{i}y^{an} (a guide) w^{a}-n^{a}ṣīrā (and a helper).

The phrase k^{a}fā b^{i} means “is sufficient”. The verb k^{a}fā by itself means “was sufficient”.

Verse 32, part 1

وَقَالَ ٱلَّذِينَ كَفَرُوا۟ لَوْلَا نُزِّلَ عَلَيْهِ ٱلْقُرْءَانُ جُمْلَةً وَٰحِدَةً ۚ

And those who disbelieve say, “Why was the Qur'an not revealed to him all at once?”

W^{a}-qāl^{a} (and said) *all^{a}dhīn^{a}* (those who) *k^{a}f^{a}rū* (they disbelieved, they rejected) *l^{a}wlā* (why not) *n^{u}zz^{i}l^{a}* (it was sent down) *^{a}l^{a}y-h^{i}* (upon him) *al-q^{u}r'ān^{u}* (the Quran) *j^{u}ml^{a}t^{an}* (all together, an aggregate) *wāḥ^{i}d^{a}t^{an}* (one, once).

The phrase *j^{u}ml^{a}t^{an} wāḥ^{i}d^{a}t^{an}* means "in one go", "in [the form of] one aggregate".

Verse 32, part 2

كَذَٰلِكَ لِنُثَبِّتَ بِهِۦ فُؤَادَكَ ۖ وَرَتَّلْنَٰهُ تَرْتِيلًا

Thus [it is] that We may strengthen thereby your heart. And We gave it to you in gradual revelation.

K^{a}-dhāl^{i}k^{a} ([it is] thus, [it is] that way) *l^{i}-n^{u}th^{a}bb^{i}t^{a}* (to make firm, to strengthen) *b^{i}-h^{i}* (with it) *f^{u}'ād^{a}-k^{a}* (your heart) *w^{a}-r^{a}tt^{a}lnā-h^{u}* (and We recited it) *t^{a}rtīlā* (a [grand/proper/spaced out] recitation).

Verse 33

وَلَا يَأْتُونَكَ بِمَثَلٍ إِلَّا جِئْنَٰكَ بِٱلْحَقِّ وَأَحْسَنَ تَفْسِيرًا

And they do not come to you with an argument except that We bring you the truth and the best explanation.

W^{a}-lā (and not) *y^{a}'tūn^{a}-k^{a}* (they come to you) *b^{i}-m^{a}th^{a}l^{in}* (with a similitude, with an argument) *illā* (except that) *j^{i}'nā-k^{a}* (we bring you) *b^{i}-al-ḥ^{a}qq^{i}* (the truth) *w^{a}-aḥs^{a}n^{a}* (and better) *t^{a}fsīrā* (an explanation, an interpretation).

The phrase *j^{i}'nā...b^{i}* means "we brought". Without the *b^{i}* it means "we came".

Verse 34

ٱلَّذِينَ يُحْشَرُونَ عَلَىٰ وُجُوهِهِمْ إِلَىٰ جَهَنَّمَ أُو۟لَٰٓئِكَ شَرٌّ مَّكَانًا وَأَضَلُّ سَبِيلًا

The ones who are gathered on their faces to Hell - those are the worst in position and farthest astray in [their] way

All^{a}*dhīn*^{a} (those who) *y*^{u}*ḥsh*^{a}*rūn*^{a} (they are gathered) ^{a}*lā* (on) *w*^{u}*jūh*^{i}*-h*^{i}*m* (their faces) *ilā* (to) *j*^{a}*h*^{a}*nn*^{a}*m*^{a} (Hell) *ulā*^{i}*k*^{a} (those [are]) *sh*^{a}*rr*^{un} (the worst) *m*^{a}*kān*^{an} ([in] position) *w*^{a}*-aḍ*^{a}*ll*^{u} (and most astray) *s*^{a}*bīlā* ([with regards to their] way).

Verse 35

وَلَقَدْ ءَاتَيْنَا مُوسَى ٱلْكِتَٰبَ وَجَعَلْنَا مَعَهُۥٓ أَخَاهُ هَٰرُونَ وَزِيرًا

And We had certainly given Moses the Scripture and appointed with him his brother Aaron as an assistant

W^{a}*-l*^{a}*q*^{a}*d* (and truly have) *āt*^{a}*y-nā* (we gave) *mūsā* (Moses) *al-k*^{i}*tāb*^{a} (the Book) *w*^{a}*-j*^{a}^{a}*l-nā* (and we made, and we appointed) *m*^{a}^{a}*-h*^{u} (with him) *akhā-h*^{u} (his brother) *hārūn*^{a} (Aaron) *w*^{a}*zīrā* (an assistant).

Verse 36

فَقُلْنَا ٱذْهَبَآ إِلَى ٱلْقَوْمِ ٱلَّذِينَ كَذَّبُوا۟ بِـَٔايَٰتِنَا فَدَمَّرْنَٰهُمْ تَدْمِيرًا

And We said, "Go both of you to the people who have denied Our signs." Then We destroyed them with [complete] destruction.

F^{a}*-q*^{u}*l-nā* (so we said, and we said) *idhh*^{a}*bā* (go [the two of you]) *ilā* (to) *al-q*^{a}*wm*^{i} (the people) *all*^{a}*dhīn*^{a} (those who) *k*^{a}*dhdh*^{a}*bū* (they denied) *b*^{i}*-āyāt*^{i}*-nā* (our signs) *f*^{a}*-d*^{a}*mm*^{a}*r-nā-h*^{u}*m* (so we destroyed them) *t*^{a}*dmīrā* (a [proper/complete] destruction).

Verse 37

وَقَوْمَ نُوحٍ لَّمَّا كَذَّبُوا۟ ٱلرُّسُلَ أَغْرَقْنَٰهُمْ وَجَعَلْنَٰهُمْ لِلنَّاسِ
ءَايَةً ۖ وَأَعْتَدْنَا لِلظَّٰلِمِينَ عَذَابًا أَلِيمًا

And the people of Noah—when they denied the messengers, We drowned them, and We made them for mankind a sign. And We have prepared for the wrongdoers a painful punishment

W^{a}-q^{a}wm^{a} (and the people [of]) *nūḥ^{in}* (Noah) *l^{a}mmā* (when) *k^{a}dhdh^{a}bū* (they denied) *al-r^{u}s^{u}l^{a}* (the messengers) *aghr^{a}q-nā-h^{u}m* (we drowned them) *w^{a}-j^{a}^{a}lnā-h^{u}m* (and we made them) *l^{i}-al-nās^{i}* (for the people) *āy^{a}t^{an}* (a sign) *w^{a}-a't^{a}d-nā* (and we prepared) *l^{i}-al-ẓ^{a}l^{i}mīn^{a}* (for the wrongdoers, for the transgressors) *^{a}dhāb^{an}* (a torment) *alīmā* (a painful [one]).

Verse 38

وَعَادًا وَثَمُودَا۟ وَأَصْحَـٰبَ ٱلرَّسِّ وَقُرُونًۢا بَيْنَ ذَٰلِكَ كَثِيرًا

and ʿĀd, Thamūd, and the companios of al-Rass, and many generations in between that

W^{a}-ʿād^{an} (and ʿĀd) *w^{a}-th^{a}mūd^{a}* (and Thamūd) *w^{a}-aṣḥāb^{a}* (and the companions [of]) *al-r^{a}ss^{i}* (al-Rass) *w^{a}-q^{u}rūn^{an}* (and generations) *b^{a}yn^{a}* (between) *dhāl^{i}k^{a}* (that) *k^{a}thīrā* (many).

Verse 39

وَكُلًّا ضَرَبْنَا لَهُ ٱلْأَمْثَـٰلَ ۖ وَكُلًّا تَبَّرْنَا تَتْبِيرًا

And for each We presented examples [as warnings], and each We destroyed with [total] destruction.

W^{a}-k^{u}ll^{an} (and each) *ḍ^{a}r^{a}b-nā* (we presented, we struck)) *l^{a}-h^{u}* (for it) *al-amthāl^{a}* (examples, similitudes) *w^{a}-k^{u}ll^{an}* (and each) *t^{a}bb^{a}r-nā* (we destroyed) *t^{a}tbīrā* (a [complete] destruction).

Lesson 51 Review

وَقَالَ ٱلرَّسُولُ يَٰرَبِّ إِنَّ قَوْمِى ٱتَّخَذُوا۟ هَٰذَا ٱلْقُرْءَانَ مَهْجُورًا

W^{a}-qāl^{a} (and said) *al-r^{a}sūl^{u}* (the Messenger) *yā-r^{a}bb^{i}* (O my Lord) *inn^{a}* (indeed) *q^{a}wm-ī* (my people) *itt^{a}kh^{a}dhū* (they took) *hādh^{a}* (this) *al-q^{u}r'ān^{a}* (Quran) *m^{a}hjūrā* (an abandoned [thing]).

وَكَذَٰلِكَ جَعَلْنَا لِكُلِّ نَبِىٍّ عَدُوًّا مِّنَ ٱلْمُجْرِمِينَ ۗ وَكَفَىٰ بِرَبِّكَ هَادِيًا وَنَصِيرًا

W^{a}-k^{a}dhāl^{i}k^{a} (and thus, and in that way) *j^{a} ^{a}l-nā* (we made, we assigned) *l^{i}-k^{u}ll^{i}* (for every) *n^{a}bīy^{in}* (a prophet) *^{a}dūw^{an}* (an enemy) *m^{i}n^{a}* (from, from among) *al-m^{u}jr^{i}mīn^{a}* (the criminals) *w^{a}-k^{a}fā* (and is sufficient) *b^{i}-r^{a}bb^{i}-k^{a}* (your Lord) *hād^{i}y^{an}* (a guide) *w^{a}-n^{a}ṣīrā* (and a helper).

وَقَالَ ٱلَّذِينَ كَفَرُوا۟ لَوْلَا نُزِّلَ عَلَيْهِ ٱلْقُرْءَانُ جُمْلَةً وَٰحِدَةً ۚ

W^{a}-qāl^{a} (and said) *all^{a}dhīn^{a}* (those who) *k^{a}f^{a}rū* (they disbelieved, they rejected) *l^{a}wlā* (why not) *n^{u}zz^{i}l^{a}* (it was sent down) *^{a}l^{a}y-h^{i}* (upon him) *al-q^{u}r'ān^{u}* (the Quran) *j^{u}ml^{a}t^{an}* (all together, an aggregate) *wāḥ^{i}d^{a}t^{an}* (one, once).

كَذَٰلِكَ لِنُثَبِّتَ بِهِۦ فُؤَادَكَ ۖ وَرَتَّلْنَٰهُ تَرْتِيلًا

K^{a}-dhāl^{i}k^{a} ([it is] thus, [it is] that way) *l^{i}-n^{u}th^{a}bb^{i}t^{a}* (to make firm, to strengthen) *b^{i}-h^{i}* (with it) *f^{u}'ād^{a}-k^{a}* (your heart) *w^{a}-r^{a}tt^{a}lnā-h^{u}* (and We recited it) *t^{a}rtīlā* (a [grand/proper/spaced out] recitation).

وَلَا يَأْتُونَكَ بِمَثَلٍ إِلَّا جِئْنَٰكَ بِٱلْحَقِّ وَأَحْسَنَ تَفْسِيرًا

W^{a}-lā (and not) y^{a}'tūn^{a}-k^{a} (they come to you) b^{i}-m^{a}th^{a}l^{in} (with a similitude, with an argument) illā (except that) j^{i}'nā-k^{a} (we bring you) b^{i}-al-ḥ^{a}qq^{i} (the truth) w^{a}-aḥs^{a}n^{a} (and better) t^{a}fsīrā (an explanation, an interpretation).

ٱلَّذِينَ يُحْشَرُونَ عَلَىٰ وُجُوهِهِمْ إِلَىٰ جَهَنَّمَ أُو۟لَٰٓئِكَ شَرٌّ مَّكَانًا وَأَضَلُّ سَبِيلًا

All^{a}dhīn^{a} (those who) y^{u}ḥsh^{a}rūn^{a} (they are gathered) ^{a}lā (on) w^{u}jūh^{i}-h^{i}m (their faces) ilā (to) j^{a}h^{a}nn^{a}m^{a} (Hell) ulā^{i}k^{a} (those [are]) sh^{a}rr^{un} (the worst) m^{a}kān^{an} ([in] position) w^{a}-aḍ^{a}ll^{u} (and most astray) s^{a}bīlā ([with regards to their] way).

وَلَقَدْ ءَاتَيْنَا مُوسَى ٱلْكِتَٰبَ وَجَعَلْنَا مَعَهُۥٓ أَخَاهُ هَٰرُونَ وَزِيرًا

W^{a}-l^{a}q^{a}d (and truly have) āt^{a}y-nā (we gave) mūsā (Moses) al-k^{i}tāb^{a} (the Book) w^{a}-j^{a}^{a}l-nā (and we made, and we appointed) m^{a}^{a}-h^{u} (with him) akhā-h^{u} (his brother) hārūn^{a} (Aaron) w^{a}zīrā (an assistant).

فَقُلْنَا ٱذْهَبَآ إِلَى ٱلْقَوْمِ ٱلَّذِينَ كَذَّبُوا۟ بِـَٔايَٰتِنَا فَدَمَّرْنَٰهُمْ تَدْمِيرًا

F^{a}-q^{u}l-nā (so we said, and we said) idhh^{a}bā (go [the two of you]) ilā (to) al-q^{a}wm^{i} (the people) all^{a}dhīn^{a} (those who) k^{a}dhdh^{a}bū (they denied) b^{i}-āyāt^{i}-nā (our signs) f^{a}-d^{a}mm^{a}r-nā-h^{u}m (so we destroyed them) t^{a}dmīrā (a [proper/complete] destruction).

وَقَوْمَ نُوحٍ لَّمَّا كَذَّبُوا۟ ٱلرُّسُلَ أَغْرَقْنَـٰهُمْ وَجَعَلْنَـٰهُمْ لِلنَّاسِ ءَايَةً ۖ وَأَعْتَدْنَا لِلظَّـٰلِمِينَ عَذَابًا أَلِيمًا

W^{a}-q^{a}wm^{a} (and the people [of]) *nūḥ^{in}* (Noah) *l^{a}mmā* (when) *k^{a}dhdh^{a}bū* (they denied) *al-r^{u}s^{u}l^{a}* (the messengers) *aghr^{a}q-nā-h^{u}m* (we drowned them) *w^{a}-j^{a}ʿ^{a}lnā-h^{u}m* (and we made them) *l^{i}-al-nās^{i}* (for the people) *āy^{a}t^{an}* (a sign) *w^{a}-aʿt^{a}d-nā* (and we prepared) *l^{i}-al-ẓ^{a}l^{i}mīn^{a}* (for the wrongdoers, for the transgressors) *ʿ^{a}dhāb^{an}* (a torment) *alīmā* (a painful [one]).

وَعَادًا وَثَمُودَا۟ وَأَصْحَـٰبَ ٱلرَّسِّ وَقُرُونًۢا بَيْنَ ذَٰلِكَ كَثِيرًا

W^{a}-ʿād^{an} (and ʿĀd) *w^{a}-th^{a}mūd^{a}* (and Thamūd) *w^{a}-aṣḥāb^{a}* (and the companions [of]) *al-r^{a}ss^{i}* (al-Rass) *w^{a}-q^{u}rūn^{an}* (and generations) *b^{a}yn^{a}* (between) *dhāl^{i}k^{a}* (that) *k^{a}thīrā* (many).

وَكُلًّا ضَرَبْنَا لَهُ ٱلْأَمْثَـٰلَ ۖ وَكُلًّا تَبَّرْنَا تَتْبِيرًا

W^{a}-k^{u}ll^{an} (and each) *ḍ^{a}r^{a}b-nā* (we presented, we struck)) *l^{a}-h^{u}* (for it) *al-amthāl^{a}* (examples, similitudes) *w^{a}-k^{u}ll^{an}* (and each) *t^{a}bb^{a}r-nā* (we destroyed) *t^{a}tbīrā* (a [complete] destruction).

This page intentionally left blank

Lesson 52: al-Furqān Part 5

Verse 40

وَلَقَدْ أَتَوْا۟ عَلَى ٱلْقَرْيَةِ ٱلَّتِىٓ أُمْطِرَتْ مَطَرَ ٱلسَّوْءِ ۚ أَفَلَمْ يَكُونُوا۟
يَرَوْنَهَا ۚ بَلْ كَانُوا۟ لَا يَرْجُونَ نُشُورًا

And truly they have come upon the town which was showered with a rain of evil. So have they not seen it? But they are not expecting resurrection.

W^{a}-l^{a}-q^{a}d and truly have) *at^{a}w* (they came) *ʿ^{a}lā* (upon) *al-q^{a}ry^{a}t^{i}* (the town) *all^{a}tī* (which) *umṭ^{i}r^{a}-t* (was rained on, was showered) *m^{a}ṭ^{a}r^{a}* (the rain [of]) *al-s^{a}w^{i}* (evil) *a-f^{a}-l^{a}m* (so not) *y^{a}kūnū* (they were) *y^{a}r^{a}wn^{a}-hā* (they see it) *b^{a}l* (no, but rather) *kānū* (they were) *lā* (not) *y^{a}rjūn^{a}* (they expect, they look forward to) *n^{u}shūrā* (a resurrection).

Verse 41

وَإِذَا رَأَوْكَ إِن يَتَّخِذُونَكَ إِلَّا هُزُوًا أَهَـٰذَا ٱلَّذِى بَعَثَ
ٱللَّهُ رَسُولًا

And when they see you, [O Muhammad], they take you not except in ridicule, [saying], "Is this the one whom Allah has sent as a messenger? ..."

W^{a}-idhā (and when) *r^{aa}w-k^{a}* (they see you) *in* (do not) *y^{a}tt^{a}kh^{i}dhūn^{a}-k^{a}* (they take you) *illā* (except) *h^{u}z^{u}w^{an}* (in ridicule) *a-hādhā* (is this) *all^{a}dhī* (the one whom) *b^{aa}th^{a}* (has sent) *allāh^{u}* (God) *r^{a}sūlā* ([as] a messenger).

Verse 42

إِن كَادَ لَيُضِلُّنَا عَنْ ءَالِهَتِنَا لَوْلَآ أَن صَبَرْنَا عَلَيْهَا ۚ
وَسَوْفَ يَعْلَمُونَ حِينَ يَرَوْنَ ٱلْعَذَابَ مَنْ أَضَلُّ سَبِيلًا

"Indeed he almost would have misled us from our gods had we not been steadfast in [worship of] them." But they are going to know, when they see the punishment, who is farthest astray in [his] way.

In (indeed) *kād*^{a} (he was about to) *l*^{a}*-y*^{u}*ḍ*^{i}*ll*^{u}*-nā* (truly misleads us) ^{a}*n* (from) *āl*^{i}*h*^{a}*t*^{i}*-nā* (our gods) *l*^{a}*wlā* (had [we] not) *an* (that) *ṣ*^{a}*b*^{a}*r-nā* (we were steadfast) ^{a}*l*^{a}*y-hā* (upon them) *w*^{a}*-s*^{a}*wf*^{a} (and shall) *y*^{a}^{a}*l*^{a}*mūn*^{a} (they know) *ḥīn*^{a} (when, at the moment when) *y*^{a}*r*^{a}*wn*^{a} (they see) *al-*^{a}*dhāb*^{a} (the torment) *m*^{a}*n* (who [is]) *aḍ*^{a}*ll*^{u} (most mislead) *s*^{a}*bīlā* ([in his] way).

The *in* at the beginning is a special formulation that is an abbreviation of *inn*^{a}*-h*^{u} ("he indeed").

Verse 43

أَرَءَيْتَ مَنِ ٱتَّخَذَ إِلَٰهَهُۥ هَوَىٰهُ أَفَأَنتَ تَكُونُ عَلَيْهِ وَكِيلًا

Have you seen the one who takes as his god his own desire? Then would you be a guardian for him?

A-r^{a}^{a}*y-t*^{a} (have you seen, did you see) *m*^{a}*n* (who) *itt*^{a}*kh*^{a}*dh*^{a} (he took) *ilāh*^{a}*-h*^{u} ([as] his god) *h*^{a}*wā-h*^{u} (his desire) *a-f*^{a}*-ant*^{a} (then are you) *t*^{a}*kūn*^{u} (you are, you are going to be) ^{a}*l*^{a}*y-h*^{i} (upon him) *w*^{a}*kīlā* (a guardian, a person responsible [for him]).

Verse 44

أَمْ تَحْسَبُ أَنَّ أَكْثَرَهُمْ يَسْمَعُونَ أَوْ يَعْقِلُونَ ۚ إِنْ هُمْ إِلَّا
كَالْأَنْعَٰمِ ۖ بَلْ هُمْ أَضَلُّ سَبِيلًا

Or do you think that most of them hear or reason? They are not except like livestock. Rather, they are [even] more astray in [their] way.

Am (or) *t*^{a}*ḥs*^{a}*b*^{u} (you think, you assume) *ann*^{a} (that) *akth*^{a}*r*^{a}*-h*^{u}*m* (most of them) *y*^{a}*sm*^{a}*ʿūn*^{a} (they hear) *aw* (or) *y*^{a}*ʿq*^{i}*lūn*^{a} (they reason, they comprehend) *in* (not) *h*^{u}*m* (they are) *illā* (except) *k*^{a}*-al-anʿām*^{i} (like livestock) *b*^{a}*l* (no, but rather) *h*^{u}*m* (they [are]) *aḍ*^{a}*ll*^{u} (more astray) *s*^{a}*bīlā* ([in their] way).

Verse 45

أَلَمْ تَرَ إِلَىٰ رَبِّكَ كَيْفَ مَدَّ ٱلظِّلَّ وَلَوْ شَآءَ لَجَعَلَهُۥ سَاكِنًا ثُمَّ
جَعَلْنَا ٱلشَّمْسَ عَلَيْهِ دَلِيلًا

Have you not considered your Lord—how He extends the shadow, and if He willed, He could have made it stationary? Then We made the sun for it an indication.

A-l^{a}*m* (did not) *t*^{a}*r*^{a} *ilā* (you looked at, you considered) *r*^{a}*bb*^{i}*-k*^{a} (your Lord) *k*^{a}*yf*^{a} (how) *m*^{a}*dd*^{a} (He extended) *al-ẓ*^{i}*ll*^{a} (the shadow) *w*^{a}*-l*^{a}*w* (and if) *shā*^{a} (He willed) *l*^{a}*-j*^{a}*ʿ*^{a}*l*^{a}*-h*^{u} (truly He would have made it) *sāk*^{i}*n*^{an} (stationary) *th*^{u}*mm*^{a} (then) *j*^{a}*ʿ*^{a}*l-nā* (we made, we assigned) *al-sh*^{a}*ms*^{a} (the sun) *ʿ*^{a}*l*^{a}*y-h*^{i} (upon it) *d*^{a}*līlā* (an indicator).

Verse 46

ثُمَّ قَبَضْنَٰهُ إِلَيْنَا قَبْضًا يَسِيرًا

Then We withdraw it unto Us, a gradual withdrawal

Th^{u}mm^{a} (then) *q^{a}b^{a}ḍ-nā-h^{u}* (we withdrew it, we took hold of it) *il^{a}y-nā* (toward us) *q^{a}bḍ^{an}* (a withdrawing, a taking) *y^{a}sīrā* (easy, gradual).

Verse 47

وَهُوَ ٱلَّذِى جَعَلَ لَكُمُ ٱلَّيْلَ لِبَاسًا وَٱلنَّوْمَ سُبَاتًا وَجَعَلَ
ٱلنَّهَارَ نُشُورًا

And it is He who has made the night for you as clothing and sleep [a means for] rest and has made the day a resurrection

W^{a}-h^{u}w^{a} (and He is) *all^{a}dhī* (the One Who) *j^{a}ʿ^{a}l^{a}* (He made) *l^{a}-k^{u}m* (for you) *al-l^{a}yl^{a}* (the night) *l^{i}bās^{an}* (a covering, a clothing) *w^{a}-al-n^{a}wm^{a}* (and sleep) *s^{u}bāt^{an}* (a rest) *w^{a}-j^{a}ʿ^{a}l^{a}* (and He made) *al-n^{a}hār^{a}* (the daytime) *n^{u}shūrā* (a resurrection).

Verse 48

وَهُوَ ٱلَّذِىٓ أَرْسَلَ ٱلرِّيَٰحَ بُشْرًۢا بَيْنَ يَدَىْ رَحْمَتِهِۦ ۚ
وَأَنزَلْنَا مِنَ ٱلسَّمَآءِ مَآءً طَهُورًا

And it is He who sends the winds as good tidings before His mercy, and We send down from the sky pure water

W^{a}*-h*^{u}*w*^{a} (and He is) *all*^{a}*dhī* (the One Who) *ars*^{a}*l*^{a} (He sent) *al-r*^{i}*yāḥ*^{a} (the winds) *b*^{u}*shr*^{an} (good tidings) *b*^{a}*yn*^{a} *y*^{a}*d*^{a}*y* (before, in front of) *r*^{a}*ḥm*^{a}*t*^{i}*-h*^{i} (His mercy) *w*^{a}*-anz*^{a}*l-nā* (and We sent down) *m*^{i}*n* (from) *al-s*^{a}*mā*^{i} (the sky) *mā*^{an} (a water) *ṭ*^{a}*hūrā* (pure).

The phrase *b*^{a}*yn*^{a} *y*^{a}*d*^{a}*y* literally means "between the two hands [of]", it is an idiom that means "before", "in front of".

Verse 49

لِّنُحْـِۧيَ بِهِۦ بَلْدَةً مَّيْتًا وَنُسْقِيَهُۥ مِمَّا خَلَقْنَآ أَنْعَٰمًا وَأَنَاسِىَّ
كَثِيرًا

So that We may bring to life thereby a dead land and give it as drink to those We created of numerous livestock and people.

L^{i}*-n*^{u}*ḥy*^{i}*y*^{a} (so that We may bring to life) *b*^{i}*-h*^{i} (with it) *b*^{a}*ld*^{a}*t*^{an} (a land) *m*^{a}*yt*^{an} (dead) *w*^{a}*-n*^{u}*sqī-h*^{i} (We give it as drink, We water with it) *m*^{i}*m-mā* (of what) *kh*^{a}*l*^{a}*q-nā* (we created [of]) *an'ām*^{an} (livestock) *w*^{a}*-anāsīy*^{a} (and people) *k*^{a}*thīrā* (many, numerous).

This page intentionally left blank

Lesson 52 Review

وَلَقَدْ أَتَوْا۟ عَلَى ٱلْقَرْيَةِ ٱلَّتِىٓ أُمْطِرَتْ مَطَرَ ٱلسَّوْءِ ۚ أَفَلَمْ يَكُونُوا۟
يَرَوْنَهَا ۚ بَلْ كَانُوا۟ لَا يَرْجُونَ نُشُورًا

W^{a}-l^{a}-q^{a}d and truly have) *at^{a}w* (they came) *^{a}lā* (upon) *al-q^{a}ry^{a}t^{i}* (the town) *all^{a}tī* (which) *umṭ^{i}r^{a}-t* (was rained on, was showered) *m^{a}ṭ^{a}r^{a}* (the rain [of]) *al-s^{a}w^{i}* (evil) *a-f^{a}-l^{a}m* (so not) *y^{a}kūnū* (they were) *y^{a}r^{a}wn^{a}-hā* (they see it) *b^{a}l* (no, but rather) *kānū* (they were) *lā* (not) *y^{a}rjūn^{a}* (they expect, they look forward to) *n^{u}shūrā* (a resurrection).

وَإِذَا رَأَوْكَ إِن يَتَّخِذُونَكَ إِلَّا هُزُوًا أَهَٰذَا ٱلَّذِى بَعَثَ
ٱللَّهُ رَسُولًا

W^{a}-idhā (and when) *r^{a}^{a}w-k^{a}* (they see you) *in* (do not) *y^{a}tt^{a}kh^{i}dhūn^{a}-k^{a}* (they take you) *illā* (except) *h^{u}z^{u}w^{an}* (in ridicule) *a-hādhā* (is this) *all^{a}dhī* (the one whom) *b^{a}^{a}th^{a}* (has sent) *allāh^{u}* (God) *r^{a}sūlā* ([as] a messenger).

إِن كَادَ لَيُضِلُّنَا عَنْ ءَالِهَتِنَا لَوْلَآ أَن صَبَرْنَا عَلَيْهَا ۚ
وَسَوْفَ يَعْلَمُونَ حِينَ يَرَوْنَ ٱلْعَذَابَ مَنْ أَضَلُّ سَبِيلًا

In (indeed) *kād^{a}* (he was about to) *l^{a}-y^{u}ḍ^{i}ll^{u}-nā* (truly misleads us) *^{a}n* (from) *āl^{i}h^{a}t^{i}-nā* (our gods) *l^{a}wlā* (had [we] not) *an* (that) *ṣ^{a}b^{a}r-nā* (we were steadfast) *^{a}l^{a}y-hā* (upon them) *w^{a}-s^{a}wf^{a}* (and shall) *y^{a}^{a}l^{a}mūn^{a}* (they know) *ḥīn^{a}* (when, at the moment when) *y^{a}r^{a}wn^{a}* (they see) *al-^{a}dhāb^{a}* (the torment) *m^{a}n* (who [is]) *aḍ^{a}ll^{u}* (most mislead) *s^{a}bīlā* ([in his] way).

أَرَءَيْتَ مَنِ ٱتَّخَذَ إِلَٰهَهُۥ هَوَىٰهُ أَفَأَنتَ تَكُونُ عَلَيْهِ وَكِيلًا

A-r^{a}^{a}y-t^{a} (have you seen, did you see) *m^{a}n* (who) *itt^{a}kh^{a}dh^{a}* (he took) *ilāh^{a}-h^{u}* ([as] his god) *h^{a}wā-h^{u}* (his desire) *a-f^{a}-ant^{a}* (then are you) *t^{a}kūn^{u}* (you are, you are going to be) *^{a}l^{a}y-h^{i}* (upon him) *w^{a}kīlā* (a guardian, a person responsible [for him]).

أَمْ تَحْسَبُ أَنَّ أَكْثَرَهُمْ يَسْمَعُونَ أَوْ يَعْقِلُونَ ۚ إِنْ هُمْ إِلَّا
كَٱلْأَنْعَٰمِ ۖ بَلْ هُمْ أَضَلُّ سَبِيلًا

Am (or) *t^{a}ḥs^{a}b^{u}* (you think, you assume) *ann^{a}* (that) *akth^{a}r^{a}-h^{u}m* (most of them) *y^{a}sm^{a}ʿūn^{a}* (they hear) *aw* (or) *y^{a}ʿq^{i}lūn^{a}* (they reason, they comprehend) *in* (not) *h^{u}m* (they are) *illā* (except) *k^{a}-al-anʿām^{i}* (like livestock) *b^{a}l* (no, but rather) *h^{u}m* (they [are]) *aḍ^{a}ll^{u}* (more astray) *s^{a}bīlā* ([in their] way).

أَلَمْ تَرَ إِلَىٰ رَبِّكَ كَيْفَ مَدَّ ٱلظِّلَّ وَلَوْ شَآءَ لَجَعَلَهُۥ سَاكِنًا ثُمَّ
جَعَلْنَا ٱلشَّمْسَ عَلَيْهِ دَلِيلًا

A-l^{a}m (did not) *t^{a}r^{a} ilā* (you looked at, you considered) *r^{a}bb^{i}-k^{a}* (your Lord) *k^{a}yf^{a}* (how) *m^{a}dd^{a}* (He extended) *al-ẓ^{i}ll^{a}* (the shadow) *w^{a}-l^{a}w* (and if) *shā^{a}* (He willed) *l^{a}-j^{a}ʿ^{a}l^{a}-h^{u}* (truly He would have made it) *sāk^{i}n^{an}* (stationary) *th^{u}mm^{a}* (then) *j^{a}ʿ^{a}l-nā* (we made, we assigned) *al-sh^{a}ms^{a}* (the sun) *^{a}l^{a}y-h^{i}* (upon it) *d^{a}līlā* (an indicator).

ثُمَّ قَبَضْنَٰهُ إِلَيْنَا قَبْضًا يَسِيرًا

Th^{u}mm^{a} (then) *q^{a}b^{a}ḍ-nā-h^{u}* (we withdrew it, we took hold of it) *il^{a}y-nā* (toward us) *q^{a}bḍ^{an}* (a withdrawing, a taking) *y^{a}sīrā* (easy, gradual).

وَهُوَ ٱلَّذِى جَعَلَ لَكُمُ ٱلَّيْلَ لِبَاسًا وَٱلنَّوْمَ سُبَاتًا وَجَعَلَ
ٱلنَّهَارَ نُشُورًا

W^{a}*-h*^{u}*w*^{a} (and He is) *all*^{a}*dhī* (the One Who) *j*^{a}ʿ^{a}*l*^{a} (He made) *l*^{a}*-k*^{u}*m* (for you) *al-l*^{a}*yl*^{a} (the night) *l*^{i}*bās*^{an} (a covering, a clothing) *w*^{a}*-al-n*^{a}*wm*^{a} (and sleep) *s*^{u}*bāt*^{an} (a rest) *w*^{a}*-j*^{a}ʿ^{a}*l*^{a} (and He made) *al-n*^{a}*hār*^{a} (the daytime) *n*^{u}*shūrā* (a resurrection).

وَهُوَ ٱلَّذِىٓ أَرْسَلَ ٱلرِّيَٰحَ بُشْرًۢا بَيْنَ يَدَىْ رَحْمَتِهِۦ ۚ
وَأَنزَلْنَا مِنَ ٱلسَّمَآءِ مَآءً طَهُورًا

W^{a}*-h*^{u}*w*^{a} (and He is) *all*^{a}*dhī* (the One Who) *ars*^{a}*l*^{a} (He sent) *al-r*^{i}*yāḥ*^{a} (the winds) *b*^{u}*shr*^{an} (good tidings) *b*^{a}*yn*^{a} *y*^{a}*d*^{a}*y* (before, in front of) *r*^{a}*ḥm*^{a}*t*^{i}*-h*^{i} (His mercy) *w*^{a}*-anz*^{a}*l-nā* (and We sent down) *m*^{i}*n* (from) *al-s*^{a}*mā*^{i} (the sky) *mā*^{an} (a water) *ṭ*^{a}*hūrā* (pure).

لِّنُحْـِۧىَ بِهِۦ بَلْدَةً مَّيْتًا وَنُسْقِيَهُۥ مِمَّا خَلَقْنَآ أَنْعَٰمًا وَأَنَاسِىَّ
كَثِيرًا

L^{i}*-n*^{u}*ḥy*^{i}*y*^{a} (so that We may bring to life) *b*^{i}*-h*^{i} (with it) *b*^{a}*ld*^{a}*t*^{an} (a land) *m*^{a}*yt*^{an} (dead) *w*^{a}*-n*^{u}*sqī-h*^{i} (We give it as drink, We water with it) *m*^{i}*m-mā* (of what) *kh*^{a}*l*^{a}*q-nā* (we created [of]) *anʿām*^{an} (livestock) *w*^{a}*-anāsīy*^{a} (and people) *k*^{a}*thīrā* (many, numerous).

This page intentionally left blank

Lesson 53: al-Furqān Part 6

Verse 50

وَلَقَدۡ صَرَّفۡنَٰهُ بَيۡنَهُمۡ لِيَذَّكَّرُواْ فَأَبَىٰٓ أَكۡثَرُ ٱلنَّاسِ إِلَّا كُفُورٗا

And We have certainly distributed it among them that they might be reminded, but most of the people refuse except disbelief.

W^{a}*-l*^{a}*-q*^{a}*d* (and truly have) *ṣ*^{a}*rr*^{a}*f-nā-h*^{u} (we distributed, we repeated) *b*^{a}*yn*^{a}*-h*^{u}*m* (between them) *l*^{i}*-y*^{a}*dhdh*^{a}*kk*^{a}*rū* (so that they may remember) *f*^{a}*-abā* (so refused) *akth*^{a}*r*^{u} (most [of]) *al-nās*^{i} (the people) *illā* (except) *k*^{u}*fūrā* (disbelief).

Verse 51

وَلَوۡ شِئۡنَا لَبَعَثۡنَا فِي كُلِّ قَرۡيَةٖ نَّذِيرٗا

And if We had willed, We truly could have sent into every town a warner.

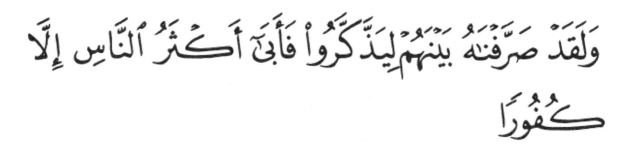

W^{a}*-l*^{a}*w* (and if) *sh*^{i}*ʾ-nā* (We willed) *l*^{a}*-b*^{a}^{a}*th-nā* (truly We sent) *fī* (in) *k*^{u}*ll*^{i} (every) *q*^{a}*ry*^{a}*t*^{in} (town) *n*^{a}*dhīrā* (a warner).

Verse 52

فَلَا تُطِعِ ٱلْكَٰفِرِينَ وَجَٰهِدْهُم بِهِۦ جِهَادًا كَبِيرًا

So do not obey the rejecters, and strive against them with it [i.e. with the Quran] a great striving.

F^{a}-lā (so do not) *t^{u}ṭi^{ʿ}* (you obey) *al-kāf^{i}rīn^{a}* (the rejecters) *w^{a}-jāh^{i}d-h^{u}m* (and strive against them) *b^{i}-h^{i}* (with it) *j^{i}hād^{an}* (a striving) *k^{a}bīrā* (great).

Verse 53

وَهُوَ ٱلَّذِى مَرَجَ ٱلْبَحْرَيْنِ هَٰذَا عَذْبٌ فُرَاتٌ وَهَٰذَا مِلْحٌ أُجَاجٌ
وَجَعَلَ بَيْنَهُمَا بَرْزَخًا وَحِجْرًا مَّحْجُورًا

And it is He who has released the two seas, one fresh and sweet and one salty and bitter, and He placed between them a barrier and prohibiting partition.

W^{a}-h^{u}w^{a} (and He [is]) *all^{a}dhī* (the One Who) *m^{a}r^{a}j^{a}* (released) *al-b^{a}ḥr^{a}yn^{i}* (the two seas) *hādhā* (this [one]) *^{a}dhb^{un}* (fresh, palatable) *f^{u}rāt^{un}* (sweet [i.e. good to drink]) *w^{a}-hādhā* (and this [one]) *m^{i}lḥ^{un}* (salty) *ujāj^{un}* (bitter) *w^{a}-j^{a}^{a}l^{a}* (and We made) *b^{a}yn^{a}-h^{u}m^{a}* (between them) *b^{a}rz^{a}kh^{an}* (a barrier) *w^{a}-ḥ^{i}jr^{an}* (and a partition) *m^{a}ḥjūrā* (prohibited).

Verse 54

وَهُوَ ٱلَّذِى خَلَقَ مِنَ ٱلْمَآءِ بَشَرًا فَجَعَلَهُۥ نَسَبًا وَصِهْرًا ۗ وَكَانَ
رَبُّكَ قَدِيرًا

And it is He who has created from water a human being and made him [a relative by] lineage and marriage. And ever is your Lord competent [concerning creation]

W^{a}*-h*^{u}*w*^{a} (and He [is]) *all*^{a}*dhī* (the One Who) *kh*^{a}*l*^{a}*q*^{a} (He created) *m*^{i}*n* (from) *al-mā*^{i} (water) *b*^{a}*sh*^{a}*r*^{an} (a human) *f*^{a}*-j*^{a}ʿ^{a}*l*^{a}*-h*^{u} (so He made him) *n*^{a}*s*^{a}*b*^{an} (a blood relation) *w*^{a}*-ṣ*^{i}*hr*^{an} (a relation by marriage) *w*^{a}*-kān*^{a} (and He was) *r*^{a}*bb*^{u}*-k*^{a} (your Lord) *q*^{a}*dīrā* (a competenet One).

Verse 55

وَيَعۡبُدُونَ مِن دُونِ ٱللَّهِ مَا لَا يَنفَعُهُمۡ وَلَا يَضُرُّهُمۡۗ وَكَانَ
ٱلۡكَافِرُ عَلَىٰ رَبِّهِۦ ظَهِيرٗا

And they worship rather than Allah that which does not benefit them or harm them, and the disbeliever is ever, against his Lord, an assistant [to Satan]

W^{a}*-y*^{a}ʿ*b*^{u}*dūn*^{a} (and they worship) *m*^{i}*n dūn*^{i} (other than, in exclusion of) *allāh*^{i} (God) *mā* (what) *lā* (does not) *y*^{a}*nf*^{a}ʿ^{u}*-h*^{u}*m* (it benefits them) *w*^{a}*-lā* (and does not) *y*^{a}*ḍ*^{u}*rr*^{u}*-h*^{u}*m* (it harms them) *w*^{a}*-kān*^{a} (and he was) *al-kāf*^{i}*r*^{u} (the rejecter) ^{a}*lā* (upon, against) *r*^{a}*bb*^{i}*-h*^{i} (his Lord) *ẓ*^{a}*hīrā* (an assistant).

Verse 56

وَمَآ أَرۡسَلۡنَٰكَ إِلَّا مُبَشِّرٗا وَنَذِيرٗا

And We have not sent you, [O Muhammad], except as a bringer of good tidings and a warner

W^{a}*-mā* (and did not) *ars*^{a}*l-nā-k*^{a} (We sent you) *illā* (except) *m*^{u}*b*^{a}*shsh*^{i}*r*^{an} ([as] a bringer of good tidings) *w*^{a}*-n*^{a}*dhīrā* (and a warner).

Verse 57

قُلْ مَآ أَسْـَٔلُكُمْ عَلَيْهِ مِنْ أَجْرٍ إِلَّا مَن شَآءَ أَن يَتَّخِذَ إِلَىٰ رَبِّهِۦ سَبِيلًا

Say, "I am not asking for any reward for it, except that anyone who wishes can take a path to his Lord [through spending in charity]."

Q^{u}l (say) *mā* (do not) *as^{a}l^{u}-k^{u}m* (I ask you) *^{a}l^{a}y-h^{i}* (upon it) *m^{i}n ajr^{in}* (any reward) *illā* (except that) *m^{a}n* (whoever) *shā^{a}* (wills, wishes) *an* (to) *y^{a}tt^{a}kh^{i}dh^{a}* (take) *ilā* (toward) *r^{a}bb^{i}-h^{i}* (his Lord) *s^{a}bīlā* (a path).

Verse 58

وَتَوَكَّلْ عَلَى ٱلْحَىِّ ٱلَّذِى لَا يَمُوتُ وَسَبِّحْ بِحَمْدِهِۦ ۚ وَكَفَىٰ بِهِۦ بِذُنُوبِ عِبَادِهِۦ خَبِيرًا

And rely upon the Ever-Living who does not die, and celebrate His praise. And sufficient is He to be, with the sins of His servants, acquainted

W^{a}-t^{a}w^{a}kk^{a}l (and rely) *^{a}lā* (upon) *al-ḥ^{a}yy^{i}* (the Living) *all^{a}dhī* (Who) *lā* (does not) *y^{a}mūt^{u}* (He dies) *w^{a}-s^{a}bb^{i}ḥ* (and celebrate, and chant) *b^{i}-ḥ^{a}md^{i}-h^{i}* (His praise) *w^{a}-k^{a}fā* (and is sufficient) *b^{i}-h^{i}* (He) *b^{i}-dh^{u}nūb^{i}* (with the sins [of]) *ʿibād^{i}-h^{i}* (His servants) *kh^{a}bīrā* (cognizant, well-acquainted).

Verse 59

ٱلَّذِى خَلَقَ ٱلسَّمَٰوَٰتِ وَٱلْأَرْضَ وَمَا بَيْنَهُمَا فِى سِتَّةِ أَيَّامٍ ثُمَّ ٱسْتَوَىٰ

عَلَى ٱلْعَرْشِ ۚ ٱلرَّحْمَٰنُ فَسْـَٔلْ بِهِۦ خَبِيرًا

The One Who created the heavens and the earth and what is between them in six days and then established Himself above the Throne—the Most Gracious, so ask about Him one well informed

All^{a}*dhī* (the One Who) *kh*^{a}*l*^{a}*q*^{a} (He created) *al-s*^{a}*māwāt*^{i} (the heavens) *w*^{a}*-al-arḍ*^{a} (and the earth) *w*^{a}*-mā* (and what [is]) *b*^{a}*yn*^{a}*-h*^{u}*mā* (between them) *fī* (in) *s*^{i}*tt*^{a}*t*^{i} (six) *ayyām*^{in} (days) *th*^{u}*mm*^{a} (then) *ist*^{a}*wā* (He established Himself) ^{a}*lā* (upon) *al-*^{a}*rsh*^{i} (the Throne) *al-r*^{a}*ḥmān*^{u} (the Most Gracious) *f*^{a}*-s*^{a}*l* (so ask) *b*^{i}*-h*^{i} (about him) *kh*^{a}*bīrā* (a well-informed one, an expert).

This page intentionally left blank

Lesson 53 Review

وَلَقَدْ صَرَّفْنَٰهُ بَيْنَهُمْ لِيَذَّكَّرُوا۟ فَأَبَىٰٓ أَكْثَرُ ٱلنَّاسِ إِلَّا كُفُورًا

W^{a}-l^{a}-q^{a}d (and truly have) *ṣ^{a}rr^{a}f-nā-h^{u}* (we distributed, we repeated) *b^{a}yn^{a}-h^{u}m* (between them) *l^{i}-y^{a}dhdh^{a}kk^{a}rū* (so that they may remember) *f^{a}-abā* (so refused) *akth^{a}r^{u}* (most [of]) *al-nās^{i}* (the people) *illā* (except) *k^{u}fūrā* (disbelief).

وَلَوْ شِئْنَا لَبَعَثْنَا فِى كُلِّ قَرْيَةٍ نَّذِيرًا

W^{a}-l^{a}w (and if) *sh^{i}ʾ-nā* (We willed) *l^{a}-b^{a}ʿ^{a}th-nā* (truly We sent) *fī* (in) *k^{u}ll^{i}* (every) *q^{a}ry^{a}t^{in}* (town) *n^{a}dhīrā* (a warner).

فَلَا تُطِعِ ٱلْكَٰفِرِينَ وَجَٰهِدْهُم بِهِۦ جِهَادًا كَبِيرًا

F^{a}-lā (so do not) *t^{u}ṭiʿ* (you obey) *al-kāf^{i}rīn^{a}* (the rejecters) *w^{a}-jāh^{i}d-h^{u}m* (and strive against them) *b^{i}-h^{i}* (with it) *j^{i}hād^{an}* (a striving) *k^{a}bīrā* (great).

وَهُوَ ٱلَّذِى مَرَجَ ٱلْبَحْرَيْنِ هَٰذَا عَذْبٌ فُرَاتٌ وَهَٰذَا مِلْحٌ أُجَاجٌ
وَجَعَلَ بَيْنَهُمَا بَرْزَخًا وَحِجْرًا مَّحْجُورًا

W^{a}-h^{u}w^{a} (and He [is]) all^{a}dhī (the One Who) m^{a}r^{a}j^{a} (released) al-b^{a}ḥr^{a}yn^{i} (the two seas) hādhā (this [one]) ^{a}dhb^{un} (fresh, palatable) f^{u}rāt^{un} (sweet [i.e. good to drink]) w^{a}-hādhā (and this [one]) m^{i}lḥ^{un} (salty) ujāj^{un} (bitter) w^{a}-j^{a}^{a}l^{a} (and We made) b^{a}yn^{a}-h^{u}m^{a} (between them) b^{a}rz^{a}kh^{an} (a barrier) w^{a}-ḥ^{i}jr^{an} (and a partition) m^{a}ḥjūrā (prohibited).

وَهُوَ ٱلَّذِى خَلَقَ مِنَ ٱلْمَآءِ بَشَرًا فَجَعَلَهُۥ نَسَبًا وَصِهْرًا ۗ وَكَانَ
رَبُّكَ قَدِيرًا

W^{a}-h^{u}w^{a} (and He [is]) all^{a}dhī (the One Who) kh^{a}l^{a}q^{a} (He created) m^{i}n (from) al-mā^{i} (water) b^{a}sh^{a}r^{an} (a human) f^{a}-j^{a}^{a}l^{a}-h^{u} (so He made him) n^{a}s^{a}b^{an} (a blood relation) w^{a}-ṣ^{i}hr^{an} (a relation by marriage) w^{a}-kān^{a} (and He was) r^{a}bb^{u}-k^{a} (your Lord) q^{a}dīrā (a competenet One).

وَيَعْبُدُونَ مِن دُونِ ٱللَّهِ مَا لَا يَنفَعُهُمْ وَلَا يَضُرُّهُمْ ۗ وَكَانَ
ٱلْكَافِرُ عَلَىٰ رَبِّهِۦ ظَهِيرًا

W^{a}-y^{a}ʿb^{u}dūn^{a} (and they worship) m^{i}n dūn^{i} (other than, in exclusion of) allāh^{i} (God) mā (what) lā (does not) y^{a}nf^{a}^{u}-h^{u}m (it benefits them) w^{a}-lā (and does not) y^{a}ḍ^{u}rr^{u}-h^{u}m (it harms them) w^{a}-kān^{a} (and he was) al-kāf^{i}r^{u} (the rejecter) ^{a}lā (upon, against) r^{a}bb^{i}-h^{i} (his Lord) ẓ^{a}hīrā (an assistant).

وَمَآ أَرْسَلْنَٰكَ إِلَّا مُبَشِّرًا وَنَذِيرًا

W^{a}-mā (and did not) *ars^{a}l-nā-k^{a}* (We sent you) *illā* (except) *m^{u}b^{a}shsh^{i}r^{an}* ([as] a bringer of good tidings) *w^{a}-n^{a}dhīrā* (and a warner).

قُلْ مَآ أَسْـَٔلُكُمْ عَلَيْهِ مِنْ أَجْرٍ إِلَّا مَن شَآءَ أَن يَتَّخِذَ إِلَىٰ
رَبِّهِۦ سَبِيلًا

Q^{u}l (say) *mā* (do not) *as^{ʿa}l^{u}-k^{u}m* (I ask you) *^{ʿa}l^{a}y-h^{i}* (upon it) *m^{i}n ajr^{in}* (any reward) *illā* (except that) *m^{a}n* (whoever) *shā^{a}* (wills, wishes) *an* (to) *y^{a}tt^{a}kh^{i}dh^{a}* (take) *ilā* (toward) *r^{a}bb^{i}-h^{i}* (his Lord) *s^{a}bīlā* (a path).

وَتَوَكَّلْ عَلَى ٱلْحَىِّ ٱلَّذِى لَا يَمُوتُ وَسَبِّحْ بِحَمْدِهِۦ ۚ وَكَفَىٰ
بِهِۦ بِذُنُوبِ عِبَادِهِۦ خَبِيرًا

W^{a}-t^{a}w^{a}kk^{a}l (and rely) *^{ʿa}lā* (upon) *al-ḥ^{a}yy^{i}* (the Living) *all^{a}dhī* (Who) *lā* (does not) *y^{a}mūt^{u}* (He dies) *w^{a}-s^{a}bb^{i}ḥ* (and celebrate, and chant) *b^{i}-ḥ^{a}md^{i}-h^{i}* (His praise) *w^{a}-k^{a}fā* (and is sufficient) *b^{i}-h^{i}* (He) *b^{i}-dh^{u}nūb^{i}* (with the sins [of]) *ʿibād^{i}-h^{i}* (His servants) *kh^{a}bīrā* (cognizant, well-acquainted).

ٱلَّذِى خَلَقَ ٱلسَّمَٰوَٰتِ وَٱلْأَرْضَ وَمَا بَيْنَهُمَا فِى سِتَّةِ أَيَّامٍ ثُمَّ ٱسْتَوَىٰ
عَلَى ٱلْعَرْشِ ۚ ٱلرَّحْمَٰنُ فَسْـَٔلْ بِهِۦ خَبِيرًا

All^{a}dhī (the One Who) *kh^{a}l^{a}q^{a}* (He created) *al-s^{a}māwāt^{i}* (the heavens) *w^{a}-al-arḍ^{a}* (and the earth) *w^{a}-mā* (and what [is]) *b^{a}yn^{a}-h^{u}mā* (between them) *fī* (in) *s^{i}tt^{a}t^{i}* (six) *ayyām^{in}* (days) *th^{u}mm^{a}* (then) *ist^{a}wā* (He established Himself) *^{ʿa}lā* (upon) *al-^{ʿa}rsh^{i}* (the Throne) *al-r^{a}ḥmān^{u}* (the Most Gracious) *f^{a}-s^{ʿa}l* (so ask) *b^{i}-h^{i}* (about him) *kh^{a}bīrā* (a well-informed one, an expert).

This page intentionally left blank

Lesson 54: al-Furqān Part 7

Verse 60

وَإِذَا قِيلَ لَهُمُ ٱسْجُدُوا۟ لِلرَّحْمَٰنِ قَالُوا۟ وَمَا ٱلرَّحْمَٰنُ أَنَسْجُدُ لِمَا تَأْمُرُنَا وَزَادَهُمْ نُفُورًا ۩

And when it is said to them, "Prostrate to the Most Gracious," they say, "And what is the Most Gracious? Should we prostrate to that which you order us?" And it increases them in aversion

W^{a}*-idhā* (and when) *qīl*^{a} (it was said) *l*^{a}*-h*^{u}*m* (to them) *usj*^{u}*dū* (prostrate) *l*^{i}*-al-r*^{a}*ḥmān*^{i} (to the Most Gracious) *qālū* (they said) *w*^{a}*-mā* (and what [is]) *al-r*^{a}*ḥmān*^{u} (the Most Gracious) *a-n*^{a}*sj*^{u}*d*^{u} (do we prostrate) *l*^{i}*-mā* (to what) *t*^{a}*ʾm*^{u}*r*^{u}*-nā* (you order us) *w*^{a}*-zād*^{a}*-h*^{u}*m* (and it increased them) *n*^{u}*fūrā* ([in] aversion).

Verse 61

تَبَارَكَ ٱلَّذِى جَعَلَ فِى ٱلسَّمَآءِ بُرُوجًا وَجَعَلَ فِيهَا سِرَٰجًا وَقَمَرًا مُّنِيرًا

Blessed is He who has placed in the sky constellations and placed therein a [burning] lamp and luminous moon

T^{a}*bār*^{a}*k*^{a} (is blessed) *all*^{a}*dhī* (the One Who) *j*^{a}*ʿ*^{a}*l*^{a} (He made, He placed, He appointed) *fī* (in) *al-s*^{a}*mā*^{i} (the sky) *b*^{u}*rūj*^{an} (constellations) *w*^{a}*-j*^{a}*ʿ*^{a}*l*^{a} (and He placed) *fī-hā* (in it) *s*^{i}*rāj*^{an} (a lamp) *w*^{a}*-q*^{a}*m*^{a}*r*^{an} (and a moon) *m*^{u}*nīrā* (luminous, radiant).

Verse 62

وَهُوَ ٱلَّذِى جَعَلَ ٱلَّيْلَ وَٱلنَّهَارَ خِلْفَةً لِّمَنْ أَرَادَ أَن
يَذَّكَّرَ أَوْ أَرَادَ شُكُورًا

And it is He who has made the night and the daytime in succession for whoever desires to remember or desires gratitude

W^{a}-h^{u}w^{a} (and He [is]) *all^{a}dhī* (the One Who) *j^{a}^{a}l^{a}* (He made) *al-l^{a}yl^{a}* (tbe night) *w^{a}-al-n^{a}hār^{a}* (and the daytime) *kh^{i}lf^{a}t^{an}* ([in the form of a] succession) *l^{i}-m^{a}n* (for whoever) *arād^{a}* (he wants) *an* (to) *y^{a}dhdh^{a}kk^{a}r^{a}* (he remembers) *aw* (or) *arād^{a}* (he wants) *sh^{u}kūrā* (gratitude).

Verse 63

وَعِبَادُ ٱلرَّحْمَٰنِ ٱلَّذِينَ يَمْشُونَ عَلَى ٱلْأَرْضِ هَوْنًا وَإِذَا
خَاطَبَهُمُ ٱلْجَٰهِلُونَ قَالُوا۟ سَلَٰمًا

And the servants of the Most Gracious are those who walk upon the earth modestly, and when the ignorant address them [harshly], they say [words of] peace,

W^{a}-^{i}bād^{u} (and the servants [of]) *al-r^{a}ḥmān^{i}* (the Most Gracious [are]) *all^{a}dhīn^{a}* (those who) *y^{a}mshūn^{a}* (they walk) *^{a}lā* (upon) *al-arḍ^{i}* (the earth) *h^{a}wn^{an}* (modestly, lightly) *w^{a}-idhā* (and when) *khāṭ^{a}b^{a}-h^{u}m* (they speak to them, they address them) *al-jāh^{i}lūn^{a}* (the ignorant ones) *qālū* (they said) *s^{a}lāmā* (peace).

Verse 64

وَٱلَّذِينَ يَبِيتُونَ لِرَبِّهِمْ سُجَّدًا وَقِيَٰمًا

And those who spend [part of] the night to their Lord prostrating and standing [in prayer]

W^{a}-all^{a}dhīn^{a} (and those who) *y^{a}bītūn^{a}* (they spend the night) *l^{i}-r^{a}bb^{i}-h^{i}m* (to their Lord) *s^{u}jj^{a}d^{an}* (prostrating, as ones who prostrate) *w^{a}-q^{i}yāmā* (and standing, as ones who stand).

Verse 65

وَٱلَّذِينَ يَقُولُونَ رَبَّنَا ٱصْرِفْ عَنَّا عَذَابَ جَهَنَّمَ ۖ إِنَّ
عَذَابَهَا كَانَ غَرَامًا

And those who say, "Our Lord, avert from us the punishment of Hell. Indeed, its punishment is ever adhering ..."

W^{a}-all^{a}dhīn^{a} (and those who) *y^{a}qūlūn^{a}* (they say) *r^{a}bb^{a}-nā* (our Lord) *iṣr^{i}f* (avert) *^{a}n-nā* (from us) *^{a}dhāb^{a}* (to torment [of]) *j^{a}h^{a}nn^{a}m^{a}* (Hell) *inn^{a}* (indeed) *^{a}dhāb^{a}-hā* (its torment) *kān^{a}* (was) *gh^{a}rāmā* (ever adhering, never leaving).

Verse 66

إِنَّهَا سَآءَتْ مُسْتَقَرًّا وَمُقَامًا

“Indeed, it is evil as a settlement and residence."

Inn^{a}-hā (indeed it) *sā^{ʔa}-t* (was evil) *m^{u}st^{a}q^{a}rr^{an}* ([as] an abode, [as] a place of settlement) *w^{a}-m^{u}qāmā* (and [as] a residence).

Verse 67

وَٱلَّذِينَ إِذَآ أَنفَقُوا۟ لَمْ يُسْرِفُوا۟ وَلَمْ يَقْتُرُوا۟ وَكَانَ بَيْنَ
ذَٰلِكَ قَوَامًا

And [they are] those who, when they spend, do so not excessively or sparingly but are ever, between that, [justly] moderate

W^{a}-all^{a}dhīn^{a} (and those who) *idhā* (when) *anf^{a}qū* (they spent) *l^{a}m* (did not) *y^{u}sr^{i}fū* (they act extravagantly) *w^{a}-l^{a}m* (and did not) *y^{a}qt^{u}rū* (acted miserly, were penny-pinchers) *w^{a}-kān^{a}* (and was) *b^{a}yn^{a}* (between) *dhāl^{i}k^{a}* (that) *q^{a}wāmā* (balanced, moderate).

Verse 68

وَٱلَّذِينَ لَا يَدْعُونَ مَعَ ٱللَّهِ إِلَٰهًا ءَاخَرَ وَلَا يَقْتُلُونَ ٱلنَّفْسَ
ٱلَّتِى حَرَّمَ ٱللَّهُ إِلَّا بِٱلْحَقِّ وَلَا يَزْنُونَ ۚ وَمَن يَفْعَلْ ذَٰلِكَ يَلْقَ
أَثَامًا

And those who do not invoke with God another deity or kill the soul which God has forbidden [to be killed], except by right, and do not commit unlawful sexual intercourse. And whoever should do that will meet a penalty.

W^{a}-all^{a}dhīn^{a} (and those who) *lā* (do not) *y^{a}dʿūn^{a}* (they invoke, they call on) *m^{a}ʿ^{a}* (with) *allāh^{i}* (God) *ilāh^{an}* (a deity) *ākh^{a}r^{a}* (other) *w^{a}-lā* (and do not) *y^{a}qt^{u}lūn^{a}* (they kill) *al-n^{a}fs^{a}* (the soul) *all^{a}tī* (which, the one which) *ḥ^{a}rr^{a}m^{a}* (He forbad, He made sanctified) *allāh^{u}* (God) *illā* (except) *b^{i}-al-ḥ^{a}qq^{i}* (by right) *w^{a}-lā* (and do not) *y^{a}znūn^{a}* (they fornicate) *w^{a}-m^{a}n* (and whoever) *y^{a}fʿ^{a}l* (he does) *dhāl^{i}k^{a}* (that) *y^{a}lq^{a}* (meets, faces) *athāmā* (a penaltry).

Verse 69

يُضَٰعَفۡ لَهُ ٱلۡعَذَابُ يَوۡمَ ٱلۡقِيَٰمَةِ وَيَخۡلُدۡ فِيهِۦ مُهَانًا

Multiplied for him is the punishment on the Day of Resurrection, and he will abide eternally therein humiliated

Y[u]ḍā[a]f[u] (is multiplied) *l[a]-h[u]* (for him) *al-[a]dhāb[u]* (the torment) *y[a]wm[a]* (the Day) *al-q[i]yām[a]t[i]* ([of] Resurrection) *w[a]-y[a]khl[u]d* (and he abides eternally) *fī-h[i]* (in it) *m[u]hānā* ([as] a humiliated one).

This page intentionally left blank

Lesson 54 Review

وَإِذَا قِيلَ لَهُمُ ٱسْجُدُوا۟ لِلرَّحْمَٰنِ قَالُوا۟ وَمَا ٱلرَّحْمَٰنُ أَنَسْجُدُ لِمَا تَأْمُرُنَا
وَزَادَهُمْ نُفُورًا ۩

W^{a}-idhā (and when) *qīl^{a}* (it was said) *l^{a}-h^{u}m* (to them) *usj^{u}dū* (prostrate) *l^{i}-al-r^{a}ḥmān^{i}* (to the Most Gracious) *qālū* (they said) *w^{a}-mā* (and what [is]) *al-r^{a}ḥmān^{u}* (the Most Gracious) *a-n^{a}sj^{u}d^{u}* (do we prostrate) *l^{i}-mā* (to what) *t^{a}'m^{u}r^{u}-nā* (you order us) *w^{a}-zād^{a}-h^{u}m* (and it increased them) *n^{u}fūrā* ([in] aversion).

تَبَارَكَ ٱلَّذِى جَعَلَ فِى ٱلسَّمَآءِ بُرُوجًا وَجَعَلَ فِيهَا سِرَٰجًا
وَقَمَرًا مُّنِيرًا

T^{a}bār^{a}k^{a} (is blessed) *all^{a}dhī* (the One Who) *j^{a}^{a}l^{a}* (He made, He placed, He appointed) *fī* (in) *al-s^{a}mā^{i}* (the sky) *b^{u}rūj^{an}* (constellations) *w^{a}-j^{a}^{a}l^{a}* (and He placed) *fī-hā* (in it) *s^{i}rāj^{an}* (a lamp) *w^{a}-q^{a}m^{a}r^{an}* (and a moon) *m^{u}nīrā* (luminous, radiant).

وَهُوَ ٱلَّذِى جَعَلَ ٱلَّيْلَ وَٱلنَّهَارَ خِلْفَةً لِّمَنْ أَرَادَ أَن
يَذَّكَّرَ أَوْ أَرَادَ شُكُورًا

W^{a}-h^{u}w^{a} (and He [is]) *all^{a}dhī* (the One Who) *j^{a}^{a}l^{a}* (He made) *al-l^{a}yl^{a}* (tbe night) *w^{a}-al-n^{a}hār^{a}* (and the daytime) *kh^{i}lf^{a}t^{an}* ([in the form of a] succession) *l^{i}-m^{a}n* (for whoever) *arād^{a}* (he wants) *an* (to) *y^{a}dhdh^{a}kk^{a}r^{a}* (he remembers) *aw* (or) *arād^{a}* (he wants) *sh^{u}kūrā* (gratitude).

وَعِبَادُ ٱلرَّحْمَٰنِ ٱلَّذِينَ يَمْشُونَ عَلَى ٱلْأَرْضِ هَوْنًا وَإِذَا
خَاطَبَهُمُ ٱلْجَٰهِلُونَ قَالُوا۟ سَلَٰمًا

Wa-ibādu (and the servants [of]) *al-raḥmāni* (the Most Gracious [are]) *alladhīna* (those who) *yamshūna* (they walk) *alā* (upon) *al-arḍi* (the earth) *hawnan* (modestly, lightly) *wa-idhā* (and when) *khāṭaba-hum* (they speak to them, they address them) *al-jāhilūna* (the ignorant ones) *qālū* (they said) *salāmā* (peace).

وَٱلَّذِينَ يَبِيتُونَ لِرَبِّهِمْ سُجَّدًا وَقِيَٰمًا

Wa-alladhīna (and those who) *yabītūna* (they spend the night) *li-rabbi-him* (to their Lord) *sujjadan* (prostrating, as ones who prostrate) *wa-qiyāmā* (and standing, as ones who stand).

وَٱلَّذِينَ يَقُولُونَ رَبَّنَا ٱصْرِفْ عَنَّا عَذَابَ جَهَنَّمَ ۖ إِنَّ
عَذَابَهَا كَانَ غَرَامًا

Wa-alladhīna (and those who) *yaqūlūna* (they say) *rabba-nā* (our Lord) *iṣrif* (avert) *an-nā* (from us) *adhāba* (to torment [of]) *jahannama* (Hell) *inna* (indeed) *adhāba-hā* (its torment) *kāna* (was) *gharāmā* (ever adhering, never leaving).

إِنَّهَا سَآءَتْ مُسْتَقَرًّا وَمُقَامًا

Inna-hā (indeed it) *sāa-t* (was evil) *mustaqarran* ([as] an abode, [as] a place of settlement) *wa-muqāmā* (and [as] a residence).

وَٱلَّذِينَ إِذَآ أَنفَقُوا۟ لَمْ يُسْرِفُوا۟ وَلَمْ يَقْتُرُوا۟ وَكَانَ بَيْنَ
ذَٰلِكَ قَوَامًا

W^{a}-all^{a}dhīn^{a} (and those who) *idhā* (when) *anf^{a}qū* (they spent) *l^{a}m* (did not) *y^{u}sr^{i}fū* (they act extravagantly) *w^{a}-l^{a}m* (and did not) *y^{a}qt^{u}rū* (acted miserly, were penny-pinchers) *w^{a}-kān^{a}* (and was) *b^{a}yn^{a}* (between) *dhāl^{i}k^{a}* (that) *q^{a}wāmā* (balanced, moderate).

وَٱلَّذِينَ لَا يَدْعُونَ مَعَ ٱللَّهِ إِلَٰهًا ءَاخَرَ وَلَا يَقْتُلُونَ ٱلنَّفْسَ
ٱلَّتِى حَرَّمَ ٱللَّهُ إِلَّا بِٱلْحَقِّ وَلَا يَزْنُونَ ۚ وَمَن يَفْعَلْ ذَٰلِكَ يَلْقَ
أَثَامًا

W^{a}-all^{a}dhīn^{a} (and those who) *lā* (do not) *y^{a}d'ūn^{a}* (they invoke, they call on) *m^{a}'^{a}* (with) *allāh^{i}* (God) *ilāh^{an}* (a deity) *ākh^{a}r^{a}* (other) *w^{a}-lā* (and do not) *y^{a}qt^{u}lūn^{a}* (they kill) *al-n^{a}fs^{a}* (the soul) *all^{a}tī* (which, the one which) *ḥ^{a}rr^{a}m^{a}* (He forbad, He made sanctified) *allāh^{u}* (God) *illā* (except) *b^{i}-al-ḥ^{a}qq^{i}* (by right) *w^{a}-lā* (and do not) *y^{a}znūn^{a}* (they fornicate) *w^{a}-m^{a}n* (and whoever) *y^{a}f'^{a}l* (he does) *dhāl^{i}k^{a}* (that) *y^{a}lq^{a}* (meets, faces) *athāmā* (a penaltry).

يُضَٰعَفْ لَهُ ٱلْعَذَابُ يَوْمَ ٱلْقِيَٰمَةِ وَيَخْلُدْ فِيهِۦ مُهَانًا

Y^{u}ḍā'^{a}f^{u} (is multiplied) *l^{a}-h^{u}* (for him) *al-'^{a}dhāb^{u}* (the torment) *y^{a}wm^{a}* (the Day) *al-q^{i}yām^{a}t^{i}* ([of] Resurrection) *w^{a}-y^{a}khl^{u}d* (and he abides eternally) *fī-h^{i}* (in it) *m^{u}hānā* ([as] a humiliated one).

This page intentionally left blank

Lesson 55: al-Furqān Part 8

Verse 70

إِلَّا مَن تَابَ وَءَامَنَ وَعَمِلَ عَمَلًا صَٰلِحًا فَأُوْلَٰٓئِكَ يُبَدِّلُ
ٱللَّهُ سَيِّـَٔاتِهِمْ حَسَنَٰتٍ ۗ وَكَانَ ٱللَّهُ غَفُورًا رَّحِيمًا

Except one who repents, believes and does righteous work. For them God will replace their evil deeds with good. And ever is God Forgiving and Merciful.

Illā (except) *m^{a}n* (one who) *tāb^{a}* (he repented) *w^{a}-ām^{a}n^{a}* (and he believed) *w^{a}-^{a}m^{i}l^{a}* (and he worked) *^{a}m^{a}l^{an}* (a work) *ṣāl^{i}ḥ^{an}* (righteous, wholesome) *f^{a}-ulā^{i}k^{a}* (then those) *y^{u}b^{a}dd^{i}l^{u}* (He replaces) *allāh^{u}* (God) *s^{a}yy^{i}ʾāt^{i}-h^{i}m* (their bad deeds) *ḥ^{a}s^{a}nāt^{in}* ([with] good deeds) *w^{a}-kān^{a}* (and was) *allāh^{u}* (God) *gh^{a}fūr^{an}* (Forgiving) *r^{a}ḥīmā* (Merciful).

Verse 71

وَمَن تَابَ وَعَمِلَ صَٰلِحًا فَإِنَّهُۥ يَتُوبُ إِلَى ٱللَّهِ مَتَابًا

And he who repents and does righteousness does indeed turn to Allah with [accepted] repentance

W^{a}-m^{a}n (and who) *tāb^{a}* (he repented) *w^{a}-^{a}m^{i}l^{a}* (he worked) *ṣāl^{i}ḥ^{an}* (a wholesome [deed]) *f^{a}-inn^{a}-h^{u}* (then he indeed) *y^{a}tūb^{u}* (he repents) *ilā* (to) *allāh^{i}* (God) *m^{a}tābā* (with [true or accepted] repentance).

Verse 72

وَٱلَّذِينَ لَا يَشْهَدُونَ ٱلزُّورَ وَإِذَا مَرُّواْ بِٱللَّغْوِ مَرُّواْ كِرَامًا

And [they are] those who do not testify to falsehood, and when they pass near ill speech, they pass by with dignity.

W^{a}-all^{a}dhīn^{a} (and those who) *l^{a}* (do not) *y^{a}shh^{a}dūn^{a}* (they testify [to]) *al-zūr^{a}* (falsehood, lie) *w^{a}-idhā* (and when) *m^{a}rrū* (they pass) *b^{i}-al-l^{a}ghw^{i}* (by ill speech, by drivel, by nonsense) *m^{a}rrū* (they pass) *k^{i}rāmā* ([as] dignified [ones]).

Verse 73

وَٱلَّذِينَ إِذَا ذُكِّرُواْ بِـَٔايَٰتِ رَبِّهِمْ لَمْ يَخِرُّواْ عَلَيْهَا صُمًّا
وَعُمْيَانًا

And those who, when reminded of the verses of their Lord, do not fall upon them deaf and blind

W^{a}-all^{a}dhīn^{a} (and those wh) *idhā* (when) *dh^{u}kk^{i}rū* (they were reminded) *b^{i}-āyāt^{i}* (of the signs [of], of the verses [of]) *r^{a}bb^{i}-h^{i}m* (their Lord) *l^{a}m* (did not) *y^{a}kh^{i}rrū* (they fell down) *ʿ^{a}l^{a}y-hā* (upon it) *ṣ^{u}mm^{an}* ([as] deaf [ones]) *w^{a}-ʿ^{u}myānā* (and [as] blind [ones]).

Verse 74

وَٱلَّذِينَ يَقُولُونَ رَبَّنَا هَبْ لَنَا مِنْ أَزْوَٰجِنَا وَذُرِّيَّٰتِنَا قُرَّةَ
أَعْيُنٍ وَٱجْعَلْنَا لِلْمُتَّقِينَ إِمَامًا

And those who say, "Our Lord, grant us from among our spouses and offspring comfort to our eyes and make us good examples for the righteous."

W^{a}-all^{a}dhīn^{a} (and those who) *y^{a}qūlūn^{a}* (they say) *r^{a}bb^{a}-nā* (our Lord) *h^{a}b* (grant, bestow) *l^{a}-nā* (to us) *m^{i}n* (of) *azwāj^{i}-nā* (our spouses) *w^{a}-dh^{u}rrīyāt^{i}-nā* (our offspring) *q^{u}rr^{a}t^{a} a'y^{u}n^{in}* (comfort to the eyes) *w^{a}-ij^{a}l-nā* (and make us) *l^{i}-l-m^{u}tt^{a}qīn^{a}* (to the God-fearing ones) *imāmā* (leaders, examples to be emulated).

Verse 75

أُوْلَٰٓئِكَ يُجْزَوْنَ ٱلْغُرْفَةَ بِمَا صَبَرُواْ وَيُلَقَّوْنَ فِيهَا
تَحِيَّةً وَسَلَٰمًا

Those will be awarded the Chamber for what they patiently endured, and they will be received therein with greetings and [words of] peace

Ulā^{i}k^{a} (those) *y^{u}jz^{a}wn^{a}* (are rewarded by, are awarded) *al-gh^{u}rf^{a}t^{a}* (the Chamber) *b^{i}-mā* (by that which, for what) *ṣ^{a}b^{a}rū* (they patiently endured) *w^{a}-y^{u}l^{a}qq^{a}wn^{a}* (and they are be received) *fī-hā* (in it) *t^{a}ḥīy^{a}t^{an}* ([with] greetings) *w^{a}-salāmā* (and peace).

Verse 76

خَٰلِدِينَ فِيهَا ۚ حَسُنَتْ مُسْتَقَرًّا وَمُقَامًا

Abiding eternally therein. Good is the settlement and residence

Khāl^{i}dīn^{a} (abiding eternally) *fī-hā* (in it) *ḥ^{a}s^{u}n^{a}t* (is good, is beautiful) *m^{u}st^{a}q^{a}rr^{an}* ([as] a settlement) *w^{a}-m^{u}qāmā* (and [as] a residence).

Verse 77

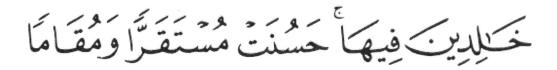

قُلْ مَا يَعْبَؤُا۟ بِكُمْ رَبِّى لَوْلَا دُعَآؤُكُمْ ۖ فَقَدْ كَذَّبْتُمْ فَسَوْفَ يَكُونُ لِزَامًۢا

Say, "My Lord does not concern Himself with you if not for your supplication." For you [disbelievers] have denied, so it [i.e. the judgment or punishment] is going to be inevitable.

$Q^{u}l$ (say) *mā* (does not) *y^{a}ʿb^{a}ʾ^{u}* (He concerns Himself) *b^{i}-$k^{u}m$* (with you) *$r^{a}bb$-ī* (my Lord) *l^{a}wlā d^{u}ʿā^{ʾu}-$k^{u}m$ f^{a}-$q^{a}d$ $k^{a}dhdh^{a}b$-$t^{u}m$ f^{a}-$s^{a}wf^{a}$ y^{a}kūn^{u} l^{i}zāmā*

This beginning statement can also be interpreted as, "Why would my Lord concern Himself with you if it was not for your supplication?"

Lesson 55 Review

إِلَّا مَن تَابَ وَءَامَنَ وَعَمِلَ عَمَلًا صَٰلِحًا فَأُوْلَٰٓئِكَ يُبَدِّلُ
ٱللَّهُ سَيِّـَٔاتِهِمْ حَسَنَٰتٍ ۗ وَكَانَ ٱللَّهُ غَفُورًا رَّحِيمًا

Illā (except) *m^{a}n* (one who) *tāb^{a}* (he repented) *w^{a}-ām^{a}n^{a}* (and he believed) *w^{a}-^{a}m^{i}l^{a}* (and he worked) *^{a}m^{a}l^{an}* (a work) *ṣāl^{i}ḥ^{an}* (righteous, wholesome) *f^{a}-ulā^{i}k^{a}* (then those) *y^{u}b^{a}dd^{i}l^{u}* (He replaces) *allāh^{u}* (God) *s^{a}yy^{i}'āt^{i}-h^{i}m* (their bad deeds) *ḥ^{a}s^{a}nāt^{in}* ([with] good deeds) *w^{a}-kān^{a}* (and was) *allāh^{u}* (God) *gh^{a}fūr^{an}* (Forgiving) *r^{a}ḥīmā* (Merciful).

وَمَن تَابَ وَعَمِلَ صَٰلِحًا فَإِنَّهُۥ يَتُوبُ إِلَى ٱللَّهِ مَتَابًا

W^{a}-m^{a}n (and who) *tāb^{a}* (he repented) *w^{a}-^{a}m^{i}l^{a}* (he worked) *ṣāl^{i}ḥ^{an}* (a wholesome [deed]) *f^{a}-inn^{a}-h^{u}* (then he indeed) *y^{a}tūb^{u}* (he repents) *ilā* (to) *allāh^{i}* (God) *m^{a}tābā* (with [true or accepted] repentance).

وَٱلَّذِينَ لَا يَشْهَدُونَ ٱلزُّورَ وَإِذَا مَرُّوا۟ بِٱللَّغْوِ مَرُّوا۟ كِرَامًا

W^{a}-all^{a}dhīn^{a} (and those who) *l^{a}* (do not) *y^{a}shh^{a}dūn^{a}* (they testify [to]) *al-zūr^{a}* (falsehood, lie) *w^{a}-idhā* (and when) *m^{a}rrū* (they pass) *b^{i}-al-l^{a}ghw^{i}* (by ill speech, by drivel, by nonsense) *m^{a}rrū* (they pass) *k^{i}rāmā* ([as] dignified [ones]).

وَٱلَّذِينَ إِذَا ذُكِّرُوا۟ بِـَٔايَٰتِ رَبِّهِمْ لَمْ يَخِرُّوا۟ عَلَيْهَا صُمًّا
وَعُمْيَانًا

W^{a}-all^{a}dhīn^{a} (and those wh) *idhā* (when) *dh^{u}kk^{i}rū* (they were reminded) *b^{i}-āyāt^{i}* (of the signs [of], of the verses [of]) *r^{a}bb^{i}-h^{i}m* (their Lord) *l^{a}m* (did not) *y^{a}kh^{i}rrū* (they fell down) *^{a}l^{a}y-hā* (upon it) *ṣ^{u}mm^{an}* ([as] deaf [ones]) *w^{a}-^{u}myānā* (and [as] blind [ones]).

وَٱلَّذِينَ يَقُولُونَ رَبَّنَا هَبْ لَنَا مِنْ أَزْوَٰجِنَا وَذُرِّيَّٰتِنَا قُرَّةَ أَعْيُنٍ وَٱجْعَلْنَا لِلْمُتَّقِينَ إِمَامًا

W^{a}-all^{a}dhīn^{a} (and those who) *y^{a}qūlūn^{a}* (they say) *r^{a}bb^{a}-nā* (our Lord) *h^{a}b* (grant, bestow) *l^{a}-nā* (to us) *m^{i}n* (of) *azwāj^{i}-nā* (our spouses) *w^{a}-dh^{u}rrīyāt^{i}-nā* (our offspring) *q^{u}rr^{a}t^{a} aʿy^{u}n^{in}* (comfort to the eyes) *w^{a}-ij^{a}l-nā* (and make us) *l^{i}-l-m^{u}tt^{a}qīn^{a}* (to the God-fearing ones) *imāmā* (leaders, examples to be emulated).

أُو۟لَٰٓئِكَ يُجْزَوْنَ ٱلْغُرْفَةَ بِمَا صَبَرُوا۟ وَيُلَقَّوْنَ فِيهَا تَحِيَّةً وَسَلَٰمًا

Ulā^{i}k^{a} (those) *y^{u}jz^{a}wn^{a}* (are rewarded by, are awarded) *al-gh^{u}rf^{a}t^{a}* (the Chamber) *b^{i}-mā* (by that which, for what) *ṣ^{a}b^{a}rū* (they patiently endured) *w^{a}-y^{u}l^{a}qq^{a}wn^{a}* (and they are be received) *fī-hā* (in it) *t^{a}ḥīy^{a}t^{an}* ([with] greetings) *w^{a}-salāmā* (and peace).

خَٰلِدِينَ فِيهَا ۚ حَسُنَتْ مُسْتَقَرًّا وَمُقَامًا

Khāl^{i}dīn^{a} (abiding eternally) *fī-hā* (in it) *ḥ^{a}s^{u}n^{a}t* (is good, is beautiful) *m^{u}st^{a}q^{a}rr^{an}* ([as] a settlement) *w^{a}-m^{u}qāmā* (and [as] a residence).

Made in the USA
Las Vegas, NV
12 April 2024

88592143R00273